EASTERN BODY

WESTERN MIND

"A book of profound and practical compassion. Judith's ideas are as essential and important as Freud's insights were a hundred years ago. She offers specific and varied strategies to understand your ways of coping, so that you can let go of those that no longer serve you and make better use of those that do."

—James Fadiman, Ph.D., author of *Unlimit Your Life* and *The Other Side of Haight*

"This very readable yet scholarly book provides a comprehensive picture of healthy human development and the development of human consciousness. We are taken, step by step, on a journey toward the integration of body, mind, and spirit. A groundbreaking contribution."

—Susan Campbell, author of *Getting Real* and *Truth in Dating*

"Rather than presenting an esoteric borrowing from Indian culture, Judith employs the metaphoric language of the chakra system within the context of modern psychology. Her clear organization and numerous charts make browsing for subjects of personal relevance a breeze. . . . The book provides a useful tool for contemplating our strengths, weaknesses, and appropriate approaches to growth."

—*Yoga Journal*

". . . sparkles with insight. Spiritual seeker, client, and therapist alike will find treasures here."

—*PanGaia* magazine

EASTERN BODY

WESTERN MIND

Psychology and the Chakra System
as a Path to the Self

REVISED

ANODEA JUDITH

CELESTIAL ARTS
Berkeley

For information on the author's workshops, please contact:

SACRED CENTERS
708 Gravenstein Hwy N. #109, Sebastopol, CA 95472
www.sacredcenters.com

Copyright © 1996, 2004 by Anodea Judith

All rights reserved. Published in the United States by Celstial Arts, an imprint of the Crown Publishing Group, a division of Random House, Inc., New York.
www.crownpublishing.com
www.tenspeed.com

Celestial Arts and the Celestial Arts colophon are registered trademarks of Random House, Inc.

Library of Congress Cataloging-in-Publication Data

Judith, Anodea, 1952–
    Eastern body, Western mind : psychology and the chakra system as a path to the self / Anodea Judith Celestial Arts.—Rev. ed.
        p.   cm.
    Includes bibliographical references and index.
    1. Chakras—Miscellanea. I. Title.
    BF1442.C53J8 2004
    150.19'8—dc22   2004010256
                                                       CIP

ISBN 978-1-58761-225-1
Printed in the United States of America

Design by Lynn Bell, Monroe Street Studios
Cover illustration copyright © by Robert McIntosh/Corbis

21

Second Edition

CONTENTS

ACKNOWLEDGMENTS

Iris, the Greek Goddess of the Rainbow, was the first deity I ever encountered. It is to Her that I owe my discovery of the chakras and the Rainbow Bridge. However, in my journey across this bridge I have been supported by a great number of people—my clients, students, teachers, friends, and family.

Of particular importance, I thank my immediate family who lived with me while I wrote this book. My son, Alex Wayne, allowed me to tell stories about him in the text and helped draw up the computer graphics. My husband, Richard Ely, gave me love, support, and patient editing. Selene Vega, coauthor of *The Sevenfold Journey* and coteacher of the *Nine Month Chakra Intensive*, helped develop this work over the years, as well as giving me wonderful support, editing, and feedback. I would like to thank Lisa Green for her feedback on child development, Jack Ingersoll for his lengthy discussions on Jungian psychology, and Nancy Gnecco for her contributions to the charts. I would also like to thank my agent, Peter Beren, for making this publication possible, and David Hinds of Celestial Arts.

Most of all, I'd like to thank those who have dared to engage in the healing process with me as your guide. From you I have learned the most. It has been a privilege to serve you.

PREFACE TO THIS EDITION

Since this book was originally published in 1996, the chakra system has come of age in the West. Yoga centers are growing exponentially, teaching *asanas* and meditations that open the chakras. Theories of "energy healing" are influencing the practice of both medicine and psychotherapy, creating a hunger for new models. Chakras now appear on T-shirts, candles, and jewelry, in sitcom conversations and articles in *Time* magazine. The idea that mind and body exist on a spiritual continuum has finally entered the mainstream. The good news is that it makes the chakra system accessible to more people as a template for transformation. The shadow side of this exposure is that, at least in the West, any cultural meme that gets seized by the collective consciousness runs the risk of trivialization, thus diluting its power.

At every workshop, lecture, or book signing, people come up to me asking whether I have a simple way to "clear their chakras." Few of them understand what a chakra actually is, fewer still have familiarity with the ancient Tantric yoga tradition from which this system originates, and even fewer still are willing to delve into the depths of their own psyches and actually do the work required to make lasting changes in their inner and outer life. While some of the modern techniques of chakra energy work can bring tangible shifts in the way we feel, it is my opinion that these changes are often short-lived if we don't roll up our sleeves and do deeper work on the soul's journey of healing and awakening.

It is to this challenge that I address this book. It will teach you an elegant system for understanding your health and imbalances, yet one that is richly complex. You will not find "one-size-fits-all" formulas that apply equally to all people or all situations. Instead, you will learn universal principles that can be effectively applied with careful consideration and understanding. You will learn, for example, that some of your chakras may be too open, with poor discrimination and filters, while other chakras can get mired in avoidance patterns and remain closed. You will learn how these unconscious defense patterns create excessive and deficient coping strategies that over time throw your system out of balance and alignment, affecting the body's health and your quality of life. You will learn that these vital energy centers open sequentially during crucial stages of childhood, and can be unwittingly shut down by well-meaning parents whose own centers were compromised. You will learn about your upward and downward currents of energy, and how each has a different purpose in the liberation and manifestation of your life force. And you will learn about the work required to reclaim the true aliveness that is your birthright.

The most frequent comment I've received from my readers about this book is that they wonder how I could possibly have written so pointedly about their private life and personal issues. This highlights how universal these ancient principles are. Yet, in a rapidly changing world, we need to continually upgrade our operating systems and learn new applications of these universal principles. Few people live in ashrams with leisure for the contemplative life. Instead, most of us live fast-paced lives, full of complex challenges. We meet these challenges through the veil of enormous emotional wounds that compromise our aliveness. We live in a culture in which that compromise is taken for granted. To heal this rift, many of us have been working on ourselves for decades, undergoing the journey to heal ourselves and find our life's purpose, the journey of individuation and awakening.

The chakra system is a map for that journey. With this map in hand, your journey can be more direct, more profound, and more deliberate. This system maps onto the body through the human nervous system, maps onto the psyche through developmental stages of childhood, maps onto the spiritual quest through states of consciousness, and transforms the culture through planes of external reality. The chakras are truly a set of portals between the inner and outer worlds.

If the outer world is to be transformed, the process must begin within. If the inner world is to be transformed, it must be understood in light of the outer forces that shaped it. These realms are not separate, yet we lack a systematic means of tying them together. The value of the chakra system is that as the inner and outer worlds connect, we become aligned—spiritually, mentally, emotionally, and physically.

In the Western world, there are somatic therapies that connect mind and body, yet ignore the spiritual aspects of our being. There are spiritually oriented psychologies that connect psyche and spirit, yet ignore the body. And there are disciplines, such as yoga, that connect spirit and body, yet fail to address the wounds of the psyche.

Through the lens of the chakra system, this book presents an integration of psychology, spirituality, and physicality within one comprehensive system. It says mind, body, and spirit are equally important facets of every one of us, yet comprise one unified entity. In honoring the full spectrum of human aliveness, this book is a contribution toward the restoration of your wondrously divine potential. With map in hand, may you enjoy the journey.

PREFACE TO THE FIRST EDITION

Eastern Body, Western Mind focuses on vital issues in therapy today: addiction, codependence, physical and sexual abuse, family dynamics, character structures, personal empowerment, feminism, male emancipation, sexuality, politics, and spirituality. It integrates techniques from bioenergetics to visualization, depth psychology to spiritual practice.

After working in the healing field for over two decades, I have seen far too much suffering of the human soul. I have sat with my tissue, drying the tears of people deeply wounded by the horrendous ignorance of emotionally crippled caretakers—people trying to limp their way through a troubled world, filled with others as wounded as themselves. I have seen how the healing process can overwhelm and frighten those engaged in this heroic journey. Yet I have also witnessed the incredible transformations and hopes that this journey brings to its travelers, as well as the transformation of the world around them.

It is to this hope of transformation that I dedicate this work. As a guidebook for the journey of awakening, it presents a systematic model for addressing the issues that plague us. It is written for individuals engaged in their own healing process, as well as for therapists, counselors, and bodyworkers who become guides along the way. It is also addressed to parents who want to raise conscious and healthy children, and to those who simply want to wake up and further their own evolution.

Eastern Body, Western Mind shows how to use the chakra system as a tool for diagnosis and healing. My primary purpose is to present the system itself, as a lens through which we can view the complex problems of the soul's evolution, both individually and collectively. The system is presented through its major components, the individual chakras, examining how they shape and are shaped by human behavior and culture.

In presenting this material, I have woven together three basic threads of philosophical thought:

1. The *Enlightenment philosophies*, whose movement is upward and beyond, toward the mental and spiritual realms. They are derived primarily from Eastern cultures and their focus on transcendence. They seek to escape the trials and tribulations of the mundane world by ascending to higher planes of consciousness that transcend suffering.

2. The *embodiment philosophies*, whose movement is down and in, toward the realms of manifestation, soul, body, and engagement with the world around us. They are reflected in the practice of somatic therapy, bioenergetics, and earth-centered spirituality. Their focus is on immanence, or the presence of the divine within. They seek to end suffering by engaging with the forces that cause it.

3. The *integrative philosophies*, whose movement is toward integration of opposites: mind and body, Heaven and Earth, spirit and matter, light and shadow, male and female. For this thread, I have chosen to focus on the depth psychology of Carl Gustav Jung, specifically, his understanding of the soul's journey toward individuation. The goal of integrative philosophies is transformation and wholeness.

The chakra system is a profound representation of the universe. Each of the seven levels represents such major areas of human life that they could fill volumes all by themselves. Issues of love and relationship, power and spirituality, emotion and instinct all beg to be examined and understood. Sexuality, for example, is just one aspect of the second chakra, and sexual abuse is just one aspect of sexuality. It cannot be the purpose of this book to detail the complexities of any particular abuse, but to place each one in the context of a larger system in which they can be understood energetically and spiritually. From this context, you can orient your healing process. For further information, please see the references listed at the end of the book.

I have wanted the book to be as user-friendly as possible. In today's fast-paced world, I know that many people do not have time to read a book of this size from cover to cover. Therefore, the text is divided by numerous subtitles and reference charts to make the information easily accessible—you can read the parts that are pertinent to you and skim the rest. Some sections are more clinically oriented, using language specific to psychotherapy, while others are directed toward a general audience.

This work is definitely a Western approach to the chakras. It places modern psychosocial issues within a spiritual context, based on the esoteric interpretations of the chakras that can be found in Eastern texts. Rather than presenting an otherworldly discipline borrowed from the cultures of the East, I have created a down-to-earth, practical application for contemporary members of Western civilization. Yet the inevitable result is a blending of East and West.

The chakra system describes the energetic structure through which we organize our life force. By understanding this internal arrangement, we can understand our defenses and needs, and learn how to restore balance. The chakra system is every bit as valid as any psychological theory, and I feel, far more versatile—one that is capable of spanning mind, body, and spirit. I invite you to explore it with me and thereby deepen your own healing process.

NOTE: The personal stories related here are combinations of real people—sometimes several people's stories overlap to make the best illustrations. All names and specific details have been changed to protect anonymity. I give deep thanks to my clients, students, and friends who have risked themselves in the service of transformation and taught me so much about this material.

INTRODUCTION

Sacred Centers of the Self

DISCOVERING THE RAINBOW BRIDGE

You are about to go on a journey through the many dimensions of your own Self. This journey will take you through a transformation of consciousness—across a vital bridge—connecting spirit and matter, Heaven and Earth, mind and body. As you transform yourself, you transform the world.

This journey is a colorful one, as life itself is colorful. It offers an alternative to the drab, gray mentality of the modern era, where color is limited to the realm of children. By contrast, too many "grown-ups" live in dark, tailored suits, riding gray subways and highways through black-and-white

> You may grind their souls in the self-same mill
> You may bind them heart and brow;
> But the poet will follow the rainbow still,
> And his brother will follow the plow.
>
> JOHN BOYLE O'REILLY

realities of grim choices and limited options. Reclaiming the multidimensional diversity of the human experience is the task of this journey—no less than a quest for our wholeness and the renewal of our collective spirit.

The seven colors of the rainbow represent an alternative to our binary black-and-white consciousness, offering us a world of multiple opportunities. The rainbow expresses the diversity of light as it moves from source to manifestation. Its seven colors represent seven vibratory modalities of human existence, related to the seven chakras of Indian yogic tradition—energy centers that exist within each one of us.

Yoga philosophy teaches us that the serpent goddess, Kundalini, represents the evolutionary life force within each person. She awakens from her slumber in the earth to dance her way through each chakra, reestablishing the rainbow as a metaphysical bridge between matter and consciousness. Through this dance of transformation, the rainbow becomes the *axis mundi*—the central axis of the world that runs through the vertical core of each one of us. On our journey through life, the chakras are the wheels along this axis that take the vehicle of the Self along our evolutionary quest, across the Rainbow Bridge, to reclaim our divine nature once again.

This Rainbow Bridge can also span the cultures of East and West, as each has something to learn from the other. The treasures of the East bring Westerners a vast spiritual wealth. The elaborate practices of yoga, the abundance of Buddhist and Hindu scriptures, and the rich imagery of Eastern deities bring Westerners new dimensions of spiritual experience. Yet despite this spiritual wealth, there is a predominance of material poverty in many of the Eastern countries, especially in India, where yoga and the chakra system originated. By comparison, most Westerners live among material wealth, but spiritual poverty. Greed and violence dominate our news, fear and emptiness plague our youth, and mindless materialism consumes the world's resources. I believe it is possible to have both material abundance and spiritual wealth. We can embrace all the chakras at once, at last achieving some kind of personal and cultural balance.

Crossing the Rainbow Bridge is a mythic metaphor for the evolution of consciousness. To reclaim a myth is to put our personal work into a larger context—a context which deepens the meaning of our individual struggle. To restore the Rainbow Bridge is to reconnect to our own divinity, anchoring it in the world around us and healing the rifts that so plague our world.

Mythologically, the rainbow has always been a sign of hope—a connection between Heaven and Earth, a sign of harmony and peace. It was once believed that deities, spirits, and mortals passed along its bands of color both during life and after, protecting the indivisibility of sky and Earth. In Norse mythology, the Rainbow Bridge connected humans to the gods, and provided the link to Valhalla, the celestial palace where the gods had their dwelling.

The rainbow, as archetypal symbol, appears in many mythologies throughout the world. In Hindu mythology, the goddess Maya created the world out of seven rainbow-hued veils. In Egyptian myth, it was the seven stoles of Isis; in Christianity, the seven veils of Salome; for the Babylonians, it was Ishtar's rainbow-jeweled necklace; and for the Greeks, the winged Iris, who carried the gods' messages to humans on Earth.

From Celtic myth, the pot of gold at the rainbow's end represents a kind of Holy Grail—the lost vessel of spiritual renewal and fulfillment. Carl Jung referred to gold as the symbolic end product of inner alchemical transformation. Passage through the chakras is an alchemical process of increasing refinement that unites light and shadow, male and female, spirit and matter, all in the crucible of the body and psyche. The pot of gold is indeed the elusive philosopher's stone that lures us into the heroic journey of transformation.

> The soul is greater than the hum of its parts.
>
> DOUGLAS HOFSTADTER

In the Turkish language, the word for rainbow literally means "bridge." Ancient myths tell us that as doomsday approaches, the Rainbow Bridge will be broken down, severing forever the connection between Heaven and Earth. As we face an uncertain future in the dawning of a new millennium, perhaps doomsday can be averted by reestablishing the Rainbow Bridge once again through the medium of our own consciousness. Thus the journey becomes a sacred quest—one that restores hope and connection, renewing ourselves, and preserving the world.

WHEELS THAT HEAL

The chakra system is a seven-leveled philosophical model of the universe. Chakras have come to the West through the tradition and practice of yoga. Yoga (which means "yoke") is a discipline designed to yoke together the individual with the divine, using mental and physical practices that join our mundane and spiritual lives. This goal is achieved by passing through steps of ever-expanding states of consciousness. The chakras represent these steps.

A chakra is a center of organization that receives, assimilates, and expresses life force energy. The word *chakra* literally translates as "wheel" or "disk" and refers to a spinning sphere of bioenergetic activity emanating from the major nerve ganglia branching forward from the spinal column. There are seven of these wheels stacked in a column of energy that spans from the base of the spine to the top of the head (see figure 0.1). There are also minor chakras in the hands, feet, fingertips, and shoulders. Literally, any vortex of activity could be called a chakra. It is the seven major chakras that correlate with basic states of consciousness, and it is these that we will examine in this book.

The chakra system originated in India, more than four thousand years ago. Chakras were referred to in the ancient literature of the Vedas, the later Upanishads, the *Yoga Sutras of Patanjali*, and most thoroughly in the sixteenth century by an Indian yogi in a text called the *Sat-Chakra-Nirupana*.[1] In the 1920s, chakras were brought to the West by Arthur Avalon with his book *The Serpent Power*.[2] Today, they are a popular concept linking areas of the body and psyche with associated metaphysical realms.

> Whether the symbol of the circle appears in a primitive sun worship or modern religion, in myths or in dreams, in the mandalas drawn by Tibetan monks, in the ground plan of cities, or in the spherical concepts of early astronomers, it always points to the single most vital aspect of life—its ultimate wholeness.
>
> C. G. JUNG

Chakras are not physical entities in and of themselves. Like feelings or ideas, they cannot be held like a physical object, yet they have a strong effect upon the body as they express the embodiment of spiritual energy on the physical plane. Chakra patterns are programmed deep in the core of the mind-body interface and have a strong relationship with our physical functioning. Just as the emotions can and do affect our breathing, heart rate, and metabolism, the activities in the various chakras influence our glandular processes, body shape, chronic physical ailments, thoughts, and behavior. By using techniques such as yoga, breathing, bioenergetics, physical exercises, meditation, and visualization, we can, in turn, influence our chakras, our health, and our lives. This is one of the essential values of this system—that it maps onto both the body and the mind, and can be accessed through either.

Thus the chakras are said to have a *location*, even though they do not exist in the physical sense. Figure 0.1 shows the relative locations of the seven major chakras. These locations may vary slightly from person to person, but remain consistent in their overall relationship to one another.

While they cannot be seen or held as material entities, the chakras are evident in the shape of our physical bodies, the patterns manifested in our

7
6

5

4

3

2

1

FIGURE 0.1. CHAKRA LOCATIONS IN THE BODY

lives, and the way we think, feel, and handle situations that life presents us. Just as we see the wind through movement of the leaves and branches, the chakras can be seen by what we create around us.

Based on their location in the body, the chakras have become associated with various states of consciousness, archetypal elements, and philosophical constructs. The lower chakras, for example, which are physically closer to the earth, are related to the more practical matters of our lives—survival, movement, action. They are ruled by physical and social law. The upper chakras represent mental realms and work on a symbolic level through words, images, and concepts. Each of the seven chakras has also come to represent a major area of human psychological health, which can be briefly summarized as follows: (1) survival, (2) sexuality, (3) power, (4) love, (5) communication, (6) intuition, and (7) consciousness itself (see figure 0.2).

Metaphorically, the chakras relate to the following archetypal elements: (1) earth, (2) water, (3) fire, (4) air, (5) sound, (6) light, and (7) thought.

7		COGNITION	THOUGHT
			Consciousness
6		INTUITION	LIGHT
			Luminescence
5		COMMUNICATION	SOUND
			Vibration
4		LOVE	AIR
			Equilibrium
3		POWER	FIRE
			Combustion
2		SEXUALITY	WATER
			Polarity
1		SURVIVAL	EARTH
			Gravitation

FIGURE 0.2. BASIC ISSUES AND ELEMENTS OF THE CHAKRAS

(This is my own interpretation; classic texts only list the five elements earth, water, fire, air, and ether.) These elements, in turn, represent the universal principles of gravitation, polarity, combustion, equilibrium, vibration, luminescence, and consciousness itself, respectively (see figure 0.2). Understanding these formative principles and the essence of the associated elements gives us a key to understanding the unique nature of each chakra. Earth is solid and dense; water is formless and fluid; fire is radiating and transforming; air is soft and spacious; sound is rhythmic pulsation; light is illuminating; while thought is the medium of consciousness. Meditating on the elements gives us a profound sense of the distinct flavor of each chakra.

Together the chakras describe a kind of Jacob's ladder connecting the polarities of Heaven and Earth, mind and body, spirit and matter. These polarities exist on a continuum, with the chakras as incremental steps that are embodied within all life processes. Each step upward moves from a heavy, well-defined vibrational state to a higher, subtler, and freer form. Each step downward brings us into form and solidity.

As there are seven levels to the chakras and seven colors in the rainbow, the slowest vibration of visible light, red, is associated with the base chakra, and the fastest and shortest, violet, with the crown. Each of the other colors (orange, yellow, green, blue, indigo) represent the steps between.[3] As we learn to open and heal the chakras within us, we *become* the Rainbow Bridge—the living link between Heaven and Earth.

Each of the chakras' principles and attributes will be discussed in the following chapters. The *Table of Correspondences* (figure 0.3) groups some of the basic information for you.

THE HUMAN BIOCOMPUTER

The word *chakra* literally means "disk." How fitting that in modern times, disks are the common storage unit of programmed information. We can use this analogy and think of chakras as floppy disks that contain vital programs. We have a survival program that tells us when we need to eat, how many hours to sleep, and when to put on a sweater. It contains details such as how much money we think we need, what we are willing to do for that money, what constitutes a threat to our survival, and what makes us feel secure. Likewise, we have programs for sexuality, power, love, and communication. In this analogy, the seventh chakra can be thought of as the operating system. It represents how we organize and interpret all our other programs.

In the computer world, technology is advancing so rapidly that programs written ten years ago are sorely out of date today. So, too, with many of the programs we were given as children. For example, old-fashioned gender roles are incompatible with egalitarian relationships, and new models are evolving from the struggles of modern couples. An alcoholic follows a program for recovery, and programs are necessary to achieve weight loss or gain academic degrees. We all function by sets of programs, which may or may not be conscious. The challenge before us is to find the appropriate program and get the bugs out.

In this analogy the body is the hardware, our programming is the software, and the Self is the user. However, we did not write all of these programs, and some of their language is so archaic it is unintelligible. It is a heroic challenge, indeed, to identify our programs and rewrite them all while continuing to live our lives, yet this is the task of healing. It becomes even more difficult when we realize that each of our personal programs is part of a larger cultural system over which we have had little or no control.

The chakra system is an evolutionary program and can be used to reprogram our lives. If we can learn this on an individual level, perhaps we can apply the same methods to our culture and environment.

There is another important aspect to this analogy that we often take for granted, namely, the basic energy that makes it all work. The most elaborate computer with megabytes of software is useless without electricity. What activates any and all of our programs is the energy we pour into the system. Intricate internal flowcharts decide which areas to energize and when. Hunger centers are activated when the stomach is empty and sexual centers awaken with certain stimuli.

In order to understand a human being, we have to examine the flow of energy through the system. We can think of this energy as excitement, charge, attention, awareness, or simply the life force. (Some spiritual systems describe it as *chi*, *ki*, or *prana*.) Our understanding of the chakras comes from a pattern analysis of energy flowing through a person's body, behavior, and environment.

Sally's pattern might be to ignore her body and live entirely in her head. George's pattern might be to push people away whenever they get close, while simultaneously talking too much in an attempt to keep them engaged.

FIGURE 0.3. TABLE OF CORRESPONDENCES

	CHAKRA ONE	CHAKRA TWO	CHAKRA THREE
SANSKRIT NAME (MEANING)	*Muladhara* (root)	*Svadhisthana* (sweetness)	*Manipura* (lustrous gem)
LOCATION	Base of spine, coccygeal plexus	Abdomen, genitals, low back, hips	Solar plexus
CENTRAL ISSUE	Survival	Sexuality, emotions	Power, will
ORIENTATION TO SELF	Self-preservation	Self-gratification	Self-definition
GOALS	Stability, grounding, physical health, prosperity, trust	Fluidity, pleasure, healthy sexuality, feeling	Vitality, spontaneity, strength of will, purpose, self-esteem
RIGHTS	To be here, to have	To feel, to want	To act
DEVELOPMENTAL STAGE	Womb to 12 months	6 months to 2 years	18 months to 4 years
IDENTITY	Physical identity	Emotional identity	Ego identity
DEMON	Fear	Guilt	Shame
ELEMENT	Earth	Water	Fire
EXCESSIVE CHARACTERISTICS	Heaviness, sluggish, monotony, obesity, hoarding, materialism, greed	Overly emotional, poor boundaries, sex addiction, obsessive attachments	Dominating, controlling, aggressive, scattered, constantly active
DEFICIENT CHARACTERISTICS	Fearful, undisciplined, restless, underweight, spacey	Frigid, impotent, rigid, emotionally numb, fearful of pleasure	Weak will, poor self-esteem, passive, sluggish, fearful

CHAKRA FOUR	CHAKRA FIVE	CHAKRA SIX	CHAKRA SEVEN
Anahata (unstruck)	*Vissudha* (purification)	*Ajna* (to perceive)	*Sahasrara* (thousandfold)
Heart area	Throat	Brow	Top of head, cerebral cortex
Love, relationships	Communication	Intuition, imagination	Awareness
Self-acceptance	Self-expression	Self-reflection	Self-knowledge
Balance, compassion, self-acceptance, good relationships	Clear communication, creativity, resonance	Psychic perception, accurate interpretation, imagination, clear seeing	Wisdom, knowledge, consciousness, spiritual connection
To love and be loved	To speak and to be heard	To see	To know
4 to 7 years	7 to 12 years	Adolescence	Throughout life
Social identity	Creative identity	Archetypal identity	Universal identity
Grief	Lies	Illusion	Attachment
Air	Sound	Light	Thought
Codependency, poor boundaries, possessive, jealous	Excessive talking, inability to listen, stuttering	Headaches, nightmares, hallucinations, delusions, difficulty concentrating	Overly intellectual, spiritual addiction, confusion, dissociation
Shy, lonely, isolated, lack of empathy, bitter, critical	Fear of speaking, poor rhythm, aphasia	Poor memory, poor vision, unimaginative, denial	Learning difficulties, spiritual skepticism, limited beliefs, materialism, apathy

In our spirituality, we reach for consciousness, awareness, and the highest values; in
our soulfulness, we endure the most pleasurable and exhausting of human experiences and emotions. These two directions
make up the fundamental pulse of human
life, and to an extent, they have an attraction for each other.

THOMAS MOORE

Jane might move from one job to another, never staying long enough to get a promotion, and might carry a poor self-image because of her lack of success. These patterns can be seen as expressions of the way chakra programs run our human biocomputers.

It is quite common to have a perfectly good program and not know how to activate it. People with weight problems often know exactly what they should and should not eat or how they should exercise. Yet getting such programs activated is another question entirely. Activation requires a charge of energy moving through the psychic currents of the body.

In order to run any of our programs, we have to activate our energy currents (see figure 0.4). Human bodies are taller than they are wide, so our major energy pathways run vertically while subtler currents run in other directions. This leaves us with two essential poles: the earth-centered pole, which we contact through our bodies, and the pole of consciousness, which we experience through our minds. Between these poles runs a dynamic flow of energy that we experience as our life force.

When energetic contact is made through the body, it is called *grounding*. Grounding comes from the solid contact we make with the earth, especially through our feet and legs. It is rooted in sensation, feeling, action, and the solidity of the material world. Grounding provides a connection that makes us feel safe, alive, centered in ourselves, and rooted in our environment.

Consciousness, on the other hand, comes through that elusive entity we call the mind. It is our inner understanding, our memory, our dreams and beliefs. It also organizes our sensate information. When consciousness is detached from the body, it is wide and vague, dreamy and empty, but capable of great journeys. When it is connected to our body, then we have a dynamic energy flow throughout our entire being. In this way, the spiritual realm

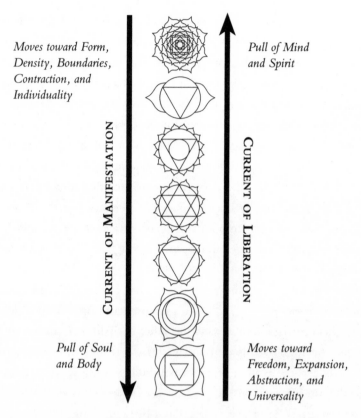

Moves toward Form,
Density, Boundaries,
Contraction, and
Individuality

Pull of Mind
and Spirit

CURRENT OF MANIFESTATION

CURRENT OF LIBERATION

Pull of Soul
and Body

Moves toward
Freedom, Expansion,
Abstraction, and
Universality

FIGURE 0.4. ENERGETIC CURRENTS

becomes *embodied*, making it tangible and effective. In effect, we have plugged in the system, just as we plug in our radio, so we can tune in to various frequencies. The chakras then become like channels, receiving and broadcasting at different frequencies.

Soul and spirit are expressions of these polarities. In my use of these terms, I see soul as tending to coalesce toward the body, leaning toward form, attachment, and feeling, whereas spirit tends to move toward freedom and expanded consciousness. *Soul is the individual expression of spirit, and spirit is the universal expression of soul.* They each connect and are enhanced by the other. (This discussion is picked up again in the chakra seven chapter.)

Liberation and Manifestation

The seven vortices of the chakras are created by the combination of these two active principles: consciousness and matter. We can think of the flow of consciousness as entering through the crown chakra and moving downward through the body. Since the chakras represent elements that become increasingly dense as they descend (from thought down to earth), I call this downward flow of energy *the current of manifestation*. When we take thoughts and turn them into visualizations, then words, and finally into form, we are engaged in the process of manifesting. Only through embodiment can consciousness manifest. This means that the energy current must be run through the body/hardware to activate the necessary programs.

> Liberation is the path of transcendence. Manifestation is the path of immanence. Both lead to the same place: the divine.

The upward current, moving from dense earth to ethereal consciousness, is the *current of liberation*. As we move incrementally upward through the chakras, we become less restricted. Water is less defined than earth; thoughts are less specific than words or pictures. Historically, the chakras were thought of as a path to liberation—a path where one is freed from the restrictions of the material world.

It is a basic premise in this work that a human being needs a balance between both of these currents in order to be whole. If we cannot liberate, we cannot change, grow, or expand. We become like automatons, unconsciously stuck in monotonous routines, our consciousness lulled to sleep from boredom. By contrast, without the current of manifestation we become aimless and empty—dreamers flying into vast realms but unable to land, full of ideas but unable to make commitments or completions. When we combine both currents, we have the mating of cosmic polarities known as the *hieros gamos*, or sacred marriage. This union of opposites creates limitless possibilities. It is the metaphoric source of *conception*—a word that implies both the birth of an idea and the beginning of life.

Unfortunately, both currents are affected by negative experiences. Physical pain, childhood traumas, social programming, and oppressive environments or activities all cut us off from our ground, and hence from the liberating current that originates at the base. Our culture, so proud of its mind-over-matter philosophy, cuts us off from our bodily experience and from the earth itself. In this severance, our sexuality is negated, our senses assaulted, our environment abused, and our power manipulated. Our ground is our form, and without it we lose our individuality.

At the other end of the pole, misinformation and indoctrination invalidate our consciousness. The child who is told he did not see what he just saw or could not have felt what he was feeling learns to doubt his own awareness. Instincts and memories may become disconnected from the body. This can produce phobias and compulsive activity, where behavior does not necessarily match the intentions of the conscious mind.

> For the archetype, as Jung conceived it, is a precondition and coexistent of life itself; its manifestations not only reach upward to the spiritual heights of religion, art, and metaphysics, but also down into the dark realms of organic and inorganic matter.

Fortunately, information and experience are stored in *both* physical and mental states. When one side is cut off, the other side can often be accessed. Our bodies can recover memories our minds have forgotten, as when incest memories appear to people during bodywork or sexual activity. Bringing consciousness into our ground activates various memories and experiences that reveal the lies and misunderstandings blocked from memory and deadening our consciousness.

Likewise, sensation can return to the body when attention is focused on certain mental material—the elements of a dream, characters in a novel, or images in a picture. Often when a client or friend talks about a vital issue, they will experience a streaming of energy in their body as a part previously deadened comes to life. Both lead to profound insight.

Integration of mind, body, and energy makes healing possible. It is not enough to merely understand without action or to merely move energy without understanding. It is the integration of these two currents that creates the changes we seek in our lives.

RECEPTION AND EXPRESSION

There are also two horizontal currents flowing into and out of each chakra—*the current of reception* and *the current of expression*. We mix our two vertical currents together in order to express ourselves at different chakra levels. For example, the speech I express through my throat chakra is a mixture of my thoughts, my will, and my breath. My love is a mixture of feelings and understanding. Likewise, what we receive through these horizontal currents enters the system and travels up and down between the chakras. For instance, an insight that I receive may release something in my body or change my thinking.

When a chakra is blocked, reception and expression become distorted. If we think of the chakras as analogous to holes in a flute, then you can see how we need to be able to open and close each one in order to play a full range. How to make this a reality is the subject of this book.

CHAKRA BLOCKAGE

We have all experienced times when the free flow of our energy seems blocked. Habitual blocks may fall into categories that relate to chakra function. For instance, if communication is difficult for us, we have a block in the fifth chakra. If we live in fear and submission, we could say our power chakra is blocked. If our physical health or personal finances are in constant crisis, then we have a block in the first chakra.

What blocks a chakra? Childhood traumas, cultural conditioning, limited belief systems, restrictive or exhausting habits, physical and emotional injuries, or even just lack of attention all contribute to chakra blockage. Difficulties abound in life, and for each one, we develop a coping strategy. When difficulties persist,

Taking and giving are the common principles of all life. Both are essential factors in open systems, in connection with the world, and in one's personal evolution. If they are out of balance, the system becomes either overwhelmed or empty and can no longer function.

A block develops from equal and opposing forces meeting on a particular plane. We cannot merely eliminate one or the other force. They must be integrated.

these coping strategies become chronic patterns, anchored in the body and psyche as defense structures.

Eventually these defenses create holding patterns in our musculature that restrict the free flow of energy, even when real threats cease to exist. This chronic tension is known as *body armor*. It effects our posture, breathing, metabolism, and our emotional states, as well as our perceptions, interpretations, and belief systems. Obviously, since the body-mind system is so affected, we see manifestations in our relationships, work, creativity, and belief systems—all of which tend to perpetuate the pattern.

Like a rock in a streambed that collects sticks and leaves, a block of any significant degree gains severity over time. What begins as a small fear grows into a full-blown phobia, severely limiting one's freedom. Habitual anger may alienate a person from his or her friends, and that isolation may produce depression and more anger. Clinging in relationships creates abandonment, which increases one's tendency to hold on.

> Without entering and leaving there is no development; without ascending and descending, no transformation, absorption, and storing.
>
> NEI CHING

Furthermore, any block in a specific chakra affects the flow of the four basic currents. We may be unable to get our liberating current "off the ground," finding ourselves continually thrown back to survival issues. Or we may be unable to fully ground our manifesting current, and remain lost in a flood of ideas, unable to make connections in the real world. If we are unable to *receive* a particular kind of energy (like love or new information), then the chakra atrophies and becomes further limited in its functioning. If we are unable to *express* energy, we stagnate and become a closed system.

In any of these cases, we are incomplete or unbalanced in our experience of life. For this reason, it is important to recognize the blocks we carry, find ways to understand their source and meaning, and develop tools to heal them.

Unblocking a chakra requires addressing the problem on multiple levels.

1. *Understand the dynamics of that particular chakra.* This means knowing the chakra system well enough to understand both the nature of each

chakra and its function in the system as a whole. This way we know what the chakra is trying to accomplish, and how it behaves in its optimal functioning.

2. *Examine the personal history related to that chakra's issues*. Each chakra has a developmental stage, with traumas and abuses that affect its functioning. Understanding your programming from each particular stage gives vital information about the nature of the block.

3. *Apply exercises and techniques*. As the chakras are physically embodied, there are specific physical exercises designed to open particular parts of the body. There are also meditations, real-world tasks, and visualization techniques to help influence change in a chakra.

4. *Balance excess and deficiency*. If a chakra is blocked by chronic holding, we learn to let go. If it is blocked by perpetual avoidance, we learn to focus on that area in both our bodies and our lives.

Not all blocks are the same, however, even in the same chakra. Different blocks require different kinds of healing. The discussion below makes an important distinction between two basic kinds of chakra imbalances. The chapters ahead look closely at what causes blocks in specific areas, and analyzes the nature of their different manifestations.

EXCESS AND DEFICIENCY

The way an individual copes with stress, negative experiences, or trauma usually falls into one of two categories: increasing one's energy and attention in order to fight the stress, or decreasing it in order to withdraw from the situation. This results in an *excessive* or *deficient* coping strategy. You can tell which way a person has decided to go by looking at their body and examining their habits. Is their body well-toned to the point of chronic tension? Do they worry every point excessively? Are they compulsive about details, overly organized? If so, they are generally overbound or excessive. By contrast, if their pattern is to withdraw from situations, to be vague, unreliable, or overly changeable, with a

So many of life's problems stem from too much or too little of something. We spend our lives searching for balance.

body that is undertoned, loose, or pasty, then they are likely to be underbound or deficient. The somatic therapist Stanley Keleman describes it this way:

> In an overbound response the membranes of the structure thicken or stiffen in such a way that the environment cannot be penetrated either from outside-in or inside-out. Underbounded structures involve membranes that become unglued; there is porosity in which the world invades the person or he leaks out into the world.[4]

We can also view this as a pattern of avoidance or overcompensation. Avoidance leads to chakra deficiency and overcompensation leads to chakra excess. A bully who compensates for insecurity by dominating others exhibits an excessive third chakra. A frightened person who talks constantly would have an excessive fifth chakra. A densely overweight person may have an excessive first chakra, using body weight to feel protected and grounded. Excessive chakras overcompensate for loss or damage by focusing excessively on that issue—usually in a dysfunctional way that fails to heal the loss.

An avoidant response in a particular area occurs when one does not have enough development to fully function on that level, so they avoid situations that might engage that area. Someone who has had early physical trauma may withdraw from their body and have trouble dealing with the physical world. A person who feels powerless will make every effort to avoid conflict. Someone who grew up in isolation and neglect may not have learned how to create relationships and will close down their heart chakra and withdraw socially.

An excessive chakra is too cluttered to be functionally useful. Like a traffic jam, the chakra is blocked by overcrowding, and the energy becomes dense and stagnant. A deficient chakra restricts energy and remains cramped, empty, and useless.

As we develop through life we are likely to become excessive in some areas and deficient in others. If a person is deficient in their first chakra, it is likely they will be excessive in their upper chakras. If they are excessively attached to power over others, they will have trouble in relationships. It is even possible to exhibit both deficient and excessive patterns in the same chakra. For example, someone who is highly emotional but sexually frigid exhibits both excess and deficiency in the second chakra.

Excessive and deficient chakras do, however, have some things in common. They are both a result of coping strategies designed to deal with stress, trauma, or unpleasant circumstances. They both restrict the flow of energy through the system, and block the complete expression of both the liberating and manifesting currents. Eventually, they both result in dysfunctional behavior and health problems.

Healing these imbalances is theoretically very simple. An excessive chakra needs to discharge energy, and a deficient chakra needs to receive energy. However, it is difficult to open a chakra which has been closed for forty years, or to get an excessive person to let go. In addition, there are many subtleties that create exceptions to the above rule. For instance, if someone talks too much as a way of discharging, it may not help to encourage them to talk more. Instead, they need to strengthen an underlying deficiency, such as poor grounding or emotional numbness. In this way, an excessive chakra can feed a deficient one. Someone who is a strong visualizer can use that same strength to imagine (and create) a healthier body. In strengthening a deficient chakra, it may also be necessary to create support by strengthening a chakra below it. Our sense of power (third chakra) increases when we are grounded (first chakra). Good relationships (chakra four) require emotional sensitivity (chakra two). These subtleties emerge as one works with the system over time.

The beauty of the chakra system lies in its multidimensionality. These imbalances can be approached verbally through discussion, physically through work with the body and movement, spiritually through meditation, emotionally through exploration of feelings, visually through images, aurally through sounds, and actualized through outer-world tasks that strengthen certain areas of our lives.

CHARACTER ARMOR

As excess and deficiency become part of our chronic holding patterns, they can become *character armor*. This bio-energetic term describes types of coping strategies and their chronic holding patterns locked in the posture and tissues of the body. Character armor typically develops from difficulties experienced during developmental stages of life. Our ways of coping become defenses that get "hardwired" into the system as it develops, beyond conscious awareness. They are not what we *decide* to do, but rather are like default programs that run automatically.

> Character provides a meeting place for psyche and soma. . . . Character represents a practice of self-care, an ongoing hasty, rigid solution imposed over our instability to maintain an intact sense of self.
>
> JOHN CONGER

Character structure describes overall patterns of armoring in the body. Alexander Lowen describes six basic character structures, each with distinctive characteristics, based on the pioneering work of Wilhelm Reich.[5] Most people exhibit at least one of these six patterns, with shades and overtones of the other structures. For instance, we may work through one layer of a character structure only to find another one underneath, or sometimes a structure becomes activated by life situations, such as loss of a loved one activating our "oral" issues or the demands of graduate school activating our need to achieve. Understanding character armor is very useful in working with the interface between body and mind, and correlates directly with the distribution of energy through the chakras.

Lowen has given the six character structures specific names, some of which make them seem quite pathological. I believe that these character structures are common to us all and for this reason I prefer to use names that are less demeaning. They are described *briefly* here, using both names, with more detailed discussion in their appropriate chapters.

THE SCHIZOID/CREATIVE. Lowen named this structure Schizoid because of its characteristic split between mind and body that results from first chakra alienation. People with this structure are highly creative and intelligent, with upper chakras that are overdeveloped. Their issues center around the right to exist, so this structure is discussed in the first chakra chapter.

THE ORAL/LOVER. The Oral structure is discussed in the second chakra chapter as it results from deprivation in the nurturing/nourishment stage of dependency related to chakras one and two. Since Oral types are strongly oriented toward emotional merging and giving, they are also referred to as Lovers.

THE MASOCHIST/ENDURER. The Masochist structure is fixated at chakra three with energy bound at the will. Robbed of their autonomy, masochists tend to hold everything inside in a conflicting pattern of pleasing and resisting, turning their blocked energy inward against the Self. They are strong and loyal, and can endure difficulty well, so they are more positively referred to as the Endurer structure.

THE RIGID/ACHIEVER. Wounded at the heart by lack of approval, this type tends to focus their energy on achievement. They are highly functional but often afraid of relationships, commitment, and feelings of intimacy. The Achiever structure is discussed in the chapter on chakra four.

THE HYSTERIC. This structure is a variation on the Rigid/Achiever and tends to occur more often in women, who have more cultural permission to be emotional. The wounds and patterns are similar to the Achiever, but where the emotions are initially held back, they later erupt with an intensity that gives this structure its name.

THE PSYCHOPATH/CHALLENGER-DEFENDER. The Psychopathic structure is also developmentally related to the third chakra, but the result is excessive rather than deficient. This type is oriented toward power-over and is also called the Challenger-Defender, as they defend the meek and challenge the strong. Since their holding pattern brings energy upward in the body, especially to the neck and shoulders, I discuss the Challenger in the fifth chakra chapter.

You can see pictures of the different body types in figure 0.5. A chart of their characteristics appears in figure 0.6 for easy reference. Other charts follow in the more detailed discussions that show their relationship to the excess and deficiency patterns of all seven chakras.

FIGURE 0.5. TYPES OF BODY ARMOR

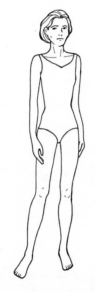

A. SCHIZOID CHARACTER

B. ORAL CHARACTER

C. ENDURER CHARACTER

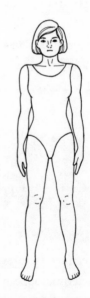

D. RIGID CHARACTER

E. HYSTERIC CHARACTER

F. CHALLENGER-DEFENDER
CHARACTER

FIGURE 0.6. FIVE CHARACTER STRUCTURES

LOWEN'S TERMS	SCHIZOID	ORAL
ALTERNATE TERMS	Creative	Lover
AGE OF DEPRIVATION	Utero to 6 months	6 months to 2½ years
HOLDING PATTERN	Holding together	Holding on (clinging)
FEAR	Falling apart, going crazy	Abandonment, rejection
DOUBTS	Right to exist	Right to have
ILLUSION	My mind is my body.	I can't do it alone. Love will solve everything.
PARENT	Angry, frightened	Depriving
PERSONALITY SYMPTOMS	Lacks sense of self	Depressed, needy, dependent
EYES	Vacant, fixed, scared	Pleading, puppy dog
POSITIVE ASPECTS	Highly creative	Loving
BODY SIGNS	Tension in joints, constricted, jumpy	Sunken chest, too fat or thin, pale, soft
CHAKRAS MOST AFFECTED	Deficient 1st	Excessive 2nd, excessive 4th

MASOCHIST	RIGID	PSYCHOPATHIC
Endurer	Achiever	Challenger–Defender
1½ to 3 years	3½ to 5 years	2½ to 4 years
Holding in	Holding back	Holding up
Humiliation, exposure	Surrender (to feelings)	Submission (to another)
Right to act (autonomy)	Right to want, right to feel	Right to be free, right to love
I'm trying to please you.	Performance is everything.	It's all a matter of will.
Instrusive, authoritarian	Sexually rejecting, cold	One parent seductive, one authoritarian
Feels stuck, moody	Agressive, proud, competitive	Power hungry, obstinate, contrary
Suffering, confused	Sparkling, bright, present	Compelling
Steady, patient, diplomatic	Good achiever, highly functional	Keep their heads, kind to underdogs
Compressed, ass held tightly, jerky movement	High head, closed heart, active pelvis, blocked middle	Attractive, upwardly displaced, loose pelvis
Blocked 3rd	Deficient 4th	Excessive 3rd, strong 5th

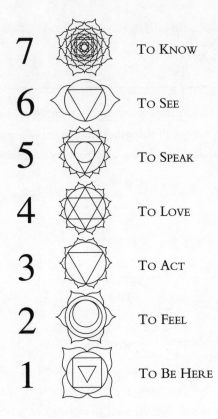

7		To Know
6		To See
5		To Speak
4		To Love
3		To Act
2		To Feel
1		To Be Here

FIGURE 0.7. THE SEVEN RIGHTS

THE SEVEN RIGHTS

The quickest way to minimize the divine within is to interfere with its basic rights.

Each one of the chakras reflects a basic, inalienable right, as listed below and in figure 0.7. Loss of these rights blocks the chakra. Reclaiming these rights is a necessary part of healing the chakra.

CHAKRA ONE: *The right to be here.* To find solidity in the first chakra, we must have an instinctual sense of our right to exist. In my workshops I find that a large majority of people have trouble with this right, as basic as it may seem. Without the right to be here, few other rights can be reclaimed. Do we have the right to take up space? Do we have the right to establish individuality? Do we have the right to take care of ourselves? The right to be here is the foundation of our survival and security.

A corollary to this right is *the right to have*, especially to have what we need to survive. I may have grasped my right to be here, but still have trouble allowing myself to *have* such things as time to myself, pleasure, money, possessions, love, or praise. Not being able to have something is like owning a bookcase without shelves. If there is no place in the system in which to store things, and no effective process for obtaining them, then we find ourselves in a constant state of deprivation—even when help is offered.

An unwanted child doubts his or her right to be here, and may have difficulty obtaining necessities later in life. When we are denied food, clothing, shelter, warmth, medical care, or a healthy environment, our right to have has been curtailed. Consequently, we may question that right many times in life. The right to have underlies the ability to contain, hold, keep, and manifest—all aspects of a healthy first chakra.

CHAKRA TWO: *The right to feel*. A culture that frowns upon emotional expression or considers sensitivity a weakness infringes upon our basic right to feel. "You have no right to be angry." "How can you express your emotions like that? You should be ashamed of yourself!" "Boys don't cry." These kinds of injunctions infringe upon our right to feel. Feeling is the way we obtain important information about our well-being. When the right to feel is impaired, we become out of touch with ourselves, numb, and disconnected. A corollary of this right is *the right to want*, since if we cannot feel, it is very difficult to know what we want. Our right to enjoy healthy sexuality is intimately connected with our right to feel.

CHAKRA THREE: *The right to act*. Cultures with narrowly defined behavior patterns impair the right to act through fear of punishment and the enforcement of blind obedience. Most people follow in the footsteps of others, afraid to innovate, afraid to be free. When the right to act is restricted, will and spontaneity go with it and our vitality decreases. This does not imply that the third chakra profits by senseless or whimsical acts, but that we do need freedom to develop our inner authority. A corollary to this right is *the right to be free*.

CHAKRA FOUR: *The right to love and be loved.* In a family this can be damaged by any dysfunction in the parents' ability to love and care for their child. Culturally, the damage appears in judgmental attitudes toward men loving men and women loving women. The right to love is further damaged by racial strife, cultural prejudice, war, or anything that forces enmity between groups as well as by poor self-esteem, broken will, and inability to feel or communicate. As the central chakra in a system of seven, the right to love is harmed when any of the other rights are lost or damaged.

CHAKRA FIVE: *The right to speak and hear truth.* This right is damaged when we are not allowed to speak truthfully in our family. "Don't talk to me like that, young man!" "We don't discuss that subject in this family." This includes not being heard when we do speak, keeping family secrets, and not being spoken to honestly. When our parents, culture, or government lie to us, there is abuse of this right. Learning clear communication is essential to reclaiming this right.

CHAKRA SIX: *The right to see.* This right is damaged when we are told that what we perceive is not real, when things are deliberately hidden or denied (such as parental drinking), or when the breadth of our vision is discounted. When children see things that are beyond the scope of their understanding, or when angry or frightening scenes occur frequently, children diminish their own ability to see. This may affect both physical vision and subtler psychic perceptions.

CHAKRA SEVEN: *The right to know.* This includes the right to accurate information, the right to truth, the right to knowledge, and the right to simply know what's going on. Certainly education is an important part of knowledge. Equally important are one's spiritual rights—the right to connect with the divine in whatever way we find most appropriate. To force on another a spiritual dogma infringes upon our seventh chakra personal and spiritual rights. To deny information and education is to close down the natural questing of the seventh chakra.

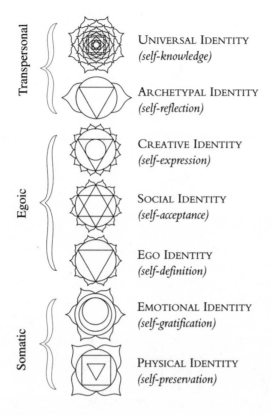

Transpersonal

UNIVERSAL IDENTITY
(self-knowledge)

ARCHETYPAL IDENTITY
(self-reflection)

Egoic

CREATIVE IDENTITY
(self-expression)

SOCIAL IDENTITY
(self-acceptance)

EGO IDENTITY
(self-definition)

Somatic

EMOTIONAL IDENTITY
(self-gratification)

PHYSICAL IDENTITY
(self-preservation)

FIGURE 0.8. IDENTITIES

THE SEVEN IDENTITIES

If our rights remain intact, or if we have managed to reclaim them, then we have a good chance at embracing our seven basic chakra identities, each of which builds upon the one below in an ever-expanding pattern of larger systems. Before listing the identities, it is worthwhile to reflect on the concept of identity itself, for it is a slippery but important concept in both psychology and spirituality.

Identity is a constantly changing and expanding manifestation of spirit. Without it, our power is too diffuse, but if we cling to it, we become limited.

Identity gives us *meaning*. We are constantly in search of meaning, for it tells us how to operate. By identifying rain clouds, we know to roll up the windows in the car. If we are ill or out of sorts, we want to identify the cause.

Each of the chakras is associated with a particular identity that emerges developmentally as we mature through life. Each identity contains within it the identities of the previous stages. Expanding our sense of identity is one of the keys to expanding our mode of consciousness from one chakra to the next.

The identities can be seen as metaphoric layers of clothing, as ways to cover the essential soul underneath. It is not a problem to have clothing—we need different outfits for different occasions, from jeans to tuxedos to sexy lingerie. It *is* a problem if we think the clothing is who we actually are, and never remove it.

When we are so immersed in these identities that we confuse them with the underlying Self, then we have gotten stuck at a particular level. We have confused the clothing for the body itself—unwilling to remove it, scared to expose the nakedness underneath. If, on the other hand, we cannot identify at all with a level, then we know we have some work to do there. Job hunting in dirty jeans or gardening in formal wear is inappropriate—if that is all we can do, we are severely limited.

The chakra identities (see figure 0.8) can be positive or negative, liberating or imprisoning. They are simultaneously real and false. They are real in that they are real parts, yet they are false because they are not the whole.

CHAKRA ONE: Our first identity level is known as the *physical identity*, and its job is *self-preservation*. Here we learn to identify with the body—when my body is hungry, *I* am hungry, when it hurts, *I* hurt. The body cloaks the invisible soul, and reveals its shape and expression. When we identify with the body, we identify with the soul's expression in physical form, as well as its physical qualities of male, female, young, old, fat, thin, healthy, or sick.

Physical identification is necessary for dealing with the physical world. If I don't realize that I *cannot* lift one hundred pounds of paper in a carton, I can seriously hurt my back. If I don't recognize when I'm hungry or need to rest, I can seriously compromise my health over time. To go without this identity is to be dissociated from the body and disconnected from the physical world.

CHAKRA TWO: Beneath the surface of the body churn the emotions. The emotions are the clothing of our feelings. When we experience a strong emotion, we feel our aliveness and often identify with the feeling involved. Even our language makes this identification: I *am* angry, I *am* scared. (Other languages say, I *have* fear or anger.) This is the identity that says, *I feel therefore I am*, and whatever I feel *is* what I am. Some people identify their main sense of self in this way.

The second chakra, then, is our *emotional identity*, and its job is *self-gratification*. Emotion emerges from our physical identity and yet brings in an added dimension. We have to feel our bodies in order to feel our emotions and learn to interpret their messages. Emotional identity expands the experience of the body and gives it dimension and texture, connecting us to the flow of the world.

CHAKRA THREE: In the third chakra, we identify with our will, behavior, and our actions. This is where we realize that we are a separate entity with the power to choose our own actions and consequences. This is the *ego identity*, oriented towards *self-definition*.[6] This type of identification says, "I am what I do." When we do something right or achieve something difficult, we feel good about ourselves. When we make mistakes or fail, then we think we're bad. We think that what we do is a statement of who we are. Ego identity emerges from physical and emotional identity and can be thought of as the *inner executive*, as it executes our intentions. This is the identity most often in charge. But we have to remember—it is only a middle manager.

CHAKRA FOUR: In the fourth chakra, we create a *social identity*, also known as the *persona*. The persona is the personality created to interact with others—it is the part of ourselves that the ego allows to rise above the surface, separated off from the shadow. Our social identity may be the compulsive helper, the seductive lover, the pleaser, or the entertainer. In our families we may take on the role of the lost child, the hero, the good girl, or the rebel. Initially, our self-concept is based on how others react to us—

whether we are popular or an outcast, admired or criticized, loved or rejected—identifying ourselves primarily through our relationships. As we mature, the identity shifts to include how we perceive our role of service to others, or how we have learned to give and embrace a world beyond our ego-oriented self. This becomes our basis for *self-acceptance*.

The social identity has the ego as its base, yet continually expands beyond the realm of self-centered needs to embrace an awareness of others. As I transcend my ego identity to care more about others, my social identity emerges. Yet, how I present myself to others depends a great deal on underlying ego strength.

CHAKRA FIVE: The fifth chakra is the center of our *creative identity*. Here we identify with our *self-expression*—what we say and produce. Initially, we identify with our word through the commitments we make. I have committed myself in marriage and by that commitment I am a wife. I have given my word to write a book, and in that commitment I am a writer. In this identity, we take responsibility for what we say by embodying it in our actions. Through our creativity, we identify ourselves as artists, teachers, entrepreneurs, politicians, mothers, or fathers. (We may also identify with our mistakes and failures.) The creative identity expands outward, through its ability to contribute and give back to the larger system.

> The most basic hypothesis about the human psyche . . . is that of a pattern of wholeness that can only be described symbolically.
>
> EDWARD WHITMONT

As this level matures, we begin to identify with larger possibilities and reach for inspiration from the great works of civilization, from the inspiring acts of heroes and saints, poets and painters. As we expand into the creative flux of the world around us, we identify with our path. Our path is the realization of our personal contribution to the larger system. Ideally, the path leads to an ever-expanding growth of consciousness and an eventual transcendence of the personal self into the transpersonal self. Its foundation is a healthy ego, social confidence, and a sense of compassion for others.

CHAKRA SIX: In the sixth chakra, we expand into our *archetypal identity*, transforming the individual *I* into something transpersonal. Our personal story is now seen as an event in a larger story. If we suffered from poor mothering because our mothers were not supported, we carry a piece of the archetypal story of the degradation of the Mother Goddess—the loss of the archetypal Mother. The power that our mothers lacked was the same power that has been stripped from women over millennia, stripped from the archetype itself. Those who suffered from distant fathers carry a piece of the larger story of industrial revolution, of disempowered men removed from their families, and the distant Father-God archetype.

We enlarge our understanding of Self as we find our own life themes reflected in fairy tales, mythology, movies, and news stories. We experience *self-reflection* in the larger system. We realize we are players in a much larger drama, riding the waves of the cultural tide's ebb and flow. As we mature at this level, we consciously embrace the evolution of the archetypal symbols that speak to us. If we take on a crusade for the preservation of the ancient forests, we are doing more than just saving trees—we contribute to a larger archetypal cause.

CHAKRA SEVEN: In the crown chakra, we come to the final and largest identity: our *universal identity*. The more our consciousness expands, the larger our identity can become. As we realize the magnificent scope of the cosmos, we have the opportunity to transcend our smaller, more limited world, and identify with the entire universe. This is a common theme in mystical experiences where the identification with the smaller ego states gives way to recognition of a unitary identity with all of life, indeed of all creation. In Eastern philosophy, this is the basis of true *self-knowledge*—the knowledge of divinity within.

The chakra levels move from exclusively individual identities—as unique and singular as our bodies—toward a universal commonality. At the outer extreme of the crown chakra, individuality is transcended and absorbed in the larger field of the divine. This is expressed by the Buddhist maxim: Thou Art That. The purpose of the crown chakra, meditation, and indeed, of most spiritual disciplines, is to break through the bonding with the smaller identities and to achieve realization of the universal identity. This does not deny the reality of the smaller identities; it just means that we see them as part of a unified and integrated whole.

Each identity is primary when our developmental process is centered there. Like Maslow's hierarchy of needs, we must consolidate our identities on the lower levels before we can sustain the larger identities, even though we may catch glimpses of them from time to time quite out of order. As we experience the higher, more inclusive identities, our lower identities slide into appropriate perspective—no less important, yet taking their place as pieces supporting a much larger, more powerful whole.

DEMONS OF THE CHAKRAS

The unconscious is not just evil by nature, it is also the source of the highest good; not only dark but also light, not only bestial, semihuman, and demonic but superhuman, spiritual, and, in the classical sense of the word, "divine."

C. G. JUNG

Each of the chakras has what I have come to call a specific demon that interferes with its health and undermines its identity. I use the word *demon* not to denote some kind of evil creature, but as a way of naming the counterforce that seemingly opposes the natural activity of the chakra. The reason I say seemingly is that demons arise to teach us something. A counterforce usually results in strengthening whatever it opposes. The presence of the demon keeps the chakra from doing its job, but that challenge also forces us to bring more awareness to that job, so eventually we can do it better.

When unacknowledged, the demons keep us from moving forward. They fixate our energy at a particular chakra level, short-circuiting our activities and expression, blocking resolution. If we acknowledge the demon and explore its reason for being there, we gain a deeper understanding of ourselves. To acknowledge that we have fear, for example, enables us to face

7		ATTACHMENT
6		ILLUSION
5		LIES
4		GRIEF
3		SHAME
2		GUILT
1		FEAR

FIGURE 0.9. DEMONS OF THE CHAKRAS

that fear and understand its origins, eventually making us more confident. To acknowledge grief enables healing, and allows the heart to lighten.

The demons are discussed in detail in each of their respective chakras. What follows is a brief description of each to give you an overall idea of their range (see figure 0.9).

The demon of chakra one is *fear*. Fear arises when something threatens our survival. It prevents us from feeling secure, focused, and calm. It creates hypervigilance, which forces energy into the upper chakras.

The demon of chakra two is *guilt*. Guilt undermines the natural flow of emotional and sexual energy through the body, and inhibits us from reaching out, diminishing emotional and sexual connections with others.

Chakra three has *shame* as its demon. Shame undermines self-esteem, personal power, spontaneous activity, and joy. Shame collapses the third chakra and turns its radiating energy inward against the self.

Grief is the demon of the heart chakra. Grief counteracts the heart's lightness and expansion, and makes it feel heavy and closed. Grief results from hurts to the heart.

Lies are the demonic antithesis to the communication of truth in the fifth chakra. Lies twist our relationship to the outside world through distorted information.

Illusion is the demon of chakra six. Illusion fixates the attention and keeps us from seeing accurately.

And finally, *attachment* is the demon of the seventh chakra. Attachment is the small focus of attention that obscures realization and unity with cosmic consciousness.

DEVELOPMENTAL STAGES

Development of the skills and concepts related to each chakra occur progressively in life, each completed stage supporting the healthy awakening of the next chakra. Although we function through all of our chakras most of the time, there are specific developmental stages in which the various chakra skills are learned and incorporated into the personality. Typically, the chakras evolve sequentially, from bottom to top, along with our chronological age (see figure 0.10). It is sometimes necessary for the next chakra phase to begin in order for the one below it to complete.

All the world's a stage, and all the men and women merely players. They have their exits and their entrances. And one man in his time plays many parts; his acts being seven ages.

WILLIAM SHAKESPEARE

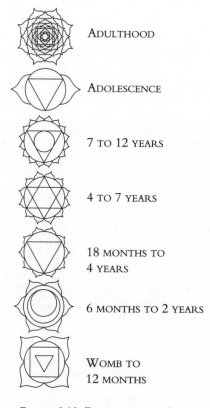

ADULTHOOD

ADOLESCENCE

7 TO 12 YEARS

4 TO 7 YEARS

18 MONTHS TO 4 YEARS

6 MONTHS TO 2 YEARS

WOMB TO 12 MONTHS

FIGURE 0.10. DEVELOPMENTAL STAGES

FIGURE 0.11. COMPARATIVE THEORIES OF DEVELOPMENT

CHAKRA	1 - *Muladhara*	2 - *Svadhisthana*	3 - *Manipura*
IDENTITY	Physical	Emotional	Ego
AGE	Womb to 12 months	6 months to 2 years	18 months to 4 years
FREUD	Oral	Oral	Anal
REICH/ LOWEN	Schizoid (Creative)	Oral (Lover)	Masochist (Endurer) Psychopath Challenger-Defender
PIAGET	Sensory-motor (Stages 1 & 2)	Sensory-motor (Stages 3 to 6)	Preoperational
ERIKSON	Trust vs. mistrust	Trust vs. mistrust★	Autonomy vs. shame and doubt
MASLOW	Physiological	Safety	Belonging★★
WILBER	Pleromatic, uroboric	Typhonic (axial, pranic, image-bodies)	Membership self
KOHLBERG	Punishment/ obedience	Instrumental/ hedonism	Good boy/ nice girl
PSYCHO- SYNTHESIS	Lower collective unconscious	Lower personal unconscious	Conscious self

★ I would add a stage to Erikson, corresponding to chakra 2, called separation vs. attachment, leaving trust vs. mistrust to chakra 1.

★★ This is Maslow's order. To more appropriately reflect the chakras, self-esteem would correspond to third chakra and belonging to fourth chakra.

4 - *Anahata*	5 - *Vissudha*	6 - *Ajna*	7 - *Sahasrara*
Social	Creative	Archetypal	Universal
3 to 7 years	7 to 12 years	Adolescence	Adulthood
Phallic	Latency	Adolescence	Genital
Rigid (Achiever/Hysteric) Psychopath Challenger/Defender			
Preoperational	Concrete operations	Formal operations	Formal operations
Initiative vs. guilt	Industry vs. inferiority	Identity vs. role confusion	Intimacy vs. isolation, generativity vs. self-absorption, integrity vs. despair
Self-esteem★★	Self-actualization	Transcendence	Transcendence
Early egoic personic	Middle egoic personic	Centaur/existential, late egoic, mature ego, low subtle	High subtle, causal, ultimate
Law and order	Social contract	Universalism	Universalism
Conscious self	Conscious self	Higher unconscious, higher collective, unconscious	Transpersonal

Therefore, there is some overlap between the development of one chakra and the next. There is also, of course, variation from person to person, a discrepancy which gets broader in the upper chakras.

The first complete round of chakra development takes roughly twenty years, with the whole cycle starting over again on a more complex level when the child leaves home and begins his or her adult life. Descriptions of the stages listed below are necessarily brief, with more detail given in subsequent chapters—this is meant to outline the unfolding developmental process. These stages can be compared with other developmental models, as shown in figure 0.11.

CHAKRA ONE
Mid-pregnancy to 12 months after birth,
peaking at 4 to 5 months

The first chakra relates to the formation of the physical body and takes place during prenatal development and infancy. In this stage body growth is most rapid, and is therefore the main focus of the life force. The infant's developmental task is to learn how to operate the body—how to suck, eat, digest, grasp, sit, crawl, stand, walk, and manipulate objects—in general, to deal with the physical world and the challenging force of gravity. These tasks are incredibly demanding and occupy the bulk of consciousness throughout the first year.

> If there is anything we wish to change in the child, we should first examine and see whether it is not something that could better be changed in ourselves.
>
> C. G. JUNG

Consciousness in the infant is focused internally, with little awareness of the outside world. The baby lives in a fused symbiosis with the mother, not yet realizing a separate sense of self. Until the child moves under his own steam, even minimal independence is impossible. Discovery and mastery of motor functions is the first step toward this independence.

Awareness in this stage focuses mainly on survival and physical comfort. When these needs are properly met, it anchors the spirit into the physical body, and the child feels welcomed into the world. Erik Erikson, in his eight stages of psychosocial development, defines the struggle of this age as one of *trust vs. mistrust.* Successful progress through this stage gives us a sense of hope and affirms our right to be here and our right to have. This stage builds the foundation of security and groundedness that enables *self-preservation* and forms the *physical identity*.

CHAKRA TWO
6 months to 2 years, peaking at 12 to 18 months

The second chakra, which is typified by duality, sensation, feeling, and mobility, comes into conscious attention at about six months when visual acuity allows the child to focus on outside objects and gain a wider visual perspective. A noticeable state of alertness occurs when the child sits up and for the first time becomes aware of things out of immediate range.[7]

As the child learns to crawl and walk, she develops the ability to move away from her mother and experience brief episodes of independence. Called *hatching* by Margaret Mahler, the infant is just beginning to discover that she is a separate self, hatching from the egglike symbiosis of chakra one. As she is still very dependent upon the mother, this discovery is simultaneously frightening and exciting, and therefore fraught with ambivalence as she plunges into a world of diversity and choices. Although Erikson's first stage of *trust vs. mistrust* extends into this period, I would give this stage a separate name, characterized by the conflict of *separation vs. attachment*.

As the child explores, she experiences her first distinctions as binary choices—good and bad, pleasure and pain, closeness and distance, self and other. In this stage, these distinctions are felt, rather than understood. At this point, the child is all need, sensation, and desire. Needs want to be satisfied. Sensation gives way to desire. Needs and desires mark the motivation for locomotion—seeing something and moving toward it, merging with it, and incorporating it (most often through the mouth). As language is not yet developed, the prime means of communication is through emotion, which hopefully is responded to in a caring and meaningful way.

This stage focuses on the formation of an *emotional identity* which is mainly interested in *self-gratification*.

CHAKRA THREE

18 months to approximately 4 years

Chakra three begins with the period of attempted autonomy that occurs with the "terrible twos" (also known as the willful stage). The child has now successfully "hatched" from the mother, and is secure enough in this separateness to want to experiment with his own volition. What was only powerless wishing in the second chakra now becomes an act of will, with some small hope of success. The development of language allows the child to conceive of time in terms of cause and effect. This realization makes it possible to begin controlling impulses and delaying gratification. (If I eat my vegetables, I will get dessert.) Here the unconscious, instinctual states of the lower two chakras start to come under conscious control, signaling the emergence of the conscious self and the awakening of the ego.

> The strength of our ego boundaries is the result of each properly resolved developmental crisis.
>
> JOHN BRADSHAW

The child at this stage is naturally self-centered, and wishes to establish a sense of personhood, power, and the ability to self-create and self-define. He is aware of himself as a separate entity, and is now focused on power dynamics through exploration and development of his personal will.

The important achievement here is a sense of autonomy and will, balanced harmoniously with the will of others. Breaking the child's will is extremely damaging, as is allowing the child an excessive sense of control without setting limits. Erikson refers to this stage as *autonomy vs. shame and doubt*. Healthy resolution brings about power and will.

This is the formation of a personal *ego identity*, mainly focused on *self-definition*.

CHAKRA FOUR

4 to 7 years

Chakra four develops as one leaves the stubborn egocentricity of the third chakra and begins to show interest in relationships outside of the primary ones with Mother and Father. This does not mean that the heart has not already been open, as any parent of a toddler will attest. In earlier phases, the heart is open but not intelligent, being unconscious of its loving. As chakra four awakens, loving becomes more conscious, meaning that behaviors are consciously adapted to gain or express love.

The autonomy developed in chakra three forms a foundation for relationships with others. Relationships within the family provide the child's first model of how to form her own relationships. The child now internalizes these family relationships and begins to have playmates her own age. The nature of any of these relationships greatly affects the child's self-esteem, and for this reason, rejection or loss can be particularly damaging at this stage.

The world of the family is the social foundation for entering the larger world of school or day care. Conceptual thinking makes it possible to perceive the world as a complex set of relationships, and learning these relationships is the dominant task at hand. "Why does the fire make it warm?" "Why does Susie's mommy drive a different car?" "Why does Daddy have a beard and you don't?" Learning how things relate to each other is the main focus of consciousness at this stage.

This stage heralds the formation of our relationship programs and our *social identity*. The successful formation of a healthy social identity rests on *self-acceptance*, which simultaneously allows for the acceptance of others. Erikson called this stage *initiative vs. guilt*, with resolution bringing about direction and purpose, essential to the next level above.

CHAKRA FIVE
7 to 12 years

This is the stage of creative expression. Once the social identity is developed and one understands basic relationships between Self and world, a period of personal creativity unfolds. If preceding stages have gone well, then the child has a solid sense of self, and is filled up energetically and emotionally. Now there is a desire to move that energy forward into creativity, into the act of giving something back, of making one's own offering to the world. The ability to make this offer and be appreciated for it is essential for maintaining ego strength. The child's thinking now operates on a more symbolic level, allowing creativity and more abstract thinking (Piaget's *concrete operations*).

Erikson called this stage *industry vs. inferiority*, where resolution results in a sense of competence. This is a period of expansion, experimentation, and creativity. For this reason it is important to support the child's natural curiosity and creativity. It is also important to model healthy forms of communication.

This is the formation of a *creative identity*, with the important property of *self-expression*.

CHAKRA SIX
Adolescence

The awakening of this chakra requires an ability to recognize patterns and apply them to life decisions. This is the emergence of Piaget's *formal operations* stage, where imagination helps the child develop his symbolic conception of the world.

For adolescents, it marks a period of reexamining their social identity—this time making it a more conscious choice, whereas the fourth chakra social identity is largely created in unconscious reaction to family dynamics. There may be a dawning interest in spiritual matters, mythology, or symbolism, whether through music, lyrics, popular movie icons, or the latest fashion at school. When allowed to mature, this leads to the formation of *archetypal identity*, whose interest is *self-reflection*. Erikson named the conflict of adolescence as *identity vs. role confusion*.

CHAKRA SEVEN
Early adulthood and beyond

The seventh chakra is related to the pursuit of knowledge, the formation of a worldview, and the awakening of spiritual pursuits. Each new piece of information is filtered through the developing worldview (a constantly changing structure), forming the basis of all future behavior. The seventh chakra is largely concerned with the search for meaning—asking questions about the nature of life, the universe, and the Self within.

This leads to the formation of a *universal identity*, which is found at the core of the awakened Self through *self-knowledge*.

INTERACTIVE DEVELOPMENT:
THE CHAKRA SYSTEM AS A WHOLE

It is important to note the role of both ascending and descending energy currents as development takes place. Borrowing some from Ken Wilber's developmental psychology, we can see how the descent of consciousness from the crown couples with the organization of raw energy from below, and stimulates the ability to move on to the next stage[8] (see figure 0.12). Having an awareness (chakra seven) of the body (chakra one) allows us to differentiate from the body, and in so doing, to be able to operate on it and hence operate on the physical world. The dawning of images (chakra six) allows us to perceive a world outside of ourselves, and gives rise to a sense of otherness and the desire to move and explore (chakra two). The development of language skills (chakra five) allows us to exert our will (chakra three) as we say yes, no, I will, or I won't. Language interaction gives us *concepts* to go with our movements, feelings, or actions, and thus the conceptual world of relationships, characteristic of chakra four, is born.

Difficulties occurring during any of these crucial stages can affect the chakra that is developing at that time, as well as the chakras that follow. For example, one's sense of power is positively affected by the security of getting survival needs properly met, ease of the heart is supported by the nurturance of touch in the first and second chakra stages, and our ability to communicate is supported by a balanced ego and a sense of love and acceptance.

ADULT DEVELOPMENT

THE PROCESS OF INDIVIDUATION

Chakra development during childhood is relatively unconscious. Adult development, by contrast, is largely conscious—we have to want to develop, or it may not happen at all. For many people, adult chakra development never occurs as they remain in dependency and powerlessness and never break from their programmed instinctual patterns. They may never have spiritual cravings and may never discover the potential of their higher selves. As the process of awakening is often fraught with challenge and

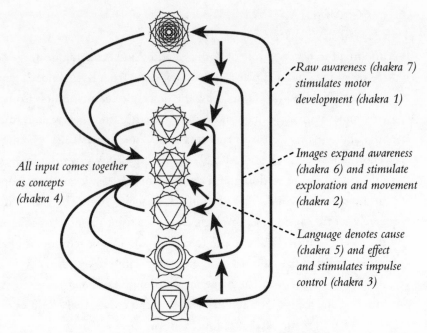

Raw awareness (chakra 7) stimulates motor development (chakra 1)

Images expand awareness (chakra 6) and stimulate exploration and movement (chakra 2)

All input comes together as concepts (chakra 4)

Language denotes cause (chakra 5) and effect and stimulates impulse control (chakra 3)

FIGURE 0.12. COMBINED CURRENTS IN DEVELOPMENT

difficulty, who is to say whether they are better or worse off? But for those who are unsatisfied with the script given them, who long for something greater, here is a description of the second round of personal evolution through the chakras.

Once the child leaves home and begins to live independently (early adulthood), the chakra stages begin again. The second round is not as clearly defined, as there is much more potential for variation in the developmental order. Some people have children before they develop a job skill, others go to school for years and years. Some begin with spirituality and have a family later, or never have a family at all. Some spend a short time establishing an economic base, a relationship, or a mode of creative expression, while others spend their whole

Individuation means becoming a single, homogeneous being, and in so far as individuality embraces our innermost, last, and incomparable uniqueness, it also implies becoming one's own self... or "self-realization."

C. G. JUNG

life at any one these tasks. What follows is a general guideline—and could perhaps be seen as optimal rather than actual. For this reason, ages are not listed.

CHAKRA ONE: The first issue to solve is one of survival—getting a place to live, learning to care for yourself, and finding a means of independent income. The time spent on this stage clearly varies from person to person— for some it is a lifelong struggle. Successful completion marks basic independence and self-sufficiency.

CHAKRA TWO: Once this is accomplished (or simultaneously) one forms sexual relationships. This is not to say that sexuality has not been occurring for many years, but awareness of "other" now becomes more acute and the need for partnership may become primary. Satisfaction of emotional needs is the underlying drive, usually projected on the partner. Emotional frustration may awaken unconscious patterns from the shadow, which may sabotage early relationships, often with misunderstandings, blaming, and emotional turmoil. This is even more acute when the adult senses of personal will and responsibility have not yet awakened.

CHAKRA THREE: In adults, the individuation process liberates us from having to conform to the expectations of parents, friends, or culture, and allows us to become a true individual operating under our own power and will. Here we move from dependency, powerlessness, and obedience to the creation of our own path and future. This may or may not awaken in one's life. It is often triggered by meaningless jobs, or the enslavement of relationships in which we are defined by the needs and expectations of the other person.

Here begins the task of making our own way in the world—developing a personal career, building skills to meet challenges, and controlling our destiny. This may be a time of political involvement, of seeking affinity with others who are fighting their own powerlessness, whether through political affinity groups, recovery groups, or spiritual groups. The misaligned third chakra seeks power *over* others; the awakened third chakra seeks power *with* others.

CHAKRA FOUR: The focus on relationships eventually matures into true empathy and altruism and the maintenance of lasting partnerships.

Relationships that have gotten past the hormone stage usually require a serious reevaluation of one's behavior toward others. Sometimes the loss of a previous relationship causes us to examine the nature of *all* our relationships, including our family of origin. If there are children, there is an emphasis on family dynamics. Relationships with colleagues, coworkers, friends, and community add to the complexity of this midlife stage.

We may also examine ourselves in terms of our relationship to the world around us. What role have we been playing? What role do we want to play? What do we seek from relationships? What parts of ourselves have been repressed and need to be reclaimed? Jung marked the fourth chakra as the midlife beginning of individuation, focused initially on the balance between inner masculine and feminine, or *animus* and *anima*.[9]

CHAKRA FIVE: Once again, creative and personal expression come into play. This is the stage where one makes their personal contribution to the community. It may mean creating a business, writing a book or thesis, building one's own house, or seriously pursuing an artistic hobby. This creative expression helps coalesce issues experienced in the previous stages. With most people it occurs around midlife. With more creative personalities, it happens much sooner and may precede or dominate other activities. It may also be a period of marking our contribution through public service.

CHAKRA SIX: This stage involves the reflection and study of patterns through exploration of mythology, religion, and philosophy. There may be a period of searching in the form of travel or renewed study of inner paths. This is an introverted stage of taking in from outside, having satisfied one's extroverted urges and wanting further inner development. (For those who begin in introversion, it may be time to communicate what has been learned to the outside world.) This is also a time of spiritual interest and development, if such has not already occurred. Such searching intensifies when children are grown and the adult has more time and freedom for contemplation and spiritual practice.

CHAKRA SEVEN: This is the time of wisdom, spiritual understanding, knowledge, and teaching. Now we bring together information gathered throughout life, and pass it on to others. For some this means leaving the mundane world for a spiritual pursuit, while for others it is a time of teaching and sharing, a time to develop mastery.

Again, it must be stressed that these developmental stages, especially the second cycle, are not the same for everyone, nor are they experienced in the same order. Adult development is often arrested by unresolved childhood conflicts. If you find that you have not gotten very far on some of these levels, then this book is for you. It will help you find where you might have gotten stuck and explain how to proceed on the path of liberation toward wholeness.

In the following chapters, the preceding principles are applied to each chakra in detail. It must be remembered, however, that this is a model, rather than a rigid dogma. Individual people are very complex and, in order to be valid, one's whole chakra pattern must be examined. Whenever I teach my workshops, I always get a host of questions along the lines of, "My friend has or does so and so. What chakra is that?" It is seldom that simple. Linking specific symptoms to specific chakras is not enough. For instance, a timid person (deficient third chakra), may be suffering from poor grounding (deficient first chakra), tumultuous feeling states (excessive second chakra), or any number of other possibilities. What is important is to first understand the complete system and then to examine each person as a whole, using reason, intelligence, competence, and compassion. Only then will the assessment be complete.

CHAKRA ONE

Reclaiming the Temple of the Body

FIRST CHAKRA AT A GLANCE

ELEMENT
Earth

NAME
Muladhara (root)

PURPOSE
Foundation

ISSUES
Roots
Grounding
Nourishment
Trust
Health
Home
Family
Prosperity
Appropriate boundaries

COLOR
Red

LOCATION
Base of spine
Coccygeal plexus

IDENTITY
Physical

ORIENTATION
Self-preservation

DEMON
Fear

DEVELOPMENTAL STAGE
2nd trimester to 12 months

DEVELOPMENTAL TASKS
Physical growth
Motor skills
Object permanence

BASIC RIGHTS
To be here and have

BALANCED CHARACTERISTICS
Good health
Vitality
Well grounded
Comfortable in body
Sense of trust in the world
Feeling of safety and security
Ability to relax and be still
Stability
Prosperity
Right livelihood

TRAUMAS AND ABUSES
Birth trauma
Abandonment, physical neglect
Poor physical bonding with
    mother
Malnourishment, feeding
    difficulties

TRAUMAS AND ABUSES (CONT'D)

Major illness or surgery

Physical abuse or violent
environment

Enema abuse

Inherited traumas—parents'
survival fears (i.e., holocaust
survivors, war veterans,
poverty conditions)

DEFICIENCY

Disconnection from body

Notably underweight

Fearful, anxious, restless,
can't settle

Poor focus and discipline

Financial difficulty

Poor boundaries

Chronic disorganization

EXCESS

Obesity, overeating

Hoarding, material fixation,
greed

Sluggish, lazy, tired

Fear of change, addiction to
security

Rigid boundaries

PHYSICAL MALFUNCTIONS

Disorders of the bowel, anus,
large intestine

Disorders of solid parts of the
body: bones, teeth

Issues with legs, feet, knees,
base of spine, buttocks

Eating disorders

Frequent illness (can be
deficient and/or excessive)

HEALING PRACTICES

Reconnect with body

Physical activity (aerobics,
weights, running, dance)

Lots of touch, massage

Bioenergetic grounding

Hatha yoga

Look at earliest childhood
relationship to mother

Reclaim right to be here

AFFIRMATIONS

It is safe for me to be here.

The earth supports me and
meets my needs.

I love my body and trust its
wisdom.

I am immersed in abundance.

I'm here and I'm real.

SHADES OF RED

When Mary walked into my office, the pain in her body was palpable, yet she was unaware of it. She walked stiffly and nervously, her eyes darting about frantically, hypervigilant for her own safety. She spoke rapidly as if with great fear, and the urgency of her words revealed a deep suffering that in forty-six years had never been relieved. Her body was constricted, thin, and wiry, and her history revealed a number of self-destructive tendencies, including anorexic starvation in an attempt to annihilate her body and live entirely in her mind. She was now developing numbness in her extremities. Her hands, cut off from the waters of her soul, flitted nervously of their own accord, like fish on a line. She could not tell if she was hungry or sleepy, warm or cold. Disconnected from her body, it is no surprise that she also felt disconnected from life itself.

This woman was clearly an individual, yet her suffering had common roots with many clients I have seen over the years. She had tried other therapists who stayed entirely in the realm of conversation, and none could touch the severe separation of mind and body from which she suffered. Her plight is the plight of many, in varying degrees of severity. Separated from the experience of our bodies, we are separated from our aliveness, from the experience of the natural world, and from our most basic inner truth. This division creates a dissociative state. Disconnected from our body, our actions become compulsive—no longer ruled by consciousness or rooted in feelings, but fueled by an unconscious urge to bridge the gap between mind and body at whatever cost.

To lose our connection with the body is to become spiritually homeless. Without an anchor we float aimlessly, battered by the winds and waves of life.

Disconnection from the body is a cultural epidemic. Of all the losses rupturing the human soul today, this alienation may be the most alarming because it separates us from the very roots of existence. With jobs that are degrading, routines that are automatic, and environments that annihilate our senses, we lose the joy that arises from the dynamic connection with the only living presence we are guaranteed to have for the whole of our lives: our body.

Dissociation produces dangerously disconnected actions. Senseless killings and drive-by shootings (where another's body is seen as lifeless and meaningless, a thing of one's own) pervade our newscasts, met with morbid fascination by anonymous viewers. Women annihilate or silicone their curves to meet the cultural norm of model figures plastered on billboards and magazines. Men pound their flesh into submission to build a sense of power, often numbing their sensations and feeling. Many people fall into addictions, numbing their aliveness with food, drugs, or compulsive activities. Children are beaten, molested, and marshaled into obedience, driven from their own young bodies before they even learn to understand them, driven by disembodied adults who know not what they annihilate.

Mind severed from body, culture from planet—to lose our ground is to lose our home.

We are taught to control the body by way of the mind, which is considered far superior. But the body has an intelligence whose mysteries the mind has yet to fathom. We read in books how to eat, how to make love, how much sleep to get, and impose these practices on the body rather than listening from within.

Without the body as a unifying figure of existence, we become fragmented. We repress our aliveness and become machinelike, easily manipulated. We lose our testing ground for truth.

Devaluation of the body is further perpetrated by many religious attitudes. Some religions describe the body as the root of all evil, while others tell us that it is merely an illusion or, at best, simply insignificant. Medical practices treat the body mechanically, as a set of disconnected parts divorced from the spirit that dwells within. Standard training for psychotherapists completely ignores the role of the body in mental health. Conspicuous in their absence are requirements in anatomy, nutrition, allergies, movement, yoga, neuromuscular alignment, bioenergetic character structures, or even simple massage. The use of therapeutic touch or physical contact in any form is often strictly forbidden, so great is the fear of sexual contamination. Universities educate our minds at the cost of our bodies, where we sit completely still for days, months, and years, training ourselves for sit-down jobs that continue to ignore the body's needs.

Is it any wonder that we equally ignore our physical surroundings, damaging the body of the Earth in order to perpetuate our dissociated survival? Perhaps the increasing problem of homelessness is a metaphor for our own cultural homelessness, for the body is indeed the home for the spirit. Our health care crisis extends far beyond the issue of insurance coverage—it is a crisis of connection with the biological reality of our existence.

Degradation of our physical reality is a cultural epidemic for which there is no simple cure, no pill to take, no miraculous healing. Nor can we necessarily ease the pain that comes when the numbness wears off and we awaken to the constriction and abuse we have previously accepted. Only by recovering the body can we begin to heal the world itself, for as mind is to body, so culture is to planet. Healing the split between mind and body is a necessary step in the healing of us all. It heals our home, our foundation, and the base upon which all else is built.

UNFOLDING THE PETALS

The Body

Foundation

Survival

Roots

Grounding

Nourishment

Trust

Health

Home

Family

Prosperity

THE FOUNDATION OF THE TEMPLE

All foundations rest upon the earth—the universal ground for all that we do. To connect with the body is to connect with the earth, to be grounded in the biological reality of existence. Our bodies are the home of our spirit. Situated at the base of the spine, the first chakra is the foundation for the entire chakra system. It is here we build the foundation for the temple of the body—the anchor for the Rainbow Bridge. Without a strong, rooted foundation, little else can be accomplished. We must have soil firm enough to provide stability, yet yielding enough to be penetrated by roots. The anchoring of this temple digs deep into the earth, for its Sanskrit name, *muladhara*, means "root support."

The foundation contains the temple's energy by defining its scope, edges, and boundaries. It defines a place, as a basic context of all that happens to us. It gives us a ground, a home, an anchor point for our experience. The foundation largely determines the shape of the structure above, determining what it can hold, how high it can build, what kind of stresses it can withstand. Thus damage to this chakra is reflected in each and every chakra above.

To build a strong foundation is to gain solidity. Solidity allows us to be firm and make boundaries. Solidity has consistency, repetition, accountability. Our bodies are the solid form of our existence; they have definable boundaries. To be solid is to face what is in front of us without flinching, to remain anchored in truth in the face of opposition, and to remain calm and secure.

SURVIVAL

Survival is the first challenge to being alive, the original instigator of feeling, action, creativity, and awareness. Without assuring survival, nothing is possible. By attending to survival, everything is possible.

The underlying element of consciousness that forms this foundation is the instinct to survive. This instinct is archaic, fundamental, and unavoidable and runs the baseline maintenance program of our physical existence. When satisfied, it retreats to a dronelike subroutine, allowing our consciousness to engage in other activities. When threatened, it dominates all other functions of consciousness. Where are your thoughts when you are suddenly chased by a mugger, spinning into a car accident, or facing a life-threatening illness? At these times, all available psychic energy is routed to survival and little is available for anything else.

When survival threats are frequent occurrences (as they are for someone raised amid violence or severe poverty), then consciousness becomes fixated at this level. This keeps the body in a state of hyperstimulated readiness, flooded with stress hormones that promote the instinctual fight-or-flight response. One may feel restless, tense, and unable to sleep deeply, which may lead to frequent health problems over time. This is common in post-traumatic stress disorder (PTSD), a condition where stress reactions continue to occur long after the trauma is over.

One of my clients grew up in a Guatemalan war zone. After fifteen years in a safer environment, his muscles were still constantly tensed and ready to run. He had insomnia and a serious jaw-clenching problem. He was fearful and jumpy and had trouble concentrating and difficulty manifesting prosperity. He was a highly creative, intelligent, sensitive man whose body was breaking down in his early thirties because he could never relax. He could neither satisfy nor escape the demands of his first chakra.

When the first chakra is damaged, we are plagued with issues of survival, including health, money, housing, or job problems. We may find that a basic feeling of safety and security seems to elude us no matter what we do even when there are no real threats to our survival.

The survival instincts lie at the base of the *collective unconscious*, as inherited tendencies and preferences that have developed in the human psyche over the course of evolution. These instincts form the natural impulses of the body to defend itself and to connect with the environment. When these natural instincts are denied, we have a rupture between our waking consciousness and the very core of our being. We become disembodied and disconnected from our environment. By reclaiming the first chakra, we can live harmoniously with our basic survival instincts without being unconsciously ruled by them.

THE DEMON OF FEAR

When survival is threatened, we feel afraid. Fear heightens our awareness and floods the body with natural chemicals (such as adrenalin) to energize it for action. Fear brings our attention into the here and now to address the threat, but focuses the attention outward and upward to the chakras of perception and mental activity. We become hypervigilant, restless, anxious. We can't settle, relax, or let down. It's as if we are jumping right out of our skin.

Scared is what happened when the sacred gets scrambled.

When we live in an environment of danger or deprivation, we experience fear. If danger was a frequent presence growing up, then fear pervades our baseline program for survival. The sense of fear brings a feeling of safety, as paradoxical as that might sound. We feel safe only because we are hypervigilant and become even more uncomfortable when we try to relax. The nervous system and the adrenal glands remain overworked. In this state of hyperarousal, our triggers are more sensitive and more likely to react in extremes. Our foundation is literally shaky and concentration may be difficult. As a result, the body is in a constant state of stress, which becomes normal. This may eventually create high blood pressure, heart trouble, stomach troubles, immune system depletion, weak adrenal glands, insomnia, or chronic fatigue.

Fear engages our survival instincts by getting us ready to respond. But if it becomes constant, we lose our ability to respond appropriately.

Ideally, fear wakes us up from the sleepy hypnogogic state of merging and trust, characteristic of the infant. When the threat cannot be overcome, we adapt to the fear and form ourselves around a basic contraction and shakiness. This is contrary to the healthy state of the first chakra, which is associated with safety, security, and solidity. To work through fear is to learn to relax and feel the subtle energies of the body, to have pleasure and expand our attention to a wider vista. To combat fear is to strengthen the first chakra. To live with fear is to weaken it.

In order to fully ground into a solid foundation capable of supporting the rest of our activities, the demon of fear must be overcome. This means first of all that the fear must be understood. Where did it come from? How did it serve you? Understanding is not enough, however, because the fear response is still lodged in the body. The next step is to release and integrate the instinctual responses to the fear. Does it make you want to run and hide? Does it make you angry and activated or paralyzed and confused? Allowing the body to express these responses helps complete the *gestalt* of the response to the original trauma. In its completion, the cycle of fear can be broken, and a healthier pattern created. Finally, one must develop the strength and resources to effectively meet similar threats in the future. This may include such things as building self-esteem, learning martial arts, or improving communication skills.

Although fear is the demon of the first chakra, it is also a sacred adversary, a presence that has much to teach us. Fear exists as an ally of self-preservation, teaching us of our own importance and the need to take care of ourselves. Only when we acknowledge this demon as an ally can it be truly mastered.

Ernest Holmes, who founded the Science of Mind philosophy, describes both fear and faith as having similar qualities. Fear is a belief that something awful might happen, while faith is a belief that something good will happen. Although the results are different, the causes are the same—both are beliefs that govern our behavior and influence the way we feel. If we can replace unreasonable fear with reasonable faith, then we have a natural antidote to our first chakra demon.

> This external fear is never to leave us for long as we live with it; it operates as a transpersonal stimulus for the development of consciousness, with which to oppose what is feared . . . without this fear, there would be no psychological development.
>
> EDWARD WHITMONT

RECLAIMING OUR ROOTS

The Sanskrit name for the base chakra, *muladhara*, means "root support." This chakra roots us into our bodies, the physical world, and the earth. A plant cannot survive without roots, and neither can the psyche of a human being. Our roots represent where we come from: the earth, womb, our ancestors and family, and our personal history. We cannot simultaneously deny our past and maintain our roots.

In order to create a solid foundation, we have to sort out the roots of our childhood. For better or worse, these roots nourished and sustained us in our most formative stages. Where the ground was inhospitable, we need to transplant our psyche to more fertile soil. This involves paying attention to the environments we live in and the ground we create around us.

The *muladhara* chakra corresponds to the element *earth*, which is the ground for our roots. As stated in the introduction, human life is dependent upon a supply of energy. Our roots can be seen as the way our system plugs in to the larger system of the planet, which is our source, the origin of the liberating current, from which all things grow up. The elements needed for physical survival come from the earth in various forms—the food we eat, the things we touch and see, the water we drink, the air we breathe, and the sounds we hear. We push against the earth in order to stand or move and we rest upon the earth (nurtured by gravity) when we choose to be still.

For most of us, our roots are unconscious influences on our behavior, linked to elements from our past. To bring *muladhara* to consciousness is to bring awareness to our roots, to uncover the past, to examine it, to delve into it. Everything that grows above branches out into infinity, growing more complex. Going down to our roots brings us into a singular simplicity, and anchors us into the commonality of the collective unconscious. It brings us home to the earth.

> Just as the groundedness of a tree routes the flow of sap from earth to leaves and from leaves to earth, so does our groundedness channel the flow of excitement from ourselves to the environment and from the environment to ourselves.
>
> STANLEY KELEMAN

GROUNDING

A healthy first chakra allows a person to be energetically grounded—a concept that is critical to understanding basic aliveness and well-being. Grounding orients us in time and space, and connects us to the environment. Being grounded gives us a source of strength through connection to our body and environment. Physically this happens through the legs and feet, through which excitement is passed up into the body and excess is discharged downward into the ground. This means we can stand on our own two feet and move forward in life. Only by drawing energy up from the base can we create the liberating current that flows to the crown.

Grounding brings consciousness into the body, and is essential for forming healthy boundaries. We feel more awake and alive when the downward current of consciousness connects with the body and meets the edges and boundaries of physical reality.

Many people who consider themselves spiritual have greatly improved their lives when they learned to send their energy downward as well as upward. We are typically taught that spirituality is only found in the non-physical realms, yet to truly experience our body's aliveness is to experience a profoundly spiritual state—achieved by embracing our natural tendencies rather than denying them through ascetic practices.

> The mighty oak was once a little nut that stood its ground.

When we are grounded, we can be present, focused, dynamic. Our attention is concentrated in the here and now, bringing a dynamic intensity to the way we present ourselves. Our experience is direct, sensate, immediate. We are confident yet contained, connected with our own source of support.

Without grounding we are unstable. We lose our center, fly off the handle, get swept off our feet, or daydream in the fantasy world. We lose our ability to contain, which is the ability to have and to hold. If we cannot contain, we cannot hold our boundaries and build up inner power; thus, we cannot mature. Boundaries allow the hermetic seal necessary for transformation. Without boundaries, natural excitement gets dissipated and diluted and becomes ineffectual. When we lose our ground, our attention wanders and we appear vague and insubstantial.

> To be grounded is to be connected to our emotional-electrical currents, to the waves of our needs and images and the rhythms of actions which comprise our physical-psychic processes: the rhythms of the human and natural ground.
>
> STANLEY KELEMAN

The healthy establishment of one's ground is the essential work of the first chakra, and the foundation for any further growth. Here lies the basic rights of the first chakra: the right to be here and to the right to have what we need in order to survive.

NOURISHMENT

Nourishment is our most basic form of support for the body's survival. Our past history determines how we support and nourish ourselves. Without support, we fall. Without nourishment, we collapse. Persons who embody a sense of physical collapse are revealing a lack of support in their life and their bodies show a corresponding sense of defeat. They may question their right to be here, have difficulty nourishing themselves, or suffer from abandonment issues.

> The need for nourishment forces us to remain open as a system, in constant interaction with our environment.

Eating disorders are often manifestations of first chakra issues of nourishment. My friend Connie turned to food whenever she felt lonely, trying to make solidity out of her feelings of emptiness. Mary, whom we met earlier, so questioned her right to be here that she literally doubted her right to feed herself and frequently went days without eating. Reclaiming our right to be here, learning to ground, and attending to our need for nourishment are all first chakra necessities.

MANIFESTATION AND PROSPERITY

The characteristics of good grounding, connection with our bodies and the physical world, self-nourishment, and self-preservation contribute to the ability to manifest prosperity. I am not talking about being rich here—I am talking about meeting basic survival needs in ways that offer security, stability, and enough freedom to expand beyond survival consciousness. This means being able to keep the rent or mortgage paid, keeping the car in good repair, keeping our homes relatively clean and running smoothly, and putting regular meals on the table. This is about being able to handle the basic demands of the earth plane, the requirements of living in a physical body. In order to meet these survival needs, we must be able to deal with our immediate physical environment—to extract from it what we need for our personal or familial preservation. This is the testing ground of our first chakra abilities. It gives us a means for our own independence, enabling us to stand on our own two feet, to stand in our own ground. Only by standing in our own ground can we determine our future.

The first chakra is the most specific and limited level in the system. A limitation is a boundary, separating something from what is around it in order to define it. A boundary creates a necessary limitation that allows us to have something whole, something specific.

In order to manifest, we must be able to accept limitation. We have to be able to focus on what we want, to be specific about it. We have to be able to stick with it long enough for manifestation to occur. I have to be able to sit in my chair for months on end to manifest this book. It may be necessary to stick with long periods of schooling or training to manifest a good job skill. To become proficient at something, we have to practice it over and over again, limiting ourselves to that specific activity until we master it.

I have known many highly intelligent and talented people, especially in the New Age and counterculture circles, who could not manifest prosperity.

What I have also noticed in this group is an unrealistic attachment to freedom, an unwillingness to accept limitation long enough to manifest their
basic needs. As a result, they do not have freedom at all, but enslavement
to a first chakra level of consciousness. As a freedom-loving Sagittarian, I
spent the decade of my twenties in this state. I
was free from the restrictions of a boring job, but
I also was too poor to do anything with my freedom. It was not until I accepted limits with grace
that I manifested any prosperity for myself.

Manifestation requires an acceptance of limitation. A boundary allows us to contain, and thus collect and build.

When we cooperate with first chakra limitations, our energy builds up and naturally expands to
other levels. When we rebel against these limita-
tions, we are kept in survival mode and are unable to get our liberating current up off the ground. The essential paradox here is that we must accept
limitation in order to transcend it. This theme applies to all the chakras—we
must consolidate each level in order to move on.

GROWING THE LOTUS

DEVELOPMENTAL FORMATION OF THE FIRST CHAKRA AT A GLANCE

AGE
Womb to 12 months

TASKS
Physical growth
Motor development
Bonding

NEEDS AND ISSUES
Trust
Nourishment
Safety
Right to be here

A GAME OF PRETEND

Allow yourself, for a moment, to enter the experience of the newborn infant. You have just left the warm and dark womb where everything was provided for you and emerge now into dazzling light and cold. You open your eyes and see blurred images, hear sounds louder than you have ever before heard. You are scared and hungry. Some basic instinct draws your mouth to a breast and you suck your first juices of life, warm milk flowing into your empty belly. You relax, temporarily feeling safe. You have begun your lifelong journey with the most difficult task of all—getting born.

> The task at this time is to help the child come fully into her body, develop a sense of trust in her caretakers, and a sense of safety about the world around her.
>
> STANLEY KELEMAN

For the first several months of your life, you can't do anything for yourself. You understand nothing and have almost no control over your body or surroundings. You can't speak the language, so you can neither communicate nor understand anything said around you, yet your life depends on getting your needs met.

Though you gradually master simple tasks, this is your basic state during the first year of life. The meeting of your needs is beyond your control, yet you need everything. There is a frightening feeling that was not present in the womb. Things are not provided automatically as they were in the womb. There are periods of hunger, cold, discomfort, and pain.

Whether these needs are miraculously met creates your psychological foundation for relating to the world: *trust* or *mistrust*. Because you do not understand the mechanism for getting your needs met (crying is automatic, and unintentional at this stage), the issue of *trust vs. mistrust* becomes a basic experience of your very self. This is your first vague sense of whether or not you are glad to be here.

Trust or mistrust is the basic element of your first chakra program, which is a foundation for all the other programs that follow. Trust enables your body to unfold from its cramped position, allows security and calm, and encourages connection, bonding, and exploration. With trust, the survival instinct is satisfied, and there is a sense of emotional well-being. If you are confident that the world is a friendly place, you have the sense that you will live. Without trust, your survival feels constantly threatened, and because there is nothing you can do to meet the threat, the anxiety is unbearable.

> Our family determines how we find our ground, how we form our territory. If we do not have plenty of touching and holding, we may never be sure of ourselves emotionally, of the ground we stand on, since we cannot trust others to hold us. . . . People who are not held enough have a fear of falling and hold themselves stiffly away from the earth.
>
> STANLEY KELEMAN

The substance of survival—feeding, holding, warmth, and physical comfort—must come from outside you. This is provided by your roots, meaning your parents, family, and caretakers. The degree to which parents succeed at this task depends a great deal on the kind of support they received as infants and children, and what kind of support system they have for themselves while you are young. Are grandparents helpful and supportive? Is there adequate money for the family to take care of needs? Does the mother have to work? Does she eat well while pregnant and nursing? All of these affect your first chakra development.

In the first few months of life your nervous system responds instinctually. Signals come from within your body—hunger, cold, discomfort—and are communicated spontaneously through movement or crying. Your consciousness is not developed enough to block any flow of energy. You are utterly open, as you have not yet learned to filter out anything unwanted. Your infant body is literally flooded with aliveness or charge. It is from this state that you form your first chakra and the very beginnings of self.

ENVIRONMENT AS SELF

For the developing fetus, the uterus is the first experience of body, the first home and environment, and the ground of being from which life emerges. For this reason this environment has an important and often overlooked influence on first chakra development. The mother's nutritional balance and her emotional states during pregnancy play a role in the texture of the child's personal ground. When the womb is tight, the infant learns to contract her own body. When the mother is afraid or tense, chemicals flow through the uterine environment, stimulating a level of heightened energy that becomes a normal baseline state for the fetus inside. If the mother uses substances like tobacco, alcohol, or drugs, the child inside uses them too.

> Human life begins in a state of pre-egoic embedment. The neonatal condition is one of immersion in the Dynamic Ground prior to the articulation of any sense of individuated selfhood. . . . In the state of original embedment, the neonate is, in effect, in a womb outside the womb. He is in a state of psychic gestation antecedent to the delivery and development of the ego.
>
> MICHAEL WASHBURN

Birth is the gateway into life and the beginning of individuality. It is the first step in our lifelong journey and has a marked effect on how we feel about that journey. Yet the infant is not aware of that individuality for quite some time. For the first five to six months, she remains in a state of fused identity and has no concept of a separate self. The mother's body, voice, touch, and general presence are all part of a unified, undifferentiated whole experience of life.

The state of both mother and environment become, literally, the first experience of self. If the mother is warm and attentive, the environment comfortable and supportive, then this is how we experience ourselves. The charge flowing through us is warm, exciting, and positive. If the mother is cold and cruel and the environment is painful, then our first experiences of life and of self have a negative charge. This programming provides a basic building block of all further development and is why first chakra issues show up in all the chakras that follow.

If reflexive body gestures and sounds (such as crying) produce relief in the form of food, warmth, and comfort, then the continuity between inside and outside remains unbroken and the fused state continues until there is enough awareness and motor development to begin separating. If the child is unable to get her needs met, then she develops growing distrust of the outer world, a dissociation from the inner world, and a feeling of helplessness and inadequacy at the core of her being. The need for the inner and outer worlds to remain consistent is extreme in the young child for many years to come, but especially during a period when there is no distinction. If our instinctual impulses do not get us the things we need in order to survive, we learn to distrust or ignore them, and simultaneously perceive the world as hostile. To distrust our basic instincts is to put ourselves at odds with the deep core of our physical being. It puts us at odds with our ground and the natural world.

Erikson named this first struggle of life *trust vs. mistrust*, and described its healthy resolution as a feeling of hope. "Hope is the enduring belief in the attainability of primal wishes."[1] Hope gives us confidence, enthusiasm, positive thinking, and excitement about life. It is the essential essence needed to thrive and move forward.

The developmental tasks at this stage center around learning to operate the body as the basic vehicle of life. Awareness, coming down from the seventh chakra, is initially focused on the body itself as the child discovers her hands, feet, fingers, and toes. She learns through instinct to suck, grasp, roll over, sit up, creep, crawl, and walk. The child also learns to make contact with the physical world by grasping and moving objects, learning to handle a bottle or cup, using the sides of the crib to pull herself upright. She eventually learns that objects continue to exist even when she cannot see them.

The first chakra program is preverbal, preconceptual, reflexive, and instinctual. Piaget called it the *sensory-motor period,* where awareness is sensory and the task is motor development.

At about six months, an amazing change takes place. The child sits up and becomes vertical on her own for the first time. The chakras are now stacked up on each other, and the energy begins to flow upward. Parents often notice an increased brightness and presence in the child. Sitting up expands the field of visual perception, and consequently the size of the world, marking the beginning of the second chakra.

Other first chakra developments continue, however, such as increasing body weight, developing motor coordination, and strengthening the legs in preparation for walking. Soon the child creeps, crawls, and walks, standing at last on her own two feet with some degree of vertical independence. The fundamental building blocks of the individual life have been created, and the child is ready to explore the world through her senses and movement, opening the exciting realm of chakra two.

TRAUMAS AND ABUSES

Anything that threatens survival, such as birth trauma, abandonment, neglect, serious illness, malnourishment, extreme poverty, or physical abuse, impacts the first chakra. The younger a child is when such things occur, the more likely these threats will undermine first chakra formation. A smooth first year of life creates a solid foundation that can better withstand or recover from difficulties later on.

When a young infant faces danger or neglect, it forces him to fall back on himself—an independence which is developmentally impossible. Instead the child falls into an intolerable pit of fear and helplessness—the experience of having no ground. When this happens, the downward current of energy is blocked. Instead, the life force moves toward the upper chakras, which feel safer. The upward movement then becomes habitual, depleting the lower chakras and sending the system out of balance.

Birth and infancy are beyond the conscious memory of most people. Yet, as primary experiences, they indirectly pervade every aspect of our being. Recovery from these traumas is a distinctly nonintellectual process. It requires returning to the messages and movements of the body, immersing ourselves in our physicality, and reconnecting to core impulses. The following is a closer look at some of the unfortunate events that damage first chakra functioning during its crucial formative stages.

As the parent was to the child, so the mind is to the body.

BIRTH TRAUMA

Birth is our first survival experience. Separation from the mother after birth is a deplorable medical custom that is fundamentally traumatic to the infant. It is no wonder that a culture practicing such a custom leaves people so out of touch with their ground that we find ourselves suicidally damaging the earth, our collective ground.

Consciousness and culture change much more rapidly than the evolution of the physical body. Only in the last century have babies been born into a technological environment, compared to millions of years of moving from the womb into an equally organic experience of contact with the mother, quiet, darkness, and containment. Technological birth, in which the infant is pulled out into bright lights, spanked, and separated from the mother, is such a shock to our ancient nervous systems that the experience is an assault to our neurological sense of ground. Those first moments communicate that something is terribly wrong, even though a newborn is not conscious of such a formulation. Male infants are even further traumatized by circumcision without anesthesia!

Fortunately, hospitals are becoming more aware of the need for continuity from womb to mother and breast. Breast-feeding is making a comeback, and postnatal contact is finally recognized as crucial to mother-child bonding. In the meantime, we have several generations that endured ground-wrenching birth experiences. For most of us, reclamation of our body and ground must be a conscious act instead of a literal birthright.

Birth traumas can set up further difficulties and weaknesses. The child of a horrible birth is more likely to cry, be needy, and have health problems. The crying may in turn inhibit parent-child bonding, causing stress in the new parents, which leads them to further neglect or abuse. When the ground is properly laid in, and the child is well received, nurtured, and cared for, then he is relatively calm, and more likely to receive the positive regard and support of others in those important first few months.

> The period immediately following birth is the most impressive part of life outside the mother's body. What a baby encounters is what he feels the nature of life to be.
>
> JEAN LIEDLOFF

Incubator babies are deprived of the mother's touching and suckling. Seeing loving faces through glass without being touched is disembodying. Adults who were incubator babies may have a tendency to view their lives as surreal and put up with distant relationships without knowing how to bring them closer. There is a vague sense that something is missing from life, but they are unable to grasp what it is. Isolation feels normal and is therefore too easily accepted; they are missing the experience of safety and bonding, and therefore of solid contact with their own body.

Abandonment

Abandonment, whether physical or emotional, directly impacts our survival. A child that is not touched enough experiences a kind of abandonment, even when other care is provided. Physical nurturing is so essential that children in institutions deprived of touch often die from a disease called *marasmus*, a Greek word for "wasting away." They simply do not have enough energy to form themselves from food alone. In the 1920s, studies revealed a death rate for institutionalized babies of 90 to 100 percent; the few that did survive were the ones graced by brief periods in foster homes.[2]

Abandonment can be subtle or blatant. Any time a young child is separated from his birth parent, he feels somewhat abandoned. Short periods of separation are normal and do not cause lasting harm. Longer periods, such as lengthy hospital stays, divorces, or long trips out of town, create profound insecurity. It is important to take time for extra attention and assurance after such separations.

Even when a child is adopted, there is still an abandonment by a birth parent. Adoptive parents need to make up for the child's separation anxiety by providing consistent love and security—more than natural children would need.

Abandonment threatens our survival. It makes us feel unwanted, and we doubt our right to be here. It elicits fear, which may inhibit appropriate responses to common situations. For instance, if we fear abandonment as adults, we may be afraid to speak up in our relationships about the things we dislike for fear of being abandoned again. Or we may accept abandonment too readily, and interpret the slightest criticism or mood change from our partner as a signal that we are unwanted. The emptiness of abandonment may be reexperienced every time it happens in adulthood, where the loss of a loved one leaves us feeling like we're falling apart. The body itself may reflect this collapse, with the muscles chronically undercharged, the legs weak, and the upper back hunched over as if the spine cannot quite hold itself upright.

Abandonment during the formative years often results in an excessive first chakra—one that overcompensates by clinging to security, food, loved ones, or routines. Janet was unhappy with her job but was terrified to lose it for fear of never finding anything else. Mariana's relationship was unful-filling, but she was convinced she would be alone forever if she left it. Marvin had plenty of money in the bank but could never spend it. Each one clung to the security of what they had, essentially putting their energy in a holding pattern that provided false security. Without basic trust, they all feared change.

Abandonment by others also creates a tendency to abandon oneself. Cindy, for example, abandons whatever task she is doing at the slightest interruption. Sam takes poor care of his body, forgetting to eat or bathe. Sarah abandons her own opinion when she meets disagreement and adopts the other's opinion. Nathan abandons his projects before he completes them, dropping out of school and leaving tasks unfinished at work and home. Abandonment undermines the trust needed to develop a sense of security, hope, and confidence. It undermines our very foundation of Self.

NEGLECT

Neglect is a subtler form of abandonment. Neglect is often intermittent, counteracting the first chakra's basic job of stabilizing the entire system. If the neglect is mild enough that we still survive, we grow up with a buried memory of helplessness that lacks a connection to anything concrete. This instability leads to a mistrust of others, causing a further alienation from those who might give support. Neglect also results in shame, which heavily impacts the third chakra senses of self-esteem and personal power, as well as the fourth chakra right to be loved. Like abandonment, neglect is often echoed in the way we treat ourselves.

FEEDING DIFFICULTIES

Malnourishment or hostile eating situations (such as Dad's outbursts of anger during dinner) affect our ability nourish ourselves—an essential first chakra function. Whether or not a child is breast-fed, the emotional state of the mother while feeding, and inherited attitudes about food all impact this vital survival function. I have had more than one female client who was not allowed to eat until her brothers were fed. Another told me of having to sit at the table for four hours until she ate a cold plate of eggs.

Some children live in constant hunger, while others are overfed foods of poor quality, forced to eat when not hungry, or manipulated by parents through food.

Adults who had these types of experiences as children have a hard time interpreting true hunger messages. They may have food allergies, avoidance, or addiction to food. This can appear as trust issues, eating disorders, digestive difficulties, or simply as the stagnant energy that results from being a closed system, unable to incorporate new input. Since nourishment comes in many forms—food, friends, or intellectual and creative stimulation—this issue may translate to many other areas of life.

ENEMAS

Another first chakra trauma, more popular a generation ago, is the trauma of enemas. Repeated use of enemas is tantamount to sexual abuse, only the abuse is to the first chakra rather than the second chakra of sexuality (though in some cases it may have sexual overtones). This invasion of the area most closely related to the root chakra destroys the trust so crucial at this stage, and literally fractures one's sense of solidity. Difficulty with boundaries is guaranteed, creating either impenetrable walls or nonexistent boundaries. The first chakra *right to have* is denied, as the child's only solid creation is taken away against their will at a time out of sync with the body. In reaction, energy is pulled upward toward the head, resulting in either an inability to hold and contain or an excessive need to do so, as well as a damaged sense of autonomy (a third chakra issue).

This does not mean, however, that any use of enemas is abusive. There are times when it may be necessary for health reasons. It becomes abusive when it is used excessively, unnecessarily, as an instrument of power or punishment to the child, or as perverse sexual sublimation on the part of the parent.

> No form of abuse is more binding than physical violence. The victim bonds to the abuser out of terror—terror for his or her life. . . . The more one is beaten, the more one's self-worth diminishes. The more one thinks they are lowly and flawed as a human being, the more one's choices diminish. One becomes bonded to violence.
>
> JOHN BRADSHAW

PHYSICAL ABUSE

Physical abuse causes pain and teaches children to dissociate from their bodily sensations. The anxiety from the abuse produces stress hormones and this heightened state may become addictive, producing a need to create crisis throughout life in order to feel alive and overcome the numbness of dissociation. Crisis puts us repeatedly in a state of survival. Bodily dissociation may make one accident-prone, where edges, boundaries, and dangers are not noticed. These minor injuries bring one home to the familiar experience of pain. Coping strategies for dealing with physical abuse can impact any and all of the chakras, with difficulties in surrendering to feelings (chakra two), power dynamics and self-esteem (chakra three), relationships (chakra four), communication (chakra five), clear seeing (chakra six), and clear thinking (chakra seven).

As physical abuse literally harms the body, it will always show up in first chakra issues in some way. It marks a profound betrayal of trust, as the child is always ill-matched for protecting himself. Physical abuse may create excessive or deficient coping strategies, either separating consciousness from the body or creating an obsession with the body as a thing. Combinations of both dissociation and obsession are common, such as numbness of feeling coupled with fastidious dieting.

Physical abuse has a fragmenting effect on the nervous system and a similar effect on the natural flow of experience. In some cases, the body is physically damaged by cuts, wounds, or broken bones. Does it not follow that the more subtle energy fields become broken and fragmented as well? This makes it hard to mend the shattered sense of stability, trust, safety, and well-being.

As physical abuse usually comes from someone within the home, daily life becomes dangerous. Fear is then a constant companion—a way of relating to the world—and as such becomes a touchstone for the experience of aliveness. This may cause one to create future crisis situations, where the familiar sense of stress is used to stimulate that sense of aliveness.

Accidents, Surgeries, Illnesses

James came from a relatively normal home without any of the apparent abuses that so often plague my clients, yet his history showed an unbelievable series of freak accidents. At age four, he was hit by a car and broke his leg. The next year he fell and fractured his skull. Another year, he had acute appendicitis. At fifteen, the jack on a car gave way while he was underneath, nearly killing him. When I saw him at age nineteen, he had just been attacked by a mugger while delivering pizza at his evening job. James was an intelligent and likable guy who had trouble sitting still, concentrating, or sticking with anything. Though he was otherwise intact, he had a traumatized nervous system from his many accidents.

Surgeries, severe illnesses, or accidental physical injuries can have traumatic effects on the body and nervous system. Even surgery necessary for survival can traumatize the body and psyche of the child going through the experience. We do not usually think of car accidents as having long-term emotional effects, but many people report unconscious fears, difficulty sleeping, changes in eating habits, prolonged nervousness, and difficulty concentrating long after their physical injuries have healed.

Effects from these events can be harder to decipher as they may have been dismissed as insignificant. Still, they leave their mark in the body, usually as post-traumatic stress symptoms that exhibit an energetic fragmentation unrelated to current events. The tendency to fragment may resemble the energetic process of the Schizoid structure (page 81), without its other physical or emotional characteristics. It is as if the impact of the accidents sent the spirit out of the body, and it has not quite found its way back in. Just as a cup that breaks and is reglued may have tiny leaks in it, the auric field does not always seal completely, and there may be difficulty with containment, focus, grounding, and other first chakra issues.

Inherited Trauma

Lucy was born two years after her sister died in the crib. Lucy's parents doted on her and gave consistent attention to her every need. What fueled this care, however, was her parent's fear that she, too, might die suddenly. Lucy absorbed this fear unconsciously, and had frequent health problems and insecurities throughout her life.

Hannah had an underlying sense of fear and insecurity that seemed unrelated to any trauma or abuse. It manifested as an excessive clinging to security and hoarding of possessions. Her parents had fled to this country during World War II under great duress and danger. Her mother was traumatized by the experience, even though it was rarely mentioned among the family. Hannah could remember her mother waking up with nightmares and coming to her for comfort. Her mother was fanatical about locking doors and maintaining provisions for emergencies, and lived with a sense of fear about Hannah's future. Inadvertently, she passed her fear onto her daughter.

It is possible to inherit first chakra issues from our parents without any direct abuse to ourselves. Parents with war trauma, poverty issues, racial persecution, those who are holocaust survivors, who have lost a previous child, or have unresolved survival issues of any kind (including the ability to be fully in their own bodies) might unconsciously pass their fears on to their children. This will most likely result in attitudes and beliefs about the world's danger, rather than physical manifestations. Still, this can contaminate the underlying ground of being with an unidentifiable layer of fear and distrust that eventually becomes part of the bodily experience.

POOR BOUNDARIES

Boundaries can be a mystery to those who have been deprived of nurturing, continuity, and safety. A client of mine who had grown up in an orphanage could not comprehend the purpose or need for any boundaries at all. His pain of separation and desire to merge were so intense that the whole concept of boundaries was loathsome to him. As a result, he repeatedly invaded others' boundaries and eventually wound up in jail with charges of child molesting.

When our own boundaries are not functioning, the world will provide them for us. Others will reject us, police will jail us, illness will confine us.

We can interfere with embodiment by not permitting boundaries to form——or by not permitting boundaries to unform. Either way, we can discourage our future, our self-forming.

STANLEY KELEMAN

We will pair up with people who have overly rigid boundaries and who will continually throw us back on ourselves. However, if lower chakra needs have been properly met, then we are not afraid to set appropriate boundaries. We have the ability to say "enough food," "enough drink," or "enough of this nonproductive relationship." We can withdraw, secure in the knowledge that our own roots will support us. We are not dependent on others. If our needs were not satisfied in the first chakra, then we are afraid to set limits—still seeking at any cost the merging and contact that we were denied, never experiencing the satisfaction of "enough."

When a person is not allowed to have their own ground but must serve the survival needs of the family, then boundaries do not form. This is the background of the codependent who may have had to care for Mommy in her illness, Daddy in his drunkenness, or the younger siblings while the parents worked. When these duties become necessary for survival, then survival is equated with no boundaries. The child grows up with a pragmatic contradiction because in today's world, survival most definitely requires boundaries.

UPPER CHAKRA DOMINANCE

Experiences that threaten survival intensify the upward movement of energy in the body. When the body is neither safe nor comfortable, the child redirects her attention away from the unpleasant experience and cuts off bodily sensations. The downward, grounding current is inhibited as much as possible, directing most of the energy to the head. Such a person may be physically numb and fail to notice when she needs to eat or rest, both of which are first chakra maintenance programs. As a result she may contract frequent illnesses—listening to the body only when it is yelling too loud to be ignored. She may not read emotions clearly (since emotions have bodily sensations) and consequently be unaware of her needs. A person with an accelerated upward current is hypervigilant to messages *outside* of herself, as if constantly searching for ways to connect with her caretaker or constantly watching for danger. This is the hallmark of a deficient first

> Without awareness of bodily feeling and attitude, a person becomes split into a disembodied spirit and a disenchanted body.
>
> ALEXANDER LOWEN

chakra: the body is deadened and the consciousness is elevated, creating a profound mind–body split.

An adult with damaged ground is usually plagued by a terrible sense that something is wrong, but cannot identify what it is. Ground is so basic and structured so young, that it literally becomes *back*ground. We are seldom aware that our ground is infertile soil, muddy landslide, or impenetrable rock. Like a fish who does not know it is in water, our ground is often invisible to us. As a result, a therapist working with this problem may feel confused about the issue and be led away from it, just as the client's own energy has led them away from their ground. The sessions may be highly intellectual, jump from topic to topic, or contain lies and omissions that cover up the true problem. Learning to develop the downward current of the body and literally building a ground just as one would build a foundation—brick by brick—is what is needed for the top-down structure in which the upper chakras dominate.

OBJECTIFYING THE BODY

One of my clients constantly referred to her body as "this thing she dragged around with her." Another worried about her figure to the point of obsession, trying to make it look just like the models. Another, who was a dancer, said, "I get so mad at my body when it doesn't perform the way it's supposed to."

> The neurotic ego dominates the body, the schizoid ego denies it, while the schizophrenic ego dissociates from it.
>
> ALEXANDER LOWEN

The body can be an alien entity to the person whose first chakra is damaged, seen as a static thing rather than a living statement of the soul. Alienation from the body results in objectifying the body, which means seeing it as an object, like a puppet master sees his puppet.

Women in this culture often regard their body as a thing even if they suffered no abuses as children. As Susan Kano writes in *Making Peace with Food*, "It is only through extensive and continual conditioning that an intelligent human being comes to see herself as an ornament, whose first priority is the attainment of a slender body, rather than as a complete human being who has a myriad of other concerns and unlimited potential."[3] As we objectify ourselves and each other, we come to see the body as a thing to be controlled and maintained, rather than as a living, dynamic statement of who we are.

OTHER CHAKRA IMBALANCES

When the first chakra is damaged, it reflects in each of the other chakras. Sexuality is affected, as it is an experience of the body, of the senses, and of contact and connection; one's sense of personal power is affected because we cannot fight or defend ourselves without ground to stand on. Without roots bringing energy and nourishment up from the earth, we are weak. Relationships are adversely affected by the lack of boundaries and a persistent insecurity that needs constant reassurance. Communication may be blocked by fear, or become excessive and disconnected from feeling.

The upper chakras are more likely to be intensified with an elaborate and creative imagination and a dedication to the intellect as a defense against feeling. In extremes, such intensification can cause confusion, vagueness, or a feeling of going crazy. The answer lies not in curtailing consciousness, but in grounding and embodying that consciousness.

CHARACTER STRUCTURE

THE SCHIZOID:
CREATIVE AND INTELLIGENT

The Schizoid character structure is also called the Creative, because of its high degree of intelligence, creativity, and interest in spiritual matters. This structure develops early in life, even in the womb, where a child may be conceived by a fearful, angry, or unwilling mother whose emotions are transmitted to the child. This structure can also be seen as the *unwanted child*[4] (see figure 1.1). If the mother is fearful or

> The schizoid defense is an emergency mechanism for coping with a danger to life and sanity. In this struggle all mental faculties are engaged in the fight for survival. Survival depends upon the absolute control and mastery of the body by the mind.
>
> ALEXANDER LOWEN

FIGURE 1.1. SCHIZOID CHARACTER STRUCTURE (CREATIVE)
THE UNWANTED CHILD

FIRST CHAKRA Highly deficient	SECOND CHAKRA Deficient	THIRD CHAKRA Paradoxical (excessive and deficient)	FOURTH CHAKRA Deficient
Trauma in utero, early life	Out of touch with feelings, sensation of body	Upward current strong, giving impression of lots of energy	Fears intimacy, isolates
Doubts right to be here, right to exist	Feelings are intellectualized, may be distorted, irregular	Downward current weak, little focus	Aloof, distant
Energy pulled upward toward head	Lacks trust in relationships, especially physically	Scattered, irregular bursts of energy, highly nervous, excitable, intense	Armored against dependency
Body contracted and compressed	Poor physical bonding	Functions poorly under pressure	Lack of self-love
Body parts feel separate	Poor sense of nurturing	Feels powerless	Not demonstrative or affectionate, fear of reaching out
Movement mechanical	Movements may be jerky, not fluid	Poor self-esteem	Paradoxical breathing (e.g., pulling stomach in while inhaling)
Tendency toward paranoia			
Fears disintegration			
Distrusts own body			

FIFTH CHAKRA Excessive	SIXTH CHAKRA Highly developed (may be excessive)	SEVENTH CHAKRA Highly developed (may be excessive)
Highly talkative but chaotic; may jump from topic to topic	Imaginative	Withdraws to spirit world, may be highly spiritual
Voice mechanical	Psychic	Strongly intellectual
Keeps speech going to feel safe	Intuitive	Highly intelligent
Energy discharged through throat	Able to think in archetypes and symbols, loves the abstract	Brilliant, innovative thinkers, not bound to old forms
May interrupt	Visually aware (hypervigilant), active fantasy life	
Difficulty listening, incorporating new information	Perceptive	
Highly creative, artistic		

resistant to being pregnant, her muscles will contract and the womb will be tight around the fetus. The growing child does not get a sense of freedom, safety, or being wanted. She contracts her own being even as she is physically growing at a rate faster than any other time. Contraction becomes a normal way of being, an energetic statement of withdrawal from life.

If the mother has pulled away from her own body, she will have difficulty transmitting a healthy sense of ground to her child. She may not touch the infant enough, which is the basic affirmation of the child's existence. Since the body is not affirmed, the creative character questions her *right to be here*, the first of our seven rights. Creative types do not feel they have the right to take up space or attend to their physical needs. They tend to deny their own bodies, ignoring signals of hunger, thirst, or fatigue. This can also happen when a mother is overtired, ill, or burdened with too many children, even if her children are wanted. Without proper support, the mother cannot give the important grounding that her child needs during the first year of life.

Mary, whom we met earlier in the chapter, had a Schizoid/Creative character structure. She was tall, thin, and wiry. Her eyes were wide open as if frozen in a startle response. She was nervous, shaky, and highly energized, even prone to manic attacks. She slept and ate very little, and had been diagnosed at one time as anorexic. When asked to draw a picture of her body (which was a difficult exercise for her) she drew a rope coiled tightly around her torso like a boa constrictor. Her torso moved very little, and was collapsed at the chest (see page 23, Schizoid Character).

She was especially blocked at the throat, which she constantly cleared as she spoke. Her speech was hurried and frightened, yet she did a lot of writing that revealed her highly sensitive and intelligent mind. She was capable of great insights and perceptions and missed very little of what went on around her. Her upper chakras were highly developed while her lower chakras had very little energy. She was out of touch with her body. She had not had a sexual partner for many years. She felt powerless in most areas of her life. She lived alone, spent much time alone, and had acquaintances but no close friends.

Mary's energetic process was fragmented. She preferred to stay in the realm of conversation, where she felt safe, and jumped from topic to topic.

She told me she felt she had "not participated in her own life," and as she began to heal, she at first scattered her energy through too many activities, afraid to invest in any one thing. Since her body was constricted, she had difficulty handling too much charge or excitement. If this occurred, she would become confused by the upward current of energy overcharging the upper chakras and flooding her with too much information without a way to sort it out. The limiting and grounding aspects of the lower chakras were not available to her, as she basically lived in fear.

I gave Mary assignments in self-care, oriented toward basics like eating and sleeping. I recommended that she get a massage each week, take walks frequently, and indulge in pleasurable things like long, hot baths. As she was unable to experience her body as a whole, single organism, we worked to reclaim it piece by piece. I used the asset of her creativity in drawing, and had her engage in movement that expressed what she drew. This gave her a feel for the connection between her body and her body image. I helped her experience and adjust her boundaries, moving them from the withdrawn space deep within her to something she could place around her for a feeling of safety. I helped her break the habit of constriction by pushing against me while I held a pillow, energetically pushing out from within. I was careful to avoid overcharging as her body could not handle it. Instead, we worked with grounding exercises and gentle, safe, physical exploration.

Gradually Mary learned to pay attention to her body. In an ongoing therapy group, she slowly learned to trust more people and open up to them. She learned to value herself and reclaim her right to be here. She began getting involved in activities that brought personal satisfaction. Her process of recovery went through many turns and stages, but once begun, she could no longer continue the self-denial that had been her pattern for over forty years. She was now participating in her own life.

EXCESS AND DEFICIENCY

Determining excess and deficiency within the chakra in question is a necessary assessment to make before using most of the exercises. An excessive chakra will benefit most from relaxing or discharging exercises, while a deficient chakra will benefit from stimulating or charging exercises.

Charge is a bioenergetic word for the body's basic excitement. We feel charge when we are angry, excited, sexually aroused, scared, in love, or any of a number of intense emotional states. We feel charge whenever our survival is threatened, when we get a profound spiritual connection, when we watch an exciting movie, or when we are creating a work of art. Charge can be felt as intensity, enthusiasm, or heightened awareness. Issues from our childhood hold a lot of charge, some positive and some negative. For children of alcoholics or divorced parents, holidays are often charged with anxiety. We become hypersensitive to issues that have a lot of charge and we may overreact or compulsively avoid such situations. Positive experiences hold charge too. We may get a charge of energy from seeing an old friend, getting a promotion, or remembering a good vacation.

Charge can be invoked through grounding exercises, increased breathing, fantasy, visualization, or talking about charged material. Dream images may hold a lot of charge, and this charge may spontaneously arise in the body as one discusses his dream. Truth also has a charge, especially when it has been previously hidden, as if a gate opens in the body.

Increasing charge increases one's awareness of the body by increasing its aliveness. If a person is depressed, or his body seems weak or unformed, increasing the charge can give him a sense of well-being, and is a fairly safe process. Depression is basically a state of undercharge, a lack of excitement or enthusiasm.

Not all charge is pleasurable however. When a body is rigidly compressed, as it is in the Schizoid/Creative structure, increased charge may be felt as anxiety. Chronic muscular tension is designed to defend *against* charge, as a way of avoiding or dispelling unwanted feelings. In this case, one must be careful not to overcharge or load the body with more energy than it has the capacity to safely handle. When one is overcharged, he may feel anxious, restless, scared, or out of control. Excess charge of this type is experienced as stress (see figure 1.2).

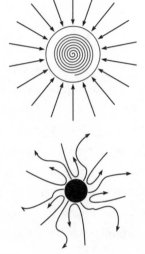

An excessive first chakra draws so much energy that it cannot move the energy downward to ground, or upward to the rest of the body. This creates excess solidity that has trouble embracing change.

A deficient first chakra is so contracted that energy moving inward is deflected and dispersed randomly throughout the body, without grounding. This creates chaotic movement with little consistency.

FIGURE 1.2. FIRST CHAKRA EXCESS AND DEFICIENCY

DEFICIENCY

A deficient first chakra is contracted, vacant, weak, sloppy, or unformed. This is usually recognizable by simply looking at the body. Contraction pulls inward, as if the person were trying to make himself as small as possible. He may sit cross-legged and hunched over, with arms pulled inward across his body, making tight, small movements. In assessing contraction, it is important to see if you can determine its center. A person may be contracting his energy upward into his head, backward into his solar plexus or heart area, or occasionally downward into his ground.

If the contraction pulls away from the ground, the first chakra becomes empty and vacant and the person may be totally out of touch with feeling in this area. If a person's energy is very disorganized, the first chakra will be weak and disappear at the slightest challenge. It may appear to be grounded at times and not at others. The person may shift his position constantly as if fidgeting, or move from foot to foot while standing. There is a restlessness to the energy in general, often with difficulty concentrating.

There is also a kind of deficiency that may appear in either a thin body or with a large, overweight one (which would seem like an excess) where the body is very loose and unformed. Since the first chakra is about solidity, the unformed body has a hard time solidifying itself or holding its shape, ground, or basic structure. There is poor muscle tone, circulation, color, and boundary formation. This is a state that is undernourished and undercharged.

A person with a deficient first chakra does not recognize the body's importance. Grooming and hygiene may be poor; dressing may be sloppy. Details about life are not important, whereas fantasies, dreams, knowledge, and spirituality are very important (balanced by upper chakra dominance).

Deficient first chakra types need to discover their ground. They respond well to working while standing and using exercises that charge the body (see *Grounding Exercise*, page 98). They need encouragement to form themselves and maintain that form, which can be strengthened through challenge. Boundary exercises are very useful.

Excess

An excessive first chakra feels heavy. It has solidity, but with a sluggish and massive feeling. The body is more likely to be large and dense, with excess weight distributed especially around the hips, thighs, and buttocks. The weight itself is solid and thick rather than loose and flabby. If there is no weight problem, you may find that the muscles are hard and rigid.

The body is quite solidly formed and seems resistant to change. The person may not move his body very often in the session (whereas the deficient may shift constantly) and the eyes are defensive, with the head held steady. He may complain about being stiff, sluggish, bored, afraid of change, or unable to get off the ground. There may be a hardness about the person's character. He likes routine, security, and possessions, and may be driven toward financial achievement. He may appear cynical about spiritual subjects, preferring the concrete. His appearance may be meticulous, well-dressed, and well-groomed. Movements, when they occur, may be repetitive or compulsive. His boundaries are overformed, more like brick walls. He complains about being stuck.

Excessive first chakra types need to discharge, let go, and shift from excessive stability to movement and flow. Since energy is fixated at the base of the spine, movement is needed to distribute the energy more effectively and leave the first chakra in better balance. Physical movements such as dancing, walking, swimming, or simply stretching are usually successful with the excessive first chakra because the physical realm is one that is familiar and comfortable. Yoga is especially recommended, as it allows for peaceful relaxation and subtle movement of energy within.

BALANCE

A balanced first chakra is solidly grounded yet dynamically alive. There is both flexibility and consistency, an ease with both expansion and contraction. There is a sense of form without rigidity, a feeling of bodily comfort, and a healthy distribution of energy throughout. This gives a sense of inner security, good self-care, an affirmed right to be here, and a strong sense of presence.

I am often asked if a chakra can be simultaneously excessive and deficient. This actually happens quite frequently, where some coping strategies overcompensate while other aspects are avoided. This is an attempt to balance the energy *within* a chakra, rather than throughout the system as a whole. A chakra balanced within itself is less likely to affect other chakras in the system than a chakra that manifests one-sided patterns. We integrate by bringing the extremes back toward a common center, anchored in the physical body. For example, overeating is often an attempt to ground the body. By increasing the function that is underdeveloped (in this case, appropriate grounding) we create a possibility for the compensating function to decrease.

ASSESSING YOUR HISTORY

Uncovering developmental life experiences can also shed light on a given chakra's structure. What is known about one's birth, breast-feeding, or early infancy? What else was going on in the family at that time? Were there any major illnesses, surgeries, or hardships? What kind of bonding and nurturing came from the mother? How did the mother relate to her own body? Were there any threats to one's survival or the survival of family members? And how were these factors addressed? Using common sense, these questions usually reveal excessive and deficient strategies.

Neglect and rejection usually result in deficiency, where not enough energy comes into the system to form a solid foundation. Stressful situations, smothering, or numerous challenges are more likely to result in excess. The ground needs to hold on for dear life in order to survive and therefore over-compensates. It is possible, however, that the same situation can produce equal and opposite reactions in two different people—physical abuse may send one person completely out of touch with her body, while another becomes overly focused on it.

Persistent problems are examples of the processes in place. "My health is a constant problem." "I can't seem to get going." "I'm afraid all the time." "My finances are always deplorable." These can usually be sorted into problems of excess or deficiency. Compare these statements with the chart at the beginning of the chapter for more help assessing your own processes.

RESTORING THE LOTUS

HEALING THE FIRST CHAKRA

The following is an outline of suggestions, techniques, and interventions for addressing first chakra imbalances. I want to stress that each technique should be used with discretion and in combination with your own therapeutic style. No two people are alike, and the space here is not adequate for elaborate diagnosis.

It is first important to determine the state of a person's connection with their body, the ground beneath them, and the environment around them. The shape and form of the body and the characteristic style of connection with the outside world are where we find clues. Careful observation of the way a person walks, talks, moves, breathes, sits, and looks

To heal our relationship to our bodies is to heal our relationship with the earth. To regain our ground is to regain our aliveness, and the foundation of all that follows.

out from behind their eyes tells us about the underlying patterns. Here we are looking at the body's statement of inner process—such as contraction, expansion, conflict, freezing, collapse, activation, deadening, or dissociation.

Notice that these are energetic statements rather than emotional states, even though they are caused and often accompanied by emotions, such as fear resulting in contraction, helplessness in collapse, excitement or anger in activation. These states will change according to what is going on at the moment. Describing a past trauma may bring activation into some parts of the body.

In first chakra work, however, the energetic statement made by the body is more important than the emotion itself. Keeping the person in touch with bodily sensations rather than focusing on the emotions helps provide containment for difficult, traumatic material. The person can focus on what her body is *doing* without getting lost in the feelings, which are more characteristic of the second chakra. This is done through constant reference to and mirroring of the physical processes that are experienced during the session. "When you feel scared, what does your body do? What happens in your belly, or your breathing?" A person can learn to gain some relief from painful emotions simply by changing their *physical* expression, without tumbling down the labyrinth of historical content and emotional soup. A simple grounding suggestion can also bring greater strength and calm, such as "What happens when you put your feet back down on the floor and press your weight into them?" "What happens when you stand up?"

DRAWING THE BODY

I find it useful to have clients draw their own body on a large piece of newsprint with an assortment of colored crayons. The instructions given are to draw what your body *feels* like without trying to make a realistic picture of it. A pencil-thin anorexic may draw her body as a puffy balloon if that is the way she experiences it. A rigid person may draw dark squares and hard angles. A fearful, contracted person may draw a very tiny body, using only a quarter of the page, where an overly expanded person may need several sheets of paper. An underformed, collapsed person may draw ethereal swirls with no concrete form at all.

The beauty of this exercise is that it shows graphically, without intellectualization, what is going on energetically. The client can look at her own picture and see forms that normally remain unconscious. After first asking the client to talk about her drawing, the therapist can then ask questions and point out overlooked aspects such as, "What does this heavy black line going through your middle section represent to you?" "I notice your drawing looks very fluid but has no boundaries. Does this fit your life?" "It seems you are afraid to take up space." "You draw the body as if it were very fat, but you are actually very thin." Sometimes whole parts of the body get left out—how does the client relate to these parts? One person left out her head because she ran out of room on the page and was afraid to ask for another piece of paper. Does she often lose her head out of fear of asking for what she needs? Another person used three sheets of very large paper (24 by 36 inches) but made only a very few pale marks. Her energy was too diffuse.

If possible, have the client stand before a full-length mirror and hold her drawing in front of her torso. This has the effect of giving a kind of X-ray vision into the internal schema of the energetic structure. How does she feel about this person? What conclusions would she draw if she saw only the picture? What are the areas that most need attention and healing? If there is no mirror in the office, give this as a home assignment. As people grow and change, they can make these pictures periodically, providing a graphic representation of their progress.

BODY DIALOG

The first step out of dissociation is to reestablish communication with the body. This exercise gives voice to various parts of the body and allows the mind to dialog with these parts and learn about their experience.

I usually begin by having the person lay down in a relaxed, comfortable position while I sit beside her with a pad and pencil, ready to write down everything that is said. I first ask her to pretend that her body is a corporation and that she is a visiting consultant, sent to interview the workers about how they each feel about their job and their position in the company. Each body part is a member of the corporation, and I ask her to work her way from the feet to the face. After I name a part of the body the client begins with "I am my feet and I . . ." and then completes the sentence with their emotional experience. "I am my feet and I feel like the weight of the world is on me." "I am my belly and I feel afraid." "I am my head and I run the show." Sometimes one part of the body may wish to tell a whole story, linking several statements. Other times it may not be able to find its voice, or it may feel numb.

When the whole body has had a chance to speak, I then read back what I have written, omitting the actual body parts. "I feel the weight of the world is on me. I feel afraid. I am running the show. I feel numb, tense." The client then gets a chance to see how the body is expressing her life experience.

Following this exercise (which usually comprises a whole session) one can then go back and have dialog with the parts that seem most significant. "So you, chest, feel constricted and empty. What would make you feel fuller?" "So, stomach, you feel like you have to be big to get noticed. How does it feel being big and full? How does it feel when you're empty?" The stomach might answer, "It feels scary when I'm empty. But I feel numb when I'm full." Then the question might be, "What do you feel scared of?"

The dialog can occur between the client and herself, or between the therapist and the client. The goal is to develop a relationship through communication and acknowledgment—a relationship that can then lead to action and change.

AFFIRM THE PHYSICAL

The first chakra represents our physical reality. When it is damaged, our relationship to the physical world is damaged. Therefore, in cases of both excess and deficiency, healing occurs through creating a new relationship with the physical—with our bodies, the earth, and our surroundings. This can be an act of reunion or an exploration of a marvelous mystery.

For the Schizoid structure with a deficient first chakra, touch and nurturing are crucial for developing a relationship with the body that is affirming and pleasurable. Regular massage and physical exercise are indispensable.

Massage helps break down contracted body armor while simultaneously providing a nurturing and pleasurable experience. Exercise actually pumps energy through the body and develops strength, promoting a sense of connection and pride.

As stated earlier, it is important to continually refer the client to his bodily experience. "What happens in your belly when you talk about this incident?" "Can you feel the change in your breathing whenever you speak about your mother?" If the client reports that he feels nervous or scared or angry, encourage him to anchor these feelings in the body by asking him to describe their physical sensations. "What do you feel in your body when you're nervous?" The answer might be, "I get butterflies in my stomach, my breath gets shallower, I tighten my shoulders."

Every feeling has a physical sensation. Once the physical response is clarified, the feeling can be deepened by exaggerating that response or lessened by creating an equal and opposite response. One might say, "Tighten your shoulders and constrict your breath even more." Intensifying the feeling can help bring it from the unconscious into conscious awareness, where it can be reclaimed, examined, or expressed. This is especially crucial when working with body numbness, where the physical sensations have to be exaggerated in order to be noticed.

A negative feeling can be lessened by instructing the client in an opposite movement. For example, Joanie, who was physically abused as a child, has an unconscious response to painful material, which is to draw her legs up into her body and bring her knees close to her chest. When asked to exaggerate this, she curls into a ball as if to hide. As she does this, she feels intense fear, which she recognizes as a frequent feeling from childhood. To encourage her to uncurl, I ask her to deepen her breathing, put her feet on the ground, and then push down into her feet. This encourages an opposite reaction that creates an entirely different feeling. This gives Joanie a sense of her ground and a place from which to affirm a new way of being in her body.

Sometimes, changing body movements in this way evokes a cathartic release, which may or may not be advisable, depending on the level of trauma. One needs to proceed carefully. If the trauma is severe, activating a release may overwhelm the system, *especially* if the grounding is weak. If grounding has been adequately developed during previous sessions, with a strong sense of trust in the therapeutic relationship, then gentle release may bring relief by discharging the feelings held in the body armor and allowing new feeling to enter.

In order for Joanie to maintain this grounded position and feel comfortable with it, she needs to reorganize her usual way of handling things. It is not as easy to retreat energetically when the feet are planted firmly on the floor. To support the new structure, she must instead confront, say no, get angry, or defend. This response needs to be encouraged, but from a bodily position that supports it in small, manageable steps.

The emotional and physical structures are interdependent. Change in the physical structure helps support a new emotional response, and change in emotional expression helps support new physical postures. Both sides must be worked simultaneously, but emotions are more appropriate to the realm of the second chakra, so we will focus here on the physical.

WORK ON THE FEET

We connect to our ground through our feet and legs. Working on the feet can imply two things: working directly with the feet themselves, as in foot massage, flexing and arching, kicking, or pushing with the feet (see my book *The Sevenfold Journey* for more physical exercises) or working while standing on the feet (literally getting on one's own two feet).

As I begin grounding work with the feet, I ask the client to remove his shoes and socks and stand on a tennis ball or a footsie roller to open up the muscles in the feet. The client stands on one foot while pressing the other into the tennis ball, applying enough weight to loosen tension. A footsie roller is a wooden dowel with ridges sold at many natural food stores or health spas. The footsie roller is harder than the tennis ball but penetrates more deeply.

Sometimes I have the client walk across a plain wooden dowel, about the size of a closet bar, moving his feet one inch at a time. This last exercise can be quite painful to the feet if there is a lot of blocked energy, so I only use it when working on more advanced stages of grounding.

Unfortunately, most psychotherapy occurs as a verbal dialog, sitting in a chair, and is essentially nonphysical. This is clearly not the best approach for someone who wants to work on lower chakra issues, especially if their cognitive faculties are overdeveloped as a defense. In this kind of situation there are still some simple things that can be done to support grounding. At the very minimum, one can teach a client to keep his feet on the ground, preferably with shoes off. This helps him maintain a deeper energetic connection to his body and a greater presence in the session. This is essential for people who have grounding problems (which, in reality, is most of the population). Asking the client to occasionally press into his feet reaffirms and strengthens the grounding connection and is especially useful when dealing with fear and nervousness. Pressing into the feet helps push energy through the body where it can be released. The client can be asked to continually monitor his bodily experience as explained earlier. Exercises that involve drawing the body or speaking for body parts as if they were subpersonalities, and assigning body-supportive homework, are essential adjuncts to working with the first chakra.

Once the feet have been opened up, I ask the person to stand and experience them in a whole new way. I ask him to feel his feet holding up the body's weight and to feel the texture of the floor beneath. Most are astonished at how much more awareness they have of their feet and immediately feel a bit more grounded.

Doing psychological work while standing increases the body's energy, allows greater assertiveness, overcomes passivity, and supports independence. The mere act of standing is an assertion of autonomy. Standing takes one out of the baby stage and allows the adult to emerge. Standing establishes a ground, and literally manifests the metaphor "to take a stand." Many of our expressions reflect this important energetic concept: "to put one's foot down," "to have a leg to stand on," "to refuse to stand for something," "to withstand," and finally, "to understand." Having a client stand on his feet embodies any and all of these concepts. In this case, the stand he takes is for himself.

Careful attention is also paid to the way in which he stands. Is the pelvis tipped forward or held back? Are the knees flexible or locked? Does the belly hang forward or the chest collapse? These are all indications of the client's holding pattern and should be noted and worked with over time. It helps to explore both conscious and unconscious body postures. Conscious body posture is the one we have when we are watched. We hold in our stomach, lift our shoulders and chest, and straighten our spine. Unconscious body posture is the one that happens without thinking. We may slump, tighten, or stand habitually on one leg.

How does the client feel when trying to ground? Does it make him feel jittery or secure? Is there a focus of tension that occurs in the body or does the body relax? Does it require much concentration or does it come naturally? Do the eyes express excitement, fear, or sadness? These are the things to ask about and observe, or to offer as feedback to the client. "Your eyes are suddenly showing fear, is that what you're feeling?" Next direct that identification to the body. "So what sensation in your body lets you know you're afraid and when did this sensation start to occur?" Other questions or statements might include: "What do you experience in this position?" "Your pelvis is pulled backward. What happens if you allow it to move forward?" "It seems you have a need to lock your knees. What happens when you bend them?" These statements are not designed to be analytical as much as to invite deeper experience. Look for breaks in the flow of energy, places that are held stiffly, or parts that move awkwardly. Then focus and exaggerate these unconscious processes until they become conscious.

Locking the knees is a way to throw the body into passive weight, where we withdraw energetically while still giving the outer appearance of being present. Passive weight can also be thought of as dead weight—locking the knees cuts down on the energetic connection between the legs and the ground and deadens bodily sensations. When the knees are locked, the belly pushes forward, the chest collapses, the head falls downward, and the breathing lessens. This is the posture of defeat, and defeat is allegorical to falling; therefore, we lock our knees to remain standing. The posture of alertness, by contrast, holds the knees slightly bent and keeps the center of gravity low, much like the stance used by martial artists.

GROUNDING EXERCISE

To increase the sense of dynamic contact with the ground, I ask the client to place his feet shoulder width apart with toes slightly inward and knees slightly bent. Sometimes I tell him to push into his feet as if trying to part the floorboards, increasing leg solidity. A person cannot easily be pushed off their ground when holding a position like this. Asking him to maintain this position while the therapist pushes slightly on the sternum requires him to dig his feet into the floor, which increases the energy in the legs.

Once the basic position is established, I then ask him to bend and straighten his knees several times slowly, inhaling while bending and exhaling while straightening and pushing them into the floor. The knees should not straighten all the way. If this exercise is done correctly, a mild trembling in the legs will begin. With some people this takes only seconds, with others several minutes. The trembling is a sign that new energy is coming into the legs and feet. If the exercise is continued, this energy will gradually increase and the trembling will become stronger. As it does, it can be used to enliven parts of the body that are deadened and move through blocks, or it can be passed upward to the rest of the body. Every time we push against something solid, we increase energy flow in our body. Increased contact with the ground builds up charge. One must be careful to observe how the client deals with the increased charge. If anxiety arises, which it often does, it must be either processed or curtailed. It can be curtailed by slowing down or stopping the exercise, kicking the legs into the air in front, or sitting in a chair with the head lowered. It can be processed by working with the material it illuminates. Sally, for example, got very anxious during her first grounding experience. This was observable through her eyes and breathing, and through elucidating frequent descriptions of her experience.

"I'm getting very uncomfortable," she said.

"Fine, let's hold the position right there and see what the discomfort is about. What are the sensations in your body?"

"I'm getting a tingling in my hands and lips." (This is not an uncommon response to charge.)

"OK. Pay attention to your hands. What do they want to do? What is their impulse?"

"I don't know. I can't tell. I feel confused."

I could see the arms trembling, as if locked in place. "Try reaching forward with your arms. Reach out in front of you." Sally reached out in front and the charge ran up her torso and out her hands. She began to sob. The sense of anxiety changed and she was suddenly immersed in the memory of wanting to reach for her mother when her mother was not there. She was able to express her feelings of sadness and her inhibition around reaching out. I allowed her to grab my hands and feel a solid contact with someone. The end result was a feeling of calm.

In this case, anxiety arose from the confusion she felt about her instinctual (core) response to needing someone when they were not there, a response that had been shut off for lack of satisfaction. In other cases, it may not be resolved so simply. My rule is to take the person as far as she can handle, and only push when I feel confident there is a possibility of some resolution within the session. I determine this by intense observation and constant dialog that keeps me in touch with both her physical and emotional states.

As a person begins to resolve the issues brought to light by the exercises, the grounding gains solidity. She is literally resolving that which has stood between herself and her ground. As this occurs, problems with jobs, housing, and physical ailments—all first chakra issues—begin to resolve.

REGRESSIVE TECHNIQUES

Since the first stages of life are preambulatory, not all first chakra work can be done while standing. If there are traumas that occurred in the earliest stages of childhood, it may be necessary to use postures that simulate these earlier stages.

Rebirthing techniques are done while laying down and use certain kinds of breathing to trigger memories of the womb and birth experience.

Holotropic breath work (created by Stanislav Grof) is a technique that releases deep tensions held in the body. These are not techniques that can be adequately described here, but one might want to refer a client to a trained rebirther or holotropic breath worker for a few sessions to access material from these early stages. These methods are very powerful however, and should not be used lightly with a client who has serious trauma or with one whose history you do not yet know well.

When doing work with early childhood stages, I have the client lie down on his back, on a fold-out futon, keeping the knees bent so that the feet are flat against the foam. I then facilitate relaxation and encourage deeper breathing, watching closely for signs of energetic changes or blocks. The following exercise, *pushing the feet*, pushes energy down into the legs.

I ask the client to raise his legs into the air and wave them around, much as an infant might. I also encourage him to make abstract sounds as he breathes—easy for some and difficult for others. The sounds help the client to surrender to the movement of energy, but are not a focus at this time.

I then ask him to push outward with his feet with the toes flexed back toward the body. As the client pushes into his heels, the legs will soon begin to vibrate just as they would in the standing position, and I encourage them to surrender to this trembling and to continue breathing fully. After building up the charge, I ask the client to kick his legs rapidly in order to discharge, with knees bent for the younger stages, knees straight for a more mature assertion. Sound is encouraged here, and if the arms seem energized, he can also strike the mat with his hands or fists. The kicking lasts until the client is tired (usually a minute or so) and is followed by rest.

This is an expressive charge-discharge cycle that pushes out but does not encourage the act of taking in. It will open up the energy and get it flowing, but does not teach the client to contain. It is good for a basic anger release and breaking up rigidity, but is not advised for issues of abandonment, lack of nurturing, or neglect, which are softer and quieter experiences.

NOTE: Many of these exercises have what I call an *afterflow*. This means that the energetic flow in the body is more likely to occur immediately *after* the exercise than during it. Therefore it is crucially important for the client to take a few moments of quiet to really feel the streaming of energy in his body before moving on to something else.

For the tenderer emotions, I allow the client to begin by lying down and work with the hands and lips. I gently massage the shoulder and back muscles and ask the client to reach forward with his hands as if reaching for a person. I also encourage the suckling response by asking him to push his lips outward (especially good for the Oral/Lover structure). It rekindles the oral experience, and through renegotiation of past memories can help satisfy the endless oral cravings. It is important to end with the client getting slowly to his feet, feeling the ability to support himself in an active and adult way.

Some of these techniques have profound boundary implications and should not to be used before establishing clear boundaries and a sense of safety and trust between practitioner and client. The practitioner must stay aware of transference and countertransference issues. I always completely describe the exercise ahead of time, and ask the client if he feels comfortable with it before beginning, assuring him that we can stop at any time. I do not even suggest such exercises to a client who has just begun therapy, or to one who, in my assessment, is not good at saying no (such as sexual abuse survivors and clients with an extreme need to please). As with any therapeutic technique, caution and discretion are imperative.

CONCLUSION

Without the healthy functioning of the first chakra, we are hopelessly trapped on a mundane level of existence, forever avoiding and forever dealing with the same issue—a need to solidify the ground level from which all else grows. It is my belief that if a person's ground is not somewhat intact, all other work is less effective. If the ground is intact, subsequent work proceeds in a more coherent fashion and strengthens the ground. Grounding is a slow and cumulative process. It is where we begin, yet it is always changing as a result of what we build above it.

One can never work on grounding too much. Our culture, so very removed from the ground of the planet, and with values that hold the body and the physical world in such low esteem, continually separates us from our ground. Regardless of childhood development, there is always work to be done to overcome the cultural programming that weakens our first chakra connection.

Reclaiming the sacred temple of our bodies, our right to be here, and our right to have what we need in order to survive can be a joyous reunion with the very ground of our own being and a solid beginning to the exciting journey of recovery through the chakras.

CHAKRA TWO

Swimming in the Waters of Difference

SECOND CHAKRA AT A GLANCE

ELEMENT
 Water

NAME
 Svadhisthana (sweetness)

PURPOSE
 Movement and connection

ISSUES
 Movement
 Sensation
 Emotions
 Sexuality
 Desire
 Need
 Pleasure

COLOR
 Orange

LOCATION
 Lower abdomen
 Sacral plexus

IDENTITY
 Emotional

ORIENTATION
 Self-gratification

DEMON
 Guilt

DEVELOPMENTAL STAGE
 6 months to 2 years

DEVELOPMENTAL TASKS
 Sensate exploration of
  the world
 Locomotion

BASIC RIGHTS
 To feel and have pleasure

BALANCED CHARACTERISTICS
 Graceful movement
 Emotional intelligence
 Ability to experience pleasure
 Nurturance of self and others
 Ability to change
 Healthy boundaries

TRAUMAS AND ABUSES
 Sexual abuse (covert or overt)
 Emotional abuse
 Volatile situations
 Neglect, coldness, rejection
 Denial of child's feeling states,
  lack of mirroring
 Enmeshment
 Emotional manipulation
 Overuse of playpen or
  restricting normal movement
 Religious or moral severity
  (antipleasure)
 Physical abuse
 Alcoholic families

TRAUMAS AND ABUSES (CONT'D)
Inherited issues—parents who have not worked out their own issues around sexuality; untreated incest cases

DEFICIENCY
Rigidity in body and attitudes
Frigidity, fear of sex
Poor social skills
Denial of pleasure
Excessive boundaries
Fear of change
Lack of desire, passion, excitement

EXCESS
Sexual acting out, sexual addiction
Pleasure addiction
Excessively strong emotions, ruled by emotions (hysteria, bipolar mood swings, crisis junkies)
Oversensitive
Poor boundaries, invasion of others
Seductive manipulation
Emotional dependency
Obsessive attachment

PHYSICAL MALFUNCTIONS
Disorders of reproductive organs, spleen, urinary system
Menstrual difficulties
Sexual dysfunction: impotence, premature ejaculation, frigidity, nonorgasmic
Low back pain, knee trouble, lack of flexibility
Deadened senses, loss of appetite for food, sex, life

HEALING PRACTICES
Movement therapy
Emotional release or containment as appropriate
Inner child work
Boundary work
12-step programs for addictions
Assign healthy pleasures
Develop sensate intelligence

AFFIRMATIONS
I deserve pleasure in my life.
I absorb information from my feelings.
I embrace and celebrate my sexuality.
My sexuality is sacred.
I move easily and effortlessly.
Life is pleasurable.

SHADES OF ORANGE

I seldom find a client or even a friend without sexuality issues. Too little, too much, afraid, addicted, ashamed, deprived, or compulsive—the cries of sexual wounding echo through many lives, bringing pain and frustration, anger and fear—all to an experience meant for pleasure. Collectively, these wounds reverberate through our culture in struggles over a vast range of sexual issues: birth control, abortion, gay rights, nudity, fidelity, celibacy, child molestation, rape, and pornography. In a binding paradox, sexuality is simultaneously rejected and magnified.

> Lose your mind and
> come to your senses.
>
> FRITZ PERLS

This wounding takes its toll. Emotional numbness is the approved ideal for public behavior. Emotional reactions are frowned upon as a sign of losing control. The function of *feeling*, in the Jungian sense, is considered an inferior function in our culture, associated with the inferior status of women. Passion, an essential motivating force for vitality, power, and creativity, is suppressed, viewed as a petulant child needing to be controlled by our will. Without passion and pleasure, our lives blur into senseless sameness, our feelings dulled behind the daily subroutines of expected behavior.

The second chakra—center of sensation and feeling, emotion and pleasure, intimacy and connection, movement and change—is instead turned and twisted, squashed and squandered, further severing the perceptual cognition of the mind from the sensate ground of the body. Without touch, we become literally out of touch. Dulled in our senses, behavior becomes *senseless* instead of *sensible*.

In recovering the second chakra, we reclaim our *right to feel*. We also reclaim passion and pleasure, neediness and vulnerability, and our sensate connection to both inner and outer reality. We free the flow of dynamic energy that is essential for growth, change, and transformation and release the armor that separates us. We can then reclaim the intimacy that we long for, ending our fragmented isolation.

Sexuality and spirituality have long had a conflicted relationship. Many people see them as polarized rivals for consciousness—that to pursue one is to deny the other. Such philosophies tell us that to become spiritual we need to overcome desire, to renounce sexuality, to rise above our feelings. Other practices, such as Tantra, see sexuality and spirituality as an indivisible whole, each one enhancing the other.

To deny the qualities of the second chakra is to deny an essential piece of our wholeness, a piece that has an important part to play in the expansion and awakening of consciousness. To make it more or less important than the other chakras is to unbalance the whole system. Let us honor the second chakra as an exciting and necessary part of our journey, and in that honoring free ourselves to both enjoy it and embrace the realms beyond it.

UNFOLDING THE PETALS

Change

Movement

Flow

Sensation

Pleasure

Emotion

Need

Desire

The Shadow

Guilt

Duality

Sexuality

DIVING IN THE WATERS

The myth of going under water, of being drowned and born again . . . the myth of baptism . . . is a daring leap into non-being with the prospect of achieving new being.

ROLLO MAY

As we enter the second chakra, we encounter the watery realm of emotions and sexuality. Where we have worked for grounding and stability in the first chakra, we now cultivate feelings and movement; where we have been concerned with survival and structure, we now focus on sexuality and pleasure. Our associated element has shifted from *earth* to *water*, from solid to liquid. In this transmutation we encounter *change*. Through consistency, consciousness finds meaning; through change it finds stimulation and expansion.

If we think of the body as a vessel for the soul and spirit, then the element of earth in chakra one provides support and containment for the fluid essence of chakra two, much like a cup holds water. Without appropriate containment, water flows out and the cup runs dry. With excessive containment, however, water cannot flow at all and becomes stagnant and dull. Ideally, we want to have a cup that is capable of filling, holding, and emptying. The task of the first chakra was to build this container. In the second chakra we look to its contents.

> Emotional fulfillment comes from balancing the emotional flow and emotional containment within the sensate and structural forms of the body.

LETTING GO TO MOVEMENT

In the first chakra, we learned to ground, stabilize, and focus. Now, in the second chakra, our challenge is just the opposite—*to let go*—to flow and move, to feel, and to yield. Movement and change stimulate consciousness. They stir the watery essence of feelings that flow through the body.

On the physical plane, movement literally gets us up off our butts, where we rise from the anchor of chakra one and expand outward. Through movement, we extend our field of perception, increasing our sensory input. By moving the body, we build muscle tissue, increase circulation, stimulate nerve endings, and generally enhance the body's flexibility and aliveness. The flow of pleasure and excitation through the nervous system bathes the organism in sensation and awareness. Movement has its own pleasure.

By paying attention to the way we move, we can uncover previously buried issues and feelings. In the first chakra, the *structural forms* of the body gave us clues to unconscious process. In the second chakra we observe the way these forms *move and make contact*.

> The universe exists only through a constant dance of consistency and change. Through consistency, consciousness finds meaning; through change it finds stimulation and expansion. To find consistency within change is to embrace the unfolding flow.

SENSATION

The senses are the gateway between the internal and external world. Sight, sound, touch, taste, and hearing give us a constantly changing inner matrix of the world around us. The senses are the data input of our overall system. They allow us to connect and give meaning to our experience. Through our senses, we differentiate between pleasure and pain, we expand or contract, move forward or backward, react or enact. When there is pain or emptiness, our senses shut down.

The complex combination of sensation and feeling gives us the emotional texture of experience. Senses, as the language of feeling, form the basis of our values. How we perceive something and how we feel about it determine our values. Without a sensual connection to what is around us, we lose our sense of values and distinctions.

PLEASURE

What do you do after completing a hard day of work? Most people try to relax and turn toward pleasure of some kind. Once an organism has taken care of its survival needs, the next thing on the agenda is usually pleasure. It is biologically natural to move toward pleasure and away from pain. Pain makes us contract, withdraw, or shut down, whereas pleasure invites us to extend, expand, and tune in to our senses. If our overall purpose in the second chakra is to stimulate movement, then pleasure is the most inviting way to accomplish this.[1]

As children, pleasure comes to us through touching and closeness, play and stimulation, and validation of our emotional experience. Children take pleasure in being alive and reaching out with that aliveness to encounter the world. To be met with love and encouragement in that reaching is to meet life as a pleasurable experience.

Unfortunately, not all children have this luxury. My client Jennifer came from a home where pleasure was frowned upon as an indulgent waste of time and energy. Her mother was an overburdened single parent of five children who had to sacrifice pleasure simply to survive. There was never enough

> Just as logic leads the mind, desire guides the soul.
>
> THOMAS MOORE

time or money for those little extras that bring pleasure to life. As the eldest, Jennifer was expected to shoulder adult responsibilities. Time spent with her friends was seen as taking away from her job with the family. She was not allowed to pursue her own pleasures. She grew up to feel she had no right to indulgences of her own while her mother was working so hard just to survive. To this day, even though she has a well-paying job, she can only let herself buy clothes at the thrift store, rarely takes a vacation, and allows herself little time for sexual pleasure. Life to her is grim, and she looks older than her years.

For Oliver, pleasure came with manipulative strings attached. Oliver was given treats of pleasure, such as cookies, extra time watching TV, or snuggles with Mom, only when he behaved according to his mother's needs. When he was sad, angry, or needy himself, these treats were denied. While this may seem like a common use of reward and punishment, Oliver now has trouble feeling his anger and expressing his needs for fear that his wife will deny him affection, or that some unseen punishment will fall from the sky and take away everything he values. In fact, Oliver has trouble figuring out what he wants at all, because long ago he learned to deny his wants. Oliver feels guilty about having pleasure in his life—always wondering if he deserves it.

For Samantha, pleasure was provided in a healthy atmosphere. She was loved and touched without being invaded. Her body was respected and cared for. Her parents took pleasure in her curiosity and delight and there was a spirit of fun in the household. She has a healthy sense of pleasure. She tunes in to her body and can tell when she has had enough. She is positive and enthusiastic about life.

How was pleasure regarded in your family? Was it frowned upon or indulged in? Did your family take time for vacations, laugh together, and play? Was there a predominant message that hard work and self-sacrifice were necessary for survival or the means to spiritual fortitude? Were work and play, self-discipline and pleasure, brought into balance? How do these attitudes reflect in your own orientation toward pleasure?

Pleasure invites us to pay attention to our senses, to live fully in the present, to enjoy the experience of being alive. Pleasure invites us to relax, which dispels stress. Pleasure makes us more receptive to new ideas, more enthusiastic about new tasks or demands. Through pleasure, we extend our awareness throughout the intricate network of nerve endings that constantly connect the inner and outer worlds through the medium of consciousness.

Pleasure invites us to integrate something, while pain pushes us to separate and disown. If someone or something is pleasurable to me, I am more likely to want to explore it further, move toward it, make it part of my life. If something is not pleasurable (as in a job that we dread) there is a tendency to avoid or deny it.

Our culture equates maturity with the ability to deny pleasure. We are often told to put our pleasures away as we grow older—to sit still, work hard, deny or control our feelings. Pleasures we once knew become regulated by guilt, held inside by rigidity in the body and rigidity in our thinking. What becomes rigid also becomes brittle and fragile. Because of its fragility, a rigid system needs to be strongly defended, and that defense results in a closed state.

When we are constricted, the flow of the life force is limited. When we let go and flow freely, we can literally carry more "charge" or excitement in the body. Getting the energy to move through the body is one of the major purposes of the second chakra. Pleasure is a primal means of inviting that flow. When pleasure is denied, an essential part of our second chakra program never gets installed. This creates a person who is missing a vital ingredient to wholeness but does not know what it is, how to find it, or even that it is missing. The result is rigidity in the body and disconnection from the outer world.

We filter experience through the realm of feeling. When pleasure is denied, we disown our right to it, we feel guilty for wanting it, ashamed of having it. Then all feelings are subject to question. The child no longer has the screen of his own feelings to filter incoming stimulation, and consequently loses the discriminating capacity of healthy boundaries. The result is excessive defenses or the inability to protect oneself at all. Boundary issues are then prevalent in each of the lower three chakras.

When primary, healthy pleasures are denied, secondary pleasures take over, such as the pleasure of drinking, drugs, avoiding responsibility, sexually acting out, or overeating. Since secondary pleasures cannot really satisfy our longing for primary pleasures, our lack of satisfaction makes us crave more, forming a basis for addictions. There is a ravenous hunger to feel good, a hunger that is never truly satisfied. Healthy pleasure brings satisfaction; addictive pleasure brings a craving for more.

EMOTIONS

Emotions are instinctual reactions to sensory data. If the senses bring in raw information, feelings are the unconscious reaction to this information, and emotions are the way we organize our feelings. Without consciousness, emotions govern our reactions. We may get angry, fall in or out of love, feel depressed or afraid, but these emotions generally arise from the depths of our psyche quite of their own accord. We may choose the way we respond to these emotions, but the feelings have a life of their own.

> Emotion is the chief source of all becoming conscious. There can be no transforming of darkness into light and of apathy into movement without emotion.
>
> C. G. JUNG

I believe that ultimately, emotions have a spiritual function as the language of the soul. This language is spoken through the body. We can think of sensations as the words, feelings as the sentences, and emotions as the paragraphs. These building blocks are the primary levels of our experience through which our story unfolds, giving us meaning. Meaning integrates our felt sense of experiencing the world.

Most therapies focus strongly on emotions. Pervasive feelings of fear, frustration, shame, or anxiety initiate the quest for change and the beginnings of transformation. If we run from these emotions (something that is culturally supported) we run from the very gateway to our transformation.

Once on our quest, emotions help unravel the story of our soul's journey. Feelings emerge from the unconscious, from the instinctual core of the body, and move up from the lower chakras to enter consciousness. We react in certain ways, but we do not always know why. Feelings captivate our consciousness, fixating our attention until we unravel their mystery. Feelings are the key to buried memories, to events that have a significance our conscious mind may have denied. Initially, emotions are subconscious organizations of impulses to move away from harm and toward pleasure.

It is difficult to feel emotions without some kind of movement. It's hard to hold still when we're angry or excited. Nervousness makes us shake. Sadness can leave us heaving in long, shaking sighs. We control emotion by freezing our body movement. We stiffen our jaw, tighten our neck and belly, inhibit our breathing, and generally contract. Feeling the emotion at a later time is usually accompanied by some kind of movement, a release of the held tension, that allows us to open and expand once again. Anger is released through hitting or kicking, fear through shaking, yearning through reaching, sadness through sobbing.

Just as releasing emotions frees the body, the converse is also true; we can free emotions by consciously moving the body. Reaching out may trigger buried longing and sadness; hitting a pillow may access deeper levels of anger. The way we hold our body tells us a lot about what kind of emotions are stored beneath our awareness. Encouraging movement where the body is frozen helps to free the emotions and restore aliveness and motility.

NEED

Needs are necessities. They are not idle longings. I need to put gas in my car in order for it to run. I need to have training to do a particular job. My child needs love if he is to become emotionally balanced. These are requirements for healthy functioning.

As children we are often shamed for our needs. Our parents may have been unable to meet them, or may have had unmet needs of their own. As a result, we were taught that they were not necessities, and we learned to disown them. One woman I worked with could never let herself eat until she was absolutely starving, could not fill her gas tank until she was close to empty, and could not take the next breath until she had held her exhale empty for several moments. She saw her needs as dismissible desires, something she should overcome. She felt guilty for having them, and tried

Needs are the basic requirements of the system, necessary for it to run. They are the nonnegotiable bottom line.

to keep them hidden. As a result, she kept herself deprived and depleted, unable to fill her basic needs and move on to other things.

When we reclaim our needs, we take responsibility for our own fulfillment.

DESIRE

Desire is a spiritual/emotional impulse that inspires us to move to something greater, to embrace change. If we do not desire anything, the senses shut down. We lose our aliveness. We have no impetus to move forward. The object of desire may not be necessary, but the feeling of desire is the soul's longing to move forward.

Desire is often frowned upon by spiritual disciplines. We are taught that desires are a trap, a distraction from our true path, bound to lead us astray. We are told that desires lead to frustration and suffering and that only by denying them can we truly find God, enlightenment, or peace. But finding God is also a desire, a longing, and a need. Without desire, we are unable to put forth enough effort to attain what is difficult. Without desire, we have no energy, inspiration, or seed for the will. Desire may lead to frustration, but that frustration gives us powerful lessons for growth. Desire is not the trap, but the fuel for action. It is the *object* of our desires that often gets confused.

> You are what your deep driving desire is. As your desire is, so is your will. As your will, so is your deed. As your deed is, so is your destiny.
>
> BRIHADARANYAKA
> UPANISHAD IV.4.5

When we understand the deeper needs behind our desires, we are more able to satisfy ourselves at the core level.

Desire is a combination of sensation and feeling. Desire is the fuel for the will, which is related to chakra three. It is the seed of passion and enthusiasm, essential for developing energy and power. It is the essential thrusting forward that leads us to action. Only by staying in touch with our feelings can we truly know our soul's desire; only by knowing our deepest desires can our will have clarity. Otherwise, the unacknowledged desires sabotage the will by fighting against it. This brings us to *the shadow.*

THE SHADOW

Since the second chakra produces the first major change of consciousness, the first experience of opposites, and represents literally, the number two, it is associated with duality and polarity. Thus, one of the tasks of second chakra adult development is to integrate previously polarized or one-sided aspects of our personality into an indivisible whole. This is an essential step in our alchemical quest: the reclaiming of the shadow and the integration of such polarities as masculine and feminine, mind and body, inner and outer experience. As it is with Jung's individuation process, we often have to move downward into the unconscious to pick up lost remnants of the lower chakras in order to become whole. In the second chakra, our work is to reclaim the shadow.

> One does not become enlightened by imagining figures of light, but by making the darkness conscious.
>
> C. G. JUNG

The shadow represents repressed instinctual energies that are locked away in the realm of the unconscious. They do not die or cease to function, but they are no longer part of conscious awareness, no longer directly expressed through our conscious activity. Consequently, they are enacted unconsciously, sometimes with great force. We may think we never get angry but enact a passive stubbornness that infuriates others. We may deny our own neediness, but subtly manipulate ourselves into the center of attention.

Keeping the shadow in chains requires a great deal of energy and robs the whole of its grace and power. Furthermore, it doesn't work. The shadow chases us in our dreams. It sabotages our work and relationships. It energizes compulsive activities. When the shadow is repressed we are cut off from our wholeness and from our ground. As the instinctual energies are a large part of the child psyche, we are also removed from the innocence and spontaneity of the inner child.

When the shadow remains unacknowledged, it is projected onto others. Like a hidden shape over which we shine our inflated light, the shadow is seen parading shamelessly in the behavior of those around us, while we remain righteously virtuous. Maria, who repressed her sexuality, saw every man as trying to get sexual favors from her. Sandy's foster mother, a benevolent leader in her church community, was punishing and controlling at home, constantly accusing Sandy of immoral activity.

When we become polarized, we are like a magnet, drawing toward us the opposite pole. We invariably attract those who embody our rejected shadow—as mates, bosses, coworkers, neighbors, or children, who insinuate themselves into our lives through relationships we cannot easily escape. If we have rejected our personal power, our boss will be a tyrant. If we are an ever-giving codependent, we will marry someone cold and withholding. If we are quiet and considerate, our neighbor or roommate will be noisy and inconsiderate.

Shadow qualities are met with intense criticism and judgment as they are projected onto others. The presence of this judgment is our clue to the shadow as a *rejected self*. If sexuality is a rejected self, then overt sexuality in others will produce a highly charged negative reaction (much like what we see in some religious sects fixated on the sexual behavior of others). If anger is a rejected self, we will fear and criticize it in others. If we suppress our emotions, we will have little tolerance for those who are needy, crying, or strongly expressive. It makes us very uncomfortable to be around someone expressing our shadow energies. Our judgment is an attempt to negate the source of our discomfort.

Psychologist Hal Stone suggests that this judgment arises out of the resonance between the rejected self and the behavior of the other.[2] It is hard for the unemotional, rational type to be around someone who is emotional because it awakens his rejected emotions. Since this aspect of his personality is not allowed expression, the stimulus must be removed at all costs. If it's not removed, his rejected self will awaken to the point where he can no longer keep it in check—a point that seems dangerous to the ego's concept of self. Through judgment, we attempt to remove stimuli that might awaken our shadow.

Reclaiming the shadow dissolves judgment, and brings greater acceptance of self and others and

> Repression will always call forth a compensatory counter activity of the unconscious which will, through the back door, force upon us the very thing we are trying to repress.
>
> EDWARD WHITMONT

restores an essential wholeness. One of my rejected selves was the slacker. Unable to relax, I had to push myself all the time to be constantly accomplishing something. I felt critical of those who were not working as hard as I was and judgmental of my husband reading the Sunday paper (while I worked)—until I learned to acknowledge how much I needed time off to sit and simply relax. My judgment of others' laziness gave me the clue to my rejected self. Allowing myself to be lazy at times and to relax and enjoy life eliminated my judgment of others and greatly improved my health and relationships.

Reclaiming the shadow does not mean that we become thieves, killers, rapists, or rageaholics. Such aspects are more likely to emerge when the shadow is repressed and its energy builds to the point of taking over the conscious self. The greater the repression, the louder our shadow has to yell to be heard and the greater its chance to become demonic.

You can think of this in terms of bringing some fruit and a sandwich to work for lunch. In order to keep yourself from eating too soon, you stuff the lunch in the back of your desk drawer and forget about it. You send it to the shadow realm, where it is out of sight, out of mind. You get so busy you forget about it entirely until two weeks later, when an odd smell starts coming out of your drawer and you discover this decaying piece of garbage. It did not start out that way, but lost in the shadows it degenerated into something quite unpleasant.

Elements of our personality can do the same thing. Without expression, they don't get to evolve. Our childish tempers don't get to become sophisticated communication. Our neediness doesn't get met with love and intimacy; our sexual urges become compulsive fantasies. Our shadow elements, like rejected children, resort to more and more extreme behavior to get attention.

Reclaiming the shadow means that we reclaim the instinctual energies of our needs and desires so that they can be channeled in appropriate ways. It does not mean we surrender consciousness to the shadow, but that we instead bring the shadow into consciousness.

GUILT

Guilt is the demon of the second chakra because it curtails the free flow of movement, largely by taking the pleasure out of it. If I feel guilty about what I am doing, I do not fully enjoy it. I cannot fully sense the experience as one part of me is frozen off, restricting or trying to control what I am doing. In constant struggles with my weight, I used to feel guilty whenever I ate. As a result, I took no satisfaction from eating and I wanted to do it again. Compulsive activities are often instincts of the pleasure principle, driven to repetition because the guilt prevents satisfaction.

Guilt sequesters the shadow into its dark and unconscious realm. We might say that guilt is the prison guard that keeps the shadow caged, keeping it from coming into the light of consciousness. As a result, the caged shadow becomes even more insistent and the prison guard must tighten his control.

Guilt polarizes the personality. It divides light against dark, good against bad. We are wonderful one day and horrible the next, all because of something we did. The brighter the light, the darker the shadow. The greater the guilt, the more we try to emancipate ourselves by flawless behavior. Flawless behavior inhibits the natural flow of energy moving up from the lower chakras and tends to polarize mind and body.

A polarized personality is characterized by either-or thinking. Without the multiplicity of the rainbow, we find ourselves locked in black-and-white choices. Morals taught to a young child without a genuine sense of connection to others tend to be given in black-and-white terms. This is good, that is bad. For young children with a limited understanding of the world, this is quite necessary. To stay there is to remain in an immature cognitive process.

> If we were all to sit in a circle and confess our sins, we would laugh at each other for lack originality.
>
> KAHLIL GIBRAN

Children who live in fear of punishment get frozen in this either-or thinking. Understandably, they want the rules to be clear so they can behave accordingly and remain safe. They want it spelled out in black and white, and will tend to look at all life in polarized terms. But what happens to those cases that are in-between?

Stacy, for example, was having a difficult time deciding whether or not to leave her boyfriend. To her, the only choices were either to live with him or completely stop the relationship and never see him again. Neither of those choices appealed to her. It never occurred to her that there were a number of choices between those two extremes. She could move out and date him, and maybe date other people for a while. She could end the relationship as she knew it and reestablish a friendship. Because she felt guilty about her negative feelings, she thought she had to overcome them completely or withdraw from the relationship.

Feelings are usually ambiguous. To fully embrace our feelings is to embrace that ambiguity. Black-and-white choices are seldom acceptable. Unacceptable choices keep us from making decisions and trap us in paralysis. When we can't move forward, the second chakra aspect of movement is thwarted. When you feel trapped in either-or thinking, take a moment to ask yourself what you feel guilty about.

A new kind of mathematics called *fuzzy logic* is being introduced into the binary logic of computers to make them smarter. Fuzzy logic is able to approximate the states between polarities, rather than work only with off and on, zero and one. Fuzzy logic defines places between the apple core and the whole apple as half eaten, nearly gone, almost whole, or any number of states in between. These states are usually more accurate and enable better decisions.

We have to develop our ability to feel in order to discern the subtle nuances between polarities. When feelings are numb, we can only discern the obvious differences, the more blatant black-and-white choices. When there is guilt, we think we have to make clear decisions and are uncomfortable with approximations. As a result, it may be harder to get to the truth, harder to communicate that truth to others, and harder to work through it to a sound decision.

> Ambiguity has a destabilizing effect. . . . Very few have the courage or the strength to hold the tension between opposites until a completely new standpoint emerges. . . . This is because, in acknowledging contradictory truths, one has to create an inner equilibrium to keep from being torn in two.
>
> ALDO CAROTENUTO

There is, of course, a healthy place for guilt: as a feeling that allows us to examine our behavior before, during, or after our actions. When it's not distorted, guilt tells us where the boundaries are and where we need to make change. In its appropriate place as feedback, guilt is not a demon but a guide. It is only when guilt becomes excessive, habitual, internalized, and toxic that it dominates the free flow of movement and the full sensate experience of life that is so necessary to the second chakra. Guilt is a teacher when it guides us, but a demon when it binds us.

SEXUALITY

Sexuality is the ultimate expression of the many issues associated with the second chakra: movement, sensation, pleasure, desire, emotions, and polarity. It is the resolution of difference, the union of opposites, and the connecting experience that transcends isolation and forms the foundation for the next chakra level: power. It is the grounds for much of our growth, as it brings us into contact with others who are by nature different from us.

Sexuality is the incorporation of Eros, the basic force of attraction. Eros is an ancient god, the connecting force that unites and delights, bridges and soothes. In Hindu mythology, Eros is the god *Kama*, the originator of all the gods, the binding power of allurement that holds the universe together. Since the force of Eros brings things together, its denial can pull things apart. In a culture this leads to destructive activities.

To embrace Eros is to have the capacity for surrender, to be able to flow with the biological nature of the instinctual/ emotional body. To dance with Eros is to dance with the life force in the liberating current of the lower chakras. Sexuality is the ecstatic expression of that force.

Sexuality, as stated earlier, has been massively misunderstood by our culture. The wounds of mismanaged sexuality are deep and pervasive, affecting the natural flow of excitation through the body. Guilt, as demon of the second chakra, is a direct antidote to

> That unity of culture and nature, work and love, morality and sexuality for which mankind is forever longing, this unity will remain a dream as long as man does not permit the satisfaction of the biological demands of natural (orgastic) sexual gratification.
>
> WILHELM REICH

pleasure and self-esteem. Guilt has been poured through the sexual gates from which Eros flows with such force that for many this portal no longer opens. Thus an essential gateway to pleasure and transformation becomes locked. Sexuality is rejected and sent to the realm of the shadow, where it takes on its demonic form of dissociation and perpetration, desperately seeking connection at any cost.

To reclaim the second chakra is to reclaim our right to feel and our right to healthy sexuality. It is the reclamation of the force of Eros as it flows through all aspects of life. This does not mean that this energy always culminates in the sexual act. Eros is alive and well in every aspect of our existence—the smell of food cooking in the kitchen, the colors of a sunset, eating ice cream on a hot day. Eros needs to be an honored part of our experience, honored for the powerful god that he is.

BALANCED CHARACTERISTICS

A balanced second chakra has the capacity for sexual satisfaction, physical pleasure, general enjoyment of life, comfort with intimacy, and the ability to accept movement and change gracefully, including graceful physical movements. There is steadiness and clarity in emotional states. One can feel deeply without excessive histrionics. Balance involves the ability to nurture self and others while still maintaining healthy sexual and emotional boundaries.

Sexuality in a balanced second chakra is a healthy expression of intimacy, pleasure, and joy, with sensitive boundaries and a true sense of connection. This balance or lack of it can occur in any and all styles of sexuality—heterosexual, transsexual, gay, straight, bisexual. The qualifications for healthy sexuality can only be decided by the persons in question; however, the general guidelines of consenting adults, mutual enhancement, integration with one's life, and stimulation of growth are a good place to start. Ultimately, sexuality should serve the enhancement of the whole chakra system, within and without.

GROWING THE LOTUS

DEVELOPMENTAL FORMATION OF
THE SECOND CHAKRA AT A GLANCE

AGE
6 months to 2 years

TASKS
Sensate exploration of the world
Locomotion
Separation from symbiotic fusion

NEEDS AND ISSUES
Separation vs. attachment
Safety and support to explore
Emotional security
Stimulating environment
Self-gratification

When my son, Alex took his first steps across the room on his first birthday, it was a remarkable moment. He was truly delighted with himself and the glee on both his face and mine was unmistakable. To the pride of us all, he was entering a new state of maturity. He now had an increased level of independence, which brought both excitement and danger. He could move faster in his explorations of the world and he could also get himself hurt. His first steps were shaky and uncertain—upright, he had farther to fall. He immediately wanted me to hold him and reassure him that he was safe, that what he had done was OK. This dilemma, *separation vs. attachment*, typifies the second chakra stage of development.[3]

We have described earlier the increased alertness that appears when the child is able to sit up on his own at approximately six months. At this time, the eyes are better able to focus, bringing the external world into the child's awareness in a way that was previously impossible and stimulating a new influx of consciousness. The external world is an unexplored mystery at this age, discoverable only through the senses. He now has the desire to move outward and explore, to taste and touch at a close range what he sees and hears from a distance. This stimulates the urge to move, which develops locomotion.

The primary focus on the mother slowly begins to wane, as exploration of the environment captures the child's attention. The discovery of the external world shatters the blissful psychic unity characteristic of chakra one. The child is now plunged into a world of duality, making his first distinctions binary—inner and outer, self and other, pleasure and pain. Sometimes Mother's presence feels warm and wonderful while at other times she seems angry or depriving—what psychologists call the "good mother" and the "bad mother." The task now is to connect these dualities.

As the cognitive abilities of language and reasoning are not yet developed, the primary means of making this connection is through feelings. The world outside stimulates feeling states inside. Expressing internal feelings creates external changes, such as Mother coming to comfort the child when he cries. Feelings are the dawning of psychic awareness and the beginning of value formation. What feels pleasurable is considered good, what is unpleasant, bad. These binary distinctions give direction to the child's movement. He wants to move toward that which feels good and away from discomfort. The senses are the stimulus for these feelings; hence, delighting his senses becomes the child's driving interest. It is important to have an environment that brings pleasure to the child as he explores, with colorful shapes, toys that make sounds, and textures to touch.

As the body develops and grows stronger, locomotion becomes more efficient. Sensate stimulation, feeling, and movement become inseparably linked. A child needs to be allowed (when safe) to move according to his feelings for this link to be solid, such as pulling away from a stranger he does not trust or being allowed to keep a toy that brings pleasure. This links the emotions with body instincts.

As movement becomes more efficient, the child's world widens even more and at times he finds himself moving away from the mother. At first this is frightening and he wants to immediately run back and assure himself that she is still there. As this dance is repeated, security is established, which allows

> The infant's inner sensations form the core of the self. They appear to remain the central crystallization point of the "feeling of self" around which a "sense of identity" will become established.
>
> MARGARET MAHLER

the child to gradually emerge as a separate self, setting the ground for chakra three. The child development researcher Margaret Mahler has called this phase *hatching*, for the child is hatching from the egglike symbiosis with the mother to emerge as a distinct individual.[4]

Touch, comfort, and nurturance give the security and connectedness that make it safe to become separate. "Lack of touch is experienced as separation anxiety—lack of contact, of connection," says Ashley Montagu, author of *Touching: The Human Significance of the Skin*.[5] This lack of connection feels like a threat to survival and throws one back to the panic and fear of the first chakra, preventing development from moving upward appropriately. Touch gives us our kinesthetic orientation and is the first sensate experience we learn. Can the child learn to trust his own senses? Can he learn to interpret them accurately? Are his feelings mirrored appropriately? Is he protected from danger? Is he exposed to a toxic emotional field in the family? Since the exploration of the immediate environment can be a scary and dangerous quest, supporting guidance from caregivers is essential.

Meeting survival needs and promoting healthy emotional bonds between parents and child help develop the second chakra by providing a pleasurable and safe experience of outer world exploration. The flow of energy between mother and child gives this transition stability; the constancy of Mother makes it safe to explore. The ground becomes a springboard for upward development. Without a solid ground to push away from, we cannot push very far, as if we were jumping on a sandy beach.

The *emotional climate* of the family is a crucial influence at this stage. If the mother is fearful, angry, or anxious, the child will absorb these emotions on a nonverbal, somatic level. Somatic experiences become hardwired into the system, meaning they become emotional states that are biochemically anchored into the musculature beyond the control of the conscious mind. The language of emotions (which later becomes the *emotional repertoire*) is being programmed at this stage through responsive mirroring. Such mirroring involves reflecting to the child what it seems he might be feeling. "You don't look very happy. Is something wrong?" "I see that you are very excited!" "Are you angry at Daddy?" If a child is preverbal, emotional mirroring happens through comfort and voice tone—a reflection and response to the child's feeling state. This may be as simple as picking up the child when he cries, rocking him when he's upset, or letting him have a place to appropriately express his anger.

The tasks of this developmental stage are to develop a sensate connection between the inner and outer world, to provide bonding and a supportive emotional environment for both closeness and separation, to create a feeling of pleasure and connection with the body, and to awaken the developing consciousness through sensory stimulation. If these tasks are handled correctly, the child will develop a healthy second chakra, with the accompanying qualities of graceful movement, deep emotion, sensitivity, passion for life, and sexual health.

TRAUMAS AND ABUSES

TACTILE AND SENSATE DEPRIVATION

David grew up in a comfortable middle-class family. His mother was a devoted career mother who had no life outside the home. She did everything expected of a mother—she cooked and cleaned, drove her children to baseball games, laid out their clothes in the morning, and joined the PTA. Still, she rarely touched her children. She did not give them hugs, read them stories on her lap, or display physical affection. In fact, no one in the family displayed affection. As a result, David carries a soul wound that makes it hard for him to connect with himself or understand what he really wants in life. He tends to be a loner, putting his energy into his career and avoiding the closeness of relationships.

When body identity is not affirmed through touch, it is often replaced with a frozen image—a split between the sixth and second chakra. When image takes over the feeling self (as it does in the narcissistic personality), the person may achieve external success yet still be internally disconnected. As life progresses, this split becomes more pronounced until there is a breakdown. The narcissistic wound is a soul wound. The deeper, more vulnerable, feeling self is ignored, while the shallower external self is praised and rewarded.

> Loss of the essential condition of well-being that should have grown out of one's time in arms leads to searches and substitutions for it. Happiness ceases to be a normal condition of being alive, and becomes a goal.
>
> JEAN LIEDLOFF

Children need a certain amount of sensory input in order to develop the important connection between mind and body. Appropriate sensate stimulation increases intelligence, coordination, and alertness. If there are a variety of toys to play with, colors to see, sounds to hear, and textures to touch, the mind has more input to stimulate its process. Daniel Goleman, in his book *Emotional Intelligence*, describes how rats with fancier cages (more ladders and treadmills) not only solve mazes better, but also develop heavier brains than rats with sparse cages.[6] Important neural circuitry is developing as sensate awareness comes into play.

Jean Liedloff, author of *The Continuum Concept*, notes profound developmental differences between children that are held and carried and those who are not. Since the child's innate instinctual expectation is to be held, a feeling of rightness occurs, which settles the nervous system, when touched. Without this experience, the overwhelming sense of longing to be held arises, and the sensate attention extends beyond itself and looks for the missing experience. After too much disappointment, it becomes numb. Liedloff says that the difference between a child's expectations and her actual reality correlates to her sense of well-being.[7] The greater the difference, the more a child experiences doubt, suspicion, fear of being wounded, and resignation—all of which undermine emotional well-being.

Too much or too little stimulation generates serious conflicts in the internal mapping of the outside world, the forming of relationships, and the development of grace and movement. Children deprived of touch cope paradoxically by distancing themselves from others, denying their need for closeness. When hugged, they often feel stiff and wooden, unable to fully receive the hug.

Lack of touch can result in autoerotic stimulation such as habitual rocking, compulsive masturbation, and eating disorders. All of these are attempts to fill that second chakra gap with some kind of movement and pleasurable sensation. Marion Woodman, in *Addiction to Perfection*, describes obesity as wrapping one's body with soft flesh in an attempt to replace an absent or rejecting mother.[8]

Lack of touch prohibits the development of the principle channels of sensory reception. When there is too little or too much stimulation of the senses, then the sensory channels shut down. Failing to learn the sensate language is like failing to learn to read—we lose an essential channel of information. Sensations are the building blocks of emotional intelligence and allow us to get along well with others.

The other senses gradually develop in conjunction with tactile experience. The sound of the mother's calm or angry voice connects with the warmth of being held, the loneliness of neglect, or the fear of being hit. Visual cues such as facial expressions, light and dark, or the decor of different rooms are connected with bodily experiences of sleeping and waking, eating and bathing. These associations link the internal mapping system that is developing through the child's sensate experience of the world. If the experience is painful, then the senses shut down and the world becomes definitively smaller. The child retreats to the inner world of fantasy and imagination.

If the stimulation is more than the child can handle, she becomes over-charged and the excess energy will try to find a way to discharge. Since this is a period when emotions are the primary language, this discharge occurs through emotional expression, such as crying or anger. This habit may get firmly established and exist throughout life.

Between the ages of nine and eighteen months, the baby is learning to string together sensations, actions, and reactions into an organized sense of self. Linking different senses into a single gestalt of experience marks the primary connection between mind and body. If the senses do not logically flow from experience, then the child learns to distrust her own senses. If the sense of hunger does not result in being fed, if a mother's soothing voice does not connect with being held, if a child is shamed or rejected for her natural needs, then the senses seem to have failed to give proper information to the individual. When we distrust our senses, we shut them down. Hence the abused child, even in adulthood, may not be able to tell whether she's hungry or full, tired or in danger, overstimulated or coming down with a cold. The senses have lost their reliability as information gatherers.

According to Jung, an underdeveloped sensate function leads to frequent misjudging of situations, relying instead on excessive intuition, which may often be far removed from reality. What becomes deficient in the second chakra often shows up as an excess in chakra six.

Whereas understimulation fails to awaken the curiosity of the developing mind and leaves the child disconnected and alone, overstimulation may overwhelm the nervous system and create anxiety. If we are in tune with our child, we can hopefully achieve a balance.

EMOTIONAL ENVIRONMENT

Rebecca was a toddler when her parents were getting divorced. It was an angry and painful time in her family. Still in a high chair (so her mother tells me), she witnessed violent fights between her parents. Though Rebecca was not hit, she witnessed her father's constant rage at his wife until her mother finally took Rebecca and her siblings and left the marriage. It was at that point that Rebecca became a little hellion, carrying the rage of her now-absent father. Immersed in a field of violence, Rebecca learned anger as a primary way of relating. Ten years later, when her mother first came to me, that pattern still persisted. It was now impacting Rebecca's social relationships, her schoolwork, and her mother's well-being.

Sometimes small children seem like little reaction machines. Energy comes in; energy goes out. Without the maturity to temper their emotions, the feelings that run through a family run through the children with very little change. Children do not decide to be angry or fearful, loving or calm. They merely reflect the emotional climate in which they are helplessly immersed.

Yet, the emotions that pass through the child affect her physiological state, sense of the world, and growing sense of herself. If the household is saturated in anger, she may get used to the high adrenalin state that anger creates and learn that anger is the normal way to express oneself. If Mom or Dad are fearful, that fear is communicated to the child non-verbally and becomes part of the child's emotional repertoire. If the environment is loving, their developing sense of self is centered around expecting, receiving, and expressing that love with its attendant feelings.

This is the stage where the child develops the part of his identity that is associated with chakra two: the *emotional identity*. The emotions that are most familiar become a core complex within the developing Self—a way that we feel consistent with our internal being later on. If anger is the emotional field that surrounds him, then the child learns to identify with that anger and carries the biochemical state that goes with it. If it was sadness or fear, then the child feels most "himself" when experiencing these states. Even extreme emotions can become normal over time, so that later in life one creates situations (such as danger, conflict, or loss) that produce similar emotions. In order to break this cycle, the emotions must be identified and understood, while creating new, more productive patterns of expression.

However, the emotions children express in reaction to their situations are often met with punishment, rejection, or shame. Rebecca was punished for her temper tantrums. David became emotionally withdrawn, and was ridiculed for being shy. Sarah was naturally exuberant, but was shamed into being quiet. The expression of feelings then becomes a mistrusted impulse.

Unable to trust our own feelings, we instead hold them in, shut them down, or dissociate from them. Since emotions are an instinctual response to experience, we lose a vital connection to experience and to life. Alcohol or drugs may be used to create distance from experience. Behavior may be compulsive, devoid of feelings. An abusive parent is unable to feel the pain of the child. Since our feelings are so immersed in sensation, inhibiting them requires us to deaden the sensations of our body and hence deaden our aliveness as well.

Emotions are the first language of the child, spoken through the instinctual reactions of the body. The child learns her emotional language through effective mirroring and positive response to her raw feeling state. If the parent responds to the child's emotional expression, then the child learns that her innate reactive language is effective and pays more attention to it. If she learns to understand her emotions, she becomes *emotionally literate*, which means she can read and communicate with her own emotions and those of others. Emotions can then evolve into meaning (i.e., mature through the chakras).

Empathy promotes emotional literacy. Effective mirroring lets a child attach consciousness to her instinctual feelings. She learns that a certain internal state is called *anger*, while other feelings may be called *sadness* or *fear*. In this way she learns to express her feelings in a more mature way. When Johnny looks sad, his mother says, "Oh you look sad today. What's the matter?" This teaches him to name his feelings, to read them, and later communicate them through language instead of acting out.

Being told not to feel a certain way negates our second chakra *right to feel*. "Oh, you mustn't feel that way about your uncle." "Wipe that smirk off your face!" "You've no right to be angry!" If we believe these injunctions, we institute the domination of mind over feeling. We feel guilty about our feelings and repress them, even to the point where they are no longer recognizable.

Emotions are an instinctual movement of psychic energy. Only our mind interprets some emotions as "good" and others as "bad." When we repress the emotions related to abuse, we simultaneously repress all our emotions, and with them the movement of the spirit.

Susan, for example, was never allowed to be angry. Nothing in her life made her angry, so this did not seem to be a problem. She complained instead of the isolation she created by continually withdrawing from people. She did not see that her withdrawal was a result of the anger she was unable express. If she could only express what she disliked, she might be able to make changes in her relationships instead of withdraw.

To a person who is emotionally illiterate, watching someone in an emotional state is a complete mystery, as if that person is speaking a foreign language. The emotional one is criticized for making no sense or acting foolishly, while an emotional illiterate finds his own feelings an equal mystery. When the feeling function is underdeveloped, it comes out in its shadow form as *moodiness*. The moods are not consciously connected to feelings but, nevertheless, carry emotional tones that are usually quite apparent to anyone else. When asked what is wrong, the moody person usually answers with a grumpy "Nothing!" which is actually meant to be a true statement. Their illiteracy prevents them from being able to read their own emotions and learn their important meaning.

In a family where feelings are simply not expressed, there is no opportunity to learn emotional language. Without emotional literacy, a whole dimension of human experience and connection is lost. Without the ability to read our own needs and feelings, we are unable to meet them, and remain trapped until the message is finally interpreted.

Your children are not your children. They are the sons and daughters of life's longing for itself. They come through you, but not of you. And though they are with you yet, they belong not to you.

KAHLIL GIBRAN

ENMESHMENT

Second chakra development begins with a fused identity between mother and child and ends with the emergence of autonomy. The child first learns his emotions as an extension of those of the family, but later learns to have his own. When the child is not allowed to emerge and express himself as a unique individual, he is enmeshed. When emotions arise that are not pleasing to the mother, such as anger, dependency, or fear, and they are met with punishment, rejection, or shame, then the child learns that he can only have feelings that correspond to his parent's wishes or feeling states. He is not allowed to develop a separate identity grounded in his own sensate/emotional experience. The child's life is defined in terms of family needs, but the family is not there to supply the child's needs. An enmeshed child will therefore feel guilty when pursuing his own needs and interests.

The enmeshed child is given a false sense of self. He takes his cues from outside himself, defines his feeling state by the reactions of others, and forms an outer persona that may be at profound odds with his inner needs. This is the basis of the narcissistic personality described so well by Alice Miller in *The Drama of the Gifted Child*.[9] The outer persona is believed to be the real self. The result is a life lived without individuation or authenticity.

An enmeshed child will be highly aware of everyone else's feelings. Clairsentience (the ability to sense others' emotions) comes from a second chakra that is too other-directed and not grounded enough in one's bodily experience. A clairsentient walks into a party and feels responsible for the woman in the corner who is being ignored, or he can feel the jealousy of his neighbor, whose wife is flirting, all without awareness of his own needs. A little clairsentience gives us sensitivity to others but too much separates us from our ground and leaves us ruled by a tumultuous blend of others' emotions that we cannot control.

SEXUAL ABUSE

Sexual abuse hits at the very core of the second chakra. Whether mild or severe, within the family or outside, sexual abuse has long-lasting effects on all aspects of the second chakra: the free flow of energy within the body, the ability to have intimacy, pleasure, and healthy sexuality as an adult, comfort with emotions, a healthy sense of boundaries, and a positive relationship with one's own body. Nor is sexual abuse limited only to second chakra damage—it affects our sense of trust, our experience of power (or lack thereof), our future relationships, and often, because of the secrecy

> I have come to realize that sexual assault is an imposed death experience for the victim. That is, the victim experiences her life as having been taken by somebody else.
>
> EVANGELINE KANE

involved, our ability to communicate. Since it assaults the feeling and sensate functions of the body, chakras six and seven often compensate by an excess of intuition and thinking.

Sexual abuse comprises anything that does not respect the natural development of a child's sexuality. Sexual abuse could be slapping or punishing a child for touching his own genitals, or pushing sexuality onto a child who is not developmentally able or interested. Sexual abuse includes exhibitionism, voyeurism, exposure to pornography, sexual teasing, invasion of privacy, unwanted physical affection, age-inappropriate sexual language or jokes, as well as the obvious genital fondling or sexual engagement with a child by an adult, parent, or older sibling. Enticing a child through exposure, flirtation, or promises of rewards to express sexual interest in ways he or she might not otherwise, also comprises sexual abuse. It does not allow the child's sexuality to develop at its own pace. Adults who push themselves on unwilling adult victims are also engaging in sexual abuse, but I am concerning myself here with activities that affect us at more developmentally sensitive ages. The younger such an event occurs, the more devastating its effects.

The stimulation of erogenous zones is meant to dissolve boundaries. For adults, this is usually a pleasurable experience. The child's original state, however, is without boundaries. Early childhood development is oriented toward developing an ego that can *make* boundaries and distinctions, rather than toward dissolving them. If erogenous zones are stimulated at these sensitive ages, boundaries may not form and the child may have difficulty blocking or even sorting out influences coming in from outside. This difficulty with boundaries is often a lifelong struggle for victims of childhood sexual abuse. Without good boundaries, they fail to protect themselves against future invasions, and the incidence of further traumatic sexual experience is very high. Internally, this can even affect the immune system, which may fail to appropriately recognize invading organisms.

Sexual abuse can produce emotional numbness, dissociation, various addictions, eating disorders, or phobias, sexual dysfunction, guilt and shame, depression, hostility, dependency, sleep disorders, psychosomatic disorders, and many other difficulties with life. It wreaks havoc on relationships where issues of trust and intimacy come into play, and many abuse survivors choose celibacy and isolation rather than take the risk of further betrayal. Others may become highly sexual or promiscuous, repeatedly seeking the high erotic charge that was imposed upon them as children. For this reason, some untreated sexual abuse survivors become subsequent perpetrators, failing to respect the boundaries of others and unconsciously acting out the abuse they suffered. Often, sexual abuse is so traumatic that the events are repressed from memory, making them hard to effectively recognize and treat. For others, the memories are all too intrusive and arise spontaneously at unwanted times, such as during moments of intimacy, relaxation, meditation, or social interaction.

Sexual abuse confuses the pleasure/pain dynamic and distorts the interpretation of emotion. Because the physical experience may be pleasurable while the emotional betrayal is painful, there can be a continued confusion around pleasure and pain. One may feel sad or ashamed when feeling pleasure, or limit pleasure for fear of the emotions it brings up. In other cases, where the perpetrator was a trusted family member and the abuse occurred in the guise of intimacy and closeness (sometimes the only closeness the child received), emotional pleasure can be coupled with guilt and shame. The whole arena of the second chakra gets immensely scrambled. Abuse survivors often feel betrayed by their own bodies and may choose to ignore its signals altogether. Sorting out these conflicting messages buried in sensation and emotion is a long and difficult process.

Bringing the abuse to consciousness, learning about its effects, and engaging the healing process promotes profound changes in every aspect of one's life. It *is* possible to heal the effects of sexual abuse and there are now many trained therapists, groups, and books out to assist the healing process (see the bibliography at the end of the book).

RAPE

Rape is such obvious assault to the second chakra that it nearly speaks for itself. The use of sexuality for power and violence, the violation of one's boundaries and one's dignity, the intimidation and annihilation of the spirit within—all assault the entire chakra system. As the second chakra is the first place in the system where the outside comes in (an essential gateway to being an open system), the violation of rape may force the entire system to close. Any of the effects listed for child sexual abuse can also occur with adult experiences of rape. When there are unhealed wounds from childhood abuse, rape is not only a traumatic event in and of itself, but also a reenactment of earlier events. The stronger our basic lower chakra foundations, the better our resources for recovery.

ABORTION

Abortion is not an abuse that happens to a young child, yet it needs to be considered here as it can have profound effects on a woman's second chakra. On an emotional level, abortion constitutes a moral struggle, and no matter how liberal one's views, the decision is never easy. It is nearly always accompanied by emotional turmoil, often by guilt and fear, and may entail a profound sense of grief and loss. In addition, abortion halts the natural process of the body that is geared toward continuing the pregnancy. Even with anesthesia, there is assault on the second chakra organs, and such a wound takes time to heal, time which is seldom acknowledged.

A woman who has just had an abortion needs to treat herself with the tenderness she would give to a rape victim, because in a sense, the womb gets raped in an abortion. Not only is it helpful to create ritual or dialog around the possible spirit of the child, but it is also important to dialog with the body before, during, and after the operation. We can tell the body what is going to happen, comfort the body during the process, and soothe the body after it is over. It is important to have a friend who can hear your grief and take time to write in your journal or be alone with your feelings.

It does not help that the political climate around abortion is so stormy. A woman goes through enough pain and trauma just dealing with an unwanted pregnancy; if she comes to the difficult decision to have an abortion, she needs love and support, not further degradation and shame.

GENERAL EFFECTS OF ABUSES

In a world that both seeks and denies pleasure, where sexuality has become confused, misaligned, and mistreated, and where mechanization denies the sensate experiences of the body, the wounds to the second chakra are many and profound. Anything that blocks development of the second chakra severs two essential connections: the *internal* connection between mind and body, and the *external* connection that joins inner and outer worlds, self and other, soul and environment. Without these connections, we become, as Alexander Lowen states, "split into a disembodied spirit and a disenchanted body."[10]

Lacking tactile stimulation and nurturing, we become literally out of touch, fragmented, isolated, removed, disconnected, and ultimately misinformed. If our sensate channels close down, we block the bulk of our information input and become closed off in our own world. Out of touch with our own feelings, we are necessarily out of touch with the feelings of others and lack the basis for empathy and compassion necessary to get to the fourth chakra.

If expression through movement is denied, our bodies become rigid, yet blocking this requires a great deal of energy. A child who monitors all his actions for fear of rejection or criticism becomes heavily armored, with a rigidity that is reflected in physical awkwardness and personal discomfort. Often there is a similar lack of flexibility and openness to new ideas, alternative lifestyles, adventures, or possibilities. What is *rejected* then becomes *projected*—rigidity can be vehemently judgmental, fueled by the passion that is forbidden in the feeling realm.

CHARACTER STRUCTURE

THE ORAL: THE LOVER

Samantha sat on my couch with tears streaming down her face. Her voice, like her body, was heavy and slow. She had first come to me for depression and overeating, but now she was facing a dark despair over the sudden loss of her primary relationship with a woman she had hoped to share her life with. She felt abandoned and betrayed. She felt like she was falling apart. She had trouble getting a deep breath. She could not stop thinking about her lover and was desperately hanging on to the slightest hope for reconciliation. She was having trouble taking care of herself, having trouble concentrating

FIGURE 2.1. ORAL CHARACTER STRUCTURE (THE LOVER)
    THE UNDERNOURISHED CHILD

FIRST CHAKRA Deficient	SECOND CHAKRA Excessive	THIRD CHAKRA Deficient	FOURTH CHAKRA Excessive
Feeling of emptiness, abandonment	Dependent, clingy	Undercharged, lethargic	Believes that love will solve everything
Difficulty forming oneself, body appears collapsed	Needy	Lack of aggression, fear of anger	Very attached in relationships, loyal
Legs don't support; can't stand on own two feet; knees locked	Craves touch, nurturance, sex	Poor muscle tone	Very loving, kind, compassionate, understanding
Scarcity—there's never enough	Emotionally responsive	Doesn't recognize power options	Codependent
Fear of letting go	Wants to merge	Debases oneself, especially in relationships	Feels rejected easily
	Feels deprived	Poor self-esteem	
		Easily discouraged, demands feel impossible	

FIFTH CHAKRA Excessive	SIXTH CHAKRA May be balanced	SEVENTH CHAKRA Deficient
Fills emptiness with oral activity, such as talking	Can manifest in either direction	Spiritual connection about seeking union, more to heal heart wound
Engages people through conversation and uses it to hold their attention (get love)	Focus on others makes for highly sensitive intuition	Spirituality may mirror parent-child relationship (i.e., infantile), wants to get taken care of
Immature communication— doesn't ask directly for needs	Lack of energy from the ground may not make it to the upper chakras	Intelligence is calculating— fixated on meeting needs
Voice may be childlike or sad	Daydreams to fill emptiness	

> The oral character does not make a strong effort to reach out for what he wants. In part this is due to a lack of strong desire, in part to the fear of reaching.... He hopes to get what he wants somehow without reaching for it; in this way he can circumvent the feared disappointment.
>
> ALEXANDER LOWEN

at work, and at times felt suicidal. On this day, she felt like all hopes for her future were dashed—that without her lover she was forever lost.

Samantha is an example of an Oral character structure. Her feelings of loss and despair are quite real. If we could be in her body, we would feel the devastating emptiness, as if someone had just turned a switch and cut off all our vital supplies. It would be difficult to sit up straight. We would want to collapse, curl up in a ball, and have someone hold us. Our arms might hang lifeless at our sides. We would want to cling, forgive, plead with our lover to stay and take care of us. The abandonment would be all too real and familiar because we have been here before in other relationships. We would be lost in our grief.

In Freud's psychosexual stages, the first and second chakras correlate developmentally to the oral stage, where the primary focus is on nourishment and physical contact. When there is deprivation at this stage, the child does not get the energy she needs, and literally has trouble forming herself. The deprivation is usually emotional—too much separation from the mother, too little touch, too little attention—but it can also be physical, in terms of not getting enough to eat, losing access to the breast too soon, or having a mother without enough energy to nourish her child. In this day and age, where working and single mothers are common, there are many reasons why a mother may not be able to provide adequately for her child, either emotionally or physically. The result is deficiency in the first chakra's ability to ground and form, and an excessive neediness in the second chakra. We can think of the Oral character as the *undernourished child* (see figure 2.1).

In bioenergetics, the Oral character is seen as dependent, addictive, and needy. The body tends to be soft and underformed, sometimes thin and collapsed, other times overweight, but loosely bound. There is usually collapse in the chest, and the muscles and flesh seem to sag with resignation (see page 23, Oral Character). From their deprivation, Orals remain chronically undercharged. They are prone to depression and generally have too little energy. They question not so much their *right to exist* (as it was for the Schizoid/Creative structure) but rather the *right to have*. They are less concerned with the question of "Will I survive?" but instead ask, "Am I wanted?" Their issues center around satisfactory nourishment from food or love. They desperately want to be loved; when this longing is frustrated, as it usually is, they turn to food and oral activities for comfort.

Where the Schizoid withdraws, the Oral seeks dependence and merging as a defense against deprivation. This relates to the infant's inability to provide for her own emotional needs and must receive energy from outside herself in order to feel normal. Therefore, the focus of energy as an adult is also fixated outside the self. When loved, the Oral personality feels energized and whole. She is nurturing and giving, a loyal partner who is perceptive and understanding. She bonds well and loves deeply, and for this reason her kinder name is the Lover. Lovers are not afraid to love, dissolve boundaries, or be close, even though they tend to get hurt. Since they love so deeply, losing a relationship is especially baffling and they wonder why another's love is not as deep as their own. Their dependency is often clinging, which, of course, drives people away and perpetuates the problem. Rejection becomes their greatest fear.

As Lover types perk up when interacting with others, they often find definition through service to others, though this defense can also be a trap. Through service, one ostensibly earns the right to have their needs met as well as the sense of being wanted. The Oral personality is a prime candidate for codependence—with a compulsive need to fix and fixate on others.

The exhaustion that results from constant giving creates an even greater emptiness inside, and this is the vicious cycle of the Oral structure. They give in order to receive, but seldom receive in kind, and so keep themselves depleted and feeling even needier. Often, the more an Oral character is deprived, the harder she tries to give. Breaking this cycle involves learning to nourish oneself physically, emotionally, and spiritually. By filling our own vessel, our neediness decreases and we are better able to receive. Our giving then comes from a more mature place of fullness rather than emptiness.

As the name might imply, the Oral character is often fixated on cooking and eating food, or other oral activities such as smoking, drinking, excessive talking, or biting. Food, being the only solid substance we ingest, provides a sense of support and solidity and is a substitute for the emotional nurturing that was lacking. In actuality, it *is* a kind of nourishment—it gives support, strength, and a feeling of inner presence to fill the intolerable emptiness. Unfortunately, excessive eating can lead to lethargy and inertia and prevents healthy grounding. Having a heavy body is a way of feeling heavy enough to be anchored in the world, wrapping oneself with the body of the mother and producing the comfort that was not supplied when it was necessary. Curtailing the eating may produce anxiety or depression and may reveal an emptiness that has no specific focus or content.

Oral/Lover types believe that love can solve everything. They can be the sacrificial mother, the devoted wife, the loyal worker. They can be good at breaking down another's walls, as they do not experience a great need for boundaries in their interpersonal relationships. They are mystified when others erect boundaries, say no, or create separation. This lack of boundaries causes rejection from others and perpetuates the vicious cycle of dependency-rejection-insecurity-clinging-rejection.

Oral types have poorly developed aggression and seldom get angry, partly because their energy levels are low, and because getting angry risks rejection, their greatest fear. Without aggression, the Oral character has difficulty forming the hard, definitive edges characteristic of first chakra solidity and so necessary for survival. Focus and self-discipline, boundary formation, and acceptance of enforced structure (such as a job or school) require immense effort and may seem like alien concepts with unfair demands that Orals resent and resist.

Healing those with an Oral character structure involves teaching them to stand on their own two feet and feel power and completion in their separateness and independence. It helps to encourage their aggression, which energizes the body and moves the liberating current upward to nourish the upper chakras. They do not need to develop the second chakra, which is usually excessive, but instead need to balance this excess by developing the chakras directly above and below it, namely, those of will and grounding.

Their strong ability to love needs to be turned back upon themselves in self-care and spiritual nourishment. The first step is to move them out of their excessive emotional state, and back in touch with solid ground.

An excessive second chakra has a weak boundary and poor containment. There may be too little discretion about sexual and emotional expression, with a stronger movement outward than inward.

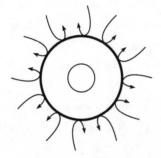

A deficient second chakra has a rigid boundary and lets very little energy pass into its core. Depleted, there is little drive to reach outward.

FIGURE 2.2. SECOND CHAKRA EXCESS AND DEFICIENCY

EXCESS AND DEFICIENCY

Since the second chakra is about movement, excess and deficiency reflect the amount of internal and external movement of the body, as well as emotional identification and sexual expression. As we are passing through the realm of duality, a healthy balance is essential for progress to the third chakra center of power. Maintaining two poles requires enough flexibility to expand to either pole as situations require. There is no power with only one pole.

Many people vacillate between excess and deficiency in this chakra—some over a period of years marking major cycles of sexual activity or celibacy, for example, while others may experience extreme emotional fluctuations within a single day. Holding one's center (related to the grounding of chakra one) is essential to finding a healthy balance. This balance is not a matter of rigid restriction to a fixed center, but of homeostatic fluctuation around an inner stability, much as those toys with weights on the bottom always return to an upright position because the heaviness of the base always brings them back home. Finding our center in the tumultuous oceans of the second chakra is a sign of resolution that allows us to move on (see figure 2.2).

DEFICIENCY

Dave found it hard to know what he was feeling. He would go into depressive moods, sometimes for days, but could rarely decipher what was bothering him. His marriage was stable but lacked passion. Sex to him often felt like a duty rather than a pleasure. Having been rarely touched as a child, he was uncomfortable with displays of affection. He complained of feeling emotionally numb in life, while his wife's emotional fluctuations were a complete mystery to him. He was not particularly happy in his job but was terrified to contemplate making a change. His body was well formed but rigid. Dave's second chakra program was very sparsely written. As a result, the chakra was closed down.

Second chakra deficiency results, above all, in restricted movement, physically, emotionally, and sexually. In the body this can be seen as rigid or jerky motions, stiff joints, and a rigid musculature that has trouble yielding to softness and feeling. Such a person walks stiffly, with little motion in the hips and with difficulty bending the knees and pelvis. (This varies according to severity; not all deficiencies are so obvious.) Try walking while holding your pelvis rigid and you get an idea of what it might feel like. You can feel the rigidity that is required by the entire rest of the body.

Restricted movement inhibits the flow of excitation through the body, inhibits the nourishment of *chi*, or vital energy, lowers the breathing and metabolic rate, and diminishes the emotions. Since movement and change are essential to the system's resilience, the rigidity of second chakra deficiency makes us fragile. To protect this fragility, boundaries are kept very strong in order to keep out unwanted energy that might induce change and threaten stability. There is a belief that if we let feelings flow, we will fall down the rabbit hole with nothing to support us. For many, this feels like disintegration, and until there is adequate ground to support new movement, this may be a very real fear.

On a mental level, restricted movement and fear of change may create a monopolarization of ideas—the belief in only one way to do things. This, too, must be defended by rigid and hostile boundaries (often seen with religious and political fanaticism). New input is resisted, and the single pointed focus can create an intensity that may appear powerful, but is really brittle and fragile.

Since pleasure invites an expansion of energy from the core to the periphery, then someone with a deficient second chakra remains in a contracted state. Such a person tends to avoid pleasure, often because of a harsh inner critic that cannot allow fun without self-condemnation. This denial may send energy to higher chakras, with either positive or negative results. The energy may move upward to the third chakra as frantic activity or workaholism, or to the higher chakras as increased creativity, religious fervor, obsession with purity, or intellectual pursuits. As pleasure becomes a rejected self, the pleasure of others meets with harsh judgment.

Deficiency on the emotional level can result from either a complete lack of programming (as in growing up in an emotionally cold household) or from suppressing emotions in order to tolerate an intense situation. In either case, a lack of feeling and a corresponding lack of bodily sensation are avoidant strategies that lead to second chakra deficiency. This produces a feeling of emptiness, a dullness about life, a feeling of being stuck (no inner movement), and a sense of isolation. There may be a kind of resignation, apathy, or pessimism, and an inability to sense one's own needs.

Sexually, a deficient second chakra manifests in repressed, diminished, or nonexistent sexual feelings. It may be difficult to connect emotionally during sex, with numbness in the lower body, or difficulty achieving arousal or climax. There may be shame around sex, judgment, or simply intense shyness that contracts the energy at a time when it would otherwise expand and merge with another. As sexuality is such a complex issue, fear of sex may, in fact, be fear of the feelings that sex opens up—internalized shame about not being good enough, shame about our bodies, panic around weak boundaries, inability to communicate well, or any number of related issues from past wounds.

Contraction in the second chakra may also affect the social realm, as social skills require emotional literacy. Internalized guilt and shame can produce intense awkwardness in social situations, making one seem stiff or cold when interacting with others. One may be perceived as having no feelings, when actually the feelings may merely be hidden. Deficiency in the second chakra usually results in introversion.

EXCESS

Dana was always in an emotional state. To her, everything seemed like a crisis that had to be dealt with immediately. She was sometimes exuberant, full of energy, and inspiring to be around. At other times she was gripped by anger or torrents of tears, as if her world were falling apart. She was highly social and spent much of her time on the phone or going to parties. In her relationships, she was highly sexual and very giving. She loved to get deeply involved and her relationships had dramatic ups and downs. She had trouble sitting still, concentrating on tasks, or delaying gratification in any way. When I worked with her, she was two years sober but had been an alcoholic for over a decade. Dana's excessive second chakra overcompensated for her lack of emotional fulfillment as a child.

With an excessive second chakra, one feels most alive in intense emotional states. The phrase "I am angry" implies that we *are* that emotion, rather than merely having a momentary feeling. For some people, the only time they feel they *are* anything is when they are feeling some kind of intense emotion. The range may fluctuate from rage to tears, excitement to fears—each one the center around which everyone else must dance. It is difficult for such a person to separate their feelings from the realities of the situation. If they feel threatened, they can't tell whether the threat is real. They cannot see that their fear may be related to something in their own past, or that they have choices in how they react. They may also be excessively sensitive emotionally, unable to let things roll off their back, and take everything to heart. Emotions may range wildly from one state to another within a relatively short time period.

In this type, the upward current, based in unconscious instincts, is more active than the downward current of conscious understanding. In a family, the ones with strong emotions may dictate the behavior of the rest of the family. This excess also creates deficiency in the other members. The emotional dictator takes up all the emotional space and everyone else must dance around their volatile or depressive moods, stripped of the right to their own feelings.

In contrast to the isolation of the deficient state, the person with a second chakra excess has an intense need to be connected at all times. There may be an addiction to people and partying, with an inability to be alone, form boundaries, or say no. As the corresponding developmental stage is still one of merging and dependence, being stuck in the second chakra keeps us in a state that is still trying to find completion through others.

Without the ability to comprehend separateness, there is difficulty separating one's own feelings from those of others (clairsentience). People with high clairsentience are so aware of what everyone else is feeling, they have trouble getting in touch with their own feelings. If they are around someone depressed, they take on the depression, as if it is their fault. They are happy if others are happy. This may result in social, sexual, and emotional dependencies.

Often this social dependency results from an attempt to block out the intensity of one's deeper emotions. When we are with others, busily interacting and attending to their needs, we are distracted from our own fears and sadness. Since emotional needs at this developmental stage must be met from outside, fixation at this level results in a fixation on others at the cost of oneself—a state commonly known as *codependency*.

Stimulation of the senses is craved by a system that is excessive in this chakra. In contrast to the deficient who might prefer bland colors, foods, or uniformity in surroundings, the excessive wants constant stimulation, change, and excitement. These people have a highly dramatic sense of being alive, which may initially appear as a kind of thriving, yet their stimulation seldom gets channeled into real output, and the person may feel lost or alone when they try to be in a quieter state.

Sexually, the excessive second chakra seems to lead the rest of the system around by its gonads. Often wonderful lovers, they are responsive to the instinctual energy of Eros, and thrive on the intimacy, connection, and ego validation they feel in sexual situations. While there is nothing wrong with this in and of itself, it becomes a problem when it wins out over good discrimination in the choice of lovers, creates sexual addiction to the point of neglecting other elements of life, or results in a conquest of lovers rather than real intimacy. Quantity may become more important than quality.

The second chakra relates to the element water, and an excessive second chakra has a container that is weak due to poor boundaries, spilling and scattering the water before it can nourish growth inside. There may be a need for constant movement, making it difficult to stick to one thing long enough to manifest.

In terms of the pleasure principle, the excessive second chakra may be so oriented toward pleasure that it prevents anything else from being accomplished. When faced with difficulty, the pleasure addict says simply, "It's too hard. I want to go out and have fun and feel better." An excessive chakra grabs the energy and does not let it pass on to other chakras. Therefore, the energy needed to fuel the will gets grabbed by the need for immediate gratification. If that gratification could be eventually satisfied, it would be fine, but when the cycle becomes addictive, it is never satisfied and always dominates any other urges.

ADDICTIONS

Addictions are difficult to classify in terms of chakras because different substances produce different states. Even addiction in general cannot be classified in any single chakra. In chemical dependency, the drug of choice gives us important clues about chakra imbalances. For example, stimulants or depressants relate primarily to the energy dynamics of the third chakra, while alcohol creates the merging and lessening of inhibition more closely related to the second chakra. Excessive eating may be an attempt to ground, related to chakra one; a move toward pleasure (chakra two); or blocked anger in the third. But all addictions are initially an attempt to create or deny a feeling or a state of consciousness. The attempt to create a particular state is a compensation, while denial is an avoidance. This gives us our basic excessive and deficient coping strategies.

Alcohol lessens the inhibiting control of the conscious mind, which allows the liberating current to come up from below and move unhindered toward the crown, releasing energy and discharging the system. When the downward current, which focuses and limits, becomes excessive, the life force can feel restricted and relief is felt by overthrowing its dominating influence. An alcoholic may free up his anger or say things that were previously blocked as the energy moves upward. Free of inhibition, he can be spontaneous, share his feelings, make jokes, and feel alive. Unfortunately, there is no integration with this release. There is expression but little reception. The relief is only temporary and must be repeated again and again—a cycle that leads to addiction. Here is a clear example of where sending energy upward is not always beneficial.

While the treatment of addictions is a complicated process beyond the scope of this book, the need to reroute the cyclic repetitive patterns and discharge the underlying emotional force falls under the domain of the second chakra. Since addiction is so often the result of an emotional wound, the general principles of second chakra healing apply. They are reconnecting with the sensations of the body, discharging and/or learning to contain pervading emotions, completing blocked movements frozen by trauma, and learning to decipher and appropriately meet needs.

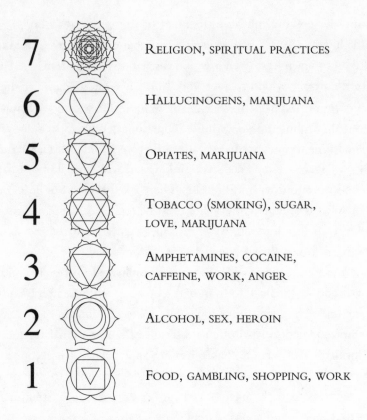

7	RELIGION, SPIRITUAL PRACTICES
6	HALLUCINOGENS, MARIJUANA
5	OPIATES, MARIJUANA
4	TOBACCO (SMOKING), SUGAR, LOVE, MARIJUANA
3	AMPHETAMINES, COCAINE, CAFFEINE, WORK, ANGER
2	ALCOHOL, SEX, HEROIN
1	FOOD, GAMBLING, SHOPPING, WORK

FIGURE 2.3. ADDICTIONS AND RELATED CHAKRAS

RESTORING THE LOTUS

HEALING THE SECOND CHAKRA

There is so much amiss in our cultural attitudes about emotions and sexuality that healing this chakra becomes a monumental task that extends beyond our personal selves. Who has the final word on what healthy sexuality really looks like? What is an appropriate level of emotional response? When have we ever completed our emotional work? How do we fully open our sensate channels in a world that is full of assaulting sounds and images? How do we hold a healthy and

> We cannot heal
> what we cannot feel.
>
> JOHN BRADSHAW

potent sexuality that by nature involves others, when others are wounded in their own sexuality? If there were a touchstone for a healed second chakra, it might be the ability to embrace change without losing one's core stability.

It would take a whole book to describe all the intricacies of healing second chakra issues. Indeed, there are many volumes on healing from sexual abuse alone, not to mention emotional abuse, inner child work, object relations, enmeshment, and movement-oriented therapies, all of which also relate directly to the second chakra. My discussion of healing techniques will be limited to those related specifically to chakra theory.

Healing the second chakra is largely a matter of encouraging the excess or deficiency to move toward the center. The basic premise is simple: Where movement is restricted, identify holding patterns and encourage movement. Where movement is excessive, learn to contain, either by releasing emotions so the pressure is lessened or by learning to tolerate increased sensation and excitement. This requires learning to pay attention to the subtle currents and impulses that flow through the body.

REINSTATE THE NATURAL HEALING PROCESS

It must be understood that the body has its own healing process. When we cut ourselves, it is important to clean and bandage the wound, but the natural healing process takes place on its own beneath the bandage. We are biologically equipped with innate instincts for healing and self-preservation, and when these instincts get interrupted by trauma or ongoing stress, then our whole foundation is upset, and with it the free flow of energy.

The streaming of energy through the body is the body's way of restoring balance. Freeing this stream while simultaneously providing a safe container will promote much of the healing. This reestablishes the flow of liberation that allows us to leave constricting patterns and expand. As the liberating flow rises into consciousness, its meaning is integrated into a larger context. This helps bring the manifesting current downward, channeling the emotional energy toward constructive ends.

In healing the second chakra, we always act on behalf of the body's natural healing process, where movement and emotion are essential. When that movement is restricted, so too is the healing process. If one's innate reaction to a given situation has been thwarted, then there is a constant tendency to recreate similar situations so as to complete the initial pattern. If the block is severe, similar situations may not allow completion, leaving us in a hopeless cycle of repeating negative traumas without being able to resolve them and move on.

THAWING THE ICE—
RESTORING THE FREE FLOW OF MOVEMENT

Ray first came into my office complaining about a recurrent pain in his neck. He had tried physical therapy, chiropractic work, massage, standard psychotherapy, and a variety of other methods to no avail. As there was no organic cause for the pain, he knew some mind–body issue was at work. I could see that he held his body rigidly, that his neck moved very little, and that his hands and arms were held close to his chest. His energy was contracted.

When we first began bioenergetic work, he responded very favorably. He charged up easily and discharged with a shaking motion that soon evolved into intense but random movements of his arms and shoulders. Knowing that there was a fair degree of trauma behind his frozen response, I proceeded carefully and spent several weeks gently charging and discharging through movement before getting into the content of the trauma. Like a pressure cooker, this energy needed to be released slowly before taking off the lid. I encouraged various movements of the arms and shoulders, which allowed him to connect more deeply to his body's ability to move.

Understanding the block as trapped energy, I knew I needed to open things up in order to clear out the energy. Allowing the arms to regain their mobility created an opening and decreased his feeling of powerlessness. Gradually I began weaving his historical material and emerging emotions into the movement, which soon changed from random motions to purposeful

> Trauma occurs only when an individual adapts to threat (a normal response) but is then unable to adapt again or unable to return to pre-threat functioning.... It is the inhibited (or thwarted) flight or fight that results in the freezing response which will lead to traumatic symptoms.
>
> PETER LEVINE

expression. He learned to use his arms in accordance with his inner needs, alternately reaching out for support or pushing away to establish boundaries. With boundaries and a sense of power and grounding established, it became safe to work more deeply on the emotional material. We gradually thawed the ice in his body and restored emotional flow.

When an organism is threatened, the flow of energy in the body is increased in preparation for fight or flight. If neither running nor fighting are possible (as with a child getting beaten by his father), then we have to override these impulses, even while the body is being energized. Repeated trauma that we cannot overcome forces us to live in this energetic contradiction of activation and inhibition. This results in a kind of frozen intensity known as *tonic immobility* or the *freezing response*. The ability to play dead as a way to fool predators or lessen the effect of the trauma is a natural biological response throughout the animal kingdom. Freezing enables us to partially check out of the body and dissociate from the painful sensations that are likely to occur. If we cannot prevent trauma, dissociation is a valuable defense. It keeps us from being overwhelmed by deadening our awareness in the immediate experience.

Somatic therapist Peter Levine has studied the way repeated traumas and abuse create a chronic freezing response in the body. When a trauma is activated, one shakes slightly as if cold. Actually, we are frozen stiff, frozen in our movement, contracted and withdrawn into ourselves, and using up a great deal of energy in the process. In the animal kingdom, this freezing response is not meant to be permanent. When the trauma is over, an animal may shake and move erratically, discharging the frozen energy and eventually returning to its natural state.

If trauma is repeated or constant, or if there is no comfort or safe space in which to discharge, then we do not get to release this extra frozen energy. A certain portion of our being remains locked in the trauma and free expression of energy becomes inhibited. Peter Levine's description is graphic:

> When we are unable to respond effectively to danger, our nervous system experiences the danger as an ongoing event which then becomes frozen in our psyche. When the nervous system is overwhelmed,

conflicting messages go out to the muscles. They cannot act in concert. Movements lose their fluidity. They become jerky, rigid, and uncoordinated which only intensifies the anxiety induced by the event. When the experience is intense enough the organism collapses. The body/mind experiences this as anxiety, helpessness, defeat, and depression.[11]

If freezing produces immobility, then thawing involves freeing up the body's natural movement. Just as restoring circulation after frostbite can produce intense pain and must be done slowly, so, too, with release from the traumatic effects of immobility. The more pervasive the block, the greater the trauma, and the greater the energy that is stored there. Release must be done slowly and with great care.

To avoid overwhelming the nervous system, it is important to first establish some kind of anchor or ground that can be accessed when the going gets rough. This can be a safe and familiar memory, a body position that feels comfortable, or a connection with an inner source of power, either real or imagined. When the dam in the stream is removed, there can be such a rush of energy that we need a big rock to hold onto to keep from being washed too quickly downstream. Anchoring the energy as it is released grounds it into the solidity of chakra one. This is done by translating emotion into sensation and impulse. "When you feel this rage, what are the sensations in your body?" "What do your hands want to do with this energy?" Anchored in the sensation of the body, the energy can move upward into consciousness to find meaning. "Is this rage similar to the rage directed at you from your father when you were a child?" "Can you see this shame as a result of your abandonment, rather than your level of achievement?"

It is also important to proceed slowly, reintegrating different parts of the experience piece by piece. Levine calls this slow integration *titration*. Titrating combines chemicals a little bit at a time, in amounts too small to explode. In this way, the whole volume comes together without mishap. In traumatic situations, the nervous system needs to gradually stabilize its reaction to the event. Small pieces that the nervous system can handle without getting overwhelmed can eventually lead to complete healing. This is a complex procedure, and is described in Peter Levine's book, *Waking the Tiger: Healing Trauma through the Body*.

WORKING THROUGH GUILT

Working through guilt begins with examining the forces that influenced our actions at a given time. For the child who feels guilty about doing poorly in school, it is important to recognize how volatile family situations may have prevented concentration in his studies. For the person who feels guilty about feeling needy, it is important to determine if needs were met in the past. Only by acknowledging past forces can we truly change present behavior about which we feel guilty. This does not mean we should not take responsibility for what we may have caused, but rather it allows us to see that responsibility in its appropriate context. Here are some steps you can take to move through guilt:

> The individual who has enduring repeated traumatic encounters will be susceptible to a pervasive sense of guilt that he himself is somehow responsible for causing the trauma—no matter what it is. Guilt is a nearly universal imprint left by trauma.
>
> PETER LEVINE

1. Put the guilty behavior in context. What were the forces acting on you at the time?

2. Examine the motives, drives, and needs underlying your behavior. What were you trying to satisfy or accomplish?

3. Look for ways that the behavior may have been modeled for you. (My mother always handled arguments like this. That's how I was taught to get the job done. My father never finished school.)

4. See how your underlying needs can be more directly and appropriately filled.

5. Take stock of any harm caused and find ways of making amends. If you are not sure of how to make amends, you can usually ask. If the person who received harm is no longer accessible, try to address the situation in a more global way. Give money or time to a battered women's shelter. Pay for someone's therapy. Help someone through school. Volunteer labor at a charity.

6. Make a plan for new behavior.

7. Forgive yourself and move on.

If you continue to be plagued by guilt for innocent behaviors such as pleasure or time to yourself, then examine the belief system that supports those values by asking yourself the following questions:

What is the belief system that says, for example, that sex is bad, or that time alone is selfish? What is its origin? Where did you learn it? Who does that belief serve?

What are the effects of the values inherent in that belief?

What is your own belief, and on what is it based?

What are the results of your actions? Is harm caused to yourself or others? How can you get support for your actions if you believe them to be right?

> Healthy guilt is the emotional core of our conscience. It is emotion which results from behaving in a manner contrary to our beliefs and values.
>
> JOHN BRADSHAW

EMOTIONAL WORK: RECLAIMING OUR RIGHT TO FEEL

Healing the second chakra involves reclaiming our right to feel. The first step in reclaiming this right is to remove the guilt that blocks our feelings. We learn to see them as natural responses to the situations that affect us.

The emotions related to abuse can be overwhelming and often conflicting. We may feel both intense longing and betrayal, with a simultaneous urge to both reach out and withdraw. We may feel expansive anger and contracting fear at the same time. We may feel strong emotions at some times and numbness at others.

Emotions are the precursors to action (chakra three), so it is difficult to allow an emotion to flow if the action it inspires is dangerous or frightening. For instance, if allowing ourselves to feel our anger makes us want to kill someone, it can be dangerous to experience the feeling. If experiencing the sadness of a past separation makes our present solitude unbearable, we will find ways to avoid it. If feeling our need for someone makes us subject to their abuse, we cannot acknowledge our need.

When the force behind an emotion builds up without being expressed or released, it creates an emotional excess. We need to create a safe way to lessen emotional force and allow it to be better contained and channeled. The energy of an emotion can be channeled into appropriate movements or activities. I often use my anger to clean house because when I am angry I have a lot of energy, but I cannot concentrate on anything difficult. Grief can be channeled into writing poetry, fear into heightened awareness, and longing into creative activities.

When emotions are excessive, we can shift our awareness to the sensations in our body. Emotions want to move out, to take action and be recognized. We need to balance that by moving in and paying attention to the self inside. By consciously bringing our attention inward, the emotions soften and bring us a richer tapestry of information and connection.

> Feeling is the dimensional texture of experience. Without feelings, life is flat, experience is empty, and meaning is elusive.

EMOTIONAL RELEASE—PROS AND CONS

In a world where repressed emotions are the cultural norm, it has often been the goal of therapy to facilitate emotional release. Sometimes simple catharsis can bring about profound healing and transformation. Simply letting go of something that has been long held in the body can allow the body to reform itself in new ways. Emotional release does not always bring healing, however. In some cases, where trauma is severe or emotional patterns such as anger or tears are too well established, it may overwhelm the person, create further feelings of helplessness, or drive the emotional grooves even deeper into habitual response. When emotional release is simply a discharge of energy without cognitive integration, it brings short-term relief, but seldom permanent change. The person then seeks this release again and again.

Emotional release is the instinctual psychic movement from the unconscious to the conscious, completing actions that have been interrupted. If we could not fully feel or express our emotions the first time around, we create new situations where we *can* feel them. Emotions held in the body fixate our energy in holding patterns, making it unavailable to us. Once an emotion is released, we can reclaim that energy and create a new orientation to the situation. Once we have grieved a death, we can let go. Once we have acknowledged a fear, we can take steps to overcome it.

Emotional release fully involves the body. It is not enough for the head to simply acknowledge sadness or anger. There is movement associated with each emotion, and until the movement is freed up, the energy vortex of the emotion will remain. Many clients come to me from other therapists who helped them considerably in understanding their patterns and behavior in light of their history. They say, "I know my sexual attitudes are a result of the abuse from my father. I've worked on it for years, *but it hasn't changed.*" Change is movement, and in order to create change there has to be both internal and external movement in the body.

Blocked emotion is bound into the structure of the body. When I work to free up buried feelings, I ask the person to exaggerate what I see her body doing unconsciously. If I see her fidgeting, I ask her to exaggerate those movements. If I see her contracted, I ask her to exaggerate the contraction. This brings unconscious movements and their attendant feelings into consciousness. While she holds the exaggerated position I ask her what kind of feeling this elicits. If an answer is not apparent, I ask her to verbalize what her body is saying. Someone contracted might be saying, "Don't touch me." Someone who is fidgeting might be saying, "I don't want to be here." I then ask her to express the same statement or feeling through movement. "If you were on a stage and had to express this feeling without any words, what would you do?" This embodies the feeling, and simultaneously brings it into conscious awareness.

This process usually taps the natural flow of feeling in the body sooner or later. At this point, I become a facilitator for the feeling. If there is anger, I give them a bat to hit the couch. If it is sadness, I offer comfort and sympathy. If there is fear, I offer resources for strength, invite movements that are opposite to the contraction, and stabilize their energy through grounding techniques.

CONTAINMENT

As an Oral character with characteristic lack of charge, my early somatic therapists all encouraged me to "get it out." I cried my tears, kicked and screamed, beat pillows, and certainly freed up my energy flow. But as an essentially undercharged vessel, I was simultaneously depleting myself and I lost some of my ability to tolerate and focus. I found later that a more profound lesson for me was to learn to contain.

There are times when emotional release is not advisable. When the ground is too weak to provide stability, safety, and containment, emotional release can leave one disintegrated, rather than integrated. When past traumas are severe, the emotions of rage or helplessness can retraumatize and trigger the nervous system into its familiar traumatic stress patterns. When damaging emotional habits are a presenting complaint (raging uncontrollably, crying too easily, feeling paralyzed by fears), it does not help to dig these emotional habits into deeper grooves. When any of these factors are present, it is better to facilitate containment and behavior modification than it is to release.

> To contain our energy is to embrace our excitement bodily, to let feelings unfold within our containing body and to let ourselves be formed by these feelings. By living with and from our bodily feelings, they change us, culturing our love.
>
> STANLEY KELEMAN

If the second chakra is excessive, balance is found by containment. Containment means not acting immediately upon a feeling, urge, desire, or need. Often this excessive behavior is an unconscious way to discharge energy before it can come fully into consciousness, where it might be too threatening. Without containment, there is no storage of energy and virtually no power.

Energy follows habitual paths of expression. Containment invites the creation of alternative paths. If our habitual path of release is to have sex, take a drink, or yell at someone whenever we feel anxious, then we become addicted to that activity and never understand the anxiety or effectively resolve it. If we can learn to contain the anxiety, we can find another way of resolving it.

Learning to contain does not mean that we deny or negate an experience. It is not a willful mind-over-matter affair, but a conscious penetration of mind *in* matter. Containment is a deeper focus of attention on the emotional process and where it is trying to go. Learning to contain means that we allow the energy to fill up our tissues, expand our sensation, and build our excitement. This way we get to keep our excitement rather than spend it.

Jeannette had a habit of compulsively eating small snacks throughout the day. At the slightest hint of frustration in her tasks at work, she would want to put something in her mouth to distract her from her feelings. I asked her to sit with her feelings without her "pacifier" and chart the sensations that arose. "I couldn't sit still. I wanted to pace the office, throw things at my boss, pull out the phone plug, and yell at somebody." As we worked through and resisted these discharging impulses, we became aware of the way she felt small and had too much responsibility at too young an age. She did not have the first chakra support necessary to accomplish the tasks that were expected of her. Instinctively, she reached for food to give her extra energy and as a first chakra substitute for support. Only by understanding the motivation underneath the action could we plan more appropriate coping strategies. This understanding arose through resisting the addictive impulses so that buried memories could come to consciousness.

Still water runs deep. Through containment our feelings reach greater depth. While we do not want to become stagnant, a healthy second chakra has the ability to both express and contain emotion as needed and appropriate. To contain is to build up the energy for transformation, rather than disperse it and suffer depletion.

SEXUAL HEALING—COURTING EROS

It is unfortunate that our culture tries to separate sexuality from the rest of life. As the cosmic force of connection leading toward union and expansion, it is paradoxical that we remove sexuality from the conversation and activity of the rest of our lives. In so doing we have encouraged sexual wounds to go unacknowledged and unhealed, hidden by guilt and shame.

Sexual healing is not limited to what we do in bed, but involves our entire approach to life. To achieve sexual healing is to engage with life fully on an emotional/sensate level—to make love with our eyes and ears and noses; to embrace our yearning for poetry, texture, and closeness; to become intimate with the subtle nuances of the inner self. Sexual healing cannot occur in isolation, as healthy sex involves many levels of consciousness. It cannot be separated from emotional healing, for it opens up the emotions. It is essentially tied to the senses and the pull of yearning and desire. It requires a fluid flow of energy in the body. To heal ourselves in each petal of the second chakra lotus—emotion, desire, movement, sensation, pleasure, and need—is to simultaneously heal our sexuality.

> Eros is the binding element par excellence. It is the bridge between being and becoming, and it binds fact and value together.
>
> ROLLO MAY

Sexual healing requires a balance between containment and flow. Most mechanical sexual dysfunctions, such as impotence, inability to reach orgasm, or premature ejaculation, reflect a failure to either contain one's excitement or surrender to it. These issues are energetic rather than merely sexual, and are usually reflected in the rest of the personality. Addressing these energy patterns in the body armor may simultaneously address the sexual problems.

Sexual healing involves moving from the mechanical activity of sex into the numinous quality of Eros. Sexual healing involves reweaving the union of sexuality and Eros and thus bringing sex back into the realm of the divine. Eros is a mysterious force, and the courting of Eros requires surrender to the unknown. This requires a basic emotional and physical security. Past wounds from invasions, rejections, and expectations dampen our experience of Eros. They make us afraid of ourselves, afraid of opening, afraid to trust the natural erotic impulse that unites psyche and soma, self and other, Heaven and Earth in an arc of energy that joins and sparks each of the chakras. Healing emotional wounds helps restore appropriate discrimination and trust so we can surrender to feeling once again. Eros has no goal but to enhance and connect, but we must have the trust and grounding of the first chakra and the emotional confidence of the second to open fully to this enhancement.

Sex without Eros is empty and mechanical, functioning by a push from the will, which often exhausts it. Sex with Eros nourishes the will. We become infused with energy, inspired to change, learn, and reach beyond the limits we have previously accepted. Sexuality infused with Eros brings the divine into the act of pleasure, drawing us upward and outward.

Sexual healing, by nature, involves another person—a sacred lover with whom there is trust and patience, understanding and skill. This is perhaps the most difficult element to attain, since we cannot simply order up the appropriate lover. When dealing with sexual issues, it is important to be able to stop at any point in the experience and have our lover encourage us to process whatever we are feeling at the moment. When a partner falls into numbness, mechanical routines, or fear, it is time to stop and say, "What are you feeling right now? How can I help?" As sex brings us into the most intimate and vulnerable experiences of our lives, the sexual arena is often where our deepest feelings arise. This is profound ground for healing in general.

Nor is sexual healing limited just to the second chakra. The sexual experience enhances and is affected by each of the other chakras. Our relationship to the health of our bodies (staying in shape and in touch) is the important contribution from chakra one. From the third chakra, a healthy ego and sense of power allows us to remain centered and balanced in our engagement with others. The fourth chakra, with its emphasis on relationships, has an obvious impact on sexuality. Healthy relationship with open hearts and clear communication (chakra five) can only enhance sexual connection. Imagination (chakra six) plays a powerful role in sexual enhancement, as does the ability to experience sex as a spiritual union (seventh chakra).

Sexual healing brings the sacred back into the sexual act. It is a mutual worship of the divine within, a restoring of wholeness through the unfolding of pleasure, and a nourishment of the soul in preparation for the rest of the journey across the Rainbow Bridge.

CONCLUSION

In our journey from base to crown, the second chakra is the prime mover of energy in the chakra system. As the vital forces begin their journey upward, the soul is carried on the currents of emotion and desire toward growth. If we have a secure base, we are able to yield to this inner flow of *prana* (vital energy) and follow its natural course without losing our center. Analogous to the water element of this chakra, we need to be moved by the currents but not drown in them. It is water that makes things grow, move, and change. Water makes life juicy.

A balanced second chakra has a deep emotional core that is grounded enough to be contained and open enough to flow and connect. Healing our wounds in this chakra creates the necessary emotional depth for developing true power, compassion, creativity, insight, and awareness—all aspects that are ahead of us on the chakra journey.

CHAKRA THREE

Burning Our Way into Power

THIRD CHAKRA AT A GLANCE

ELEMENT
Fire

NAME
Manipura (lustrous gem)

PURPOSE
Transformation

ISSUES
Energy
Activity
Autonomy
Individuation
Will
Self-esteem
Proactivity
Power

COLOR
Yellow

LOCATION
Solar plexus

IDENTITY
Ego identity

ORIENTATION
Self-definition

DEMON
Shame

DEVELOPMENTAL STAGE
18 months to 4 years

DEVELOPMENTAL TASKS
Realization of separateness
Estabishment of autonomy

BASIC RIGHTS
To act and be an individual

BALANCED CHARACTERISTICS
Responsible, reliable
Balanced, effective will
Good self-esteem, balanced
    ego-strength
Warmth in personality
Confidence
Spontaneity, playfulness, sense
    of humor
Appropriate self-discipline
Sense of one's personal power
Able to meet challenges

TRAUMAS AND ABUSES
Shaming
Authoritarianism
Volatile situations
Domination of will
Physical abuse, dangerous
    environment, fear of
    punishment
Enmeshment
Age inappropriate responsi-
    bilities (parentified child)
Inherited shame from parent

DEFICIENCY

Low energy

Weak will, easily manipulated

Poor self-discipline and
follow-through

Low self-esteem

Cold, emotionally and/or
physically

Poor digestion

Collapsed middle

Attraction to stimulants

Victim mentality, blaming of
others

Passive

Unreliable

EXCESS

Overly aggressive, dominating,
controlling

Need to be right, have last word

Manipulative, power hungry,
deceitful

Attraction to sedatives

Temper tantrums, violent outbursts

Stubbornness

Driving ambition (type A
personality)

Competitive

Arrogant

Hyperactive

PHYSICAL MALFUNCTIONS

Eating disorders

Digestive disorders, ulcers

Hypoglycemia, diabetes

Muscle spasms, muscular disorders

Chronic fatigue

Hypertension

Disorders of stomach, pancreas,
gall bladder, liver

HEALING PRACTICES

Risk taking (deficiency)

Grounding and emotional contact

Deep relaxation, stress control
(excess)

Vigorous exercise (running,
aerobics, etc.)

Martial arts

Sit-ups

Psychotherapy: Build ego
strength; release or contain
anger; work on shame issues;
strengthen the will;
encourage autonomy

AFFIRMATIONS

I honor the power within me.

I accomplish tasks easily and
effortlessly.

The fire within me burns
through all blocks and fears.

I can do whatever I will to do.

SHADES OF YELLOW

One need only pick up the daily newspaper to see that we are a culture obsessed with power. Headlines of violence, warfare, victimization, and dominance reveal a world continually beset by conflict. Strength is often defined as dominance; sensitivity as weakness. Taking time to consider important decisions is considered waffling, while swift, bold strokes are touted as brilliant accomplishments. Political news reads more like the sports page than as informed analysis: "President scores points over divided Congress." "GOP wins seat over Democrats." "Loggers defeat environmentalists." We put the hopes of many into the leadership of a few, remaining in passive helplessness while those in whom we invest our power spend it fighting each other, creating stagnation and political gridlock, or waging war.

> No human being can stand the perpetually numbing experience of his own powerlessness.
>
> ROLLO MAY

Immersed in our own feelings of powerlessness, we are fascinated by the triumphs of others, and glean a perverse satisfaction from following the continual struggles for supremacy and control—over ourselves, other people, other nations, and Nature herself—but always power *over* something.

What is power? Where do we get it? How do we use it? Why do we need it? How do we avoid its unbalanced duality of victimization and abuse, aggression and passivity, dominance and submission? Where do we find our own empowerment without diminishing that of others? How do we reclaim, with full responsibility, enthusiasm, and pride, our innate *right to act*, free from inhibition and shame?

These questions are central issues to anyone undergoing a healing process. Raised into obedience by parents and teachers, trained for cooperation with larger corporate, legal, military, and political power structures, we have become a society of victims and controllers. In polarized, either-or thinking, we see power in terms of eat or be eaten, control or be controlled, winners or losers, one up or one down.

The popular model of power that exists in today's world is one that can be described as "power-over," based on struggle and opposition between dualities, where one side eventually wins *over* the other side. In society, we see this in racism, sexism, classism, agism, and almost any other "ism" we could name. Power is found with the guns and the money, and our culture is obsessed with both. In a land where the American dream is for each person to become, in the words of Laurence Boldt, a "little king," we see power as having a dominion to rule over—the larger the dominion, the greater the power.[1]

In the inner world, the struggle continues. We think power is gained by fighting our inferior parts with the strength of our superior parts. If the right side wins, then we have a sense of power. If we lose, we feel powerless. We are asked to exert mind over matter, to prove our strength by dominating our basic instincts, suppressing the raw energy of the core self, which is the psychic source of our power. Struggle itself becomes the focus of our life force.

There is no doubt that at times, winning this kind of inner battle is important. But the victory of one part over another does not lead to wholeness, but further fragmentation. Such battles rob the system of energy and usually reemerge to be fought again and again. It is no wonder that the recovery movement is full of victims, scapegoating their evil persecutors, hoping to regain their lost power, not always realizing that we are all victims of an oppressive social system, of cultural values that belittle us, and of an outdated concept of power itself. We have lost the sense of our own sacredness; lost contact with the power within.

> It is not power we seek so much as the overcoming of victimization—the ability to determine our own lives. For what greater responsibility than to allow the divine within the freedom of its unique unfoldment?

To restructure the way we think of power and to channel and contain that power within our own being is the challenge of the third chakra. It transforms us, igniting our life with purpose. To have true power emanating from within renews the joy of being alive.

What is needed to reclaim our power is to enter into an entirely new dynamic, a new definition of power that lifts us out of struggle and into transformation, out of the past and into the future, one that inspires, strengthens, and empowers individuals without diminishing others.

The dynamics of power within the chakra system are also built on duality, but in a way that emphasizes *combination and synergy* rather than *separation and struggle*. Raw energy is created from a combination of the first and second chakras' attributes of matter and movement. The expression of that energy as action is motivated by survival and pleasure, the instinctual forces that combine to create our ascending liberating current.

Transforming the instinctual impulses into willed activity is made possible by the *descent* of consciousness, which gives form and direction through understanding as it meets and mediates the ascending current of liberation (see figure 3.1). When the ascending and descending currents combine, the raw energy of power is focused into activity. Only through this combination do we realize that the true purpose of power is transformation.

So we enter the third chakra through the gates of duality. By successfully integrating both sides of polarity, we emerge into a third realm that simultaneously includes and transcends polarity by creating a new dynamic. Here we reach beyond the oscillating realms of either-or—win/lose, black/white—and enter the rainbow realm of multiplicity. Once we have ventured out toward the middle of the Rainbow Bridge, our choices expand, our horizons widen. As our options increase, so do our strength and our freedom.

As we exercise choice, we initiate the will. Through exercising our will, we develop our individuality, discover our strengths and weaknesses, and begin to build the power that will steer our lives. We leave the realm of safety and security, carrying our safety within the ground of our own body. So many people in recovery are understandably concerned about feeling safe. But power is not created from staying safe; power comes from the willingness to leave the world of safety and move forward into the unknown. As we meet challenge, it strengthens us by forcing us to grow. Power, like a muscle, will not increase by doing nothing.

In the chakra system as a whole, the purpose of the third chakra is to transform the inertia of matter and movement into a conscious direction of willed activity. Earth and water are passive and dense. They move downward. Chakras one and two are instinctual. They follow the paths of least resistance. The fire of chakra three is dynamic and light, rising upward,

FIGURE 3.1. COMBINATION OF VERTICAL CURRENTS AND THIRD CHAKRA LEVEL

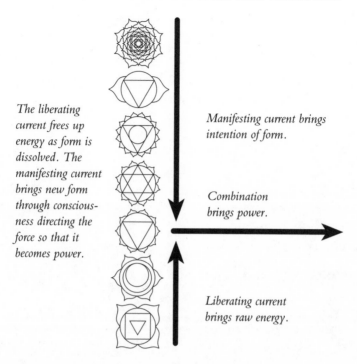

The liberating current frees up energy as form is dissolved. The manifesting current brings new form through consciousness directing the force so that it becomes power.

Manifesting current brings intention of form.

Combination brings power.

Liberating current brings raw energy.

moving away from gravity. This change is necessary to reach the upper chakras and complete our journey.

We must be willing to leave passivity behind. We must be willing to leave the way it has always been, to transform our habits, set a new course and enter chakra three. We must be willing to individuate—to step out of the familiar and expected and confront the challenge of uncertainty. "Thus to be independent of public opinion is the first formal condition of achieving anything great," says Hegel.[2] "You must be the change you wish to see in the world," says Gandhi.[3]

Friction makes sparks. Fire transforms matter to heat and light, and gives us the ability to see and to act. Fire awakens us from our passive slumber, sparking consciousness into understanding. Understanding tempers the fire, binding raw energy into power, direction, and transformation. Thus we enter the fiery yellow section of our Rainbow Bridge on the unfolding journey from matter to consciousness.

UNFOLDING THE PETALS

BASIC ISSUES OF THE THIRD CHAKRA

Energy

Activity

Autonomy

Authority

Individuation

Will

Self-Esteem

Shame

Proactivity

Power

ENERGY AND ACTIVITY

If our grounding is strong and solid and the natural flow of emotion and movement is not thwarted, then we have the means to convert energy into action. As we continue to receive input from our surroundings, the energy within the system builds and begins, like any open system, to need reorganization, expression, and discharge.

> Increased excitation is perceived as an urge to organize feeling into action.
>
> STANLEY KELEMAN

The natural expression of this energy is activity. It engages us with our surroundings, allowing us to charge and discharge our excitement. It teaches us about the world and about ourselves. Activity can invite delight or disaster depending on its results. As we mature, we begin to choose which impulses to act upon and which ones to control. Thus begins the emergence of a conscious self where mind acts upon instincts, the emergence of personal responsibility, and the birth of the ego.

A healthy third chakra exhibits energetic vitality. There is enjoyment and enthusiasm about life. Our sense of personal power gives us hope that we can make things viable for ourselves, and with this positive outlook we are not afraid to venture into the unknown, to take risks, or to make mistakes. When our energy field is strong, we do not get bogged down by obstacles. We do not lose our direction when challenged, but go forth with strength and will. We enjoy engaging in activity, tackling challenges, and grappling with the world. Activity develops our sense of power through constant presentation of new challenges.

When activity meets with shame and disapproval, however, then it diminishes our sense of power. We distrust our abilities and fear the consequence of our own energy. To avoid further shame, we inhibit our impulses and become constricted and self-conscious. We lose our spontaneity and playfulness. Unable to trust our own basic impulses and needing to constantly monitor what comes from within, the personality becomes divided against itself. It takes energy to maintain this division, a loss that robs us of our basic vitality and wholeness.

AUTONOMY

The progression from lower to higher chakras is a progression from individuality to universality. We begin in a merged state, then separate ourselves and become independent, eventually to emerge again into a larger world, this time as a conscious individual.

> The privilege of a lifetime is being who you are.
>
> JOSEPH CAMPBELL

We can think of the first three chakras as the lower gears of the system. They keep us grounded and engaged, motivated and active. They preserve the individual self as it interacts with the world. The upper chakras connect us to the universal through communication, vision, and understanding. Looking ahead, we see that at the heart chakra we make a quantum leap into the middle of the Rainbow Bridge to a place where the individual and universal meet in perfect balance. But before this meeting can occur, we need a firm grasp of ourselves as a separate, unique individual. Without a strong sense of self, our love is still an unconscious merging. Without our unique individuality, we get overwhelmed by the vastness of the universal.

I recently counseled a nineteen-year-old woman who was in a borderline psychotic state one month after a strong LSD experience. She had seen a parade of her past lives, a display of archetypal energies, a wide-eyed view of the cosmos. But her individual ego was still so unformed that she completely lost who she was in this journey. She was overwhelmed and lost from her ground in the limitless upper chakras. Simple grounding exercises produced a profound change in consciousness and brought her back to herself, at least temporarily. Returning to a solid sense of herself took time and much reconstruction.

In much of the New Age and spiritual movement, personal ego and autonomy are frowned upon along with sexuality, passion, desire, need, and the sacredness of the body. While letting go of attachment and transcending the smallness of the ego are essential steps for obtaining a universal consciousness, this achievement is pure diffusion and possibly escape if we lack a healthy ego to support such transcendence.

Therefore, autonomy becomes a necessary third chakra achievement. Without autonomy, we cannot get to the heart, for our love comes from need rather than strength, a desire to escape rather than to expand. A balanced relationship allows the persons involved to be separate beings, retain their individuality, follow their own growth, *and* come together by choice and by will, in freedom and wholeness. This right cannot be granted by a partner (or anyone else for that matter) if we do not *first* have it within ourselves.

Autonomy is *essential* for personal responsibility. If we cannot see ourselves as separate beings, we cannot take responsibility for our actions. We remain passive and irresponsible, often whining and complaining about the state of our affairs, ruled by the transitory whim of the group, the culture, our partners, or parents.

Lack of autonomy is often characterized by *blaming*. If we still blame others for our problems, we have not yet individuated. This is often seen in couples who are overly enmeshed with each other. Blaming places both will and responsibility outside ourselves. If we are grounded in our autonomy, then we are the cause of our lives and we are able to take appropriate responsibility and power. Only when we take responsibility can we really make change. If it is someone else's fault, we can only wait for them to change. We might wait forever.

INDIVIDUATION

The soul's journey toward realization is a process that Carl Jung called *individuation*. It is a journey toward wholeness and awakening, a journey across the Rainbow Bridge. On this journey the person awakens from the small world they previously inhabited to embrace the larger world of the personal and collective unconscious by reclaiming their shadow, their inner masculine and feminine, and their connection with mythic and archetypal energies. The purpose of individuation is to integrate previously undeveloped aspects of oneself into a larger, comprehensive *Self* that is simultaneously personal and universal.

As the lower realms of the first and second chakras are largely unconscious and correspond to the child's merged state with the mother and family, the third chakra becomes the point where the individuation process really begins. It is here that the ego awakens and begins to differentiate from outer expectations. What has been largely a passive experience now becomes a willed enactment. To individuate, we must break away from the gravitational fields of earth and water, mother and father, group and society and bring forth the unique, divine individual that lives within.

The third chakra aspect of individuation involves overcoming unconscious habits that allow us to be defined by others. Here we break away from internalized parents, peers, and culture, and begin to define ourselves. It is about daring to be unique, risking disapproval for the integrity of your own truth. Individuation is the unfolding of our unique destiny, the unfolding of the soul. We cannot change the world if we have not yet individuated from the way the

> The individuation process, however, cannot be grasped in its deepest essence, for it is a part of the mystery of transformation that pervades all creation. It includes within it the secret of life, which is ceaselessly reborn in passing through an ever-renewed "death."
>
> JOLANDE JACOBI

world expects us to be. We cannot truly claim our power without a willingness to individuate.

Jung's concept of individuation parallels the adult developmental process through the chakras. Where Jung thought that individuation began in the heart chakra, with the integration of the inner masculine and feminine (animus and anima), I believe it begins with the third chakra birth of psychic autonomy. Many people do not awaken this chakra at all, and spend their whole lives following the path of least resistance, giving their power to others, and defining themselves in terms of what is expected. They remain in the less differentiated aspects of the lower chakras. Damage to the lower chakras or lack of developmental completion keeps us from maturing to this point, and keeps us from true psychic freedom.

> Our ego consciousness might well be enclosed within a more complete consciousness like a smaller circle within a larger.
>
> C. G. JUNG

EGO IDENTITY

After we identify with our physical body and our emotional experience, we begin to form an autonomous new identity. This marks the birth of the *ego*— a conscious realization of oneself as a self-determining separate entity.

Freud first postulated the ego when he divided the personality into three major components: the *id*, representing our innate biological and instinctual drives; the *superego*, representing the consciousness that controls these drives; and the *ego*, which mediates between the two. The ego manages the division between conscious and unconscious, interior and exterior, and operates the gates between the many worlds of the Self.

Jung saw the ego as the *conscious* element of the Self. This does not necessarily include our unconscious hopes and dreams, fantasies and fears. Since the ego is, by definition, unaware of the unconscious, it is not the center of the whole Self but acts as an operating principle, combining inner and outer experience. The ego is an organizer of instinctual energies.

John Pierrakos, in *Core Energetics*, defines the ego in terms of somatic energy, calling it "the human faculty that mediates the flow of energy out of and into the core of the human being. It is the faculty which chooses, discriminates, analyzes, and regulates the flow of energy and experience."[4]

In terms of chakras, the ego is an organizer of instinctive energy coming up from chakras one and two as it combines with consciousness coming down from above. We shape the ego with consciousness. Life energy is its substance.

The ego functions as an *executive identity*, or CEO of the Self. It sorts out which impulses to express or repress and orients the movement of our energy toward a goal. The ego forms the statement of who we are, the statement we make to the world. It creates defenses to protect the vulnerable, core Self and develops the strategies and behaviors to meet the needs of that core self as it grows and develops. Finally, the ego organizes consciousness toward self-definition.

A well-functioning ego has a tough job. It must allow guidance by core energies that are largely unconscious while still considering the transpersonal, spiritual energies that are beyond normal consciousness, all while keeping the Self consistent, safe, engaged, and effective in the mundane world. This requires ego strength. A strong ego is able to integrate diverse and difficult experiences *and* maintain consistency in the Self.

Yet the ego divides as well as unites, for it sequesters the less favorable instinctual energies into the shadow realm. While the ego is oriented toward love and achievement, its shadow is made of those elements that seem to interfere with this. Thus the ego creates the division between conscious and unconscious, between shadow elements of the lower chakras and the developing persona that emerges in the fourth chakra. The good news is that because the ego creates the initial division, it can also integrate. Thus, our concept of Self becomes a container for the work of individuation. It spurs us onward to act in the world, and inward to pick up lost pieces.

Individuation is an expansion of the Self beyond the realms of the ego, yet the ego is necessary to anchor this growth. The word *ego* is a combination of the Greek roots for "I" (*e*) and "earth" (*go*). Thus the ego is the grounded self, the individualized roots of consciousness.

The ego is like a house. It is where we live. It contains us, gives us a place to grow and change, and creates boundaries, which are necessary for forming

> The Self is born, but the ego is made; and in the beginning of all is Self.
>
> EDWARD EDINGER

ourselves as an entity. It balances energy in the system, keeping us in homeostasis. Many spiritual disciplines advise us to transcend the ego, and consider it something bad, limiting, or false. The problem of ego is not that it is limiting—but that we let ourselves be confined by it at all times. We stay confined out of fear, guilt, or shame, and never go outside to the larger world, never open our windows and doors. It is not wrong to have a home, but it should be an anchor for experience, not a limitation. Keeping this in perspective enables us to both have a strong ego and transcend it as well.

> The striking thing about love and will in our day is that, whereas in the past they were always held up to us as the answer to life's predicaments, they have now themselves become the problem.
>
> ROLLO MAY

WILL

A woman in my chakra therapy group volunteered to work on third chakra issues. When her turn came around, she looked at me and said, "OK, tell me what I'm supposed to do." This defined her problem more than anything that followed. She had addressed something *outside herself* to tell her what she was *supposed* to do in relation to her own needs, even before those needs were stated. How many of us dutifully live our lives the way we are "supposed to," forever looking outside ourselves for clues without questioning the source of those suppositions? "Supposed to, according to what?" I asked her in return.

"Well, I thought you had some kind of process in mind for me," she answered.

"I'm more interested in the process you're already in. I can only assist you in removing what blocks it."

"But, I don't know what that is."

"Believing there is a way already prescribed for you might be a big part of it. Look instead at what you want and need. There's your fuel for the will. Your passion and desire give it strength and direction."

From here we proceeded to work on what happened to her will as a child—how it was thwarted, how she was punished for acts of autonomy, and how her maternal role model was one of a selfless people pleaser.

Learning to recognize the true will did not come easily at first. The question, "What would I do if there was nothing I was *supposed* to do?" often meets with a mysterious blank when first considered.

As children we were rewarded for doing what we were "supposed to do" and punished when we don't comply. At a crucial time of developing autonomy, our will becomes structured by things outside ourselves, without regard for the needs and direction of the Self within. We are trained to be obedient. Obedience requires will, but it is will given to another, or *disembodied will*. It no longer originates in our own body, but in someone else's—our parent's body, our lover's, the school, corporation, or military body. The will we cannot claim opens us to manipulation by others.

Obedience removes us from responsibility as we are just following orders. If the orders are wrong, it's someone else's fault. When we accept obedience as a habit or given, we become like slaves. We forget to question. We drop bombs on innocent people because those are our orders. We casually dump our lovers without thinking about how it feels, because that's how our buddies do it. We accept what we see without questioning whether there is another way.

The answer is not to become willful individualists simply seeking our own satisfaction, as pure selfishness is equally damaging. We remain trapped in the smaller ego self, unable to enter the yielding love of the heart chakra.

> The human will is intensity of desire raised to the level of action.
>
> JOHN BRADSHAW

Yet unless this cooperation is voluntary, meaning that it comes from our own will, it has no real power or enthusiasm. Without the supporting desire from the chakra below, we become meek and obedient automatons, empty of vitality and authenticity. In suppressing our will, we invite its shadow, which is either passive-aggressive sabotage or reactive rebellion rather than strategic action.

Rollo May, in his classic book *Love and Will*, asks what underlies the disordered will: "I believe it is a state of feelinglessness, the despairing possibility that nothing matters, a condition very close to apathy."[5] He goes on to describe will as "the capacity to organize one's self so that movement in a certain direction or toward a certain goal may take place."[6] Its foundation is wish, the second chakra longing for what we are missing. Desire fuels the will; consciousness descending from above gives it direction and form through intentionality. There is no will without intention—only whim.

Our longing points us toward the future. It is no coincidence that the word *will* is used in the future tense of all English verbs: I *will* go, I *will* talk to them, I *will* finish my book. It is through the will that we bring that future into reality.

It is interesting to note that the third chakra is located in the softest part of the torso. There are no bones in the front of the solar plexus. This means that the only thing that holds our body upright, with our chakras aligned on top of each other, is an *act of will* from the energetic source of the body. When self-esteem is low, when the will is broken, when we are tired and have no vitality, then this area of the body collapses. The chakra is not full enough to support the upper body. Without this support, the chest collapses, restricting our air intake, the head comes out of alignment with the body, and the knees lock, throwing us out of our true ground. It is helpful when developing the will to do exercises such as sit-ups that strengthen the stomach muscles and support this vulnerable part of the torso.

SELF-ESTEEM

Energetic vitality requires self-esteem. With a basic trust in ourselves, we can better face the unknown. We have a sense of self that does not fall apart when things go wrong, that can still maintain consistency in the face of challenge. For a healthy ego, it's OK to make mistakes. For a shame-bound personality, there is no room to err, and expansion is severely restricted. How can we reach and grow if we can't make mistakes? And without growth, how can we develop a sense of our own power? When self-esteem is low, we have a paralyzing uncertainty where there should be confidence and power.

In the many years of my practice, I have seldom found much correlation between high self-esteem and accomplishment. Often the people with successful careers, extraordinary looks, or loads of

> When one feels that it is a catastrophic event to have been wrong, one is led to avoid choice and decision. The development of an individual personality is therefore stifled.
>
> EDWARD WHITMONT

money had the lowest self-esteem. Those with healthier self-esteem seem to be the ones with fewer expectations and more permission to simply live.

Those who treated themselves well, took care of their bodies, were connected to their feelings, and allowed themselves pleasure had higher esteem because *they felt better.* They filled themselves by attending to simple first and second chakra issues. Feeling full, they felt confident. They had energy. Their sense of self was less defined by external accomplishments because there was a tangible presence inside. Conversely, if self-worth is high, we are more likely to take care of ourselves.

> Shame as a healthy human emotion can be transformed into shame as a state of being. As a state of being, shame takes over one's whole identity. To have shame as an identity is to believe that one's being is flawed, that one is defective as a human being. Once shame is transformed into an identity, it becomes toxic and dehumanizing.
>
> JOHN BRADSHAW

SHAME

Shame is the demon of the third chakra. It is inversely proportional to personal power—the greater the shame, the less we feel powerful and the harder it is for the ego to form itself. Shame blocks the liberating current and prevents energy rising from the lower chakras from forming into effective action. We feel ashamed of ourselves, and hence of our basic instincts, which must then be controlled by the mind. As a result, shame-bound personalities feel stuck and may fall into patterns of compulsive repetition and addiction.

When the ascending, liberating current gets stuck at the third chakra, the manifesting, downward current of consciousness is increased. The mind runs the show, *binding* the biological energy into controlled patterns, creating the term *shame-bound.* Shame-bound people honor their thoughts more than their instincts, especially the internal voices that constantly tell them how worthless and inferior they are. Spontaneity is limited by internal scrutiny, which binds and disempowers the will.

As natural instincts can never be fully repressed, they periodically erupt in shadow forms that only increase the sense of shame and inadequacy. When we misbehave, lose our temper, fall apart, or have lapses in our vigilant self-control, we are driven to deeper shame. Examples include the dieter or substance user who repeatedly binges or the entrepreneur who sabotages work and success through procrastination and passive-aggressive behavior. The block in the will keeps the downward current from entering the second chakra with its orientation toward pleasure, so these activities seldom have any real pleasure to them. Shame finds its penance in suffering, and the need to recreate misery and failure keeps one in a very unhappy false state of equilibrium.

PROACTIVITY

Janet was concerned that she would not get the promotion she wanted. As she was scarcely able to live on her current salary, this promotion was very important to her. At first she worried herself sick over it, but then she became proactive. Rather than waiting to be interviewed, she reversed the tables and interviewed her boss about his vision for the company. She spent additional time talking to people relevant to the new position, courting their favor for recommendations. She anticipated the needs that would arise in replacing her current position and took the initiative to find coworkers who were interested and began training them. With all this work, she did, indeed, get the promotion she wanted.

> It is not what happens to us, but our response to what happens to us that hurts us.
>
> STEVEN R. COVEY

Steven R. Covey, in his best-selling book *The Seven Habits of Highly Effective People*, has popularized the term *proactivity*, which is used largely in management seminars. Being proactive is an alternative to being *reactive* (third chakra excess) or *inactive* (third chakra deficiency). Proactivity is about choosing your actions, rather than controlling or being controlled by them. Proactive people take responsibility for shaping their future, for initiating behavior that will create the situations they want. A proactive person does not wait to see what will happen. Being proactive means you are a causative influence on your environment rather than a victim of its circumstances. Proactivity requires initiative and will.

POWER

All these attributes add up to personal power. From the Latin root *podere*, meaning "to be able," power is the ability to make change and exists for one reason only—transformation. When the old has outgrown its purpose, it is time to transform it into something new. Power is not a thing, but a way. It is a process of becoming real.

We have power when we dare to live authentically, when we reach inside ourselves and tell the naked truth. The more we dare to take risks, to question, to be true to ourselves, the easier it becomes. Power comes when we are willing to make mistakes and to be responsible for them, to learn from them, and to correct them.

> The terrain of the mysteries is the edge where power encounters power, for mystery is the arising of powers that are uncharted and untamed, that will not follow the logic of naked force, and so act in unexpected ways.
>
> STARHAWK

Power is the expression of the sacred in its evolutionary unfolding. Power is the awesome presence of the divine. Power is the mystery, the unknown, the confrontation with the other. Power is the transition from the past to the future. In order to escape the narrow traps of personal limitation and approach the magnificent expanse of totality we must reclaim our power. Power is the ability to determine our own destiny. Only in a path of uniqueness can the vital energy uncoil and pierce the regions of the unknown. Only with power can we move aside the obstacles that keep us imprisoned, enslaved, and unconscious.

Power begins with what is. Earth, as matter, is the container, movement is the means. Our bodies are the vehicle, our emotions its fuel, making the third chakra the engine. If we are to rise above these planes, we must carry them with us as we integrate new understanding. Earth and water anchor us in reality, forming the container that allows the alchemical fire to burn bright and hot. They are the crucible of transformation.

GROWING THE LOTUS

I was a single mother when my son was in his third chakra stage. How well I remember the challenge of getting both Alex and myself ready each morning. When Alex was younger, I had always made morning a period of quality time and he had come to expect it. Now immersed in his third chakra, our mornings became a battle of wills. He knew I needed to hurry and he knew how to get me. He would stall while getting dressed by hiding his shoes after I had put them on. He would play with his food or throw it on the floor and then ask for more. He glorified in the word *no*, giggling gleefully at his new found power over Mom. My own third chakra ached as I

fought the urge to scream at him, instead willing myself into the loving patience that only a
parent can understand.

This story is typical for one of the most
challenging stages of parenting—the "terrible
twos." Here we have an emerging autonomy
that is still immersed in dependency. The
child begins to feel separate, yet wants constant assurance that the parent will still be
there. He wants to do things for himself, but
most tasks are too difficult to do alone. He
wants to exert his will for the sheer pleasure of
it without discretion about how to use that
will. The challenge of this stage is to develop

> This stage, therefore, becomes
> decisive for the ratio of love and hate,
> cooperation and willfulness, freedom
> of self-expression and its suppression.
> From a sense of self-control without
> loss of self-esteem comes a lasting
> sense of good will and pride; from a
> sense of loss of self-control and of
> foreign overcontrol comes a lasting
> propensity for doubt and shame.
>
> ERIK ERIKSON

impulse control. Though difficult, the proper handling of this stage is crucial for self-esteem, personal autonomy, and a strong will—all aspects of a
healthy third chakra.

This tumultuous passage begins when the anxiety of separating from the
mother starts to decrease, allowing a new level of independence. At this
point language abilities have progressed to the point where simple two to
three word sentences are used. Both of these landmarks occur between eighteen and twenty-four months. We have safely reached the other side when the
child has weathered the stubborn storm of egocentricity and emerges as a relatively cooperative individual at approximately three years.

Consciousness continues to filter down from the upper chakras as we
develop up from the bottom. We recall that the seventh chakra awareness
initiated motor development in chakra one. Images from the sixth chakra
motivated feeling and movement in chakra two. Now the development of
language (fifth chakra) instills concepts that enable the mind to *operate* on the
impulses and behavior rising up from the physical/emotional body giving us
the capacity for personal will in chakra three. In other words, connection
between language and action is established, which gives us the potential for
impulse control. The child can understand a statement such as "Don't hit
your brother," and then try to hold that concept to curb his aggressive

impulses. He can remember the phrase "stove is hot," and decide not to touch it. Having moved past the natural limits imposed by infancy, the child must now internalize appropriate limits, which occurs through internalization of language. As these concepts get established, there may be a lot of testing going on that helps the child establish the language-action connection. Is pushing the same as hitting? How close can he get to the stove without getting burned? Does no really mean no?

With language comes a sense of past, present, and future, enabling him to control, postpone, plan, or reflect upon activities. He now begins to conceptualize *cause and effect*. If he uses the potty, Mommy is pleased. If he eats his vegetables, he will get dessert. If he touches the stove, he gets burned. *We cannot control impulses without a concept of time.*

Prior to this point the child has been reflexive and absorbing, rather than initiating. The sense of identity developed in the first and second chakras is a given identity. A comfortable, well-fed body, or a hungry, abused body; a calm emotional environment or a volatile one—these are elements over which we have no control but which, nevertheless, form the ground for our being. They are the *prima materia*, the raw material from which we create ourselves. It is from this given field that we individuate.

As the child learns to control and direct her impulses, she develops her will. The ego identity develops by sorting through the impulses and instincts coming up from the lower chakras and deciding which ones to activate. As mentioned earlier, the ego now becomes the mediator between the shadow and the developing *persona*. The ego sorts these out according to its growing definition of Self. If Mary gets punished for getting angry, her rebellious, angry self will become a shadow part of her, while her pleasing and quiet side may become a central part of her persona. Her ego, as the inner executive, decides which parts of the personality are "hired" and which ones are "fired"—we cultivate the parts that do the job we are expected to do.

Much of this struggle for control and self-mastery gets played out in the arena of toilet training. Often a struggle of wills between the parent and child, toilet training involves learning to control muscles previously allowed to respond in the moment. This requires the mastery of two basic energetic principles: *holding on* and *letting go*. The coordination of these principles establishes patterns for life, which become hardwired into the character structure.

If one is shamed for messing oneself or is toilet trained too soon, then letting go becomes fused with shame. One feels that what is within them is somehow bad, and must be controlled and withheld at all times. If one is invaded or forced to let go against natural timing (as through enemas or commands to perform on schedule), then holding on becomes an act of defiance, and letting go an act of submission. These fundamental energetic expressions are then no longer part of emerging autonomy, but are dictated by the authority figure. Holding on and letting go become externally regulated. We become ruled by others, even on the level of our own muscular response, and we move away from our own spontaneity and lose some of our vitality and joy. If the child's innate sense of timing is respected and supported, however, then she learns to trust her own inner control over her bodily expression, literally and figuratively. The result is self-confidence.

Erik Erikson named this stage *autonomy vs. shame and doubt*, meaning that we come through it with either autonomy or shame and doubt, depending on how this and previous stages are handled. Without autonomy, we are destined to feel shame, which makes us doubt our actions, constantly monitoring the free flow of power through our system. According to Erikson, the successful handling of this stage gives us the distinctly third chakra characteristics of power and will.

As the muscles mature, the ability to cause destruction develops along with the ability for self-control. A child can knock a lamp off the table in frenzied activity and she can learn to control the urge to hit her sister. The child's task is to learn appropriate self-control without losing spontaneity, confidence, or joy in expressing her impulses. When shame and doubt prevail, autonomy is curtailed. We grow up to be defined and controlled by others.

When the lower chakras are unfulfilled and their tasks are not completed, individuation may not happen. If the mother does not provide enough mothering or trust, or if the emotional environment is so enmeshed or volatile that the child is consumed by it, then there is no individuation. In some cases, there may be separation or even rebellion, but resistance to control is not the same as freedom from it. As long as we resist, we remain shaped and determined by the force we oppose. Rollo May states, "If will remains protest, it stays dependent on that which it is protesting against. Protest is half-developed will."[7]

This stage marks the earliest emergence of one's autonomy (however awkward or tentative it may be) and parents can easily thwart or encourage this process. If we deny our child the right to act or assert herself as an autonomous being, then we lead her to question that right throughout her life. If autonomy is thwarted at this crucial stage (as it is for so many through punishment, shaming, and overcontrol), then the individuation process gets bound up in either resistance or submission and never fully develops. We either hold on too tightly or let go too readily. The fire of spontaneity and joy is diminished, the will is weakened, and the senses of personal power and responsibility are undermined. The result is a deficient third chakra that cannot support the upper chakras adequately and is blocked from both solid manifestation and the full realization of consciousness.

If, on the other hand, a child's will is overly indulged without discretion or respect for appropriate limits there is an inflation of the ego. Such children are said to "ride on the shoulders of the parents" and have an inflated sense of their own power. They are bound to fall many times in their lives, creating an oscillation between feelings of inferiority and superiority. They lack the container, supplied by limits, that is necessary for true manifestation. Expecting results immediately, they may lack the inner discipline necessary to accomplish more difficult tasks, which give us a true sense of our power.

Therefore, if we want our children to grow up as autonomous individuals, to have power, and to accept responsibility, we need to supply appropriate guidance without suppressing the delicate, emerging ego. Like a new blade of grass, this ego is bravely but tenderly pushing its first shoots above ground, reaching for the light of the heavens. May we tread carefully, with patience and strength of will, giving it the nourishment it needs to grow. And may patience and strength of will guide us in the process. They will surely be needed.

TRAUMAS AND ABUSES

Claude Steiner, transactional analyst and radical therapist, once told the story of an ordinary man—we can call him Carl—whose favorite pastime was to go to the park on a sunny afternoon, sit down on a bench, and bask in the solar rays. One day as he sat quietly on his bench (wearing his business suit), a large man wearing a uniform and heavy boots came and stood in front of him, blocking the sun. Being a peaceful sort of guy who did not like to make trouble, Carl merely moved over on the park bench so he could once again feel the sun's rays on his face.

No sooner did he move than the uniformed man moved again to block the sun. Carl moved again. So did the man. At this point, Carl spoke up and politely asked the man to move aside. The man did not. Carl, getting angry now, tried to push him aside. The man pushed him back on the bench and, with his heavy boot, stepped on Carl's foot and mashed it into the ground. Carl, very angry now, began to scream obscenities, flailing his arms at the man and yelling for help.

> When what was done to me was done for my own good, then I am expected to accept this treatment as an essential part of life and not question it.
>
> ALICE MILLER

But his crying was in vain. No one came to his rescue. When Carl lifted his head and looked around, he suddenly saw why. He saw that each person in the park had a uniformed man standing in front of them. Many had boots stepping on their toes, while others were chained to their benches. Most people on the benches were passively sitting still, some were quietly reading, while others turned to stare at Carl disapprovingly, scorning his childish and uncooperative outburst. None of the others were complaining about the man on their foot—why should Carl? Their outrage was aimed not at the man in the uniform but at Carl. He was living the self they had long since rejected.

This is where the story ends, but we can all guess at possible outcomes. Did Carl continue to yell and scream only to be chained to his bench with the key in someone else's possession? Did he give up his rebellion and learn to sit quietly and passively like his neighbors? Did he rally support and create an uprising in the park? Did he transform his jailer? What would you have done?

We are held in our places within a culture where the personal loss of power is so epidemic that no one hears the cries of loss and outrage. Instead we are ostracized for acts of individuality, or, at best, feared. To keep our power over others, we often give up our freedom and authenticity, and conform to expectations. This is a terrible loss, for it obscures the unique divinity within ourselves that contains the seeds of evolution and transformation. Those who have made this sacrifice expect others to do the same and become highly offended when they do not. Straight men in their gray suits may be offended by flamboyantly dressed gay men. The obedient wife is offended by the militant feminism of her daughter. War veterans are offended by those who march for peace.

In the wake of this loss, we have a civilization so obsessed with its lost power that it spends enormous amounts of money and energy creating the shadow of power through warfare and technology. We have complied with the master, internalized the controller, and become accomplices in a polarized society whose main goal is to control more with less. Numb to this pain, numb to our own powerlessness, numb to the repetitive tasks believed necessary for our physical survival, we live with the emptiness inside ourselves. Empty inside, our cultural myth tells us that power lies outside of ourselves in the approval of others, in technological gadgets, or through a distant and authoritarian god. Thus we deplete ourselves, our resources, and our planet, reaching for a power outside, a power over, a power that will only enslave us.

What happened to our power? Why are we a culture so obsessed with it? Why is it so important to our development, and how do we get it back?

In order to answer these questions, we need first to understand how it was taken away. Using our life energy to move forward is a natural outgrowth of thriving. It is not instinctual to curtail our own expansion. It is, however, instinctual to protect ourselves.

Authority relieves us of the responsibility of independent action.

STARHAWK

AUTHORITY

Individuals in recovery today are fighting a legacy from previous generations that believed in the ultimate authority of God over man, man over woman, and parent over child. Children, at the bottom of the heap, were to be seen and not heard. A good child was a quiet, obedient child who would never talk back to his parents. To spare the rod was to spoil the child, and breaking the child's will was believed to be a kindness done for his own good, in an effort to make him a useful member of society.

Elaborate measures may be taken to accomplish this, ranging from rejection and coldness to verbal rage and physical beatings. Sometimes the unwitting child is made an accomplice to such punishment—ordered to go out and cut the switch for his own whipping, made to mumble unfelt apologies, or taught to tell lies in self-protection. Thus our will is robbed and twisted, and then given back to us as an instrument in our own oppression.

Child rearing beliefs that negate the safety and individuality of children ostensibly "for their own good" are called *poisonous pedagogy* by Alice Miller. People spend years in therapy trying to recover from the self-negating beliefs they thought were true—beliefs about their own badness, about how they rightfully deserved such treatment. As long as these beliefs remain they will be passed on to the next generation. Our culture is built upon denying basic instincts. To support such behavior, we teach it to our children before they have a chance to know anything different, and thus they become divided against themselves and grow up to be divided against each other.

Authority is an issue that is present in everyone's life. As children we contend with the authority of our parents, caretakers, older siblings, babysitters, and schoolteachers. These models of authority influence how we respond to it, but even more important, how we develop our *inner* authority. Only through inner authority do we organize and focus our personal energy into an effective will. We may emulate or rebel against our models of authority, but they shape our concept of power in subtle and profound ways.

To command our lives, we need this inner authority to have a solid presence. We need a part inside that sends us to bed when we are tired, gets us up in time for work in the morning, and firmly pushes us away from the table when we've had enough to eat or drink. We need a part that holds this authority appropriately in the face of challenge and can discern when to resist and when to yield to others. We need a part that can take us by the hand and help us create our future. We need an internal organizing principle that shapes, forms, and directs our growth.

Robert Bly, in *Iron John*, talks about this authority as an "inner King":

> When we were one or two years old, the inner King, we would guess, was alive and vigorous. We often knew what we wanted, and we made that clear to ourselves and to others. Some families, of course, do not care what the children want.
>
> For most of us, our King was killed early on. No King ever dies for good, but he falls over and dies. When the inner warriors are not strong enough to protect the King—and at two or three who could expect them to be?—he dies.[10]

Until we consciously form this inner part of our personality, it will be formed by the behavior of those who held authority over us. If our parent was a tyrant, our inner authority will either be tyrannical or its opposite, a complete wimp. It may even shift between the two at different times. If our parent was absent or passive, our inner authority is likely to be equally vacant. If our parent controlled through criticism and shaming, their critical voices will be etched into our minds and replayed ad nauseam, as the background of every living moment. If our parents were deceptive and indirect, we will be a master of avoidance and manipulation both to ourselves and others. The gender of this person also affects the way we carry this power and where we project it onto others. If it was our father who was authoritarian, we may project our fear onto other men with whom we relate. Daughters may model themselves after their powerless mother and project their father's authoritarianism onto their boyfriends.

To examine the influence of authority in your own life, ask yourself the following questions:

■ Who was the central authority figure during your childhood? What means did they use to establish their authority? How did you feel about this person? How did you feel about their authority? Did you obey out of respect or fear?

- How did you react to this authority? Did you rebel or obey, or did it vary at different times in your life? If it varied, what circumstances influenced that change?

- What form does the inner authority take in your life now? Who is it fashioned after? Do you cooperate with it willfully or with resistance and resentment? Does this inner authority respect the feeling self, the limitations of the body, and the need for expansion and growth? Where does this inner authority draw its strength and what would bring it greater strength? How can you bring this authority into better alignment with your life?

PUNISHMENT

When authority is won through respect it resonates with our inner truth. It invites us to willingly participate because we believe in the reason and purpose behind it. I take a workshop with a teacher I respect because I consider her an authority on a subject. I can argue or question if need be. I go to an authority not to give away my power, but to increase my own power and skill from another's expertise.

Authority that tells us to go against our own nature resonates with something deeper—fear. Fear regresses our third chakra will to the first chakra level of survival. Our behavior is no longer an act of self-definition but of self-preservation. Rather than move forward in action, we move backward in reaction. Punishment instills fear.

> They can let you out of jail now, because they've put the jail inside your mind.
>
> STARHAWK

Punishment is used by authority for controlling behavior and robbing us of our free will. It conditions us—like Pavlov's dog—to react automatically without thinking or questioning. Punishment only works when the loss or pain is severe enough to matter, severe enough to undermine our sense of self. It must take away something greater than what might be gained—something that we desperately need, such as safety, love, pleasure, freedom, or self-respect. Punishment can shame or control, deprive or invade. It can be physical or emotional, literal or symbolic. When an example is made of a sibling, friend, or member of our race or gender, it goes a long way toward controlling our own behavior.

Physical and emotional abuse, whether intended as punishment or as a mismanaged outlet for adult frustration, is interpreted by the child as punishment. Inflicting pain on a child is not only an abuse to the body and the spirit within, but also an abuse of authority. The adult, as a trusted authority, holds a position of unconditional power. The child is forced to accept whatever is dictated and develop his own third chakra accordingly.

John Bradshaw, in his TV series on the family, likened the size ratio of parent to child to the experience of our adult selves encountering a seventeen-foot giant who is towering over us, raging and telling us what to do. How small we are in the face of such power! If this advantage was used against us, we may continue to feel that small the rest of our lives, always seeing others as bigger, stronger, or smarter. One client I had, for whom a particularly severe beating stood out in his memory, was plagued with dreams about "the big guy and the little guy." This framework was apparent in the way he looked at his job situations and other aspects of his life.

Starhawk, in *Truth or Dare*, lists four basic ways we can respond to punishment: we can *comply, rebel, withdraw,* or *manipulate*.[11] Each of these reactions can make the third chakra dysfunctional if they characterize a pattern. To habitually comply or withdraw is to be deficient; to automatically rebel or manipulate is to be excessive. All of these responses are present in passive-aggressive behavior, which initially rebels by ineffective compliance and then manipulates by withdrawal. For example, if the child is beaten for "talking back," then the ego center of the third chakra will find power in less direct ways, such as lateness, failing in school, or acting out against younger siblings or friends. These attempts to balance the third chakra become, in adult life, stumbling blocks to true effectiveness and responsibility.

Punishment forces us to deny ourselves in order to protect ourselves. This creates a monumental block of equal and opposing forces in the third chakra, one that projects itself on others by denying their needs as well. "A life of compliance is a life of denial," writes Starhawk.[12] The name of this chakra, *manipura*, means "jeweled citadel." Compliance is a false citadel of power. Authenticity is the jewel.

Since the third chakra is about ego and self-definition, denying our authenticity is antithetical to building healthy ego strength. Instead the ego is built on the ability to comply, to live up to expectations, to be good, to avoid punishment. While we may get temporary feelings of power and energy from these experiences, we are still subject to the highs and lows of drawing our power from a source beyond us, one that we cannot control. If our boss is in a good mood and compliments our work, we get a lift of energy and we feel a sense of pride in ourselves. If the boss comes in feeling angry and critical, perhaps because of a situation at home unrelated to work, then our sense of power slumps meekly to the floor. Our power within will be largely undeveloped, as we have only experienced feeling weak, ineffective, and inadequate.

As personal power and ego strength are so intricately connected, the sense we develop of our own power becomes the sense we have of ourselves. If the power dynamics were such that we could not overcome the dominance imposed upon us, the conclusion is that we, ourselves, are inadequate.

THE PARENTIFIED CHILD

Sometimes the situation within a family requires that the child grow up too quickly and take on responsibilities that are beyond the maturity of her age. Parental substance abuse, poverty, illness, death, or divorce may push a child into the role of surrogate spouse or parent. This may take many forms: giving emotional support for the remaining parent, helping to raise younger siblings, earning money for the family, giving up childhood freedoms or a social life with peers, or even relating with a parent sexually. Since the expectation is that the child *can* fulfill these roles, and the reality is that

> It is better to do your own duty, however imperfectly, than to assume the duties of another person, however successfully. Prefer to die doing your duties: the duties of another will bring you into great spiritual danger.
>
> BHAGAVAD GITA

they are biologically and emotionally too young to fulfill them adequately, the child is left with an overwhelming feeling of inadequacy. Such inadequacy not only attaches itself to every task attempted in the future, but also to one's very concept of self. Only by recognizing the inappropriateness of these expectations and working through the attendant feelings can this sense of inadequacy be turned around. As Alice Miller has said: "One is free from depression when self-esteem is based on the authenticity of one's own feelings and not on the possession of certain qualities."[13]

Janet, the oldest of four children, was a child of an alcoholic mother and a father who traveled frequently on business. Her mother's pattern was to begin drinking in the afternoon and be passed out by dinnertime. This meant that Janet, at age twelve, took on the role of feeding her hungry brothers and sisters and putting them to bed, after which time she might be able to begin her homework. There was seldom appropriate food in the house to make a good dinner, nor was there any instruction on how to cook, so the dinners were neither tasty nor nutritious. No matter how hard she tried, her brothers and sisters whined and complained and resented her role of substitute parent. Her siblings were naturally angry and hard to control, and Janet felt powerless and inadequate in her assumed role. She often cried herself to sleep from the stress of the household chaos. As a result, Janet did poorly in school and subsequently never even applied to college, convinced that she was too dumb to handle the curriculum. She carried this image of herself, and the inferiority that went with it, throughout life. When she later became pregnant with her own child, she experienced panic attacks, and felt that she could not possibly provide for a child even though she had a supportive husband and enough income to get through the early years.

Such feelings can also arise from situations where support seems adequate. Jack, for example, was the son of a prominent surgeon. At age three, his parents taught him to read and do simple mathematics. They took him to classical music concerts and gave him the best that money could buy throughout his childhood. He skipped two grades in school and graduated at sixteen to enter an Ivy League college. Upon entering college, however, he had a severe nervous breakdown and was unable to attend classes. His feelings of inadequacy were so strong that even though he had done brilliantly in the past, the only possibility he could see was failure. This failure would then betray the confidence of his parents and reveal what Jack had always suspected—that he had a learning disability. He felt this way because the struggle to succeed had always been so hard for him, even though testing showed no such disability. Instead, the feeling of inadequacy came from the fact that he was constantly pushed beyond an age-appropriate level. Emotionally and physically, he was always younger than his classmates, who resented his position—something that only increased his shyness and feelings of inferiority.

OVERSTIMULATION AND SENSORY DEPRIVATION

The third chakra, as the receiver, creator, and distributor of raw energy throughout the system, has to handle whatever energy comes our way. (Feel the impact on your third chakra as you walk into a lively party or an intense argument, for example.) When a child is overstimulated, the third chakra and the system as a whole receive more energy than they can handle. Sexual and physical abuse overload children's sensory systems with the voltage of an adult system. They are not neurologically equipped to handle such intensity, and have to find ways to either armor themselves against the intrusion or discharge the energy through activity or acting-out behaviors. They may grow up hypersensitive to noises, colors, emotions, or situations in their surroundings, still unable to handle any kind of intense stimulation. Or they may become hyperactive, seeking constant activity in order to discharge the excess energy.

At the opposite, equally damaging pole is the understimulated child. Randy was left alone in his crib day after day throughout infancy. He was properly fed, clothed, and even loved by his parents in the way they thought best, but was not provided with the basics of touch, toys, or varied experience. He remembers having a stiff neck from looking out toward the only window for hours on end and feeling incredibly lonely and isolated. As a result Randy experiences himself as having too little energy and will, with inner feelings of emptiness, fear of sexual inadequacy, and fatigue. Randy feels most energized in situations with strong stimulation, such as concerts or large parties, but tends to lose steam when he spends too much time alone. Yet, it is his habit to isolate as the emptiness of isolation is most familiar to him.

SHAMING

When shame underlies the control and release it seems to intensify both sides of the tension. . . . Shame makes the control dynamic more rigidly demanding and unforgiving and the release more dynamic and self-destructive. The more intensely one controls, the more one requires the balance of release and the more abusingly or self-destructively one releases, the more intensely one requires control.

MERLE A. FOSSOM AND MARILYN J. MASON

Shame results from almost any kind of child abuse, be it of authority, age-inappropriate responsibility, neglect, abandonment, sexual, emotional, and physical abuse, or excessive criticism. To the child who cannot explain such behavior in terms of parental shortcomings, the only conclusion is that she, herself, is at fault. She concludes that somehow she caused the abuse and deserved it, that she is somehow bad or unworthy of real love and appropriate care. Although this conclusion does not occur on a conscious level, it still becomes the primary shaper of behavior as the mind learns to monitor every instinctual impulse and spontaneous expression. Thus the person becomes shame-bound by a consciousness that scrutinizes and controls in an attempt to prevent spontaneous acts from drawing more shame.

Some parental activity is directly shaming, and statements like "You ought to be ashamed of yourself!" are far too common. Failure to praise a child's accomplishments combined with excessive criticism over her failures will create a shame-bound personality. How many times have I heard of parents who constantly called their children "stupid," "ugly," "crazy," or "lazy" for behaviors that were, in actuality, appropriate to the age in which they occurred? Children who cannot understand something that has never been explained, who are not taught to care for themselves in terms of personal hygiene, or who react spontaneously to crazy situations are often shamed for responses they cannot help. As a result, their natural response becomes a liability that must be sacrificed for the sake of safety and approval. Thus the ego becomes divided against the instinctual core of the self.

John Bradshaw, in his excellent book *Healing the Shame That Binds You*, describes how the unacknowledged shame of the parent is passed down to the children. Take, for example, the mother whose only sense of accomplishment is through the behavior of her children. Her own shame is transferred to the child whenever he fails to live up to her needs for approval, and so she feels ashamed if his clothes are dirty, or if he misbehaves at Grandma's house. Or the father who dropped out of school may try to redeem himself through his son's college career, excessively shaming his son if he does not do well.

Shame collapses the third chakra, and as a result the whole torso collapses at the middle. This makes the chest cavity smaller, reduces breathing, and constricts the throat. With this collapse, the head falls out of alignment with the rest of the body and displaces chakras six and seven (perception and understanding) from the central column of the body. As a result, one's thoughts and perceptions are often out of kilter with the body's reality. The mind may try to run the body beyond its capabilities, ignoring its messages for food or rest, denying emotional needs, and keeping the whole system run-down.

Shame is often experienced as an inward spiral of energy in the belly—a sinking sensation, as if the chakra is spiraling backward into the spine rather than forward into life. Butterflies in the stomach are similar to the shame spiral—we fear we are not going to be good enough, that we will surely fail, or that we will be exposed.

Shame creates a block between the mind and the body that splits one off from the core self. Since the third chakra has such a close relationship to ego development, the sense of shame and the sense of self are fused. The child does not see her actions as faulty, but sees herself—the producer of those actions—as fatally flawed. "Only a flawed person would make such a mistake," she tells herself. Each further mistake (and life is always full of them) only reinforces this basic belief.

Eventually the shamed core becomes a self-fulfilling prophecy. We match our behavior to our self-concept. Afraid of making mistakes, we dare not venture outward and keep ourselves small and limited, giving us just cause for our feelings of inferiority. Without the belief that we can succeed, we quit without really trying, and of course, in quitting, we prove to ourselves that we cannot succeed.

BROKEN WILL

Through our will we create the world we want. Unfortunately, the willful child is more work to raise than the docile, obedient one. Willful children have lots of energy and want to do many things. They talk back when they disagree and challenge their parents. Many parents are too overworked, disengaged, or shamebound to be able to tolerate that challenge.

The blending of wills between parent and child is a complex and delicate matter. It is essential that parents, in their greater knowledge and maturity, provide the guiding principles and final authority over matters concerning the safety and well-being of the child. It is a constant struggle for the child to adapt to the parents' schedule—to be ready for day care on time, to eat what is put in front of him, hungry or not, or to stop playing in the middle of a game or cut off a TV show because it is time to go home. Parents who are too overburdened with their own schedule often have little awareness of their child's natural rhythms.

In striving for a smoothly running ship, many parents either consciously or unconsciously break the will of the child. Complete authority over the child is established—he is not encouraged to make any decisions for himself, not allowed to voice feelings or objections, and shamed for attempting to do so. A separate identity is not allowed to emerge, individuation cannot take place, and the child grows up unable to steer the course of his own life.

There was a time when it was believed proper and appropriate to break the will of the child. This was the parents' job and an obedient child was their reward. But this creates people who act without feeling, enthusiasm, or a healthy sense of their own power. Such people are easily manipulated, controlled, and pushed into the shadow realm of held resentments, passive-aggressive behavior, or sudden eruptions of violence as they try to compensate for their diminished power by victimizing others. Without a will, how can one

> The will is disabled primarily through the emotions. . . . As emotions get bound by shame, their energy is frozen, which blocks the full interaction of the mind and the will.
>
> JOHN BRADSHAW

stand up to the temptation of addictions? When we are robbed of our chance to say no, we are robbed of the ability to control our lives and of the essential assertion of the self.

The following list, from Alice Miller's rules of the poisonous pedagogy, all serve to break the will of the child:

1. Adults are the masters (not the servants!) of the dependent child.

2. They determine in godlike fashion what is right and what is wrong.

3. The child is held responsible for the parents' anger.

4. The parents must always be shielded.

5. The child's life-affirming feelings pose a threat to the autocratic adult.

6. The child's will must be broken as soon as possible.

7. All this must happen at a very early age so the child will not notice and will therefore not be able to expose the adult.[14]

Each of these abusive rules undermines the establishment of a powerful third chakra. They impact the development of will, self-esteem, personal responsibility, and personal freedom by effectively twisting them into unrecognizable forms through domination and suppression, control and violence, fear and submission. When this happens at an early age (especially during the delicate emergence of the individual self) we have a collapse at the core, for which the other chakras must protect and compensate.

CHARACTER STRUCTURE

THE ENDURER

Sam reminded me of a storm cloud. Dark and brooding, his body was dense, muscular, and heavy. His eyes revealed a plaintive sadness, as if he had silently endured great losses in his life—a sadness that reminded me of the sky when it was about to rain. His voice did not match his powerful body, but seemed to come out in a modified whine. He began his story with a long list of complaints. "I feel like I don't have any energy. I'm tired all the time. I feel stuck in my job, and nothing turns me on anymore. I just feel heavy and depressed, but I don't know why." His eyes were downcast and his body moved very little. When I asked him how long he had been feeling this way, he answered, "It seems like I've always felt this way. But the older I get, the worse it feels. Nothing I do seems to change it."

Later on, I got Sam onto his feet and did some basic grounding work to get a charge going through his body. It was soon obvious that he actually had quite a bit of energy. As it built up, I could see the veil of anger starting to come over his features, but as it grew, he announced that he did not like the exercise.

As I recognized his need for autonomy, we stopped the exercise and explored his history. His mother had been smothering, his father distant and passive, and his older brother picked on him. When he was just over two years old, his sister was born, and his mother forced him into early toilet training to avoid having two children in diapers. Since his brother was aggressive and uncontrollable, Sam was punished for defending himself so that he would not become like his brother. This meant he had to suppress his anger. As his brother was rebellious, Sam became his mother's favorite. She doted on him but also controlled him. She usurped his autonomy, and told him how wonderful he was when he pleased her, but she withdrew her love if he misbehaved. When he later dropped out of college because of poor grades, she refused to speak to him for a number of years. This was how she treated her favorite.

Sam learned to endure, feeling that he had no choice. He tried to please others, but usually failed. When he failed, he turned vicious criticism on himself. His life became grim, his energy bound, his sexuality lukewarm. He felt stuck, and indeed he was.

Sam was an example of the Masochist character structure (as termed by Lowen) or the Endurer (see figure 3.2). The Endurer's dilemma is that he is locked in a holding pattern that binds the energy of the will, restrains autonomy, and compresses his spontaneity, joy, and optimism. He is caught in a vicious cycle where activity that cannot move forward is turned against the self, creating more frustration, greater tension, and more blockage. This results in a morose feeling of hopelessness and despair, a disabled will, and a reduced energy level—in short, a deficient third chakra.

I refer to a "block" in the energy as a place in the psychic and somatic realm where two or more opposing forces meet. You may wish to get angry at your boss and also want his approval. These two needs, both valid, work at cross-purposes to each other. Since neither can be fully denied or fully expressed, their mutual antagonism results in a block. When either side of the block is triggered, it increases the energy of its opposite and the ensuing struggle produces stress. Sam, for example, had many reasons to feel angry at his mother but also wanted her love, and these needs seemed mutually exclusive, hence the feeling of being stuck.

The Endurer structure develops when the parent is overly controlling, squashing the child's emerging autonomy. Since authority is forced at a time when autonomy is naturally emerging but not strong enough to stand alone, submission is the only possible recourse. Since this authority is not in keeping with the child's will, the result is a pattern of *outer compliance* and *inner defiance*. The child says, "All right, I'll do what you want, but I won't really participate!" (If you imagine making this statement, you can feel the holding inside.) The only way to feel autonomous is to go into resistance.[8] Unfortunately, this resistance becomes a standard approach to life and the Endurer has trouble either engaging or participating in anything without these ambivalent feelings creating a block.

Yet the outer compliance makes him reliable, steady, hardworking, anxious to please, and *able to endure*. Endurers hold up well in crisis, are loyal mates, and seldom stir up trouble. They can stick to business and accomplish difficult or unpleasant tasks. Yet while they try to please on the outside, there is simultaneously a tendency to sabotage. A passive-aggressive stance toward life is the only possible expression the disabled will can have for dealing with these ambivalent feelings.

Largely, the ambivalence is between aggression and tender feelings. The Endurer, like any child or adult, wants approval and affection, but affection is won at the cost of his own autonomy, and anger arises. Since he feels both manipulated by and angry toward the person he wants

FIRST CHAKRA Excessive	SECOND CHAKRA Deficient	THIRD CHAKRA Split	FOURTH CHAKRA Deficient
Draws inward, "holding in"	Emotional numbness (feelings held in, blocked)	Energy bound at will	Autonomy needs seen as antithetical to love
Tends toward density or obesity in body	May avoid pleasure or feel guilty about it	Passive-aggressive manipulation of others	Critical, negative
Excessive boundaries	Experiences sex as work	Inner rage blocked	Isolates
Resistant, stubborn	Afraid to get intimate, to let go	Tries to please while inwardly resisting	Develops lots of grief
Feels stuck, unmoving	May feel inadequate emotionally and sexually	Whines instead of taking action	Afraid to reach out because it risks autonomy
		Stubborn	Sees love as conditional
		Low self-esteem, shame-based	Remains submissive to get love, so simultaneously resists closeness
		Feels like a victim	
		Intense focus of energy	
		Good discipline	

FIFTH CHAKRA Deficient	SIXTH CHAKRA Split	SEVENTH CHAKRA Deficient
Excessive shyness	Locked in self-scrutiny due to shame base	Usually not strongly spiritual due to fear of losing autonomy
Whining and complaining	Hypervigilant	Often intelligent and capable
Energy choked in throat area	Fantasizes rather than takes action	Skeptical
Difficulty putting feelings into words		Pragmatic—likes facts better than abstract ideas

affection from, he feels both need and anger simultaneously, and can express neither.

In the words of Lowen: ". . . the masochist does not deny reality as does the schizophrenic, nor reject its demands as does the Oral character. He accepts reality at the same time that he fights it, he admits the rationality of its demands at the same time that he fights them. Like no other character, he is in terrible conflict."[9]

In many Endurer structures, the will is not broken by violence but by seeming sweetness. "Oh, my little boy would never act like that and disappoint his mommy, now would he?" "Cathy is my favorite child, she is so obedient and quiet." "Oh, I'm so very disappointed that you did that. I thought you were better than your brother." The implication of not living up to assumed expectations is that we are somehow bad or inadequate, all because we have displeased someone. We want to be approved of, and submit our will accordingly while simultaneously resenting the hell out of it.

When conditional love is used as reward or punishment for behavior, the child's third and fourth chakras are at odds with each other: He can have love by cooperating and giving up his will or he can have autonomy by risking rejection and losing love—but in this equation he can never have both. Love and will become an either-or phenomenon. Since both are necessary, the plight is hopeless and the Endurer falls into despair. It is important to remember that this equation is false. In truth, we can only have true love and strong will when *both* are present and working in concert with each other. It is extremely hard for the Endurer to realize this.

At the root of the Endurer's conflict is the demon of shame. His greatest fear is humiliation. When punished or criticized, he often collapses into vicious self-recrimination known as a *shame attack*. This diminishes his third chakra, and makes it more difficult to protect himself. He experiences shame again when he is manipulated because of the weak ego. The Endurer is caught in a vicious cycle of shame that undermines action and further perpetuates the shame. It's a terrible mess.

We experience shame if we cannot adequately control what comes out of us. If toilet training is started before the muscles are mature enough, a feeling of failure results, which makes us think what is inside is evil and nasty, and must be held in. We are rewarded for holding in, shamed for letting go. Where the Schizoid *holds together* and the Oral *holds on*, the primary pattern of the Endurer is *holding in*. He becomes ashamed of what is inside, and this translates to shame about everything inside—his feelings, his thoughts, his needs, and essentially, his very self. Therefore, the greatest fear of the Endurer is *exposure*, which he is certain will lead to humiliation and further shame. Therefore, he must hold himself in.

The predicament of holding in creates several blocks in the chakra system as a whole. There are four places where tension is most likely to be released and that Endurers must guard and close—the legs, hands, throat, and genitals. They may be able to take in energy from the ground and crown, but are unable to release it. The buildup of energy inside often makes the body very dense and large, often with a thick, muscular padding between the throat and buttocks. The posture is one of shame, where the tail is tucked in, the head lowered, and the third chakra collapsed. The first and fifth chakras are blocked, and this pulling inside and turning against the self creates masochism. Reaching out is also blocked, and the Endurer is trapped inside a body packed with energy, unable to release (see page 23, Endurer Character).

Let us look at the way this padding is formed. Suppose one were sitting by the window on a cold day, quietly reading a book. Suddenly someone throws a rock through the window. The Endurer feels annoyed, gets up, puts on a coat and scarf, and goes back to reading his book. Then another rock comes sailing through another window. It gets colder. The Endurer puts on another coat and scarf over the first layer. Rather than tell the person to stop throwing rocks, the Endurer simply puts on heavier armor. After the third rock, there is a third coat, and after the fourth rock the Endurer may finally feel annoyed enough to say something, but when he tries, his cries are so muffled by the coats and scarves that no one can hear him. He is unable to stop the rocks, and unable to remove the armor. He feels miserable, worthless, and victimized. It is typical of the Endurer to not even *perceive* the option of stopping the rocks, let alone that of getting angry at the thrower. The unspoken assumption (based on past experiences with parental authority) is that they cannot be stopped anyway so why waste time trying? Failure only increases shame, so it is safer not to risk it, and instead just protect oneself.

Anger, aggression, and spontaneous activity do arise in the Endurer. They are not, by any means, devoid of feeling. But when they arise, their expression is stifled and the energy turns inward, against the self (hence the source of the masochism). The feeling of shame that is already present takes the form of a vicious internal critic that is always pointing out the Endurer's faults and flaws. The master-slave relationship of the parent to the child is thus repeated internally between the mind and the body or, in Freudian terms, between the superego and the id, where the ego is too weak to mediate between the two. The more the anger builds up, the more severe the internal punishment. This creates the feelings of hopeless despair and being stuck—the Endurer's chief complaint in life.

The Endurer's will is bound up in submission and resistance and seldom sees a proactive path of action that will alleviate their situation. The default assumption is that situations must be tolerated rather than changed. His basic shame convinces him that he has no right to ask for change, and if given the opportunity, he may not even know what he wants, having long since relinquished the right to ask. Endurers see their life as a series of "have-tos," to which they submit with resignation and resentment.

The liberating current cannot break through the impasse at the will to gain entry into the upper chakras. Love is seen as something that must be earned through approval and given by will rather than by feeling. What does get past the third chakra meets another block at the throat, and the Endurer's voice may sound like a suppressed whine. Since outward objection is not allowed, whining and complaining are the only permissible expressions of dissatisfaction. Blocked at the throat, much of the inner world is kept from chakras six and seven and therefore kept from consciousness. Instead, the inner world remains perpetually in the unconscious, and Endurers have a hard time seeing their own process. In their plight, they are a mystery to themselves, and they simply draw the conclusion that they are flawed and inadequate, and that this is unchangeable.

To heal, the Endurer needs to express both the angry and the tender feelings. The tyranny of the will must be vanquished by giving it something more productive to do than criticize. The anger that is turned against the self must be externalized, the feelings of need acknowledged and released from their cloak of shame. Movement breaks the holding patterns and sexuality allows nurturance to come in. Building self-esteem is the underlying theme, so that a larger ego can then stand up to the inner critic and emerge into autonomy once again. To the Endurer, this is a frightening process, but one which eventually reinstates their inner authority, strengthens the will, and reclaims joy and spontaneity.

EXCESS AND DEFICIENCY

EXCESS

Third chakra excesses may appear at first glance as an abundance of power and energy. In reality, they compensate for feelings of diminished or unrecognized power. To overcome feelings of helplessness, abandonment, neglect, and abuse, there is an excessive attachment—even obsession— with power, control, and bolstering one's self-esteem. Since the core self is undernourished, one tries to live up to an image or a false self that must be nourished by approval from others. As a result, third chakra excess may appear as constant activity, or what John Bradshaw referred to as a human doing instead of a human being. This bolsters the ego with accomplishments, engagements, and busy-ness. Such a person will be in constant motion, excitation, and the stress that goes with it, thriving on such conditions as a way of feeling alive. Such chronic pushing can eventually lead to chronic fatigue—a flip from an excessive to a deficient state (see figure 3.3).

> The demand for a false self to cover and hide the authentic self necessitates a life dominated by doing and achievement.
>
> JOHN BRADSHAW

A person with an excessive third chakra is ruled by a rigid will. An excessive will, is not necessarily a strong will for its lack of flexibility may make it brittle and fragile. An excessive will may flare in anger or retreat in fear when challenged. An excessive will has a constant need to be in control of oneself, of others, of situations. In extremes, it is the bully—dominating, aggressive, angry, and inflated. In less extreme forms it is the manager who tends to overmanage situations by obsessing about every detail, trying to control as many variables as possible. The manager always wants to

FIGURE 3.3. THIRD CHAKRA EXCESS AND DEFICIENCY

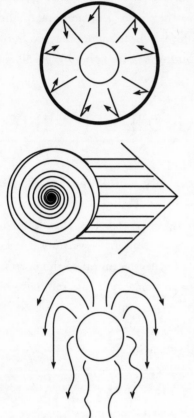

EXCESS 1: BLOCKED
Excessive energy builds up if blocked from expression and may turn against the Self.

EXCESS 2: ACTIVE
When the third chakra is open, it is focused and directed. If excessive, this expression can be dominating or obsessive.

DEFICIENCY
A deficient third chakra is depleted. Energy flowing outward is weak and aimless.

know, "Who's going to be there? What should I wear? How long will it take? What if this? What if that?"

Sometimes an excessive will can be seen in the control of one's own body. Dancers, athletes, weight trainers, runners, fastidious dieters, and even yoga practitioners sometimes run their bodies like machines, working them hard, pushing them with their will, or forcing them into submission by the rigorous regimen they have chosen. They may ostensibly choose such a program for spiritual, artistic, or health reasons, but close examination may reveal a need to bolster the ego by how well the body looks or performs. While this is certainly not true of all such endeavors, any of us can fall into this trap when working on self-improvement programs. The body is not a thing but a living vehicle. Balance between listening to the body's messages and channeling those impulses into productive activity is the integration we seek. While those with a deficient third chakra may need to develop their will with a personal regimen, those with excessive third chakras are more likely to carry it to damaging extremes.

The same self-domination by the will can also occur in one's life. We may not be engaged in excessive activity, but nevertheless push ourselves by sheer will through the challenges of daily life. In becoming an automaton we disengage from experience and feelings. We function on automatic and rarely think about what we are doing, with very little of our self involved. Here the will is disengaged from both the spirit and the body and has taken over the function of the ego, leaving experience behind. The excess will may rob vital energy from most of the other chakras, shutting down chakra two from the lack of feeling, chakra four from authentic connection, and chakra five from speaking out. The body may appear to be grounded in activity, but the spirit is not grounded in the body.

On an outward level, the excessive third chakra has a tendency to abuse power as it compensates for a weak ego and poor self-esteem. Power will seem intoxicating, and the ego may become driving, obsessive, and inflexible. Other values, such as self-nurturance, compassion, patience, and understanding, are trampled by the need for power. Life energy gets trapped in the third chakra and cannot travel to other areas.

Generally, people who have a high anxiety level are overcharged. While this may not be related to the third chakra in *cause*, it is related in effect. As the central processor for energetic expression and distribution, the third chakra works overtime when the system is overcharged. This may result in hyperactivity, muscle tension, excess stomach acid, as well as a dominating personality or ironclad will.

DEFICIENCY
People with deficient third chakras suffer from a combination of characteristics that may include lack of fire and vitality, poor self-discipline, weak will, and lack of spontaneity. They may be easily manipulated by others and often feel victimized. Depression may be frequent, as the energy of the body

is literally depressed and held back, often bound by feelings of shame. Here the weak ego copes by avoidance rather than by overcompensation. They may be intensely shy and appear cold or withdrawn. They are likely to avoid confrontation and challenge, especially when there is any risk of personal exposure. This includes performing in front of people or taking emotional risks in relationships. They are more likely to play it safe, follow the rules, let others lead, and be a people pleaser. They are passive, and control by their passivity. By letting others take the lead, they avoid vulnerability and risk and hold power over others who must take risks for them. In relationships, they let others initiate while they quietly go along, often with secret resentment. Their passivity may make their partner frustrated and upset while they, themselves, appear cool, calm, and collected. By looking good they avoid blame and responsibility. People with deficient third chakras are the lost children in the family, the quiet workers in the organization, or the devoted and selfless wife or husband.

John may agree to give his neighbor a ride to the doctor when he would really rather not, but he is too passive to say no. Instead, he shows up forty-five minutes late. This is his nonconfrontational way of expressing anger and aggression with a minimum of personal risk.

Fear, guilt, and shame (the demons of the first three chakras) are the dominating influences in the deficient third chakra. Fear contracts the energy at the base, guilt restricts the flow of movement, and as a result, there is very little energy radiating from the third chakra as it is restricted before it even gets there. The energy that does arrive is bound by shame.

The upper chakras may be excessive by contrast. The need for love is strong, as love often pulls energy up from the base into a liberation that literally increases the energy of the third chakra. The self-esteem that comes from being loved creates a feeling of safety that gradually allows power to develop. If the relationship fails, however (as it often does), then the energy falls back into a state of contraction, and the ego returns to the belief in one's own inadequacy.

Lack of outward aggression is common in third chakra deficiency. There is simply not enough energy available or the energy that is there is bound by fear and shame. If we feel we are worthless, why fight for anything? We tell ourselves that we do not matter and therefore what happens does not matter. Passivity is safer. Engagement brings fear where isolation is often more comfortable.

This isolation and passivity toward others cuts us off from the energy of the world around us. Already undercharged, we then become a closed system, further running down into depletion and monotony, which, of course, feeds low self-esteem.

Without a strong third chakra, we lack the will to run our own lives. Self-discipline is poor, follow-through is rare, and responsibility is avoided. We cannot stick to diets, build our energy through exercise, push ourselves to complete projects. The liberating current does not have enough force to escape the gravitational field of the lower chakras, and we simply do not get off the ground.

Persons suffering from chronic fatigue syndrome manifest a depletion of third chakra energy. This may be due to excessive activity that has simply run out of fuel, or chronic holding that binds the energy into exhaustion, or various medical conditions including candida overgrowth, Epstein-Barr syndrome, Lyme disease, and food allergies. In all cases, the body is calling for a rest and recharging, for contacting the deeper sources of energy that emanate from the biological core.

Both excessive and deficient third chakras may be attracted to stimulants like caffeine, amphetamines, or cocaine. Stimulants help the deficient system feel normal and help the excessive system continue its constant activity. Highly anxious personalities may also be attracted to calming drugs such as opiates, barbiturates, and alcohol.

It is possible to have a chakra that exhibits both deficient and excessive strategies. We may have a weak will but engage in constant activity, yet undermine the system over time. We may feel sluggish and lazy and yet be very manipulative. The important thing to realize is that all these behaviors attempt to deal with underlying wounds of autonomy and self-esteem.

RESTORING THE LOTUS

HEALING THE THIRD CHAKRA

Healing the third chakra is essential for maintaining healthy metabolism, balancing the distribution of energy throughout the body, and determining the course of our lives with appropriate responsibility and freedom. In order to achieve this, we need to work simultaneously on two levels: the internal management of energy within the body, and the external expression of that energy in the outer world. When both levels are addressed, our wills develop to a point where we can begin to work for social and political changes and assist in the ongoing struggle for overall human liberation.

> For in every act of love and will—and in the long run they are both present in each genuine act—we mold ourselves and our world simultaneously. This is what it means to embrace the future.
>
> ROLLO MAY

As one might expect, the inner work comes first. We cannot be very effective in the outer world if our personal energy is tied up in knots inside our own body. Untying the knots involves overcoming existing inertia—the old habit patterns that drag us downward, the binding fears from the past that rule us, the paralyzing self-scrutiny of our shame, or the compulsive acting out of unresolved conflicts. Overcoming this inertia is the first step in the individuation process.

HEALING DEFICIENCY

If the chakra is basically deficient, then energy must be built up slowly as if kindling a fire. We cannot escape the gravitational field of the first and second chakras without a burning fire to ignite and push us onward. Without the fire of confidence and enthusiasm, we cannot meet new challenges or successfully maintain disciplines such as a restrictive diet or a meditation practice. We set ourselves up for failure, which only increases the feelings of shame and powerlessness.

Building the fire means increasing metabolic energy. The first step in this process is to examine the fuel consumed to make that fire, through attention to diet. Eating foods that are low in fat, sugar, and additives yet have high levels of complex carbohydrates and sufficient protein and vegetables helps the fire burn cleanly. Eating at regular intervals keeps blood sugar levels steady and energy flowing evenly. Frequent aerobic exercise for at least thirty minutes at a time helps the body break a sweat, increases metabolic efficiency, and develops a feeling of power through increased muscle tone. As we become more physically fit, our energy flows more smoothly and our self-esteem also increases.

Deficient third chakras need to engage with life in ways that provide nourishment and support. What activities leave you feeling energized? What activities leave you feeling drained? What is it about those activities that your system responds to? Look for activities that energize you and find ways of increasing your time for them.

Challenges and difficulty can also increase our energy as long as they are not completely overwhelming and impossible. Avoidant people feel depleted and unable to meet challenges, but they seldom realize that their avoidance is precisely what keeps them undercharged. Notice what happens in your body when you confront your boss, or take a risk that plunges you into new territory. That shaky feeling may be the activation of fear or shame, but it is also a state of increased energy and aliveness. When we rise to meet challenges, we raise the psychic voltage of the system itself. Inertia keeps us in patterns that already exist. Moving into new realms forces us to create new patterns, to experience life in the now, and discover our own hidden reserves of power and strength.

Those with deficient third chakras need to work on strengthening their will by increasing physical energy as well as paying conscious attention to their goals and desires. Many of my clients do not take control of their lives because they have no master plan that outlines their long-term goals. The deficient structure does not organize very well and needs a plan to keep them on track. To stick with a plan or routine increases our feelings of power and control and boosts our confidence.

HEALING EXCESS

Excessive third chakras have more energy than the system can handle, and this energy needs to be discharged or rerouted to other chakras. Often the strategy for this type of work involves increasing the function of other chakras, rather than engaging the third chakra itself. If excess is to be redistributed it needs to have some place to go. We may need to open channels for emotional expression, soften the heart, or increase the grounding. Working directly on the third chakra in excessive cases may create a power struggle, which only creates further excess.

Instead, excessive third chakras need to relax, sit still, and let go of control. Guided meditation that takes one through deep relaxation is an excellent place to start. This is a time for quiet release and making deeper contact with the body and mind. Practicing yoga promotes relaxation and flexibility, softly dissolving blocks that bind tension. Prescribing downtime without requirements or goals allows the third chakra to disengage from its constant thrust forward and lets the person experience a deeper state of being. Taking time to do nothing can be extremely difficult for excessive third chakra types to tolerate, and they may only accept it with the idea that they are actually "doing" something to promote their own health.

OTHER GENERAL STRATEGIES FOR THIRD CHAKRA HEALING

Give Up Being Safe

The first thing I tell my clients or group members when they wish to develop their third chakra is to give up the attachment to being safe. This involves giving up wanting everything assured ahead of time and accepting that there might be criticism, challenge, misunderstanding, rejection, or a possibility of failure. While safety may be important for survival issues and for developing emotions, it is no challenge to our power if everything we do is already removed from any real risk.

We need to face the fact that the world is not safe. If we limit ourselves to what is predictably comfortable, we may as well not get out of bed in the morning. In clinging to safety and security, we remain as children—powerless and wanting the world to be shaped for us. The challenge of power is to mature, accept responsibility, and carve the shape of our future through our own proactivity. Our power increases through meeting challenges and resolving them successfully. We must be willing to take risks, venture into the unknown, and escape the gravity of the familiar in order to expand upward and outward in the journey across the Rainbow Bridge.

Work with Anger

While emotions are generally related to the second chakra, anger is particularly relevant to the third as it expresses assertive, fiery energy. Blocked anger can create both excessive and deficient conditions, but is more likely to be excessive. Those with deficient structures may not even be aware of their own anger, as they do not have enough energy to express it. Allowing a deficient structure to develop a means of expressing anger gives her permission to have this energizing and empowering emotion.

> Safety is often the comfortable euphemism we use to deny our feelings of fear. The seeker of security has found a modus operandi of sorts within an attitude of negation.
>
> JOHN PIERRAKOS

If anger is felt but not expressed, then it is more likely to result in an excessive condition. Anger is energy, as the body attempts to meet a challenge through increasing its charge. If situations that make us angry occur frequently, we live in an overcharged state. If that energy cannot be expressed, then the charge builds up in the body and becomes locked in the muscles as tension, compulsive activity, or a need to control.

Blocked anger is often a factor in obesity, which can be seen as a metabolic defect. Something is preventing the matter consumed as food from turning into energy. We might say the fires are not burning properly or that the fire energy is blocked in some way. Since food is supposed to supply us with energy, the obese person is frustrated as the food they consume does not energize them, and so they reach for more food, which only worsens the problem. I have found that releasing blocked anger often improves metabolism and helps stabilize weight problems, sometimes with little or no change in diet. When dieting is needed, reclaiming our anger often increases available energy for the will, making it easier for us to maintain the diet.

Getting anger out involves looking at what created it, examining situations we were forced to endure, and reclaiming the right to object to those abuses of power that hurt or oppressed us. Addressing our anger to these past issues helps free available energy for present challenges. It also keeps us from having an inappropriate level of charge for present issues.

In a therapeutic situation, releasing anger about our father keeps us from continually badgering our husbands or boyfriends. Standing up to our mother keeps us from resenting our wives, girlfriends, or daughters. Being able to express our anger at its source keeps it from becoming excessive or harmful, and instead increases our feeling of empowerment. In my experience as a therapist I have found that clients often fear that if they get angry in therapy, they will turn into horrible, angry people in their daily lives. In actuality, getting their anger out makes them less angry yet more effective in their lives.

> The dynamic core of your human life is grounded in your feelings, your needs, and your drives. When these are bound by shame, you are shamed to the core.
>
> JOHN BRADSHAW

Attacking the Shame Demon

In both excessive and deficient chakras, the demon of shame is usually found lurking in the shadows of the third chakra, ready to attack its poor victim the moment any mistake (or even success) arises. Thus the foundation for balanced power—healthy self-esteem—is continually undermined. For some, this results in withdrawal and collapse, for others, a fury of compensating activity.

In either case, the roots of shame need to be exposed and pulled out of our ground of being. We may feel shame about our bodies, our emotions and sexuality, our neediness, for not being "good enough," or any number of reasons. It is important to recognize the critical voice in your head, and to ask whose voice it resembles. What forces were acting on that person that drove such criticism in your direction? How did they feel about themselves?

Often when the voice rears its ugly head, the conversation is one-sided. "You're so stupid. You never do anything right. You'll never make anything of yourself." Where is the other side of this conversation? Where is the rebellion that says, "Whaddya mean, I'm stupid! You never showed me how to do anything! You never took time to teach me. You expected me to behave in ways that were beyond my maturity, to know things I couldn't possibly have known. And without the slightest support or encouragement!"

Or the rebellious voice might say, "Look, this is the first time I've tried to do this task. I'm not gonna be an expert my first time, but at least give me credit for trying. I'm doing my best. Back off!"

Shame inevitably results from abuse. Seeing the child you were in the context of that abuse and showing compassion for that child helps dissipate the shame. Inner child dialogs involve having the adult self tell the child self that they are forgiven, that it was not their fault, that they did not do anything wrong, or that they did not deserve the abuse. This replaces the overly critical, shaming programs that run us ragged and steal the joy from our lives.

CONCLUSION

Third chakra work, whether dealing with excess or deficiency, rests on building ego strength. This involves developing contact with the authentic self through the body and through its feelings and aspirations, raising self-esteem through attacking the shame demon, and creating a sense of power through meeting challenges and engaging in stimulating activities. Releasing inhibitions and fears loosens up the spontaneous, playful energy that makes life easy and enjoyable. These tactics nourish the liberating current coming up from the base chakra.

To honor the consciousness coming down from the top, it is helpful to make a list of goals and intentions and then plan the steps needed to bring those goals into manifestation. The will develops when we apply our energy to these goals or to other routines that help develop our skills and our physical energy. The results of our efforts positively reinforce the process and also ground our third chakra power in tangible reality.

Healing the third chakra brings a healthy sense of power as well as its limits. It promotes a proactive and causative approach to life, one that is confident, warm, responsible, and persevering. The person is now able to take on challenges, follow through on tasks, confront opposition effectively rather than with reactive retaliation, and take responsibility for their actions. The person with a healthy third chakra is a person with good vitality and a playful ability to laugh at themselves.

CHAKRA FOUR

Finding the Balance in Love

FOURTH CHAKRA AT A GLANCE

ELEMENT
Air

NAME
Anahata (unstruck)

PURPOSES
Love
Balance

ISSUES
Love
Balance
Self-love
Relationship
Intimacy
Anima/animus
Devotion
Reaching out and taking in

COLOR
Green

LOCATION
Chest, heart, cardiac plexus

IDENTITY
Social

ORIENTATION
Self-acceptance
Acceptance of others

DEMON
Grief

DEVELOPMENTAL STAGE
4 to 7 years

DEVELOPMENTAL TASKS
Forming peer and family
relationships
Developing persona

BASIC RIGHTS
To love and be loved

BALANCED CHARACTERISTICS
Compassionate
Loving
Empathetic
Self-loving
Altruistic
Peaceful, balanced
Good immune system

TRAUMAS AND ABUSES
Rejection, abandonment, loss
Shaming, constant criticism
Abuses to any other chakras,
especially lower chakras
Unacknowledged grief,
including parents' grief
Divorce, death of loved one
Loveless, cold environment
Conditional love
Sexual or physical abuse
Betrayal

DEFICIENCY

Antisocial, withdrawn, cold

Critical, judgmental, intolerant
of self or others

Loneliness, isolation

Depression

Fear of intimacy, fear of
relationships

Lack of empathy

Narcissism

EXCESS

Codependency

Poor boundaries

Demanding

Clinging

Jealousy

Overly sacrificing

PHYSICAL MALFUNCTIONS

Disorders of the heart, lungs,
thymus, breasts, arms

Shortness of breath

Sunken chest

Circulation problems

Asthma

Immune system deficiency

Tension between shoulder
blades, pain in chest

HEALING PRACTICES

Breathing exercises, pranayama

Work with arms, reaching out,
taking in

Journaling, self-discovery

Psychotherapy

Examine assumptions about
relationships

Emotional release of grief

Forgiveness when
appropriate

Inner child work

Codependency work

Self-acceptance

Anima-animus integration

AFFIRMATIONS

I am worthy of love.

I am loving to myself and
others.

There is an infinite supply
of love.

I live in balance with others.

SHADES OF GREEN

We may be a culture obsessed by power, but we are driven by the need for love. The basic right of the heart chakra—*to love and be loved*—is simple, profound, direct. Sadly, this chakra is easily damaged, diminished, or wounded. These wounds have profound importance as they wound both spirit and soul, affect both mind and body, and impact the very core of the self.

Why is love so elusive when it is so simple? Literature abounds with sagas of love and its loss, sagas we know only too well from personal experience. Nothing is quite so uplifting as the flowering of love, nothing so devastating as its loss. A deeply archetypal experience, love is the force that runs our lives. We cannot live without it, yet the world is crying for lack of it.

> Driven by the forces of love, the fragments of the world seek each other so that the world may come into being.
>
> PIERRE TEILHARD DE CHARDIN

All forms of child abuse are, in fact, travesties of love. They are travesties because they are not a complete absence of love, but an absence of healthy love. How many children have been spanked and abused, sexually molested, punished severely, smothered, or overmanaged while being told, "This is because I love you so much." Travesties of love occur when the most needed element of life is twisted and torn, withheld and used as a means of control. Without knowing what healthy love looks like, we have a hard time creating it in our lives. We hang on to mere shreds of love, sacrifice ourselves on its altar, run in fear when we find it.

Instead, we are turning toward the opposite of love: warfare and violence. Television violence models behavior for our children and gangs provide many of our youth with their only sense of belonging. Adolescents in my practice tell me that "cruel is cool," and to be a man you have to be mean. On a single day in America, 270,000 children carry guns to school and guns are now surpassing automobiles as the number one killer.[1] Is this not a travesty of love?

Political agendas cut funds for the downtrodden and needy, the immigrants and children, while the defense budget soars. It is alarming enough that our political leaders embody this value system—more alarming still to contemplate the number of people who support them. *What kind of cultural mythos is driving such values?*

Myths are the cultural stories of our origins and our purpose. Unconsciously, these stories influence and may even rule our lives. They define what is possible, shape who we are, and lead us to what can be. Myths are a statement of the primal relationships that exist between archetypal elements in the universe and their counterparts in our own psyches.

In the prevailing mythos, we are children of divorce. The Great Mother, a fundamental archetype of the psyche, was worshipped as a living deity for at least 25,000 years during the Paleolithic and Neolithic periods of human history.[2] She is archetypal ancestress to us all, her memory buried deeply in the collective unconscious. She mirrors our early childhood experience of our own mothers and embodies the archetypal imprint of the mothering source—nurturance, nourishment, containment, and connection.

In the collective mind of Western civilization, she has long been forgotten. Removed from our predominant mythology, she is conspicuous in her absence. She is only beginning to resurface through the growing Goddess movement, recent archeological research, and the popularity of Jungian archetypal psychology. She is the Mother we have lost and are only just beginning to find again. She is the archetypal feminine at the primal origin of our cultural history.

In her absence, the Great Father has become the sole protagonist in our dominant mythology. He is strong and powerful, but distant and ethereal. He is without a wife or daughter and is estranged from all that the feminine archetype represents. His immediate son has been crucified, ostensibly for the sins of the children. In the divorce settlement, we are the motherless children who were taken to live with the Father. In our new household, Mother was not be discussed and became forgotten.

We have inherited the myth of a broken home. We are the motherless children in our distant father's house, trying to find wholeness in a world that is longing for the magic and mystery of love. This is our story. These are our parents. We are the children of an unacknowledged marriage.

No wonder we have such a yearning for romantic love. No wonder the myth of man-meets-woman-and-lives-happily-ever-after pervades our collective fantasies, rendering other forms of love unrecognizable. If we were children of an intact and loving mythical home, *a partnership mythology*, we might seek union from an experience of cooperation, rather than through a compulsive need to complete our diminished selves through another.

Our predominant myth is one of separation. We see ourselves as separate from Nature, separate from each other, and separate from the divine. Separations are created by race, class, gender, and age. Individuals are endowed with the moral right, even encouragement, to do whatever is necessary to further their own individual existence. The environment and its coinhabitants are sacrificed for individual needs. Wealth and class create more separation, more privacy, and more individualism.

We have created vast separation between men and women, and further separation between women and women, and between men and men. Love, as the all-pervasive glue of the universe, is culturally restricted to the bonds of limited heterosexual dyads and their often lonely offspring. The model is obviously flawed, for our children are abused and our marriages repeat the pattern of our mythical parents—with epidemic divorce.

Collectively, it seems we are falling out of love with the world. We all know what deep pain we feel when we fall out of love. It pierces the very core of our being, carves a deep hole in the soul, and wounds and cripples the living spirit.

In our disconnection, we can barely relate to all the tragedies occurring in the world. Is it because the very art of relating is becoming a lost art? Is this because the time it takes to relate deeply, feel fully, and communicate and understand is no longer valued as time well spent? We are becoming alienated, hostile, defensive, self-centered, and compulsively consuming. The result is isolation, constriction, and limitation. The ground that holds us becomes shaky, and the energy that evolves us is restricted to traditional patterns that support the myth of separation. In our isolation, we are lost from our spiritual core, lost from the heart.

To cross the Rainbow Bridge connecting Heaven and Earth is to consciously reconnect severed parts of the world. It is to anchor the myth of individualism in the necessary grounding of self, while simultaneously expanding that self into a conscious unity with the world around us—socially, ecologically, and mythically. To access the divine and become as gods, we need to recognize our own divine nature as part of the greater mystery of unfolding. To heal the heart is to reunite mind and body, the mystical and mundane, self and other into an integrated whole.

This is our task in the heart chakra as it is the task for every one of us that wants to heal this world and assure its future. Without love, there is no binding force to hold our world together. Without love, there is no integration but instead *dis*-integration. Without love, our Rainbow Bridge collapses in the middle and we fall into the chasm of separation below.

UNFOLDING THE PETALS

BASIC ISSUES OF THE FOURTH CHAKRA

Love

Balance

Self-Reflection

Self-Acceptance

Relationship

Intimacy

Anima/Animus

Eros/Thanatos

Grief

Compassion

Devotion

THE MYSTERY OF LOVE

Riding on the golden flames of our power center, we now arrive at the very heart of the chakra system. Here, in a band of green, lies the center of the Rainbow Bridge, the midpoint of our journey. Like the green, growing plants, which push toward the heavens from their roots in the earth, we, too, reach outward in two directions—anchoring the manifesting current deep in our bodies and expanding the liberating current as we reach beyond ourselves. In the heart chakra, these currents

> For one human being to love another human being; that is perhaps the most difficult task that has been entrusted to us, the ultimate task, the final test and proof, the work for which all other work is merely preparation.
>
> RAINER MARIA RILKE

come to perfect balance in the center of our being. From that sacred center—the heart of the system—we enter the mystery of love.

The basic issues that we encounter in the heart chakra deal with *balance*, *love*, and *relationship*. Through balance we find a center from which we can love, through love we form relationships, and through relationships we have the opportunity to transform the self-centered ego of the lower chakras into awareness of the larger realm in which we are embedded.

It is the enchantment of love that opens the road to wider consciousness. When we fall in love, we are suddenly stripped of our defenses, lifted out of our self-centered habits, and propelled into an enlarged view of the world. Love melts our rigid attitudes and alters our psychic structure. When we fall in love, we see things anew—colors are enhanced, places take on new meaning, interests of the beloved become interests of our own.

At the same time that love expands our horizons, it also brings us into a deeper connection with ourselves. Falling in love takes us down into our bodies; desire puts us in touch with the physical self through our wants and needs. With another, we celebrate the temple of the body and honor our physicality. As we reach down inside to share our gifts with our beloved, we are forced to confront and develop our deepest nature.

> In real love, you want the other person's good. In romantic love, you want the other person.

The intimacy of love both reveals and integrates the shadow. Loving acceptance of another allows the rejected parts of our psyche to emerge safely. Not only do relationships provide a context in which the shadow is bound to emerge, intimacy invites us to share those deepest, hidden parts of ourselves. In the accepting arms of our beloved, these parts can come to consciousness. This acceptance sets the ground for the self-expression of chakra five, as only through self-acceptance can we come fully into our truth and have the courage to express it. Intimacy is the foundation for that expression.

Being loved by another increases our experience of Self, as we are reflected in the eyes, words, and behavior of our lover. Suddenly we catch a glimpse of our own divinity, our specialness, and begin in a new way to truly care for ourselves and feel a sense of pride and purpose. We take better care of our bodies, keep our houses cleaner, and dare to reach further than we might otherwise. Love brings a spiritual awakening, and the loss of it produces profound despair. Sometimes that loss severs us from our sense of divinity—a state that can hardly be tolerated after the expansion and heightened awareness that love has brought.

When love does wane, we are thrown back to our past. The loss brings us to an infantile state of vulnerability, where our needs and issues, patterns and processes are brought to light once again. We are forced to confront and heal our pain in order to go on, to delve into our childhood and psychic structure to unravel the mystery that is Self. As Jung has said, "Love is the dynamism that most infallibly brings the unconscious to light."[3] Both the presence and the loss of love force us to examine ourselves in a new light.

BALANCE

Ancient tantric diagrams depict the heart chakra as a lotus of twelve petals containing a six-pointed star made of two interlacing triangles (see figure 4.1). This represents the downward movement of spirit into matter and the upward liberation of matter into spirit, meeting in perfect balance in the heart. More than just a meeting, this is an interpenetration whose final goal is integration of spirit and mind with body and soul.

Since the heart chakra is the middle point in a system of seven centers, balance is an essential principle at this level of integration. This implies both internal balance between various aspects of ourselves (mind and body, persona and shadow, male and female), as well as balance between ourselves and the world around us (work and play, giving and receiving, socializing and being alone). Finding this equilibrium supports the basic issues of love and relationship, for without balance within ourselves it is difficult, if not impossible, to achieve healthy and long-lasting love relationships.

Balance is the underlying foundation of longevity in all things.

We will look at the concept of balance in relationships by examining dynamics in two essential kinds of relationships: the ones we have with ourselves and those we create with others.

FIGURE 4.1. CHAKRA FOUR—INTERPENETRATING TRIANGLE

INTIMACY

Intimacy, as Thomas Moore so aptly points out, is about bringing forth deeply interior aspects of the self.[4] In order to have intimacy we first need to have a sense of self. We need to be intimate with our own interior, to know our needs, wishes, fears, boundaries, and hopes. Through knowing the self within, we can honor the self that lives within another. We need to be able to love our own self enough to offer it openly to someone else. Without self-love, this cannot happen.

> To love oneself is the beginning of a life-long romance.
>
> OSCAR WILDE

The most common block in the heart chakra is the absence of self-love. How can we have intimacy with others if we are distanced from our own self? How can we reach out to others when we are drowning in shame and criticism? How can we maintain balance between ourselves and others if we have no balance within? How can we treat another with respect if we treat our own selves abusively?

Ideally, the demon of shame has been transformed in the third chakra, leaving us ready to enter the heart with an honest regard for the sacredness of our being. To love ourselves is to act respectfully and responsibly toward ourselves, to enjoy our own company when in solitude, to honor our limits and speak our truths. In general, self-love is an act of treating ourselves the way we would treat anyone else that we love—respectfully, honestly, compassionately, with feeling and understanding, pride and patience.

Our relationships with others reflect our relationship with ourselves. We will find others who treat us the way we expect to be treated, others who respond to the relationship program we carry inside our heart chakra. Self-love is the foundation for loving others.

SELF-REFLECTIVE CONSCIOUSNESS

I am continually amazed by the number of my clients who have not yet discovered the person that lives inside. They come to see me because they hurt, because their lives are not going well, or because they do not like themselves. That would seem to indicate an awareness of Self, would it not? But

> Being a friend to yourself is no mere metaphor or purely sentimental idea. It is the basis of all relationship, because it is a fundamental recognition of soul.
>
> THOMAS MOORE

when I have a client stand on her feet, do some simple grounding, and look at me and say "I," there is too often a hollow ring to the word. Sometimes it's almost a question, sometimes it's mechanical, sometimes it's barely a whisper. Sometimes she cannot meet my eyes and say "I" at the same time. When I ask such clients to expand the statement to "I am in here" (referring to the body), it often becomes apparent that the statement is

not true. Either the "I" has not truly been established, or it does not live fully in the body.

Yet, such a person may tell me long details about how she feels, what she is doing with her life, or what problems plague her. The ego self is definitely operating. What is missing?

The *beholding* of Self is missing. Beholding establishes a sacred relationship. When a teenage daughter comes downstairs for her first prom date, dressed as a woman for the first time, we simply behold her. It is an embrace, but it is not physical. To behold is not to fix, change, judge, or even want. It is simply to witness—to embrace with our awareness. In beholding the self, we witness a miraculous manifestation of divine energy living right inside us, with all its hopes and fears, joys and tears. This witnessing is "the heart of the heart." It brings us to the sacred. It is the essential realization that must be present for any real healing to occur.

It has been said that an unexamined life is not worth living. To enter the heart is to enter into self-reflective consciousness, a place of self-examination. In that reflection, we not only define ourselves (as in the third chakra) but come into *relationship* with ourselves. Self-reflective consciousness is the process of beholding. In therapy, we stop and look at ourselves—at our motives, actions, goals, hopes, and fears. While there are many who are cynical about this process, some kind of systematic self-examination is essential if we are to evolve and if we are going to rise from the power-hungry obsession of the damaged third chakra into a state of integration and peace characteristic of the fourth. Self-reflective consciousness allows us to integrate our psychic pieces, bring them into relationship, and see how they relate to each other and become whole.

It requires conscious attention to change patterns, to create something new, in short, to evolve. Without examining what has been, we are destined to repeat it. Without cultivating consciousness, our ascending current has to turn around and go back down to the base before it has reached its full expansion. In so doing, we are caught in repetitive loops, neurotic patterns that we repeat again and again.

Self-examination gives birth to a new integrated Self. This Self is no longer bound by the past, but energized by the will beneath it and headed toward the future. Self-examination is essential for establishing the balance that is the central principle of the heart chakra.

Through self-examination we give birth to the conscious being.

MIND AND BODY

One of the prime areas of balance in the heart chakra is between mind and body. This occurs through learning to decipher the body's messages. This involves distinct inner listening on the part of the mind to the body's subtle communications and often leads to recovering memories, working through traumas, releasing stored tensions, and completing unresolved emotional transactions. Through this process various parts of our experience are reconnected. Feelings are reconnected with mental images. Impulses are integrated with belief systems. Sensation is

> Love is a bodied truth, a somatic reality.
>
> STANLEY KELEMAN

connected with meaning. This is the work of self-reflection—allowing the mind to behold our experience in the body.

If work on our lower chakras has brought us fully into our body, we are now ready to integrate that awareness into higher levels of complexity and understanding.

ANIMA AND ANIMUS

In our second chakra recovery work we encountered (and hopefully integrated) our *shadow*, which contains the unconscious, rejected aspects of our personality. With an integrated shadow, we freed up energy previously used to hold the shadow back, and this newfound energy helped move us to chakra three, where we began the process of individuation. In the heart chakra, we continue our individuation by developing another essential balance—that of the inner female and male, or in Jungian terms, *anima* and *animus*.

> The mystery of two personalities is like the contact of two chemical substances. If there is any reaction, both are transformed.
>
> C. G. JUNG

The anima is the archetypal energy of the inner feminine, and the animus, the inner masculine. The anima is believed to figure more prominently in men, while the animus is the counterpart in women. Still, both genders carry each archetype.

These archetypes also exist externally as symbols in the collective consciousness, where they often become stereotypes. A stereotype is a contemporary version of an archetype, such as the docile female or the strong, silent man. Stereotypes are culturally determined versions of the original archetype—often truncated images that emphasize only a part of the archetype behind them.

Our first imprinting of these archetypes came from our mother and father, yet their behavior was influenced by the stereotypes of their time. Other stereotypes are fed to us through movies and romance novels, advertising and television, then reinforced by social pressure from peers.

It is important to realize that the images of masculine and feminine that we ascribe to anima and animus are culturally dictated, rather than innate. If our images of masculine and feminine become strongly polarized—meaning that masculine is defined by absence of the feminine and vice versa—then it is likely that either our anima or animus will be repressed. We have no permission for the opposite within ourselves to emerge.

Charles, for example, has accepted the prevailing cultural attitudes about what a man should be. He thinks a man should be strong, rational, tough, independent, successful, cool, and unemotional. To Charles, any display of vulnerability, emotion, uncertainty, or softness threatens his self-image. Since his image is so polarized, his inner feminine cannot come out at all. His anima may appear as fearful images in dreams, as depression or moodiness. It remains repressed, to be unconsciously projected onto his girlfriend. She is supposed to carry the anima for him by doing the feeling and supporting work, and maintaining the emotional quality of the relationship.

Like the shadow, the unconscious anima or animus gets projected onto others, often in idealized states, wreaking havoc on our intimate relationships. If a man has rejected his own feminine nature, he may abhor the feminine in other men while expecting his female partner to completely carry his concept of the feminine, criticizing any independent, assertive behavior she might display. Similarly, a woman who has not developed her masculine side expects her man to be flawlessly powerful, accomplished, and heroic, while she is simultaneously oppressed by these qualities. Women who claim they want a nice guy and then reject him when he shows feelings or softness are projecting their animus. If they can allow their own masculine side to increase, they can allow their men to become more gentle. If we find in our relationships that *what initially attracts us later repels us*, we might do well to look for projected anima or animus.

In both heterosexual and gay relationships, the archetypes can be reversed. A woman, gay or straight, may well live the masculine life and repress her own feminine. A man may carry the feminine in his relationship with either a woman or a man. The anima and animus are more related to the concept of opposites in the developed self than actual gender. The point is to recognize and bring forth the side that is undeveloped. The hard-edged career woman may need to develop her softer side, while the introverted, supportive male may need to develop his initiating, masculine side.

The resolution of the anima and animus represents the internal sacred marriage, or *hieros gamos*, the balancing of masculine and feminine energies within. This alchemical marriage, as Jung described it, is another step in the individuation process that leads toward wholeness. Only when this process occurs within can we hope to be free from dependence and projection and to enter cleanly and freely into relationship with another.

The *hieros gamos* stage in the individuation process usually occurs during midlife. In the earlier development of our personality, we often favor one side over the other. The scientist may have developed a noteworthy career that sacrificed home life. He may adhere to a logic and exactitude that dominates feeling and imagination, or have an extroverted personality that is constantly engaged with others through his work. At midlife, he may find himself in a crisis that calls forth his repressed feminine side. He may lose his wife, who has carried the feminine archetype for him, and be faced with his inability to supply himself with the simple arts of cooking or creating a pleasurable home environment. He may find himself unable to interpret his feelings, dried up in his creativity, exhausted from too much *yang* and not enough *yin*, or unable to spend time alone.

The woman who has given body and soul to her marriage and family may find at midlife that she has never lived for herself. She may have always followed in another's footsteps and kept her feelings within, harmoniously blending with the needs of others around her without regard for her own destiny. She has carried the archetypal feminine selflessly, but she may feel helpless and lost when it comes to striking out on her own when the children leave home and no longer define her as mother. Her husband, who has worked hard in the world to provide for her needs, may be shocked when she wants to leave him, but her need to develop her own animus may be impossible within the rigid context of her marriage. She now must learn to carry both archetypes within herself.

Though we may wish it were possible, no one else can live our unlived lives for us. Our partners never do it right and we soon find ourselves criticizing them and complaining. "If only you'd do this; if only you didn't do that." If the masculine and feminine archetypes are repressed within us, their qualities will seem very mysterious or even undesirable. We are challenged to reclaim them rather than look once again for someone to live them for us while we remain incomplete. When the anima and animus have been equally developed, our relationships have stability, mutual respect, and freedom.

RELATIONSHIPS WITH OTHERS

Nowhere is the concept of balance more important than in the success of our personal relationships. If there is a recurrent cry from couples struggling through the labyrinth of conflicted relationship, it is that they lack balance with their significant other. One partner is too distant while another feels suffocated. One partner does too much housework while the other is resentful about unequal financial earnings. One partner wants sex more than the other, initiates all the communication, or does all the emotional work. Take a moment to consider what is out of balance in your own relationship.

> Love alone is capable of uniting living beings in such a way as to complete and fulfill them, for it alone takes them and joins them by what is deepest in themselves. . . . And if that is what it can achieve daily on a small scale, why should it not repeat this one day on world-wide dimensions?
>
> PIERRE TEILHARD DE CHARDIN

Nature seeks balance. Lack of balance is experienced as pressure, frustration, and stress, leading to resentment and an erosion of openness and goodwill. If the relationship cannot eventually find an equitable balance, it is doomed to failure either through termination or resigned misery.

The following are some of the areas in which the heart seeks balance. It must be added, however, that balance is not static. It is a constantly fluctuating homeostasis, a dynamic flexibility of give-and-take that balances over time in many different ways.

REACHING OUT AND TAKING IN

As the third chakra involves mastering the energetic principles of *holding on and letting go*, the fourth chakra works with *reaching out and taking in*. Fear and grief block either or both of these responses, and can eventually block the heart chakra itself. If the heart chakra is blocked, then the arms will be blocked as well. They may habitually fold over the chest, be bound at the sides, or move awkwardly and self-consciously. If the chest is full or inflated, there may be a refusal to reach out, a fear of surrender, perhaps even a bit of narcissism, or the holding up of the Challenger-Defender structure (see page 23, Challenger-Defender Character). If the arms are weak and move aimlessly and the chest is collapsed (as in the Oral structure), then it indicates an inability to take in and nourish oneself. Reaching may have become blocked because it proved fruitless in the past.

> The ideal situation for really understanding another is not so much how a person reacts to extreme stress, but rather how he or she suffers the vulnerability of falling in love.
>
> ALDO CARATENUTO

It is easier for the child to stop reaching altogether than to reach and find emptiness. In this scenario, however, the energetic structure of the chakra gets built around that emptiness. They reach out to give, but cannot receive. The chakra is deficient.

More often, one movement will be more prevalent than the other. I often ask couples to close their eyes and express through body language the predominant energetic process of their relationship. After they have taken their positions, I ask them to open their eyes and see what each is doing. Often one will be leaning forward, arms outstretched, while the other is leaning slightly backward, with arms folded or palms facing their partner as if to hold them back. With wordless wisdom, this indicates the dynamics of the relationship.

When David and Julie did this exercise, it was clear that Julie did the reaching and David pulled back. His arms folded neatly over his chest; he stood firmly and proudly in his ground, while Julie beckoned openly to him. David's own mother had been deceptively sweet, smothering him with a love that masked her own needs. As a result, he had become mistrustful and defensive in his heart chakra. He was unable to take in the love Julie was offering, mistrusting her intentions. I asked him to open his arms and Julie to drop hers by her side, so they could experience the possibility of a different dynamic with different feelings. David felt relieved of the burden of having to defend. Julie could feel that it was possible to receive without demanding. This is the age-old dance of the pursuer and the distancer. When the pursuer stops chasing, the distancer can reach out.

For Kathy it was a matter of changing old patterns. Kathy had been nursing a broken heart from a former relationship with months of deep grieving. As springtime approached, she began a new relationship with another woman in which she was finding a profound sweetness. Yet along with the excitement of falling in love again, she was also gripped with fear. "My last two relationships ended abominably. How do I know this won't happen again? I'm terrified!"

I asked her to focus on the sweetness she had been describing in her new relationship and feel what happened in her body as she did so. "I feel like swooning. I get dizzy and light. It's the falling of falling in love." I asked her to stand and let her body express this feeling of swooning and show what it looked like, while another group member stood in for her lover. Suddenly, she was no longer in her own ground but falling toward the other woman, out of balance and out of control. She had left her own center. No wonder she was terrified!

Her concept of love was based on moving toward the other person, with a focus on the surrendering and reaching out. While this is an essential element in any relationship, it was clear that she was missing *the concept of her lover moving toward her*. She tried to assure herself that the other person was trustworthy (something we can never fully depend upon) so she could let go and surrender. But that very act of surrender was an abandonment of her own self and a recipe for eventual disaster. I had her practice pulling her lover in toward herself while holding her own ground. Only then could we move toward a mutual reaching, in which both people were centered and open to each other.

ATTACHMENT AND FREEDOM

Thomas Moore, in his book *Soul Mates*, talks about the struggle between the soul's need for attachment and the spirit's need for freedom. This struggle is a major theme in most relationships, enacted through the simultaneous longing and fear of commitment.

In the heart chakra, we seek to balance the lower chakras' pull for security with the upper chakras' pull toward novelty. When our partner constricts us, we get restless and want to push away. The spirit hates constriction and limitation, hates to be squashed.

Attachment and freedom
is the way we experience
the universal forces in their
holding on and letting go.

The soul, however, finds security in the body, in familiarity and permanence. The soul likes a container, which allows the energy to build, whereas the spirit might resent it. When our partner is pulling away, the soul becomes insecure and wants to hold on. When our partner clings, the spirit feels restless and confined. A healthy relationship needs to honor both the upward and downward movements of energy and create a balance between spirit and soul, expansion and constriction, freedom and commitment.

Moore states it plainly: "Many people seem to live the pain of togetherness and fantasize the joys of separateness; or, vice versa, they live a life of solitude and fill their heads with alluring images of intimacy. Bouncing back and forth between these two valid claims on the heart can be a frustrating, endless struggle that never bears fruit and never settles down."[5]

To decide upon one or the other is to further the divorce between the transcendence of the Father and the immanence of the Mother. As children of divorce, we search for refuge in one or the other, ignorant of the dynamic balance that serves both liberation and manifestation.

The more we allow one kind of energy, the more the other can come through. Once a commitment is made, it is easier to allow a partner their solitude or freedom. Once we know our freedom is respected, we can more easily make a commitment. Conversely, the more a partner insists on one aspect, the more his lover will yearn for its opposite. Dynamic balance is a dance between attachment and freedom.

EROS AND THANATOS

One of the hardest dynamics to accept in the realm of love and relationships is the dance between Eros, the force of life that allures and unites, and Thanatos, the force of death that divides and destroys. Eros is the son of Aphrodite, shining goddess of love and beauty, while Thanatos, born of the goddess Night, thrives on the darkness of our lack of consciousness.

When we enter into a relationship, we are joyfully swept up in the wings of Eros. We are called forth, beckoned into union, into merging and dissolving. Reaching beyond ourselves, beyond our own small ego, we touch something greater, wider, deeper. We are thrilled and expanded. This is what we long for, what we aspire to, what makes living worthwhile.

It is that which hides in the darkness of the unconscious that brings death to love. Our unconscious patterns sabotage relationships, pick fights, distance ourselves from our lover, and thrust our behavior in directions the conscious mind deplores. Our partner's lack of consciousness annoys us, and makes us want to pull away. Our own failed awareness misses those cues to our partner's needs, and we wake up one morning to the sight of our beloved standing with bags packed, saying, "It's over." It is then that we stare squarely in the face of Thanatos. Like Eros, Thanatos is a force we cannot control, one that leaves us feeling helpless.

It is not possible to have Eros without Thanatos. This does not mean that all relationships must end in tragedy, but that coming together and pulling apart are two inseparable steps in a single dance. For those who want only the coming together, Thanatos becomes extreme in his insistence. For those who honor the separation, the distancing, the misunderstandings, and estrangements as part of the flow and growth of relationships, the dance of Eros can be eternally renewed.

> To love means to open ourselves to the negative as well as the positive—to grief, sorrow, and disappointment as well as to joy, fulfillment and an intensity of consciousness we did not know was possible before.
>
> ROLLO MAY

Those who are most idealistic about love sometimes find the greatest pain. Wide-eyed they fall, giving their utmost to the beloved. Great is their dismay, when, giving all they could and valuing this love above all things, they see their lover casually mistreat what they had regarded as sacred. Denial of Thanatos invites his more unpleasant form to appear.

We can avoid the painful side of Thanatos *if* we remember to honor his presence. We must be aware of what lurks in the darkness of our unacknowledged shadow. We need to claim, not deny, our need for a certain amount of separateness, our fear of engulfment, and understand that the same fear in our partner is not a statement about us, but Thanatos's need to balance the relationship so Eros can continue the dance of love and attraction.

GRIEF: DEMON OF THE HEART

When Thanatos strikes, as it inevitably does, we experience grief. As the resident demon, grief sits on the heart chakra like a stone. When our heart is heavy with grief, it's hard to open, even hard to breathe. When grief is denied, we become numb to our feelings and our aliveness. We become hard and cold, rigid and distant. We may feel dead inside. When grief is acknowledged and expressed, however, we find a vital key to opening the heart. Tears are shed, truth expressed, and the heart lightens. The breath deepens. There is a sense of spaciousness that emerges, allowing more room inside for our spirit. Hope is reborn. Coming to terms with our own grief leads us toward compassion for others.

> Give sorrow words; the grief that does not speak whispers the o'er-fraught heart and bids it break.
>
> WILLIAM SHAKESPEARE

When we fall in love, we strip ourselves of defenses. We open to another and to the world. We expand and grow. When we are hurt in matters of love, we are hurt in our most vulnerable, trusting aspects. The purest form of self is wounded. It no longer seems safe to be authentic. Our system—wounded at the very core—shuts down and we lose not only our lover but ourselves as well. This is the deepest loss.

One of my clients called while I was working on this chapter. Her voice on the phone was shaky and tearful. "I know it's over, I just know it. He's going to leave me." I remembered that she had said this two weeks ago when I last saw her, and again two weeks before that.

"You mean it's still going?" I asked.

"Yes, and he even wants to come to therapy with me, but I know it's over. He just doesn't know how to say it. Why does this always happen to me? I feel so lost right now, like I hate myself. I just want to disappear."

"Then you're abandoning yourself," I say. "It's not that he has abandoned you, necessarily, but that you have abandoned yourself over the thought of it. So, of course, you'll think he'll abandon you, too."

There was sudden calm on the other end of the phone. "Oh," she said. "I get it. You know I haven't eaten yet today, or taken a shower. I've just been obsessing about this. What should I do?"

"Go inside to the self that's scared right now. Promise her you'll always be there. Fix her a nice lunch. Go take a shower. You can't control your boyfriend, but you can promise to be there yourself. That goes a long way."

When I saw her next it was, indeed, with her boyfriend. He had not left her, nor was he planning to. Instead he was trying to assure her of his ongoing commitment. She appeared less clinging, and we were able to facilitate some valuable communication.

Grief that occurs at the end of a relationship is easy to understand. It puts us back in touch with our primal abandonment, and makes us feel powerless. If acknowledged and expressed, it eventually passes, but sometimes we carry grief from situations that are not so obvious, as in the case of Susan.

Susan had a mother who loved her too much. She was an only child and her mother had little else to occupy her life besides being Susan's mother. Susan felt special and was never alone. She lacked for nothing in terms of attention, clothing, or toys. Yet Susan was not allowed her own independence. Her mother was subtly threatened when she played at friends' houses and later when she began to date. Susan's definition of love was shaped by her mother. When she did form relationships later in life, she was as smothering and possessive as her mother had been. When her partner did not lavish the same amount of attention on her, she felt unloved. While we might assume that Susan would grow up secure and confident, in actuality, she feared she was not enough and became quite codependent. She could never replace her mother's real needs for an authentic life, and so she always felt inadequate.

Susan thought she had had a happy childhood. But her chest was constricted and she was frequently depressed. As she learned to breathe more deeply, she contacted a vast reservoir of grief. At first she did not understand why it was there, but as she continued her grieving process, she recognized through her deeper self that the grief she carried was a mourning for the loss of her own authenticity.

If we consider that love may indeed be the most important element of well-being and spiritual growth, then any impairment in our ability to find love is a profound wound. When we further consider that this impairment affects how we treat each other in the larger social sphere, we have not only a personal problem, but a serious collective situation as well. Where grief is the wound, compassion is the healer.

COMPASSION

Compassion means "to have passion with." In the second chakra we encountered passion in the realm of feelings, through the desires of the soul reaching forward to meet its own needs. In the heart chakra, we now reach beyond ourselves and expand that passion to include an understanding of another's needs. The ego, when secure in its own autonomy and power, can now surrender willingly toward altruism. If our own needs have been met and satisfied, we can now share our fullness with another.

> Great compassion penetrates into the marrow of the bone. It is the support of all living beings. Like the love of a parent for an only child, the tenderness of the Compassionate One is all-pervasive.
>
> NAGARJUNA
> (INDIAN, FIRST CENTURY)

The ability to have compassion for others depends first on our ability to be in touch with our yearnings and pain. Pain opens us to deeper understanding of others and expands our own limited being. Thus compassion is an exquisite balance of upper and lower chakra expression. Compassion remains centered, yet open, and it quietly holds the space for change to occur, providing both the stability of a container and the freedom of release.

Compassion does not mean that we have to fix things. Most of the time, we can't, but rather than turn away we can still offer compassion to others. When I work with couples, I often see that one partner wants compassion while the other feels a demand to make it different. "I just want you to realize how hard it is for me to be alone with the kids all day," she says.

> Whoever wishes to attain Buddhahood need not follow the various practice but must only practice one thing and that is deep compassion.
>
> CHENREZIG

"What do you want me to do, quit my job?" he replies impatiently.

She looks hurt and frustrated, as that is not what she meant. What she wanted was empathy and understanding, not necessarily solutions. She wanted to hear, "I know this is hard for you. I appreciate the work you're doing." When we can't fix something, it's even more important to offer compassion.

DEVOTION

Devotion is an act of selfless love and conscious surrender to a greater force beyond oneself. In the many branches of yoga, it is the path of bhakti yoga, practiced through devotional service to a deity or teacher, through which one experiences the transcendent joy of merging with the divine. Devotion also occurs toward the beloved, within a family, or to a political cause or project. With devotion we are allowing the energy within the Self to flow beyond the Self. This transcends our perceived limitations. When we become parents, we experience selfless devotion to the newborn child as we transcend the limits of what we thought was possible in terms of loving and giving.

If everyone were perfect, there would be no need for love.

Devotion is a spiritual act of egoless surrender. When the Self binds the spirit too tightly, then devotion expands the binding by lifting us beyond ourselves. We get the powerful lesson that the Self survives even without constant attention.

Devotion can also keep us from conscious connection with the Self, especially if the ego-based stage of reflective consciousness has not already been achieved. We may find it easier to be directed by the will of another than to work through the labyrinth of our own inner yearnings. In this case, devotion depletes the ego-centered third chakra for the purpose of an excessive outpouring in the fourth. If the object of our worship should leave, fall from grace, or reject us, we are devastated. To heal, we must then reconnect responsibly to the self within, seeing it as an aspect of divinity in its own right, and much in need of love and understanding. When balanced, our devotional work becomes even deeper.

GROWING THE LOTUS

DEVELOPMENTAL FORMATION OF
THE HEART CHAKRA AT A GLANCE

AGE

4 to 7 years

TASKS

Formation of social identity and gender roles
Development of altruism
Formation of peer relationships

NEEDS AND ISSUES

Initiative vs. guilt
Love vs. rejection
Social acceptance
Self-acceptance

When Alex was about five, he came down with a stomach flu that kept him in bed for a few days. As he was sick to his stomach, I was not about to force him to eat, but wanted him to have nourishment if he wanted it. So I prepared some toast, left it on a plate next to his bed, and tucked him in with his teddy bear. He soon recovered and the incident was forgotten. A few weeks later, when I was taking an afternoon nap, I woke to find a plate of awkwardly buttered toast placed on my night table and a teddy bear on the pillow next to me. This was a true sign he was in the heart chakra stage.

> It is not so much the parent alone that is internalized, as it is the relationship between the parent and the child.
>
> KEN WILBER

The fourth chakra developmental stage begins when the child moves from the intense egocentricity and willfulness of the third chakra into a readiness to meet and cooperate with others. This generally begins between three and four years, after autonomy and basic impulse control have been established. It may happen suddenly, when the seemingly impossible child spontaneously does something sweet and kind for someone else. A child may also swing back to stubborn willfulness at three-and-a-half before finally moving on to the more loving and harmonious heart chakra stage at around four years. In the uncertainty of new behavior, a child often runs back to familiar patterns for security. Development is not always smooth.

As we climb further up the chakras, the exact timing of the developmental stages becomes less specific. It depends in part on the successful resolution of previous stages, which varies from case to case, and the variations widen as we get higher. Unfortunately, many people do not reach the upper chakra stages at all, or do so only later in life. Therefore, we will now begin to discuss both childhood and adult development.

In childhood, fourth chakra development marks the formation of our *social identity*, also known as the persona. This is the aspect of self that we create to win love, gain social approval, and get along in the larger world. In the fourth chakra we no longer see the world entirely in terms of our own needs, and so our relationships expand from being specifically one-on-one (i.e., child and mother, child and father) to include larger family and social structures. The child now finds that she is part of Mommy and Daddy's relationship with each other, and that she has brothers and sisters, classmates, neighbors, and friends of her own.

The verbal messages that were internalized during the third chakra stage centered around action and behavior. Now in the fourth chakra stage it is the parent-child relationship itself that becomes internalized. It is not only the messages Dad continually gives us about being noisy in the house, but also the context of Dad's relationship with us that becomes important. If the message was given in the context of fear, we feel fear along with the internalized message. How we behave and who we become is shaped by the way we internalize our basic family relationships.

Eric Berne outlined these internal relationships in his theories of transactional analysis, which describes how we operate from internalized parent, adult, or child scripts. If we rebel against Dad's messages, we are playing the script of the naughty child with a critical parent, and aspects of it become part of our internal dialogue. Throughout life, we may find both roles simultaneously clamoring for the driver's seat, as sometimes we will be led by rebellious urges, while at others we will be held back by our inner critic. We also repeat these relationships with others. If a friend criticizes you, they may suddenly become your critical parent. Then you find yourself reacting like a naughty child, instead of listening to what they have to say.

Children internalize relationships by *imitation*. A child who is frequently scolded may be overheard scolding her doll or best friend. Alex was imitating his mother when he brought me the toast. This imitation is called *identification*, and forms the core of the relationship program. Identification is where the child adopts the beliefs, attitudes, values, and behaviors of others, and then carries these attitudes into her relationships.

As gender roles get internalized, we develop our gender identification. Watching how parents, brothers, or sisters behave gives us our first models of how to be boys or girls. As we watch our big sister play with dolls or put on makeup, watch our brother play with trains or lizards, watch our mother give herself over to the needs of the family, and see our father relentlessly pursue his career, we are, for better or worse, developing gender-oriented behavior programs.

It is here that we take on gender roles. This is the age where boys are told not to cry and when girls are told to be nice. This splitting and repression of masculine or feminine comes to the fore again in midlife, when our one-sided development leads us into some kind of personal crisis. As stated earlier, heart chakra work includes the reintegration of anima and animus.

The child internalizes not only the relationship he has with his parents but also the entire family system. He may become an eldest child with new siblings, removed from the center of attention he once held. He may realize he is the youngest of many siblings, and learn his social identity from the way his brothers and sisters treat him. Or he may be the middle child that has to compete for attention. These dynamics took a backseat in the "it's all about me" stage of the third chakra, but emerge as part of the personality at chakra four. We then play out this family dynamic in the social arenas of school, work, clubs, and the families we form as adults. As the growing child joins the family dynamic, he takes on roles such as that of the good child, scapegoat, hero, clown, or lost child, to name but a few. These roles are like steps in a dance, unconscious patterns that form our social identities. What may begin as the conscious cultivation of a certain behavior ("Mommy likes it when I make her laugh") may grow into a lifelong role (playing the clown).

The development of a social identity prepares the child for more complex interaction with the larger world. This requires a delicate balance between maintaining and relinquishing autonomy, which should have developed in the third chakra. For the child whose autonomy is weak, there is a tendency to be swept away by others, be defined by them, or live in fear of losing the self. A kindergartner may steal someone else's cookies simply because his friend told him to, not realizing it was not his own urge until he gets in trouble for it. Then he says, "Billy told me to!" A child whose will was overly indulged may be too self-centered and may get rejected by others, such as the school bully who dominates the younger children or the egocentric classmate who always steals the center of attention.

Intellectual development also takes a monumental leap at this stage. We have entered Piaget's *preoperational period* where "intellectual development proceeds in the conceptual-symbolic rather than the earlier sensory-motor arena."[6] Having mastered the basic building blocks of language, the child now begins the task of assembling the many pieces of his experience. The child is interested in relationships not only between people, but among all the components of the world around him. He is learning to assemble raw information into larger concepts that dictate behavior. Instead of using helpfulness as a way to get a cookie, he realizes that helpfulness is a good concept. He then wants recognition for his intentions as opposed to his act. This is the *good boy/nice girl* stage of moral development described by Lawrence Kohlberg. The child is creating himself by incorporating new concepts into his growing personality.

Routines are sets of relationships. Children at this age often get upset when standard routines are disrupted—when someone sits at their place at the table, when taking a bath occurs before dinner instead of after, or when stability in the household is disrupted. The introduction of stepparents, other siblings, new households, or changes in the daily routine of school or day care can be especially disruptive at this stage. Security and identity are derived from stable relationships. When those relationships end or are threatened, as through divorce, death, or separation, then the sense of security and developing social identity can be threatened. The internalized relationship with ourselves is simultaneously affected. If we lose one of our parents, for example, we do not get to see how the two genders interact with each other, and hence may not have that balance in ourselves. (With some marriages, however, this may be a blessing.)

Finally, this is the age when peer relationships begin developing. A child enters school, chooses friends, and tries out these behavior programs in the world outside the family. The child learns whether she is well-liked or rejected, and thus her social identity gets added on to her ego identity as a new basis for self-esteem. It is interesting that the most common time for imaginary playmates occurs between ages four and six, as if this were a practice realm for real relationships.

Since relationships are the formative ground for fourth chakra development, it is important to ask some basic questions. Do relationships in the family depend on aggressive fighting for one's rights? Do they depend on giving up oneself to avoid punishment or rejection? Do they involve the expression of emotions and affection, or do the parents hide this aspect of their own relationship? Is communication modeled so that the child sees how problems get worked through, or is the rule to not talk about anything difficult? Does one parent dominate the other, or is there a sense of cooperative partnership? Are brothers and sisters given equal attention or is there favoritism, and, if so, on what is it based? Most of all—is there consistency in relationships? Is Daddy warm and giving on some days and cruelly abusive on others? These are the elements that teach the child how to behave in the world.

Erikson has described this stage as being the struggle of *initiative vs. guilt*, building on the previous stage of *autonomy vs. shame*. Autonomy gives rise to initiative in the form of reaching out toward others. Shame inhibits this reaching out, and inhibits the awakening of the heart chakra. If the child lacks initiative, she is dependent upon the reactions of others, and will play a passive role in relationships. Successful handling of this stage, according to Erikson, results in *direction and purpose*.

Socialization is where an individual acquires behavior patterns, motivations, attitudes, and values that the culture deems important. In our current social structure, this process requires that we deny many aspects of our lower chakras. To be properly socialized, the child needs to learn to control or rise above her spontaneous aggressive urges, dependencies, and fears. For males, this may also include the emotions in general. Thus the social identity often develops at the cost of previous identities. For the child whose social identity is about pleasing others, for example, the cost may be a denial of her own needs. The lost child who hides in the background denies his need for attention. Loss of contact with the original ground creates a kind of existential emptiness that then gets projected onto relationships. We end up looking to others for security, emotional fulfillment, or ego enhancement because we have denied these things within ourselves.

Between chakras three and four, the child may get the message that autonomy and love are an either-or phenomenon. This is particularly true when conditional love is used to modify behavior. Johnny soon learns what behavior pleases Mommy and what aspects of himself meet with rejection. "Mommy ignores me when I cry. She holds me when I'm quiet." We grow up believing we can either be ourselves or we can be loved, and think it is impossible to have both at once.

The appropriate completion of our social identity results in a transcendence of the ego without undue sacrifice of autonomy. The child can identify with others as equally important as the self and has the ability to cooperate with family, friends, and the larger social environment.

Every functioning adult has reached at least some basic level of ego development. Still, there are many adults who have not yet made a transition to the fourth chakra. They remain stuck in the narcissistic ego-gratification of the third chakra even in their close relationships, and have difficulty experiencing true empathy and altruism. Crises that appear in midlife (usually through the pain of failed relationships) often reveal wounds from early childhood. These lower chakra wounds can then be healed, which allows the heart chakra to open. In these cases fourth chakra development may occur in midlife, as we enter the integrative phase of our adult individuation process.

The parts of us that get ignored or outwardly rejected retreat to the realm of the unconscious. They become part of the shadow, split off from the persona. The persona is made of aspects that bring us love, while the shadow, those that seem unacceptable. As adults, part of our fourth chakra work is to reunite the persona with the rejected shadow for the purpose of balance and wholeness.

Adult development of the heart chakra results in a transcendence of the ego, an integration of the higher and lower chakras, creation of the sacred marriage of masculine and feminine, and development of social empathy and altruism. It is the achievement of balance within, as we integrate our many subpersonalities, and the expression of that balance through our relationships with others. Indeed, the fourth chakra is the gateway to spiritual fulfillment and personal mastery. Its reward is self-acceptance and self-love.

TRAUMAS AND ABUSES

There is nothing more devastating than lack of love. Love is the primal glue of the universe, the binding force par excellence. As the central integrating chamber, the heart chakra is the healer, the unifier. Love integrates and lack of love disintegrates. Without love to bind us together, we separate from the parts of ourselves that drive love away. We reject the needy parts, the angry parts, the ugly parts. Then we are no longer whole.

> Thus children…are confronted by a tormenter they love, not one they hate, and this tragic complication will have a devastating influence on their entire subsequent life.
>
> ALICE MILLER

All abuses traumatize the heart chakra as they betray love. Most of these abuses occur within the context of family relationships. It is bad enough that they happen, but worse still that they happen at the hands of people we love, people we live with, people we need to trust. So we suffer not only the abuse, but also a distortion of the relationship in which it occurs.

We shut down the connection, close off the heart, and pull back into ourselves.

When primary relationships distort, we diminish our ability to love and connect—to become *relational*. To be relational means, simply, that we are able to relate or can align our own experiences to a larger context outside. In relating, we connect to things, and see how they are connected to each other. So many of my clients, women in particular, complain about the lack of energy their partners put into their relationships. Their men, they say, act as if they live in a world of their own where the relationship is an afterthought or something they take for granted. These men (and it happens to women, too) see relationships as things rather than as living processes. Their capacity to be relational is underdeveloped.

When relationships are distorted, so is our sense of how things connect. Seeing the bigger picture—the context in which life is embedded—becomes impaired. This prevents us from rising into a larger sense of our own being.

A young child is an open, unarmored being who is completely dependent on his caretakers. In this state, the child is an uninhibited channel of love for those who care for him. His first understanding of love comes from the fulfillment of his survival and dependency needs—that he is cared for, attended to, and safe. When he is mirrored and nurtured, and when his autonomy is supported, he is also being loved. If all has gone well, a good foundation for dependent love has been built by the time the child reaches the fourth chakra stage. They perceive the parents as the ones to whom they relate for their personal needs and who help them understand the complex world around them.

It is literally heartbreaking when the trust and love that a child has for his caretakers is used against him. In adult relationships, we have the choice (perceived or not) to get up and leave when someone mistreats us; a child does not have this choice. A child does not even have the choice not to love.

The effects of this mistreatment occur simultaneously on three levels:

1. The experience of the abuse, which may create traumas that distort the natural development of the body and psyche in any of the chakras.

2. The interpretation of the abuse, which is usually attributed to our own shortcomings, as opposed to those of our parents.

3. The fusion of the abuse with love, where the two become related to each other, inseparably linked. This link perpetuates abuse in adult relationships.

If a child is attended to superficially but not touched or given specific attention, then his love for others will be equally superficial. He suffers physically from the lack of touch; emotionally, from feelings of shame; and conceptually, from a distorted concept of love. If a father sexually abuses his daughter who loves and trusts him, he is teaching her a distorted form of relating where there is no respect for boundaries. Adult survivors of such abuse often feel disembodied, have poor boundaries in their love relationships, and may define their worth in sexual terms. If a child is ignored or shamed by the very people who are most important in her life, then she internalizes that distortion in his relationship to herself. Her own internal voice will carry that criticism, and keep her in a state of utter worthlessness. In relationships with others, she will find people who will corroborate that worthlessness and perpetuate the cycle.

Any form of abuse impacts these three levels: the developmental process, our self-esteem, and relationship to others. Each of these levels will be discussed in more detail below.

THE ABUSE ITSELF

I worked with a woman who had been adopted by an aunt after her parents were suddenly killed in World War II. Her aunt constantly compared her to her natural children. "Why don't you do as well in school as your sister? You must be stupid! Why are you so lazy compared to your brother? What's wrong with you?" Even though she was cared for superficially, the original trauma of losing her parents was never addressed, leaving her at a disadvantage. There was no time to heal or repair developmental gaps before moving on to later stages. Of course, she could not compete with siblings who had not had such traumas.

> All abusive relationships teach a form of love.
>
> JOHN BRADSHAW

Abuse is the antithesis of love. If we do not get the love we need, we lack the basic ingredient necessary to assemble ourselves. Abuse of any kind undermines the natural developmental process as it interferes with the internal wiring of the physical, emotional, and psychic system. If this happened in our stereo, we would have irregular volume control, distorted sound quality, or static interference. When it happens in the psyche, we feel like defective merchandise—our fine-tuning is out of kilter.

Abuse interferes with our love of life. If life hurts, or is lonely, rejecting, empty, hostile, or dangerous, then we do not want to relate to it. Life becomes a painful experience, a process to be endured. We no longer love being alive; we no longer meet life with hope and enthusiasm. We become withdrawn, depressed, blocked. The natural flow of energy can no longer move forward.

Loss of Self-Love

Since we usually identify with our caretakers and their values, the way they treat us teaches us about our value as human beings. We take on their attitudes toward us. Abuse makes us feel unlovable, and feeling defective only adds to our shame. We become an object to ourselves, even an object of contempt. Unlovable, we are no longer in touch with our divinity, our specialness, our validity as human beings. Convinced that the fault lies in some intrinsic flaw, to which we are blind and helpless, we abandon ourselves.

Without relationship to the self, reflective consciousness is impossible. We are cut adrift, disconnected from our ground, lost and lonely, and end up seeking our ground through another. They become our reality, and the weight we impose upon them—the weight of our own self-denial—usually drives them away. We then lose all the energy we have invested in them, including pieces of ourselves. "I gave her everything! How could she possibly leave me?" When we give everything, we are bankrupting ourselves. We lack a center to which others can be attracted because, quite simply, no one is home. There is no one inside us to love because we have given ourselves away.

INTERNALIZED RELATIONSHIPS

Internalized relationships form archetypal components of our psyche. Our relationship to our mother comes to represent more than how we feel about Mom, it affects how we understand the archetypal symbol of Mother as well as the feminine in general. If our mother mistreated us, our internal relationship to the feminine and all it represents will be impaired. If she withheld these qualities, we will expect them to be withheld everywhere, even by men. If she used them as a means for control, we will fear being controlled by our need for them. As we project this impairment on the women we meet in life, we find that we are relating more to our damaged internal image of the feminine than to the actual women we meet. Our anger, expectations, defenses, and needs all get woven into the relationship and may get tangled with our partner's internal framework, which may also be just as damaged. This is grounds for a mess indeed! Then we have two people relating from their wounds and defenses, rather than from their wholeness. They see their own projections, rather than each other. Unfortunately, this is frequently par for the course.

All acts of abuse occur within the context of relationship. Relationship thus becomes the field in which all events are interpreted, and the ground in which they are later internalized.

The way our father treated us affects our relationship with all men as well as our internal masculine. How we relate to the masculine qualities of aggression, authority, logic, or initiative, and how we project these qualities onto men have major consequences for our relationships.[7] Often we pick the same kind of person as our parent yet expect different results.

Larinda had always admired her father for his successful career and his hardworking, selfless attitudes toward the family. She defended him when her mother would complain about how he was never home, or how he didn't spend much time with the children. Larinda married a man she admired for these same qualities and soon found herself a widow to workaholism, alone with her children with no one to talk to. As she had rejected her mother's feelings, she also denied her own feelings. In compensation for that denial she turned to alcohol. When she finally dealt with her alcoholism, she was forced to confront both her unmet needs as a child and the way her image of her father had masked her feelings of abandonment.

Harville Hendrix, in his best-selling book *Getting the Love You Want*, calls the internalized relationship with our mother or father an *imago*. The imago is a "composite picture of the people who have influenced you most strongly at an early age."[8] This image is not formed in the conscious mind but is like a template etched into the nervous system over years of constant interaction with our family. It programs our reactions, defenses, behaviors, and interpretations of events. It becomes part of our character armor, part of our personality.

Our relationship to internalized archetypal forces defines our relationship to the world. Whether we approach the world from a place of responsibility or rebellion, from expecting acceptance or rejection, all this remains part of our relationship program. The initial imprint shaping this program is the family. Only by unraveling these primary relationships can we hope to find the self-reflective consciousness necessary to break the habitual patterns and create new and productive relationships.

Our current relationships always provide the training ground for this process. They put us on the cutting edge of our growth, for who but our intimate partner knows best our hopes and fears, strengths and weaknesses? Who but our partner bears the brunt of our expectations and angers, our projections and manipulations? Who but our partner is the best mirror for our growth?

The heart chakra is about bonding. Unintegrated parts of ourselves that are not bonded into the heart with love will seek bonding elsewhere. Our shamed little child may bond with our partner's critical parent, and constantly recreate a dynamic that keeps us feeling worthless. Our rejected anger may seek someone who carries a temper, giving us ample opportunities to reclaim this lost piece of ourselves. Our various selves seek bonds that are permanent.

Unfortunately, bonding patterns are not always fun. We can become trapped in them, oppressed by them. We lose the freshness of seeing our partner as who they really are, and instead see only the critical parent, needy child, or rejecting aspect of their personality. The only way to break these patterns is to become conscious of these relationships within ourselves—to listen, discover, and honor the many aspects of our inner complexity.

TWISTED CONCEPTS OF LOVE

Conflicted relationships skew our conception of love. Since the child is so dependent, there is no room in the child's mind for the contradiction between love and abuse. To keep their world consistent, children deny the effects of abuse or convince themselves that they deserve it. Even acts of cruelty are seen as acts of love. When a child is being spanked and told, "This hurts me as much as it hurts you. I'm only doing it because I love you," the child is given a very strange message about what love is. They equate love with pain and with mistreatment. As recipients of that love, it becomes their duty to bear the pain and not question it. Alice Miller, in her aptly named book *For Your Own Good*, describes pointedly: "When what was done to me was done for my own good, then I am expected to accept this treatment as an essential part of life and not question it."[9] This acceptance impacts the heart chakra, as well as the upper three chakras, affecting our ability to speak our truth, to see clearly, and to question in general.

> The love a child has for his or her parents ensures that their conscious or unconscious acts of mental cruelty will go undetected.
>
> ALICE MILLER

Later, in adult relationships, we may be blind to abuse from our partner. We do not fully believe we are being mistreated, carrying in our hearts the illusion of being loved. Bradshaw has named this the *fantasy bond*. It is an illusion that keeps us believing that our partner (father, mother, friend, lover) really does love us—maybe today is just a bad day, we did something wrong, or it will be better tomorrow. We know it will change if only we could do this or did not do that. We make excuses for their behavior, and continue to accept what would normally be unacceptable. As the child has an incessant need to feel loved at all costs, he fantasizes a love when it is not really there.

REJECTION

No section on heart chakra traumas would be complete without a discussion of rejection. A universal experience that wounds us all, rejection is a fear that dwells at the core of the human heart. It brings people into their deepest despair, their darkest fears, and their heaviest grief. Fear of rejection is the prime reason we hold back our love and close down the heart chakra.

When rejection occurs, we often feel helpless. Our self-esteem plummets, our feelings mire us in unfathomable depression, and our body aches with longing. We think we cannot live, and indeed, the urge to kill oneself over the loss of love is a universal theme that has plagued people for as long as the force of love has ruled our hearts.

> At the moment of betrayal a wound is opened in our most vulnerable spot—our original trust—which is that of a totally defenseless infant who cannot survive in the world except in someone's arms.
>
> ALDO CARATENUTO

Rejection says we are unworthy and magnifies our basic shame to whatever degree we carry it. It turns us against ourselves, creating what is perhaps the deepest wound of all. Why does rejection by another so profoundly affect our inner state?

For young children, rejection is equivalent to death. Without the love of parents, what guarantee is there that we will be cared for? For many, the experience of losing love triggers the infantile state of an abandoned child, a state of intolerable helplessness totally incongruent with our adult self.

A child identifies with her parents, imitating their behavior and adopting their values as she learns about life. As adults, when we love someone deeply, we also identify with them to a certain extent. We identify with their sorrows and pains, their triumphs and joys. We often share their feelings as if they were our own. When our loved one suffers, we suffer with them in our caring. The deeper we love, the more we drop the boundaries of separateness and the stronger our identification with the other.

So what happens when we get rejected? If we are still identified with the one who is rejecting us, then we adopt the same stance and reject ourselves. For the child who is identified with his parents, he will learn to devalue himself, even to hate himself. For the adult who loses his beloved, he is left not only with the loss, but also with a negative message from someone he respects saying he is flawed, unworthy, and unwanted! If the relationship has been a close one, then he has probably shared many values and is likely to buy into his lover's rejection as a statement of truth about himself. So we identify with the deserter and dis-identify with ourselves. We move against the natural self-acceptance of this chakra and move instead toward self-rejection and grief.

Some people, when rejected, get angry instead of sad. This is often a means of self-preservation, as it breaks the negative bonding and over-identification. When we say, "You lousy sonuvabitch, how could you? I didn't deserve this!" we cease to identify with the cause of our pain and stand a better chance of reidentifying with ourselves.

Sometimes, however, rejection does uncover truths we need to face. There is seldom a louder wake-up call than the actual or threatened loss of someone we love. As a force for change, it is one of the strongest, but also one of the hardest. Too much anger may obscure the powerful lessons that are presenting themselves.

It is important to differentiate between overidentification with the lover and truths we need to learn. If there are important lessons to be learned, we need to face them with an attitude of self-compassion, as there is no time when compassion is more needed than in the depths of grief. It is compassion alone that allows us to reconnect with the self and stop identifying with the parent, lover, or friend who has betrayed, rejected, or devalued us. The grief must be shed, and in that grief, connection to the core self can be made once again.

CHARACTER STRUCTURE

THE RIGID

Henry was the character type that is least likely to enter therapy. He was a good-looking, personable, and highly successful CEO in a large company. His body radiated vitality and readiness, with well-toned muscles and erect posture. Had I not been familiar with character structures, I would have wondered what he was doing there.

After a few minutes of hearing Henry speak it became apparent that his energy, though highly charged, was held in the back of his body. As I watched him move, I could see his back was slightly arched and that his arms never reached out very far in front of him when he spoke. His impressive energy was without depth, as if caught in a loop. He admitted to being a mystery to himself. He had had a long string of relationships as many women had fallen in love with him, but somehow he always grew bored and moved on. Henry was trapped in a highly charged energy system that could not open to deeper feelings. Henry's heart was blocked.

His blocked feelings were largely due to parental rejection, which began during his fourth chakra developmental period. Although originally loving and supportive, his parents suddenly expected him to grow up and chided him for his immature need for love and security. He was no longer allowed to climb on their laps, ask for hugs, or cry when he was sad. The birth of a younger sister diverted the special attention he was used to, and he was now expected to act like a man at the tender age of five. Henry remembers that on his first day in kindergarten, he was afraid to get on the school bus. He cried and clung to his mother and later that night he was deeply scorned for his childish behavior. He was told that he was too old for that sort of thing and that it would not be tolerated. In order to stop the flow of such feelings, he stiffened his body and restricted his breath. In typical military posture, he puffed up his chest and gave the appearance of confidence. His chest, however, did not expand and contract with the breath but instead became a tight container for the emotional energy that could not flow outward through the heart (see page 23, Rigid Character).

His father, also an ambitious career man, had such high expectations for him that Henry never felt like he was good enough. In high school, he was a football star and honor roll student. He had fantasies of becoming a great scientist and finally winning his father's approval. His father, however, was still distant, focused on his own work, and paid attention to Henry only long enough to tell him how he could have done better. His mother stood by silently and supported her husband in this behavior while she poured tenderness on his younger sister.

No matter what Henry did, his authentic self was rejected. Each time he tried to win approval, his heart was broken. Forced to rise above his need for love, he channeled his aggressive energy into achievement, unconsciously hoping it would win the love and recognition he craved.

But his heart had long ago been forced to close down, and even when love was forthcoming, as it often was from women, he was unable to experience the satisfaction of being enough. In fact, love given in admiration increases the feeling that there is no love for the authentic, vulnerable self. This does not bring real satisfaction or healing and so the rigid character restlessly moves on.

At the developmental period when Henry's heart would be most open and inquisitive, he was told to shut down his feelings and perform. This rejection of the true self in favor of the achieving self is what gives this character structure its more positive name of the *Achiever*. Energetically, Henry shut down both the second and fourth chakras, while squeezing his life force tightly into the third chakra ego/activity center. There it poured out into successful business activity, fueled by drive and ambition (see figure 4.2).

Rigid character types hold back energetically. They are disconnected from their shadow and therefore afraid to surrender to their own feelings. They are out of touch with their inner child, as they were not allowed to be children for very long. No matter what they achieve, they never feel they have enough and can never get to a place where they can just let things be. They are disposed to action without satisfaction, which leaves them in a constant state of frustration. Their energy is channeled into more and greater achievement until they eventually become addicted to substances (cocaine is a particular favorite for this character type) or simply burn out with exhaustion. At this point, life forces a vulnerability that can no longer be denied and healing can begin.

Healing the Achiever requires meeting the vulnerable child on his own ground and letting him feel that he is enough just as he is. Encouragement of the softer feelings with positive mirroring helps the Rigid type discover his inner emotions and enhance their flow. Helping him release the binding in the chest and express feeling with the arms unlocks the heart chakra and helps the energy descend into the ground. General techniques will be discussed in the healing section.

> Indeed, it seems a very natural state of affairs for men to have irrational moods and women irrational opinions.
>
> C. G. JUNG

THE HYSTERIC

Since men are so often robbed of their tears and vulnerability, the Rigid character pattern tends to manifest more often in men. Women, with more cultural permission to express feelings, tend toward the Hysteric character structure. The original wound is similar—rejection from the father as the child matures, lack of empathy for the child, and high expectations for performance. For the feeling/expressive type, this rejection is met with feelings that are pushed forward, most often in melodramatic exaggeration, as a way to get the attention she craves. The tendency to express emotions hysterically becomes habitual, and she may not even notice that her reactions are extreme by other people's standards. Since she craves love, she focuses heavily on family and relationships with a desire for closeness that becomes demanding and possessive, rather than accepting and inviting. The Hysteric is changeable and highly charged, but her expression is uneven and sporadic, varying from angry outbursts to pouting withdrawal.

The Hysteric has a pear-shaped body—petite and almost childlike above the waist, with larger hips and thighs (see page 23, Hysteric Character). The wound to the heart chakra is evident in the rigidity of her chest. She may have trouble breathing when triggered emotionally, which only creates panic and even more extreme emotions. Like the Rigid type, the Hysteric lives chiefly in her persona without realizing that she is forfeiting authenticity. She feels most authentic when expressing strong emotions, as this is the way her psyche balances the habitual inhibition of the core self. Thus she identifies chiefly with her social and emotional identities, creating excess in chakra two.

On the positive side, Hysterics can be caring and supportive when their needs are met, and charming in social situations. Some find their unpredictable nature exciting. Like the Rigid type, they are highly charged and seem very alive (see figure 4.3).

Both the Hysteric and the Rigid/Achiever have developed the ability to close down their heart chakra rapidly and at will. Indeed, the heart only opens tentatively for short, intense periods, as exceptions to its basic distrustful state. They long for closeness, but feeling inadequate they fear that intimacy will reveal their shortcomings. They are usually charming and

FIGURE 4.2. RIGID CHARACTER STRUCTURE (THE ACHIEVER)
THE HURRIED CHILD

FIRST CHAKRA Solid, balanced	SECOND CHAKRA Deficient	THIRD CHAKRA Excessive	FOURTH CHAKRA Deficient
Usually has good body tone and weight balance	Fears surrendering to emotions	Child given premature responsibility, high expectations	Feels unaccepted
Good contact with reality	Unaware of own needs	Strives for perfection	Needs achievement to feel deserving of love
Hardworking	Fears intimacy	Competitive	Longs for tenderness, but has difficulty admitting it
Often prosperous	Holds back impulses to reach out	Agressive, easily angered	Needs father approval
	Difficulty relaxing	Controlled, disciplined, proud	Approval equated with love
	Unanswered wanting as a child	Takes refuge in work	Heart opens and closes rapidly
		High ego needs	Afraid of involvement, commitment
		Defensive, on guard	
		Feels opposed and challenged	

FIFTH CHAKRA Balanced	SIXTH CHAKRA May be either	SEVENTH CHAKRA Balanced overall
Strong verbally	Sixth chakra is often irrelevant, interest is in pragmatic accomplishments	More pragmatic than spiritually inclined, but longs for spiritual connection
Voice may be thin or controlled	May delight in logical abstractions, symbols, dreams, but not think of them on their own	Intelligent
Defensive verbally		Rational
Expressive, but not of inner emotions		Logical

FIGURE 4.3. HYSTERIC CHARACTER STRUCTURE (EXPRESSIVE)
THE HURRIED CHILD

FIRST CHAKRA Solid, balanced	SECOND CHAKRA Excessive	THIRD CHAKRA Excessive	FOURTH CHAKRA Deficient
Usually has good body tone and weight balance	Ruled by emotions	Child given premature responsibility, high expectations	Feels unaccepted
Childlike— wants to be taken care of	Strong emotional outbursts	Strives for perfection	Needs achievement to feel deserving of love
	Ignores needs until they get big	Competitive	Longs for tenderness, but has difficulty admitting it
	Fears intimacy	Agressive, easily angered	Needs father approval
	Difficulty relaxing	High ego needs	Approval equated with love
	Unanswered wanting as a child	Defensive, on guard	Heart opens and closes rapidly
		Feels opposed and challenged	Afraid of involvement, commitment

FIFTH CHAKRA Balanced	SIXTH CHAKRA May be either	SEVENTH CHAKRA Balanced overall
Strong verbally	Sixth chakra is often irrelevant, interest is in pragmatic accomplishments	More pragmatic than spiritually inclined, but longs for spiritual connection
Voice may be thin or controlled	May delight in logical abstractions, symbols, dreams, but not think of them on their own	Intelligent
Defensive verbally		Rational
Expressive		Logical

seductive and well-loved by others, but they seldom believe that their close relationships are authentic since they, themselves, are seldom authentic.

It can be frustrating to have relationships with either of these types. Their difficulty with reciprocating tenderness might suggest that they are often rejected, but in fact, they are so defended against rejection it is more likely that they will leave a relationship first. They unconsciously do to others what they most fear for themselves, thus keeping their heart chakras depleted and perpetuating their original patterns.

In truth, they are hungry for love—real love that is directed toward their feeling self, the nonachieving self, the simple, vulnerable, authentic self connected to the unloved child.

EXCESS AND DEFICIENCY

EXCESS

It is always somewhat disconcerting to think of an excess in the heart chakra as being a problem, and I repeatedly get questions about this in my workshops. How can we have too much love? How can the heart be too open? Do we really need to limit ourselves as we open the heart? Is there a proper level of openness to aim for?

Excess in the heart chakra is not an excess of actual love, but an excessive use of love for our own needs. Excess occurs when we overcompensate for our own wounds. Since love, by nature, involves others, then others become victims in our drama of overcompensating. Excessive love is desperate in its need for constant assurance, and does not uphold another's freedom to be who they are. It is love that is used like a drug, where the goal is to get high and remove ourselves from our responsibilities and unresolved pain. We are in excess when we use love to compensate for the incompleteness in ourselves, or when we use another to go where we cannot or will not go ourselves (see figure 4.4).

> In order to develop love——universal love, cosmic love, whatever you would like to call it——one must accept the whole situation of life as it is, both the light and the dark, the good and the bad.
>
> CHOGYAM TRUNGPA

FIGURE 4.4. FOURTH CHAKRA EXCESS AND DEFICIENCY

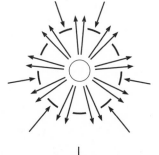

EXCESS

An excessive fourth chakra has such strong movement outward that very little energy can get in. This eventually depletes the core, which tries to replenish itself by connecting with others in the same excessive manner that caused the depletion.

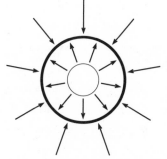

DEFICIENCY

Rigid boundaries keep the inside from coming out and the outside from coming in, resulting in isolation, which perpetuates deficiency.

Connie complained that she gained five pounds during her mother's last visit. "What happened?" I asked. "Mom kept wanting to take care of me, to feed me, to do everything for me. If I objected she got terribly hurt, claiming that I was rejecting her love. So I ate food when I wasn't hungry. I didn't do my normal workout routine. I didn't return my business calls. I got behind in everything."

What Connie's mother assumed was loving behavior was actually smothering her daughter. Her mother's hurt about having her noble efforts rejected was proof that the gifts were not really given for Connie's well-being but for her own. Connie's mother is a codependent, but in listening to the story we can see that Connie is codependent as well. Rather than risk her mother's hurt, she went against her own needs. She did not enjoy the visit, and was not looking forward to the next one.

By definition, the heart chakra is about reaching beyond the self and connecting with others. Codependency expresses an excessive heart chakra, where the emphasis on the *other* is out of balance. The compulsive need to fixate on others with excessive caretaking and meddling is a behavior that arises from our own denied needs for such care. Out of touch with our own needs, we hope this behavior will earn the right to be loved in return. Yet this denies the other's self-reliance. Codependency is not an act of love, but an obsession clothed in the guise of love.

An excessive heart chakra can be demanding and possessive. It is passionately connected, but often blindly so. Love becomes an obsession in which the loved one is more an extension of ourselves than a separate being. Jealousy is a projection of our insecurities, a product of the hungry heart. Eros and Thanatos are out of balance. We crave connection and cannot tolerate separation. A jealous person needs constant reassurance and attention and their neediness tends to result in a rejection that only deepens the underlying wound and creates even more insecurity.

Since the need for love is so strong in the excessive heart chakra, there may be poor boundaries and poor discrimination. We may fail to discern when a relationship becomes abusive and live in the fantasy bond where everything is just fine. There may be idealistic thinking about the perfection of love that continually gets betrayed by hard, cold reality. We may expect the moon from our lover—even be willing to give it ourselves—and fail to see why our expectations are not matched in kind. The excessive focus on love is like an addiction that undermines clarity and judgment.

DEFICIENCY

Alan was going through a divorce. "I'll never fall in love again," he declared. "It is not worth it. This hurts too much." His friends all told him he would find someone else before too long. "I don't want someone else!" he exclaimed. "This one was perfect. If I can't have it, I'm never going to make a commitment again!"

Alan was reacting to his wound with an avoidant response. He was closing shop—no more business, no more risk. I knew that Alan was actually a very loving person, so I knew his response was not permanent. Having had his heart opened and then broken, it was natural for him to shut down for a while. Unfortunately, some people adopt this as a basic stance during childhood and for them, shutting down becomes a more serious condition.

The deficient heart chakra responds to wounds of love by withdrawing. Having been hurt before, the heart becomes a closed system and love becomes conditional. It says, "If you don't treat me better, I won't give you any more love." "If you don't call me on time, I'll pretend I don't care." The heart plays a game of coldness, as if the withdrawal of love can manipulate someone into loving us more. Feeling depleted to begin with, a deficient heart wants others to make the first move. What a contrast to the codependent that gives compulsively whether it is wanted or not!

The deficient heart chakra is usually waiting for a knight in shining armor or a fairy godmother to come along and play rescue. He or she wants someone to see how hurt they are, and to fix it. They want energy to be poured into the system without taking any risks themselves, as risks have proved painful in the past (see figure 4.4). As the heart is basically depleted, one feels they cannot afford to open and give. Without giving, the inner economy collapses and depression sets in. Like having a dead battery, we keep waiting for a jump start. If we never let the battery charge, we need that jump start continually.

With a deficient heart chakra, there is a tendency to dwell on old relationships that ended long ago because it was a time when one felt loved. One might remain stuck in anger and betrayal and never forgive. The fact that the heart did not get filled up is seen as the other person's fault rather than one's own responsibility. Unwillingness to forgive keeps the heart closed.

The deficient heart chakra is an avoidant response to too little love. Since the unloved child did not get met with empathy for their experience, they have trouble giving empathy to others (as well as themselves). They lack compassion and remain critical and judgmental, which hurts the people they love and closes channels for expression and reception.

Past hurts may result in bitterness and cynicism—a kind of generic intolerance. Judgment is a way of justifying distance from others and defending against closeness and the risk of getting hurt again. If others are not good enough, then we can feel righteous instead of rejected. Loss of love reduces self-esteem and our righteousness gives us a false sense of pride. We are better than others who are not worthy of our love. This is a projection of our own emptiness and unworthiness. It is likely we will judge ourselves with the same lack of compassion.

David spent several sessions bemoaning the fact that he could never say, "I love you." He was capable of love, but feared expressing it. His heart chakra was so wounded that he felt he could not afford the risk of rejection. Without opening those channels, he also could not receive the love his friends had for him and remained isolated and lonely. If one complains of basic loneliness, it is likely the heart chakra is deficient. There are so many people in this world who need love—perhaps we are a bit too picky if we can't find any?

A deficient heart chakra feels basically unlovable at the core. When engaged in a relationship, one fears that intimacy may reveal this basic, unacceptable core. If there is not enough self-love to promote pride in one's interior, it remains hidden and unrevealed. Without intimacy, the heart does not get filled, and so the cycle perpetuates itself.

COMBINATIONS

You may have read these two sections and found yourself identifying with both. It is common to go back and forth at different times in life. I tend toward codependence myself, until I get hurt, at which point I withdraw and shut down. When I am in love, I am overflowing and have extra for everybody. When I feel rejected, I tell everybody to go away and leave me alone even though I secretly want someone to take care of me.

> And the day came when the need to remain closed became more painful than the risk to open.
>
> ANONYMOUS

When a heart has been too open, it is natural for it to shut down. When the heart has experienced enough loneliness, it may be ready to open up again. We may feel full of love one day, and angry and resentful the next. We may have some deficient or excessive characteristics, but not all of our characteristics are so. What is important is to examine the basic stance we take in life and to bring that stance into balance whenever we can.

RESTORING THE LOTUS

HEALING THE HEART CHAKRA

Love is the essence that heals. Patience, skill, training, and talent all play their part, but without love they are merely techniques. All wounds cry for the universal medicine of love. As the cosmic glue of the universe, love is the force that bridges the gaps that cut us asunder. In the gap between Heaven and Earth, love is the binding force that holds together the many-colored steps of the Rainbow Bridge.

> Love comforteth like sunshine after a rain.
>
> WILLIAM SHAKESPEARE

Unfortunately, due to the damage we have each received in our lives, we are not always sure how to apply love to the wounds within ourselves and others. We do not know what real love looks like or how to create it.

The following suggestions only scratch the surface of this vast subject, but give you a place to begin.

THE TASK OF SELF-ACCEPTANCE

In order to love, there has to be someone home inside. As we open up to the more universal elements of love, it is easy to forget to honor each other's individuality. Soulful love, as Thomas Moore has so aptly stated, is neither abstract nor empty, but worships the particular, the unique, the individuated self.

In honoring our individuality, we honor the subtle relationships within ourselves. We honor the individuality of every composite part: the part that seeks success, the part that fears it, the part that longs for commitment, the part that wants freedom, the inner child, the rebellious teenager, the pleaser, the nurturing parent, and all the other selves we observe as we go through life. They may want different things at different times, or even different things at the same time.

Learning to coordinate these internal relationships is the inner work of self-love. Our feelings are brought into relationship with our belief systems; our vulnerable child forms an alliance with our responsible adult; our inner masculine makes love with the inner feminine. Our inner critic, rather than permeating every thought, becomes realistically related to our self-protection. The parts are many and the combinations infinite. Only through this relational process do we form a sense of the whole.

It is not enough to merely recognize the pieces of ourselves—we need to reclaim them with that sense of bonding we call love. Recognizing each part as an essential element of the whole brings our disparate selves home to the integrating chamber of the heart. The heart's natural inclination is to create bonding. Just as heart cells under a microscope will always beat in unison, so too, our various subpersonalities will form a harmonious unity when they are brought into the loving awareness of the heart chakra. What is not brought into relationship with the core essence of the heart remains outside of the whole, an unacknowledged part. In chakra two, for example, we talked about these parts as rejected selves or the shadow.

As we reflect upon ourselves, we integrate more and more pieces of ourselves. Our sense of the whole becomes larger and stronger. Like an ecosystem whose stability and magnificence increases with diversity, the whole of a person gains beauty and stability as more and more parts become integrated. We become more complex, more mature, and capable of greater and greater possibilities. This sets the ground for creativity in chakra five, and for penetrating insight and understanding in chakras six and seven. Reflective consciousness allows this integration and it is the task usually undertaken through psychotherapy.

As we become more integrated, we become more relational. Our capacity for understanding and working with outer relationships is enhanced by the sophistication of our inner one. Instead of relating from a single part of ourselves, which makes us inflexible, we have a broader base from which to relate. There is simply more there for another to be attracted to, and more of us there to meet them. If we have accepted our own inner child, we can better accept that aspect in another.

Self-acceptance sets the stage for our social identity. It allows us to understand complex social interdependence and the sense of collective identity we all need to develop at this time in history. Having the capacity to perceive, understand, and form relationships is essential to this process. We can then see our role within the complex web of relationships around us, and can bring balance to the larger components of our culture.

EXERCISE: THE INNER FAMILY

Make a list of the various parts of yourself. You might list the inner child, the critic, the lover, the clown, the parent, the achiever, the quiet one, and so on—the possibilities are infinite. Next to each name on the list, write a few words describing how you perceive this part of yourself. The inner child might be described as playful or wounded, needy or angry, scared, cute, or awkward. The achiever might be driving, relentless, exhausted, or enthused.

After the description, write down what you think each part wants. The clown might want to be liked, the inner child might want to have fun, the critic to make sure we are always perfect. How often do these parts succeed in getting what they want? How realistic are their desires? What can be done to bring them into wholeness?

If you want to get more elaborate, you can start to look at who relates to whom. Does the hardworking adult relate to the inner child? Does the critic inhibit the artist? Does the clown entertain the sad inner child? Does the hero try and save everybody? If you see parts that clearly need to improve their relationship, write a dialog between them, as if you were writing a play. See how the dynamics develop. Let the dialog continue until some kind of resolution occurs.

LOVE OPENS WITH FEELING

Feelings are the antennae of the soul. Whenever our feelings are hurt (especially as children) we react protectively and close down our feelings. We described the realm of feelings in the second chakra as an internal flow of energy that moves through the body. In the heart chakra, we access the feelings by use of the breath. When we hold back our feelings, we hold our breath. When we hold the breath, we restrict the vital nourishment of air to our cells and muscles, and in effect, deaden ourselves. Deepening the breath allows repressed feelings to surface and be mobilized, freeing the heart from the heaviness of grief and allowing the natural balance of taking in and letting go to be restored.

It is advisable to do breath work with a trusted friend or therapist who can act as a container, catalyst, or anchor for your feelings as they emerge. If you do not have someone to work with, you can practice breathing exercises from yoga (called *pranayama*), which help to open the chest and charge the body with the vital energy of prana that is found in the element air. Some of these exercises have been described in my previous books or can be found in most books on yoga.

OBSERVING THE BREATH

Most of us do not notice how we breathe. We do not feel how we hold the breath or constrict various parts of the belly or chest. Our way of breathing is normal to us.

The first step in breath work is to feel your own breathing and have someone else watch you breathe. Let him or her give you feedback on whether you hold your breath at any part of the breathing cycle. Some people hold for a few moments before they exhale, while others hold their breath for a short time before taking the next breath. Allow the breath to become smooth and balanced in its cycle. Notice whether you breathe from your chest or your belly, and see what happens when you consciously expand the parts that are normally restricted. Notice what feelings, impulses, and desires arise. Try not to block these feelings.

REACHING OUT AND TAKING IN WITH THE BREATH

A simple but profound exercise for opening the heart coordinates the *reaching out and taking in* movement of the arms with the exhale and inhale of the breath. The instructions given here are for the facilitator.

STEP ONE: Have your friend lay down on a mat with knees bent, so that the feet have contact with the ground. Notice the breathing that is already there and become aware of its rhythms. Gently encourage awareness of the parts that are held and those that do not seem to expand or contract with the breath. If your partner is comfortable with touch, you might bring attention to the held parts by gently touching them. It also helps to lightly massage the shoulders and arms, the pectoral muscles that join the shoulders to the chest, and the area of the back behind the heart chakra. If the heart area is constricted to a point where the back is rounded forward, I sometimes put a pillow under the heart that encourages the back to arch in the opposite direction. Once the breath seems as full as possible and your friend has relaxed into it, you are ready to begin the next step.

STEP TWO: Encourage your partner to reach her arms forward with each exhale, and to pull her arms in toward the heart chakra with each inhale. These motions should be slow and conscious. When we pull in, it helps to imagine just what we are reaching for in terms of love. When we exhale, imagine what we are either letting go of, or what we are offering to the world. For example, one might suggest: "Think of the things that make you feel loved, and pull them toward you." "Imagine letting go of the fear of rejection." "Offer the love from your own heart as you push outward."

After a few moments of this, you may notice which of these motions is easier for your partner; there may be hesitation, or blockage in one direction more than another. Simply point out this observation and see if your friend is aware of it.

STEP THREE: Stand over your partner and grab onto her hands. When she pulls her arms in toward her heart, offer a bit of resistance. When she pushes away, offer resistance as well. Your resistance increases the flow of energy through the arms and often opens up blocked feelings. Again, simply observe what happens and offer feedback on what you observe.

GRIEF WORK

Unshed grief restricts the breath, and deepening the breath often releases grief. Grief is like heavy clouds in the air that obscure the sky, but once the rain is shed the sky opens up to let the sun shine again.

Grief is nearly always based on loss, especially of loved ones. It is important to reclaim that part of us that was *attached* to what we lost. The grown woman who lost her daddy when she was a little girl may have simultaneously lost her inner child. The nurturing husband who lost his wife may lose the part of himself that was tender and open. The self that feels playful, sexual, creative, or enthusiastic about life may have been lost when the lover that brought out these qualities moves on. We can tolerate the loss of a love object, but not the loss of vital pieces of ourselves.

It is important to remember that the point of grief work is to regain connection with the self inside rather than increase our attachment to what was lost. We must remember to ask ourselves, "Why was this person in particular so special to me?" "What did he or she bring to me that I am missing in myself?" "What part of me was particularly bonded to this person, and what does that part need?" "What have I lost touch with in myself as a result of this ending, and how can I nurture and regain that part of myself once again?"

We grieve because a sacred essence within ourselves has been awakened and then compromised. To grieve that essence is to reclaim it and give it the importance it deserves. Sometimes a painful situation triggers wounds from previous hurts that were never healed and indeed we may we feel like we are reexperiencing every hurt that has ever happened to us. Grief work helps us clean the wounds so that we reclaim our wholeness.

As we shed the seemingly endless tears of grief, we must remember the hope of the young boy in the stable: "With this much manure, there's got to be a pony in here somewhere!" Grief work leads us to the pony.

FORGIVENESS

When our heart is injured, we protect it from the one we believe has caused it harm. Often we blame him or her for the pain, forgetting the part we may have played in it ourselves. Blame acts as a barricade that protects us from opening to that person again. Unfortunately, when we barricade our heart we also barricade it against receiving, as well as the possibility of healing. We stay frozen in the past, unable to move forward into the future.

Likewise, when we blame ourselves for something we regret, we stay locked into that past event. We remain fixated in the state of the helpless child, the out-of-control adult, or the withdrawn lover, stuck in a pattern of shame that does not allow us to be fully present.

Forgiveness is said to be the ultimate step in healing. Forgiveness uses the compassion of the heart to understand situations in terms of the forces that were acting on both ourselves and others. We may still vehemently disagree with the actions taken. We may say, rightfully, that we would never have done such a thing. We may even need something from the other person in order to allow forgiveness—an apology, some kind of restitution, or an acknowledgment of harm. But in the end, forgiveness allows the heart to lighten and move on; it is the redemptive action of the heart.

The first step is to forgive ourselves. This is not to say we should blindly condone every thoughtless action we have ever taken. We need to look at ourselves compassionately, seeing the yearnings of the soul and what it was trying to accomplish, seeing the obstacles that were in our way, and the forces that impinged upon our journey at that time. It means that we understand why we did what we did and separate our basic essence from the mistake that was made.

Forgiving ourselves may require making amends for past action. This is an important step in recovery from addictions, for it restores balance and returns us to a position of conscious responsibility.

Look over your life and make a list of the things for which you have not forgiven yourself. Go back over each one of them and recreate the scenario that led to your actions. See if you can identify what part of you was activated at the time—the hungry child, the overworked adult, the rejected wife, the desperate teenager. Work toward an understanding of what you did and allow yourself to connect with the feelings you may not have been able to acknowledge at the time. Imagine how you might react if you saw another child (wife, husband, daughter, etc.) do the same thing and knew all about their situation. Would you be more or less judgmental? What is the expectation you had of yourself at the time? What was the expectation that was held of you by others? Were these expectations realistic?

Treat the part of you that was activated in your mind's eye with compassion. Look at what it needed, what it was trying to find. See if you can offer it forgiveness. Try to say these words to yourself, "I forgive you. You were just trying to . . . . Maybe we can help you achieve that now in a more productive way."

Forgiving others for harm they have caused is often more difficult. Some people try to forgive immediately before working through the grief and anger they have sustained. They say, "Oh, it doesn't matter. That's just how my father was. He couldn't help that he was so angry." This might be true, but it minimizes the impact such actions have on the soul and the effort it takes to stop the patterns it created in our lives.

Once we work through our feelings about a situation and reclaim pieces that were lost, then forgiveness lets us move onward. Forgiveness is an organic process and cannot be forced against its own time, although it can be encouraged.

We follow the same steps in forgiving someone else as we do for ourselves. We ask, what were the forces acting on the person at the time? What were they trying to achieve? What was driving them? What was unavailable that they needed? What blocked them from being able to respond differently? What might have been their true intentions had they been more conscious? What do I need from this person to help the forgiveness process (if it is possible)? What do I need from myself in order to forgive them and move on?

Forgiveness softens the hardening of the heart and so renews openness. It is not meant as a process that allows the same thing to happen again, but it will allow greater awareness to evolve in situations that have gone awry. It allows us to unhook the energy from the negative past and free it up for a more positive future.

LOVE MUST BE WILLED AND CREATED, AS WELL AS FELT

We tend to think of love as a feeling of which we are passive recipients. When love ebbs and flows, as surely it will, we think we are helpless to do anything about it. Stephen R. Covey, author of *The Seven Habits of Highly Effective People*, shares advice he gave to a man who felt he no longer loved his wife nor was loved in return.

"Love her," he told the man.

"I told you, the feeling just isn't there anymore," the man replied.

"Love her," Covey replied.

"You don't understand. The feeling of love just isn't there," repeated the man.

"Then love her. If the feeling isn't there, that's a good reason to love her."

"But how do you love when you do not love?" asked the man.

Covey replied: "My friend, love is a verb. Love—the feeling—is a fruit of love, the verb. So love her. Serve her. Sacrifice. Listen to her. Empathize. Appreciate. Affirm her. Are you willing to do that?"[10]

Love is a feeling, yes, but a feeling that is created out of action. The fourth chakra sits neatly above the third chakra will. Love is a daily, even hourly, conscious commitment to behave in a loving and caring fashion toward ourselves and others. When the feeling fades, it is our responsibility to find ways to create new love. Like a garden that is carefully tended, the rewards are well worth the effort.

For those of us who are unsure about what love even looks like, it is helpful to use fantasy. In fantasy, we can imagine our ideal mom or dad, or our ideal lover. We can imagine how they would speak to us, what they would do for us. In the fantasy, it is important to let the feelings fully permeate the body. As I say to my clients: "Soak your cells in this feeling. Reprogram the body with this nourishment." It is often helpful to begin this fantasy imagining ourselves at a young age and gradually growing up with this feeling present. How would it have felt at three years old to have had this kind of support and love? How would it have felt to go to school if you had had this kind of love? How would it have felt going through puberty? Would you walk, talk, or reach out differently? What would college have been like? How would your marriage or your relationship to your children be different? Fantasy helps reprogram the chakra through a succession of developmental stages.

LOVE MUST RISE BEYOND THE SELF

The purpose of the fourth chakra in the system as a whole is to get us to expand beyond our limited egos into a wider sense of connection with all life. This is the movement of the liberating current. While it is important not to deny or neglect the smaller self, it is indeed a liberating experience to rise beyond the confines of our own needs and find joy in service and altruism.

In my workshops, we give our students an assignment in the heart chakra to do something unexpected, even outrageous, for another person. It may be a favor for a neighbor you rarely speak to or a house cleaning for your wife in the middle of the night. It may be giving one hundred dollars to a panhandler or taking two days off work to spend exclusively with your children.

The joy this action imparts is contagious. Not only do you get uplifted yourself, but the person who receives your generosity will be touched in the heart, and inspired to carry it on elsewhere. How will they treat others after you make their day?

For those who consider themselves hopelessly codependent, this act of selfless service may only reinforce what they are already doing. For them, we give an even harder assignment: Do something outrageous for yourself!

LOVE MUST MAINTAIN A BALANCE OF ENERGIES

We think the heart chakra should be wide open, but in reality, few people can tolerate such a state in our crowded and traumatized social milieu. If we cannot monitor our boundaries, the heart will unconsciously shut down. The inner self will not feel protected and will simply withdraw.

Many people have difficulty balancing intimacy and autonomy in a relationship. They try to favor one side over the other and fail to realize they need both. The following exercise is similar to that of reaching out and taking in, but awakens the active rather than passive aspects of love.

COME CLOSER, GO AWAY

Seat yourself in front of your partner either cross-legged or in a chair. Let your hands meet between you at heart level. Allow your partner to pull your hands in toward his heart while he says aloud, "Come closer." Offer some resistance to the pull—not enough to block the movement, but enough to require real effort. When the hands reach the heart, allow your partner to push your hands back away from his body, saying aloud, "Go away." Again, offer some resistance to the push.

Go back and forth between these two modes, allowing any feelings or resistances to arise. Often one or the other movement will dominate and the person will realize they actually want more closeness or distance. You can then support them in their feeling by focusing on that movement.

Then change places. Now it is your turn to push and pull, and your partner's turn to offer resistance and feedback.

If you do this with someone with whom you have a relationship, ask how it mirrors what happens between the two of you. Who does the pushing, pulling, and resisting? What effect does it have? Is it balanced?

CONCLUSION

The heart chakra brings us to a place of acceptance and openness that allows the spirit inside to be still and find peace and stability without constriction. If the third chakra below has done its work correctly, we have created a place where the fourth chakra can now let go and just be. The state of being as opposed to doing is the qualitative difference between chakras four and three.

> Love is not what we become but who we already are.
>
> STEPHEN LEVINE

Healing the heart involves attending to the most vulnerable and sacred aspects within ourselves. Only through attending to their truth can we drop the protective armor that keeps us bound to the ego, bound to smaller parts of ourselves. Manipulation, derision, criticisms, or command will not work. We can only melt the armor with the combination of feeling and understanding that is love.

Through love we are able to expose our instinctual core and evolve to the next step of expressing our truth. Through love we are able to embrace and heal the larger world around us. Relationship furthers the evolution of individual souls and the collective soul of our planet.

CHAKRA FIVE

Vibrating into Expression

DEVELOPMENTAL STAGE
7 to 12 years

NAME
Vissudha (purification)

DEVELOPMENTAL TASK
Creative expression
Communication skills
Symbolic thinking

PURPOSE
Communication
Creativity

BASIC RIGHTS
To speak and be heard

ISSUES
Communication
Creativity
Listening
Resonance
Finding one's own voice

BALANCED CHARACTERISTICS
Resonant voice
Good listener
Good sense of timing and
rhythm
Clear communication
Lives creatively

COLOR
Bright blue

LOCATION
Throat, pharyngeal plexus

TRAUMAS AND ABUSES
Lies, mixed messages
Verbal abuse, constant yelling
Excessive criticism (blocks
creativity)
Secrets (threats for telling)
Authoritarian parents (don't
talk back)
Alcoholic, chemical-dependent
family (don't talk, don't trust,
don't feel)

IDENTITY
Creative

ORIENTATION
Self-expression

DEMON
Lies

DEFICIENCY

Fear of speaking

Small, weak voice

Difficulty putting feelings
into words

Introversion, shyness

Tone deaf

Poor rhythm

EXCESS

Too much talking, talking
as a defense

Inability to listen, poor
auditory comprehension

Gossiping

Dominating voice,
interruptions

PHYSICAL MALFUNCTIONS

Disorders of the throat, ears,
voice, neck

Tightness of the jaw

Toxicity (due to the chakra's
name, which means
"purification")

HEALING PRACTICES

Loosen neck and shoulders

Release voice

Singing, chanting, toning

Storytelling

Journal writing

Automatic writing

Practice silence (excess)

Non-goal-oriented creativity

Psychotherapy

Learn communication skills

Complete communications

Letter writing

Inner child communication

Voice dialog

AFFIRMATIONS

I hear and speak the truth.

I express myself with clear
intent.

Creativity flows in and
through me.

My voice is necessary.

SHADES OF BLUE

I remember an astonishing film shown in my college physics class. It featured the Tacoma Narrows Suspension Bridge, built in 1940, nicknamed the "Galloping Gertie." Only four months after completion, a remarkable and unfortunate event took place. One ordinary afternoon as a single car innocently drove across the bridge, a stiff breeze of about forty miles per hour came up. As the wind blew, it triggered subtle vibrations in the bridge, which coalesced into increasingly larger vibrations until the whole bridge started undulating like a snake. Within minutes the entire bridge collapsed in one huge, oscillating ripple, crumbling into the waters below.

> If it is true that you are what you eat, it may just as accurately be said that you are what you listen to.
>
> STEVEN HALPERN

If such an enormous structure as a steel and concrete suspension bridge can be destroyed by vibration from the wind, how are we impacted by the countless vibrations we encounter each day? Our modern world bombards us with dissonance—vibrations that we tune out of our conscious mind while our body and nervous system continue to endure. The result is a series of little stresses that can add up to larger stress with the potential to break down our entire system. What are some of these vibrations and how do they impact us?

Years ago I moved from a major city to a quiet rural area. I still remember the many auditory insults that I use to endure daily, sounds that are a normal part of urban life. There was the background drone of the nearby freeway, a constant hum periodically penetrated by blasting horns. Our house was close to the road. Cars on the street sped by, often laying rubber with a characteristic screech or blasting their stereo for all to hear. Blaring sirens sounded hourly, and in the evening they would often set off the entire neighborhood of barking dogs. Like many cities, the sounds of gunshots rang through the night air, reminding me of the lack of safety outside. Car alarms left unattended often pierced the night, just as I drifted off to sleep. Sleep was equally disturbed in the morning as the neighboring apartment building had a parking lot next to our house. Each morning, from precisely

5:40 to 5:50 A.M., one of the men would warm up the engine of his old car which had no muffler. The same apartment building had outdoor hallways and balconies from which one could hear violent arguments, kids fighting, babies crying, or, on a good day, someone else's taste in music.

As if that were not enough, we had three active teenagers living at home, and my younger son, Alex. The phone rang constantly, feet thundered up and down the stairs, and it was a rare moment when neither the stereo nor the television were on. Such household noise was frequently punctuated by the angry yelling of sibling rivalry and, on occasion, the jolting shatter of something breaking.

Unfortunately, my story is not unique.

Anyone who lives in a modern urban environment is assaulted by sound on a constant basis. Only recently in the span of human evolution are we as polluted by unwelcome sound as we are today. Two hundred years ago, in the city of Vienna, fire alarms could be given verbally by someone shouting from the top of a cathedral. In 1964, a siren needed to be 88 decibels to be heard (1 decibel or dBA is the smallest unit heard by human ears). Today a siren is 122 dBA, well over the threshold of pain. While we talk about air, water, and earth pollution, we pay little attention to sound pollution. Unable to close our ears, this is a pollution against which we have very little defense.

OSHA estimates that more than half of American production workers are exposed to an ongoing noise level of 80 dBA or higher, while the maximum intensity one can withstand over time without hearing loss is 75 dBA. When exposed to recorded industrial sound, rhesus monkeys had a 27 percent rise in blood pressure, which stayed elevated for *four months* after the noise stopped. Children living near airports are more likely than others to have learning disabilities. Babies living in noisy homes proved slower to mature in terms of sensory and motor skills and tended to keep their infantile habits longer than babies in a quieter environment.[1]

It is not just raw sound that bombards us—we also experience dissonance in mass communication. Hungry for truth, we find ourselves surrounded by the junk sound of advertising mantras that "pepsi" our thoughts, news broadcasts that obsess on violence and death, and sensationalist stories designed to fill the already agitated mind. Suppressing the urge to express ourselves truthfully, we restrict ourselves to accepted niceties, and speak the "real" truth only behind others' backs. The throat chakras of men are bound by neckties, which choke their individuality, while women are just beginning to break through centuries of public silence.

As my friend Wendy Hunter Roberts has pointed out, our news coverage brings us information without experience. News reporters rattle off deplorable facts with very little feeling. We hear about the destruction of the environment in terms of square miles of rain forest, inches of topsoil, numbers of disappearing species, but these statistics do not tell us what it is like to stand in a rain forest and hear the trees fall, or to watch the death of a lifeform that will never exist again. We read about calamities in foreign countries in terms of so many dead, so many injured, and so many dollars worth of damage. We coldly take in data without having the time or the context in which to really feel its impact. *We are receiving disembodied communication.*

Meanwhile, mass communication is proliferating. Modern communication technologies give us faster access to more information than ever before. Movies, videos, radio, books, magazines, newspapers, the Internet, cellular phones, bumper stickers, and even T-shirts—the cultural fifth chakra is an omnipresent field, influencing our consciousness at each and every moment. How can we hear our own unique vibration in a world deafened by the roars of civilization? How can we express our truth when it goes against the accepted conformity of polite conversation? In the subtle realm of the fifth chakra, how can we find the quiet necessary to listen to the truth within?

These are the issues to explore in the fifth chakra. Communication binds culture together as the primary means for sharing information, values, relationships, and behavior. Through communication we shape our future.

UNFOLDING THE PETALS

THE SUBTLE WORLD OF VIBRATIONS

As we enter the etheric level of the throat chakra, we enter a paradoxical realm of great subtlety yet powerful influence. We leave behind the balanced middle ground of the green ray and reach into the etheric range of turquoise and blue that resonate with the throat chakra. The enveloping element of air still surrounds us, yet we reach beyond it into the unknown ether—the realm of vibrations, sound, communication, and creativity.

We have passed the halfway point in our rainbow. In the dance between liberation and manifestation, we are now leaving the balance of the heart to focus more heavily on the upper chakras. We are breaking free from gravity, free from the way things have always been and from the structure and restriction of manifested form. We become more abstract, yet broader in our scope. In the first four chakras we concerned

> All sounds known through the Sanskrit alphabet are identified as the vocables sprung from the cosmic drum of Shiva, i.e., of creation itself. Sound is the paradigm of creation, and its dissolution is reabsorption into its source.
>
> AJIT MOOKERJEE

ourselves with form, movement, activity, and relationship—things that are easily observed. In chakra five, our attention moves to vibrations as the subtle, rhythmic pulsations that move through all things.

ENTERING THE SYMBOLIC

The upper chakras represent the symbolic world of the mind. Words, images, and thoughts (chakras five, six, and seven) are all symbolic reflections of the manifested plane. Each word we use is a symbol for a thing, concept, feeling, process, or relationship. Each image in our mind is a mental symbol for something real and each thought is a combination of these symbols. With symbols, we can do more with less. I can talk about a truck even though I cannot lift one. I can describe a spiral galaxy, even though I cannot travel to one. I can show you a picture of a man easier than I can describe him.

> The symbol strikes its roots in the most secret depths of the soul; language skims over the surface of the understanding like a soft breeze.... Words make the infinite finite; symbols carry the mind beyond the finite world of becoming into the realm of infinite being.
>
> J. J. BACHOFEN

Symbols can be seen as the vibrational essence of what they represent. They are the building blocks of communication and consciousness. They are like packets of meaning that can be stored in one mind and shared with others, each packet enhancing consciousness. When a symbol really speaks to us then we are said to resonate with it.

RESONANCE

All life is rhythmic. From the rise and fall of the sun to the rise and fall of our breath, from the beating of our heart to the infinite vibrations of atomic particles within our cells, we are a mass of vibrations that miraculously resonate together as a single system. In fact, our ability to function as a unified whole depends upon the coherent resonance of the many subtle vibrations within us. The task of the fifth chakra is to enhance this resonance.

Resonance is a state of synchronization among vibrational patterns. All vibrations can be thought of as wavelike movements through space and time. Each waveform has a characteristic rhythm (known as frequency) that describes how frequently the waves rise and fall. In music, the pitch of a note can be expressed as a certain frequency—higher notes have a higher frequency than lower ones.

When two or more sounds from different sources vibrate at the same frequency, they are said to resonate together. This means their waveforms oscillate back and forth at the same rhythm (see lines A and B in figure 5.1). When this happens, the height of the waves is added together (expanding the amplitude, line C) and the waves lock into phase with each other. Once in phase, they tend to remain that way. Oscillating waveforms tend to stabilize when they enter into resonance (much like members of a political movement reinforce each other's political views) because they are on the same wavelength. It is

FIGURE 5.1. EXAMPLE OF SINE WAVES IN RESONANCE

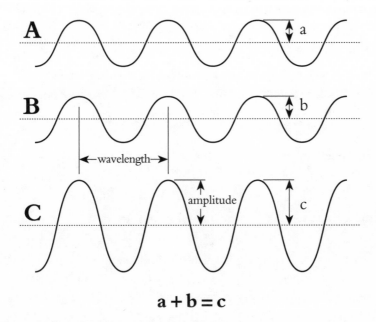

$$a + b = c$$

Sound waves A and B vibrate at the same frequency.
When added together, the frequency stays the same while the amplitude is doubled.
This maintains the same pitch but gives us increased volume.

easier, for example, to sing the same note as another than to sing a different one, as we quickly discover when we try to sing harmony. Thus resonant frequencies tend to bond together. This is also known as *rhythm entrainment* or *sympathetic vibration*.

We experience resonating wave forms in many ways. When we listen to a chorus of voices or a troupe of drummers, we are immersed in a field of resonance that vibrates every cell in our body. Such a field influences the subtler vibrations of consciousness and we feel pleasure, expansiveness, and rhythmic connection with the pulse of life itself. We enter even deeper resonance when we dance or move rhythmically to music. The rhythmic movements of the body stay in phase with the music and it actually becomes difficult to move out of phase.

The rhythmic entrainment of various frequencies within our body and consciousness forms a coherent, central vibration that we experience as a kind of resonant "hum" when we're having a good day. On those days, it seems we're in harmony with everything, as if we can't miss a beat. We're in sync with the rhythm of the universe. (It is interesting to note how much the fourth chakra state of being in love contributes to this experience.) On other days, we feel like we're out of phase or as if we can't do anything right. Then we feel out of sorts, uncomfortable in our own skin, and others may find us uncomfortable to be around. Understanding the principles of vibration and resonance helps us increase the coherence of our basic vibrational experience and realign our basic rhythm.

Resonance requires a certain balance of flexibility and tension. A string needs to be both taut and flexible in order to sound a note. In our bodies, we need to have enough flexibility to resonate with different frequencies, yet maintain enough tension to create a repeating pattern.

Human egos are multi-concentric halo-systems.

BUCKMINSTER FULLER

The state of resonance within the mind-body is a statement of our health and vitality. When we can't resonate with the world around us, we can't link with it. We are unable to expand, respond, or receive. We become isolated and ill. Opening to resonance requires both grounding for the establishment of form, and an openness of breath that yields softness and flexibility.

This balance is a delicious combination of letting and willing that allows us to both listen and respond at the same time.

> Of what is the body made? It is made of emptiness and rhythm. At the ultimate heart of the body, at the heart of the world, there is no solidity. Once again, there is only the dance.
>
> GEORGE LEONARD

It is my belief that sleep puts us back in harmony with our own resonance. When we sleep, our heart rate, breathing, and brain waves all settle into a deep, rhythmic entrainment. A discontinuous sound or sensation will wake us up—an alarm clock, someone shaking us, a noise on the street—and pull us out of a deep resonant state. At the end of the day, when we have experienced a lot of distracting vibrations, we feel tired. We want to go back to sleep.

THE ETHERIC BODY

At the level of the fifth chakra, our attention moves from the physical plane into the subtler etheric fields. Commonly known as the aura, this etheric field is generated by the totality of internal processes—from the energetic exchange of subatomic particles to the digestion of food in our cells, from the firing of neurons to our current emotional state, and on to the larger rhythms of our outer activities.

> Believe those who are seeking the truth. Doubt those who claim to have found it.

Our very life force can be seen as a stream of pulsating energy. When the stream is not fragmented by blocks in the body armor, then pulsation moves freely through the body and out into the world. This streaming creates a resonant, etheric field around the body—an aura of wholeness. A resonant field makes coherent connections with the outside world. A fragmented field makes fragmented connections.

As we interact with others, our etheric fields become engaged. The most rewarding connections occur when there is resonance between vibrational fields. Just as people who speak the same language resonate with spoken symbols, the subtle resonance between our etheric field and those of others deepens our feeling of connection. The greater our internal resonance, the more deeply we can resonate with those around us.

Kirlian photography, which allows us to see the activity of the etheric field, has revealed remarkable things about the etheric body. For example, Kirlian photographs of a cut leaf show that the etheric body of the leaf remains nearly the same even when parts of the physical leaf have been removed.[2] Yet, when a human couple merely change their thoughts toward one another, sequential Kirlian photographs reveal that their auras change dramatically. When one couple's thoughts turned from hostile to loving, the fields around their fingertips (which were not touching on the film) fused together where they had previously remained separate.[3] This tells us that the etheric body may be more responsive to the subtle vibrations of our thoughts than it is to major alterations in the physical body!

> To be a warrior is to learn to be genuine in every moment of your life.
>
> CHOGYAM TRUNGPA

Our etheric body is highly sensitive to emanations around us, even without our awareness. In the fifth chakra, we work to refine our vibrations so that we can tune into this subtlety. The name for this chakra, *vissudha*, means "purification." Purification is a vibrational refinement that takes place as we rid the body of toxins, speak truthfully and authentically, and as we work through the issues of the lower chakras. Purification prepares us to enter the even more refined energies of the chakras above.

COMMUNICATION

Communication is the essential function of the fifth chakra. As *self-expression*, it is a gateway between the inner world and the outer. Only through self-expression does the outer world get to know what's inside of us. We only know what's inside someone when they choose to tell us.

Self-expression in the fifth chakra is a counterpart to the sensate reception coming in through the second chakra. In the second chakra, we opened a gate that allowed the world *in* through our senses. In the fifth chakra, we open a gate that allows our inner self to get *out* into the world. These two chakras are often linked, such that problems in one will often be reflected in the other.

The throat chakra is also the internal gateway between mind and body. The narrowest passage within the whole chakra system, the throat is literally a bottleneck for the passage of energy. We can think of it as a kind of relay system, sorting through messages from the body and connecting them with information stored in the brain. Only when mind and body are connected do we have true resonance.

It is also through this inner gateway that the unconscious becomes conscious. If the throat is blocked, so is the upward movement of energy, which cannot pass into the conscious mind. We have impulses without strategy, whim without will. We cannot get to our higher self. If instead we live up in our head with a throat chakra block, then we cannot speak what we know. We cannot translate knowledge into feeling or action, and therefore cannot manifest.

When mind and body are not congruent, then there is a tendency to throw the head out of alignment with the body. The head may move forward with an angle at the neck, or there may be a tendency to injure the neck through accidents or build up muscle tension through stress.

Such was the case with Sarah, who complained of neck problems. Sarah grew up in a violent alcoholic family, where she was required to keep her head in order to survive frightening and crazy situations. As a result, her head was painfully out of alignment with her torso and she felt out of touch with her body. In one of our sessions we let each part of her body speak its experience, and all the parts below her neck talked about being tense or in pain. Her head and face, on the other hand, stated that they felt just fine! When I asked her to speak as if she were her neck, she said: "I'm crooked and I'm tight. I'm tilted. I relay things through the body. I feel sad. I'm not even comfortable. I'm not aware, except for a lump in the front of me." The lump in her throat was the place where communication between her mind and body stopped. If her head were to reconnect and access this knowledge, it would become aware of the pain in her body. This awareness could only take place when it became possible to actually do something about the pain and the situation that caused it. When she was a child, there was nothing she could do. In order to minimize the negative experiences, she put her head out of alignment with her own body, distorting the communication between them.

The neck is a crucial point in the mind-body connection. The body functions largely by habits, unconsciously. The mind wants to understand

and transcend. Only through a full, solid connection between mind and body, meeting at the neck, do we have the ability to break old habits, bring our physical experience to understanding, and take that vital combination into the world around us.

> The voice is a vehicle which the mind uses for its manifestations. It is the womb impregnated with the seed of the idea.
>
> LAUREL ELIZABETH KEYES

THE VOICE

The voice is a living expression of one's basic vibration. Since the fifth chakra is associated with the element *sound* and is located in the throat—the voice becomes the touchstone for the health of this chakra. If the chakra is constricted, the voice will also be constricted, sounding whiny, whispered, or mumbled. If the chakra is excessive, the voice may be loud, shrill, or the person may habitually interrupt or dominate conversation.

The sign of a healthy fifth chakra—one that is connected to both mind and body—is a resonant and rhythmic voice that speaks truthfully, clearly, and concisely. Conversation with others is balanced, with a true ability to listen and respond.

The voice not only indicates the health of the fifth chakra, but of other chakras as well. Contraction in the body (chakra one) restricts the voice. Lack of feeling (chakra two) makes the voice seem mechanical. Too little will (chakra three) makes the voice sound pinched and whiny, whereas third chakra excess makes the voice dominating. The voice also requires breath (chakra four). If the breath is constricted or uneven, the voice will not be full. If our consciousness is not open (chakras six and seven), then the voice becomes repetitive and dull. When we listen to such a voice, we have the feeling that we have heard it all before. When a person is frozen in the past, the voice does not seem fully present.

There are also many voices within us. There is the voice that tells us we are no good, the voice that wants above all to be heard, the voice that only whispers silently in the quiet moments we spend alone. Inner dialog between the various parts of ourselves helps us become more integrated. Integration creates resonance. The process of individuation honors and integrates each of our voices, and brings them together as a whole.

Only with freedom to express ourselves can we fully individuate. If the fifth chakra is blocked, we become excessively introverted and can neither express nor take in new information. If the block is severe enough, it negatively affects the whole system.

TRUTH AND LIES

To fully express our individuality is to express our truth. A nonindividuated person will express what people want to hear. A fearful person will be afraid to speak their truth. A person without ego strength will be afraid of what others think and give up their authenticity.

If your lower chakras are in good order—living in the truth of their bodies and feelings, with ego strength and accepting love—you can safely express your own personal truth. Let's look at the importance each of the lower chakras plays in this process.

If the fourth chakra brings self-acceptance, you no longer need to deny truth. This acceptance is a container that allows you to flower into creativity. Living in the field of acceptance with unconditional love and open-mindedness, your truths and individuality can emerge. You need not deny your feelings or pretend to be different.

If the ego and will are strong, you are able to express your truth even in the face of opposition. You have the courage to be different, the warrior spirit to defend your truth, even if it opposes what is around you.

If feelings are denied, we may find we have various conflicting truths. You want to move forward and you want to resist. You feel attracted to someone and do not trust them. To live in truth is to be able to live in these contradictions—to accept that each piece can be true without negating the other. To force yourself to pick one side or the other may deny a truth. Resolution of inner conflict can only come by acknowledging even conflicting truths.

> The least initial deviation from the truth is multiplied later a thousandfold.
>
> ARISTOTLE

Truth can be seen as a resonant field. Negative experiences teach us to deny and withhold our truth. We are punished for disagreeing with our parents. We are teased for admitting that we are afraid. We are misunderstood when we try to express ourselves. If our views are not consistent with the majority, we can be ostracized. Sometimes, our safety and psychic survival become dependent on restricting the truth. The child who gets hit for opening her mouth quickly learns to keep it shut. Unfortunately, this exacts a price. In repressing part of our truth, we restrict the natural resonance of the etheric field, and cease to resonate with the other parts of our truth. When we are out of our truth, we are living a lie. Lies form the demon of the fifth chakra.

Lies can be told with words, but they can also be told with actions or held by the body. When I am afraid to show someone how excited I am, I restrict the muscles of my face or hold my arms down by my side. I am then lying with my body and out of resonance with my own field. My natural process gets frozen. As long as we're frozen in this way, we are arrested in time. We can't fully participate in the streaming of the universe. We're not even in resonance with our own being.

When we live in our truth, there is a resonant continuity between ourselves and others. When this resonance is interrupted, we experience discontinuity. Perpetual discontinuity breaks down our health. Just as an engine needs all of its vibrating parts to be coordinated smoothly, so too does our basic resonance. This allows the forward progression of the self to occur gracefully.

CREATIVITY

Now that we are more distant from the established forms and patterns of the lower chakras, we not only have greater freedom to be creative, but a greater need as well. Having broken free of established patterns, we must live creatively.

Communication is the creative expression of all that is within us. Situated halfway between the third chakra of will and the seventh chakra of abstract consciousness, creativity combines will and consciousness and moves us forward into the future. When we create, we make something that has not existed before.

> To fully live our truth as individuated beings is to live life as a creative act.

Some people think of the second chakra as the center of creativity, as this is the center from which we create new life, but creativity at the second chakra level is unconscious. The creation of a child within my womb occurs on a day-to-day basis without my conscious control. I do not decide to create fingers and toes, blue eyes or brown. It happens by itself.

Creativity in the fifth chakra is a consciously willed process. We are literally *making our world* at each and every moment through our actions, expression, and communication. If I tell someone that I want them to come closer, I am creating intimacy in my life. If I tell them to go away, I am creating solitude, or maybe even alienation. Whether I tell you to pick up eggs and milk at the store or share an idea brewing in my mind, I am engaged in a creative process that is constantly shaping my reality.

Creativity is a pure expression of the spirit within us, the natural process of Self as it individuates. It allows the Self to give back to the world an assimilated form of what it has taken in. Creativity is the gateway between the past and future.

GROWING THE LOTUS

DEVELOPMENTAL FORMATION OF THE FIFTH CHAKRA AT A GLANCE

AGE
7 to 12

TASKS
Self-expression
Symbolic reasoning
Communication skills

NEEDS AND ISSUES
Industry vs. inferiority
Creativity
Access to tools for learning and creativity
Exposure to larger world

Developmental stages are less clearly defined in the higher chakras. This is especially true of the development of communication. We begin receiving vibrational and chemical communication from our mothers in the womb. As infants, we are immersed in a field of language and react to noises, voice tone, and facial expression. At nine months, we realize that sounds represent real things and begin imitating sounds around us. By twelve months, we can speak a few words, respond to simple words like *no*, or recognize our name. By two years we can express ourselves in simple sentences, with a vocabulary of about three

> Vibrations, pulsations, and streamings are basic to all human relationships, and to all concepts of freedom and social concern. . . . If a child's own streamings are allowed to develop and intensify, he becomes a living example of the paradox of individuality and connectedness.
>
> STANLEY KELEMAN

hundred words. By four or five years, there is an explosion of language and the child talks constantly to anybody who will listen!

At six years old, a child has a general command of her language. She understands words that represent abstract concepts and phrases that describe relationships between things. Back in the third chakra, we saw how the development of language gave us our first experience of time as a sequence of cause and effect. Not until age seven, however, does the child really understand time in the larger sense, such as how many weeks or months until Christmas or her birthday. A seven-year-old can now look backward *or* forward in time, a process Piaget called *reversibility*. This stage marks the point where the intellect is able to separate itself from the immediate experience long enough to consider alternate realities. Only with this realization is conscious *creativity* really possible.

Here also lies the seed of conscience. The child can conceptualize what it might be like if everyone told lies or stole from each other. In the third chakra stage, this was not possible as the level of conceptual thinking had not developed enough to see beyond immediate cause and effect. In the fourth chakra stage, a child wants to be helpful because helpfulness seems like a positive trait. During the fifth chakra stage, moral behavior has social as well as personal consequences.

It is between the ages of seven and twelve (Piaget's period of *concrete operations*) that the fifth chakra flowers. This stage is marked by more sophisticated symbolic reasoning—the ability to create a mental representation of a series of actions. A five-year-old can learn to walk a simple route from home to school, but would be unable to draw the route on paper. A concrete operational child can make this transition to symbolic representation and can reason in her head. I used to make a frequent three-hour drive that my son found long and boring. When he was four, he said to me, "Mommy, if it takes so long to get there, why don't we take a different road that will take us there right away?" When he was eight, I reminded him of that comment and he laughed at how silly he had been.

There is a shift in the child's consciousness away from the relationship-dominated fourth chakra toward a point where her social identity is fairly well formed and she begins to experiment with her own creative expression.

Erikson identifies this stage as the struggle between *industry and inferiority*, where the child "now learns to win recognition by producing things."[4] The school environment begins to replace the family as the main focus of activity as it has a wider vista and greater opportunities for creative expression. In school we find all kinds of tools, such as art supplies, books, sports equipment, audiovisual equipment, and computers. Tools give us a means of acting on the world, allowing us to do more with less. Each tool we encounter opens a wider possibility of creative expression.

If the child feels secure in her relationships, then she is more likely to feel secure enough to speak her truth and experiment creatively. She can test her ideas from a place of reasoning and imagination. She can say she would like to do something before she actually does it. She might suddenly announce that she is going to marry the boy next door when she grows up. When asked how she knows this, she may describe some rather creative deductive reasoning.

Up until now, the child has been more involved in receiving and reacting than in actual creative contribution. The system is maturing—physical growth slows down considerably and basic motor development is in place. Freud calls this the *latency period*, a time of relative peace and harmony when sexual drives are at a minimum. The enormous input of energy that the child has required and hopefully received prior to this now begins to move outward through creative expression. Susie brings home her drawings or clay figures and offers them proudly to Mommy and Daddy. It is important that she gets recognized for her contribution, because ego strength increases when we feel we have something worthwhile to offer.

With the building blocks of language and relationship in place, mental capacity now expands exponentially. We learn to use symbols to reach beyond our immediate experience. Through school, books, television, conversations, and experience, the child hungrily absorbs information about the world. The conceptual structures that organize this information are already in place, and learning proceeds rapidly. With more knowledge to play with, creative possibilities increase.

This is the awakening of the *creative identity*, whose task is *self-expression*. It is an awakening that stems from a realization of ourselves as separate beings, from our security in our social environment, and from our desire to make a personal contribution to the world around us. This requires a certain systemic fullness, hopefully gained in the previous stages of the lower chakras. Without that fullness, the child is still oriented toward taking in, rather than flowing outward. Our own shape needs to be defined before we can shape the world. When these stages have been properly fulfilled, or when the lower chakras have been relatively healed and balanced, this forward movement of communication and creativity takes place naturally.

TRAUMAS AND ABUSES

If I hit the taut string of a guitar, it makes a sound. If I hit it hard, it makes a loud sound. If I hit it softly—a quiet sound. Any beginning guitar player knows that if you don't hold the string down tightly over the frets, the sound is dull instead of resonant. When I restrict the movement of the string, I also restrict its expression.

As an event impacts us, it impacts us with a vibration. Like the guitar string, it is our nature to express what impacts us. When that expression is restricted (by whatever inhibitions we've been forced to accept), we lose our resonance and no longer vibrate in the chorus of creation. We become less fully alive, out of step, and dissonant.

If we do not express the vibration, the impact is stored in the body as stress. The natural flow of vibration through the body is interrupted and energy comes in but does not go back out. It takes effort to restrict that flow, and causes further stress to maintain the restriction.

> It is not the traumas we suffer in childhood that make us emotionally ill but the inability to express the trauma.
>
> ALICE MILLER

When the throat chakra is blocked, we separate from the chorus of life. We can't block the ears, eyes, or nerve endings of the skin as thoroughly as we can block the throat, so it is easier to block expression than it is reception, easier to block what comes out of us than what comes in. Therefore, a block in the throat chakra is most likely a block in the *discharge* of energy, creating a situation in which the input exceeds the output. This difference is experienced as stress.

If I am impacted by the humming of machinery, the ringing of telephones, the yelling of someone who is angry, the myriad of unacknowledged vibrations that impinge on me all day long, and I cannot release this energy, then I become stressed. If I have suffered a strong negative impact or an intolerable situation and I can't talk about it, these vibrations become frozen in the core of my body. Frozen at the core, my whole being is restricted from its natural rhythm of pulsation.

So what blocks us from expressing our truth, our outrage, our creativity, or our needs? What makes us close down the throat, bottling up the emotions, or annihilate our ideas before they can make it out of our mouth? What makes us hide behind silence?

Shame at the core, fear for one's safety, or simply being out of touch with the core self make us unable to bring the inside of ourselves out to meet the world. To keep this from happening, we block the essential gateway that connects inner to outer and lock the gate against the possible escape of our true feelings. We protect the vulnerable interior Self from exposure and possible harm or ridicule. We lock ourselves up, posting a censor at the door.

We do this by tightening the neck and shoulders, by throwing our head out of alignment with our body, by talking incessantly about anything except what's really bothering us. Some do it by stuffing food down their throats, as if filling the mouth will block the passage and prevent the feelings from pouring out.

Underneath each of these methods is a need to hide. In hiding we keep ourselves in isolation, keep ourselves from intimacy, and keep ourselves from evolving. In essence, we keep ourselves from meeting the truth and so we become a closed system that eventually runs out of energy and settles in inertia. When our block has reached such proportions that we are locked in inertia, it becomes even harder to get the throat to open up. Just as it's hard to write a letter to someone when you've been out of touch for a long time, it's also hard to break silence over issues that have long remained unspoken, to speak out when we are in the habit of remaining hidden, or to risk suddenly becoming conspicuous in a crowd. Much of this is kept in place by the demons of the lower chakras.

FEAR

We have a biological instinct to keep quiet when in danger. Along with the freezing response that immobilizes the body, we instinctually hold our breath as if to keep as quiet as possible. In this holding, the voice also freezes, for there is no voice without breath. Think of how common it is for people to have a nightmare and find themselves trying to scream with no sound coming out!

When someone lives in a chronic state of fear, the throat chakra closes down. Not only do we fear what might happen if we were to open up, the physiological experience of fear itself creates a block. We get choked up; we cannot speak even if we want to. We cannot take a deep breath, the mind races, and we cannot think.

Real communication reveals our interior state. Being on the receiving end of rage, physical or sexual abuse, excessive criticism, or humiliation as children teaches us to live in fear of exposing ourselves. We put ourselves in jail in order to keep safe, where the bars of the jail are our habitual muscular holding patterns. The prison guard is especially watchful at the throat chakra, for the voice inside secretly wants to come out. Silence is instilled by a voice louder than our own, which becomes a whisper permanently etched in the mind.

GUILT AND SHAME

Guilt and shame make us want to hide ourselves. Guilt and shame tell us that what is inside is in some way flawed, and that if we expose ourselves, those flaws will be conspicuously paraded for all to see. Since the outward expression of communication is blocked, the energies invested in guilt and shame become internal voices that act as vicious guardians of the sacred gate between inner and outer worlds. As we internally rehearse our words, shame rises up as the incessant critic, telling us why no one wants to

> Someone who was not allowed to be aware of what was being done to them has no way of telling about it except to repeat it.
>
> ALICE MILLER

hear what we are going to say, how we don't know what we're talking about, or how stupid we look. Suddenly our throat constricts and we find ourselves choking on our words with thoughts racing faster and faster, and only a small fraction of them making it out into expression.

We originally created this critic to save ourselves from real humiliation. Its original job was to protect the raw and vulnerable self within against outer threats. In most cases, however, the critic is imbued with all the trapped energy that cannot get out through the throat—energy that is then fed back to us in a negative way. Such critics are relentlessly overzealous and unrealistic in the severity of their criticism. Their words become self-fulfilling prophecies, creating such fear and awkwardness when we try to express ourselves that they jump back down our throats and say, "See, I was right. You're an absolute fool, and now everyone knows it."

The voice of the critic is usually a monologue. Whenever I draw forth the critic from one of my clients, I find that the conversation has only one side. The client is usually startled to even consider that there might be a second opinion. If I can make the monolog into a dialog, then another voice can come forward to combat the critic. To facilitate this dialog, I take on the voice of the critic.

"You don't know enough about gardening to teach a class on it," I taunt.

"Yes, I do! I've worked in gardening for over twenty years, and I have a lot of practical knowledge. I think my gardens are pretty!"

"But what if you make a mistake? What if you don't know how to do something?" I ask, knowing the words of the critic only too well.

"I may not know everything, but I know where to look it up. And furthermore, what do you know? You're just like my dad! You never think I can do anything right!"

Getting a second opinion is always helpful to challenge the critic. Often it is the voice of the child that never talked back to the original critical parent, and allowing this voice to emerge can be very liberating.

SECRETS

All action is communication. When we keep a secret, we not only have to monitor what comes out of our mouths, but also what we might say with our body, eyes, or facial expression. We become vigilant of our own being—separate from it rather than part of it. We are then separate from the spontaneous, streaming vibration that marks true aliveness.

Whenever we have to keep a secret, we must block the spontaneous unfolding of our true expression.

Many children are burdened with having to keep secrets. The sexually abused child who is threatened into silence about the abuse must live with a lock on her fifth chakra. "I'll kill you if you ever tell anyone about this," is a phrase far too many abuse survivors have etched into their souls. This injunction becomes so internalized that feelings of terror and even suicide may emerge when they do finally speak about the abuse even decades later.

The little boy who is told never to talk about Daddy's drinking must keep a family secret. He can't live fully in his truth. Shame in the family that is known inside but can't be shared outside—shame about money, physical diseases, mental illness, addictions, or crimes—creates an unspoken rule to never speak about this reality outside the home. He must then guard against the spontaneous expression of his fifth chakra, being careful not to talk about things that may bother him most. This can create a lifelong pattern that is especially damaging to intimate relationships.

Secrets are kept *from* children as well. I knew someone whose mother died when he was eight, but who was never allowed to discuss the reasons for her death or explore his feelings about it. It was simply never mentioned again. Another client had a brother who had committed suicide, and the family members were forbidden to speak his name.

When family problems can be seen plainly but are not talked about openly, the child picks up the unstated rule to keep secrets. This makes it impossible for him to ask questions about the problem and difficult to talk about other dilemmas later in life. Though spoken language is programmed early in life, the use of communication to solve problems is modeled throughout childhood, especially during the upper chakra developmental stages.

Sexuality is another frequently forbidden subject. In a family where sex is never discussed, the maturing child knows that his or her sexual feelings must be kept completely hidden. As sexuality and masturbation are natural in a growing child's life, walls of shame and guilt are built to keep the secret in. This pushes sexuality into the shadow realms. If a person is not comfortable talking about sexual matters, it increases the risk of unwanted pregnancies, STDs, undue shyness, shame, and acting-out behavior.

Secrets promote ignorance. They do not allow a subject to reach the light of consciousness, where new information can be gained. Secrets block the flow of energy through the fifth chakra into the upper realms of consciousness, perpetuating repetitive and compulsive behavior patterns.

LIES AND MIXED MESSAGES

Lies form the demon of the fifth chakra. We have already discussed them briefly under basic issues, but here I wish to speak of the lies we live with while growing up, lies that scramble the programming in our fifth chakras.

Being told we have no right to feel a certain way when in fact that is how we feel makes a lie of our basic experience. Hearing the words "I love you" while having the experience of being abused, neglected, or shamed makes a lie of love. Being asked to apologize for something we do not feel sorry about, to be nice to someone we clearly dislike, or to be thankful for something we didn't want are all experiences that teach us to lie. They teach us to lie to ourselves, to each other, and to our bodies. They create dissonance within the basic vibration of the self.

> The experience of one's own truth... makes it possible to return to one's world of feelings at an adult level—without paradise, but with the ability to mourn.
>
> ALICE MILLER

Daniel was the victim of his father's rage, which was inflicted on him in the form of cruel punishment. In order to prove that he was a man, Daniel was forced to endure this punishment without reaction. If he got angry, screamed, or cried, the punishment would be worse. Not only was he abused, but he was also denied the honest reaction to his abuse. He was forced to live a lie. Is it any wonder that he now has a vicious inner critic that guards the gateway of his throat chakra and regulates everything that might come out of his mouth?

YELLING AND SCREAMING

Children learn by imitation. An atmosphere of hostility expressed through constant arguing, yelling, or screaming is an abuse to the fifth chakra. What we hear around us programs our use of language and teaches us how to communicate.

When the home atmosphere is unpleasant to see or hear, we close down the aural and visual functions as much as possible. Since it is more difficult to close the ears than it is to close the eyes, a counter-dialog often occurs inside one's head where we effectively block off our listening by creating something else instead. While Mom is nagging us once more about how messy our room is, we are shutting her out by running a different set of words through our head.

Later in life, we may find it hard to listen to others, to entertain new ideas, to really be able to hear someone in their truth. We decide we already know what they are going to say, that we have heard it all before. We have our arguments and defenses ready before they even open their mouth. Instead of listening when they speak, we are busy preparing our rebuttal. Thus listening, which is absolutely essential to clear communication, becomes an impaired function.

AUTHORITARIANISM—"DON'T TALK BACK!"

When parents set rules that cannot be questioned, they leave no room for discussion. Without discussion, there is no practice ground for the child to learn communication skills. There is no place for the child's truth to be honored and no place to learn reasoning. They quickly feel devalued as no one wants to listen to them, and consequently split off from their own truth.

If we are not listened to, we shut down our fifth chakra. We get the message that our inner truth does not matter, or, in effect, that *we* do not matter. Is it any wonder that the inner voice is later drowned out by peers wanting us to do something we know is dangerous? That we cannot hear the voice of our own limits when the boss asks us to

> Children have a need to be heard and listened to. If they fail to receive this, they won't even be able to hear themselves.

work overtime, or that we fall victim to the voice of the whining spouse criticizing our behavior?

A child's inner voice must be searched for and drawn out. It must have a safe place where it can afford to be uncertain or wrong without meeting ridicule. A child's voice needs the environment of compassionate exploration to make itself heard. Without this, they may not even hear themselves.

NEGLECT

I worked with someone in her forties who said she never had an actual conversation with her father even though he lived with her throughout her childhood and saw her periodically throughout adulthood. He had spoken *to her* during that time but never *with her*. He had never asked her anything about her life, wondered what she thought, or waited for an answer when he spoke to her. It was no surprise that she had poor communication skills and kept plenty of secrets from her husband, or that she was inordinately quiet.

Children have questions, feelings, and ideas that need to be communicated with a caring adult. They need things explained to them, and need their horizons widened through conversation. Children learn to communicate by being talked with—they learn to reason, question, think for themselves, trust, and share. Through communication they have a grounding in reality, a sounding board for their ideas, a means by which to open up to something larger. This is how they gain new information, learn, and grow.

We learn to communicate by using language, seeing it modeled around us, and seeing how its power can be used to solve problems. Like learning to use a hammer, it becomes an invaluable tool for building our lives and for feeling connected, capable, and confident. To give children the gift of clear communication is to give them a key that will unlock the majority of impasses and difficulties they will face in the future.

CHARACTER STRUCTURE

THE CHALLENGER-DEFENDER

It was awe-inspiring to watch Stella perform. She was the kind of woman who made heads turn on the street—dark and sultry, with a seductive smile that could make the sun come out in your heart. Her eyes were compelling, her body lithe and graceful with wide shoulders, shapely arms, and thin waist and hips. It seemed fitting that she worked as a model, sang in nightclubs, and had hopes of eventually making it as an actress.

Needless to say, she never lacked for male attention, but her relationships were short-lived and full of frustration. She was prone to rages, after which she could allow some closeness with her partner, but she never managed to settle into a place of trust. Nervousness would follow intimacy, and she could become critical and distant. Eventually, her partners would tire of bouncing between intimacy and distance and challenge her. When this happened, she would find some way to make them appear wrong, abusive, or victimizing, and then discard them. She was prone to exaggeration, and one might even say that her penchant for acting was a love of melodrama. She did it well, both on and off stage.

Stella was very powerful in the way she conducted her work, and she was admired by the people who knew her. Few, if any, realized how fragile and lonely she was underneath. In fact, she was scarcely aware of it herself, and threw her energy into her career and into other ways that commanded admiration. She created an outer persona that was beautiful and powerful, while underneath lurked a poor self-image, vulnerable and afraid. She had a strong fifth chakra, an excessive will in the third chakra, an open but disconnected second chakra, and a weak sense of her own ground. Her heart opened and closed according to the situation—she could be very loving or cold and angry, often switching between the two with astonishing rapidity. Stella was an example of the character structure known as the Challenger-Defender (see figure 5.2).

Most character structure is set in the mind-body by the time a child reaches school age. Since the fifth chakra flowers after that, we can no longer correlate the upper chakra developmental stages so precisely to the formation

FIGURE 5.2. PSYCHOPATHIC STRUCTURE (CHALLENGER-DEFENDER)
THE BETRAYED CHILD

FIRST CHAKRA May be either	SECOND CHAKRA Excessive	THIRD CHAKRA Excessive	FOURTH CHAKRA Deficient
Usually not interested in body, taking it for granted. Some, however, become body-builders as a way of becoming powerful	Very loose pelvis	Very oriented to power, dominating yet feels powerless and victimized	Fears submission too much to trust intimacy
Unreliable	Seductive	Hyperactive followed by collapse	Views intimacy as weakness
Paranoid	Needy underneath defense	Prone to rage	Can't form equal relationships, needs to dominate and control
Self-centered	Emotional, volatile	Fears submisssion, so ready for a fight; must win	Can be close when needed by someone, defensive when challenged
	Childhood needs exploited	Thinks any difficulty is a matter of will	Good champion of the underdog
		Needs to be right	Soft and loving when they feel safe

FIFTH CHAKRA	SIXTH CHAKRA	SEVENTH CHAKRA
Excessive	Deficient	Balance to excess
Engaging, entertaining, charismatic	May appear to be insensitive of others' needs	Highly intelligent
Strong verbally, strong in arguments	Fixates on image instead of reality	Knowledgable
Prone to exaggeration	Can be monopolarized (one right way)	Difficulty surrendering to higher power
Discharges tension through talking	Especially prone to denial	Energy held high in body; strong, large head and shoulders
Dominates through talking	Difficulty seeing alternatives	
May be deceitful or secretive		

of character structure. While the Challenger-Defender structure comes from deprivation between the ages of two and a half and four years (later third chakra), I discuss it here in the fifth chakra because of its tendency to pull energy upward in the body. This generates a strong focus of energy in the upper chakras, especially the fifth. Challenger-Defenders make great actors, singers, lawyers, professors, and performers of any kind, as they are highly creative and brilliant communicators who enjoy positions of power and often handle them well. It is vulnerability that poses a problem for this structure, and most of their efforts go toward avoiding it.

A strong fifth chakra is one of the unwittingly seductive aspects of this structure. They can cajole you with sweetness, impress you with eloquence, command you with the clarity of their arguments, and stun you with their candor. Their charismatic nature makes others anxious to please them, and they are comfortable and effective when occupying positions of power.

Their upwardly displaced energy often creates broad shoulders and narrow hips, and their physical presence gives a sense of both power and grace. They are not rigid, like the Achiever type, and in fact their lower chakras (especially the pelvis) may seem excessively loose and fluid (see page 23, Challenger-Defender Character). They can be highly sexual, but are flighty and lack lasting emotional commitment. They tend to be energetically exuberant as the lower chakra energy is pushed up through the liberating current, but poorly grounded as they have too little of the manifesting current pulling toward focus and form. They are usually attractive, commanding, and confident.

Their power and well-developed communication mask a deeper sense of distrust and insecurity. Underneath the mask, the Challenger-Defender is more like an Oral—needy, hungry, and weak. These feelings are so intolerable that the Challenger-Defender goes to great lengths to avoid any situation that might reveal their hidden, vulnerable nature. They are well defended against possible challenge, but this defense also perpetuates their loneliness.

As the defender aspect of the name might imply, persons with this structure are wonderfully compassionate and supportive when defending the underdog, with whom they unconsciously relate. They make heroic champions, who will rush to your defense, fight for important causes, and generously dole out nurturing and understanding to the weak and needy. Often they find themselves in relationships with people who are younger, quieter, and emotionally dependent, choosing situations where they are least likely to be challenged.

When the meek become strong, however, and choose to question this type in any way, the supportive defender aspect suddenly turns into an attacking challenger. With white-hot verbal defensiveness, they may launch into sudden bursts of anger and attack whoever dares to challenge them. If this does not restore their sense of power, they may become rejecting and unavailable. Intimacy can only be tolerated from a position of security and advantage. They must be winners at all times, and realistic challenge cannot be tolerated. They will go to any length to preserve their position of power. It is vitally important to them to be right.

As a child, the Challenger-Defender had his or her trust broken irrevocably, usually through seductive manipulation. At a time when she was developing autonomy (third chakra) but still dependent and needing heart chakra connection, the parent used the child's vulnerability as a way to manipulate her. In this sense, the child was seduced by the parent, most often the parent of the opposite sex. This seduction may or may not be sexual, but it does convince the child to sacrifice her authentic vulnerable self for a more invincible cover persona.

The child learns that vulnerability is a danger and that seduction and manipulation are ways to overcome that vulnerability. As a result, deception may become a primary survival strategy, and Challenger-Defenders may feel perfectly justified in ignoring accepted ethics and fairness in order to live by their own rules. For this reason, and because of their penchant for power at all costs, Alexander Lowen named this structure the *Psychopath*.

In terms of authority, parents were usually inconsistent—loving and lax at times, while viciously punitive at others. The underlying result is lack of trust and certainty, which makes for a weak first chakra. There is openness but danger in the emotional center of the second chakra, a strong sense of power in the third chakra, very conditional love in the fourth chakra, and a seemingly capable, but not always honest, fifth chakra. Chakras six and seven usually reflect their high intelligence and piercing perceptiveness.

Challenger-Defenders, like all of us, need love, safety, and security. They need to have a place where their more vulnerable needs can be recognized and met, where they are loved for their imperfect self rather than their powerful image. They need to be able to see how they were dominated in childhood and then learn to direct their anger at the perpetrators as opposed to their loved ones. It is best when they have loved ones who can accept their imperfections, who are not fooled by their false persona, and do not leave them when they attack—a tall order indeed, and one that they would rarely reciprocate. In the struggle of relationship, they sometimes gain a sense of true empowerment that is anchored in feelings and the body, where they can tell the truth and have it received without judgment. It is then that they can satisfy the needs that drive them, balancing their upper chakra displacement, and move toward psychological health.

EXCESS AND DEFICIENCY

Excess and deficiency in the throat chakra are easily recognized. As this is a gateway between inner and outer worlds, we can tell just by listening how open this gateway is. Does someone ramble incessantly or are they perpetually quiet? Does the voice have resonance or is it pinched and whiny? The fast talkers are discharging energy through their throat chakras, and the quiet ones are locked inside without enough energy to break free.

Our individuality is our personal rhythm of pulsating.

STANLEY KELEMAN

DEFICIENCY

A person with a deficient fifth chakra cannot get his words together. His voice may be weak, airy, pinched, or rhythmically erratic. There is extreme self-consciousness and shyness, a need to hide, and a fear of humiliation. Sometimes there is good communication within, but it is never released through the gateway. Sometimes the communication within is restricted, and there is a great separation between mind and body.

Usually the closer a topic is to the real feelings inside, the harder it is to communicate. We may find someone who communicates very well at work when conducting business meetings, writing reports, or talking on the telephone, but has extreme difficulty talking to his wife and family about what he wants and needs. Since this chakra is about self-expression of one's truth, we judge its openness by how well we can speak about the things that are closest to the heart.

Often, it may not occur to a deficient fifth chakra person to communicate at all. He may forget to tell you he is going out of town next week until the last moment, forget to ask how your day was, or live in an interior world of conversation where he thinks that he already did all of that. It does not occur to such a person to initiate conversations about difficult situations or to use words as a way of gaining more information. He may not feel he even has the right to ask questions. Such a person may have been heavily interrogated during childhood and learned to keep this chakra private as a defense (see figure 5.3).

EXCESS

With an excessive fifth chakra, talking is a defense that is used as a way of staying in control. An excessive fifth chakra controls the conversation, the subject matter, and rhythm so as to bring its owner into the center of attention.

As the fifth chakra is one of the gateways through which stress can be discharged, excess verbiage can be a means of getting rid of energy. This was apparent with a client who flew into a torrent of words whenever we did any bioenergetic charging exercises. The words occupied her consciousness and kept her from fully feeling her body, while simultaneously discharging the excess energy. Displaced rage is often expressed through rapid talking as well.

With an excessive fifth chakra, there is much talk with little real content. Clients may go into a lengthy description of a situation that happened during the week, complete with innumerable details, and yet avoid saying anything about how they actually felt. Again, this is an attempt to discharge energy, avoid feelings, and have some sense of power over the situation (see figure 5.3).

Figure 5.3. Fifth Chakra Excess and Deficiency

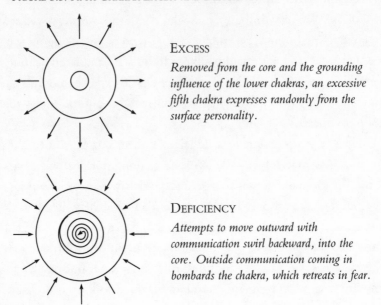

Excess

Removed from the core and the grounding influence of the lower chakras, an excessive fifth chakra expresses randomly from the surface personality.

Deficiency

Attempts to move outward with communication swirl backward, into the core. Outside communication coming in bombards the chakra, which retreats in fear.

Combinations

Lack of ground can produce either excess or deficiency within the throat chakra. For some people, lack of ground may result in excessive speech that is void of real content. For others, lack of ground creates such fear that they can scarcely get their words out at all. These people may feel swirling energy almost like vertigo when they attempt to speak, which inhibits their ability to think clearly. This closes off the throat chakra and creates a deficient condition.

It is quite common to have throat chakras with both excessive and deficient characteristics, allowing us to communicate well in some instances, and poorly in others. One person may be able to communicate feelings with grace and dignity, yet have no confidence to push outward in work and career. Others may speak well with strangers but clam up with intimate partners.

As this chakra is a gateway, it opens and closes rapidly. It is highly sensitive to the situation at hand. It coordinates many voices inside, including those from the past and from different parts of us. The throat chakra must then integrate them into one solid and whole voice, as it reaches out to communicate.

Balance

The health of the throat chakra rests in neither extreme, but in its ability to accurately communicate the truth of one's experience, witness and meet another's truth, and approach life creatively and effectively. Balanced characteristics reveal a person with good communication skills, both in self-expression and effective listening. A good listener can ask questions that elicit information, make use of that information, and let someone know that they have been heard and understood. With a healthy fifth chakra, one's voice is resonant and pleasant to listen to, and has natural rhythms with appropriate tonality and volume. They can project or speak quietly when needed. In conversation, there is a balance between speaking and listening. Since the chakra relates to rhythm, there is a sense of timing and grace in one's activities and body movements. Energetically, the pulsation of life flows freely and vibrantly, without jerky motions, self-consciousness, or agitation.

Lastly, a person with a strong fifth chakra lives life creatively. They are fairly well individuated and are not bound by fear to accepted ways of doing things. As the lower chakra energy moves into the upper chakras, form becomes less important, while intelligence, consciousness, and the ability to think become more so. Living creatively does not apply merely to the arts, but to an attitude about what is possible. We cannot assess the quality of the throat chakra by whether one paints, dances, or plays music. It is possible to do all these things by rote, without any creativity at all. Instead, the throat chakra is the gateway through which the forward-thinking mind works with the life stream of the body to create new ways of approaching life. This may be apparent in the way we dress, speak, or vary the route we take to work. Do we dare to be creative? Do we see a life full of infinite possibilities? Are we creatures of habit, or do we fully participate in each moment anew? This is the mark of true creativity.

RESTORING THE LOTUS

HEALING THE FIFTH CHAKRA

Several years ago, a friend offered me some voice lessons in exchange for bodywork. As I have always loved music but have never had a strong singing voice, I was delighted. But I soon discovered that whenever I tried to breathe deeply and project my voice fully, I started to cry. When I tried to control myself and stop the tears, my voice and breath lost their fullness.

My teacher was very patient with me and told me this was quite common. She said that the emotions are connected with the voice, and that we cannot touch one without touching the other. It was true. I could not open my mouth and simultaneously hide what I was feeling that day any more than I could reveal what I was feeling without opening my mouth. This is not only true when we try to sing, but also true of our voice projection in general. When we constrict our emotions, we simultaneously constrict our expression.

> The ability of a substance to resonate sympathetically is the result of its elasticity.
>
> RANDALL McCLELLAN

Some of my healing during that period came from simply letting out the sound of my grief and anger. At other times I needed to talk about what was going on inside of me—to put it into an intellectual context and share it with someone who would understand. Sometimes it was a combination of abstract and specific communication. In the end, I was able to arrive at a place of joy where the sound could emanate from my throat with fullness, from a place of confidence instead of fear. I did not keep up with it long enough to become a great singer, but the experience offered me a chance to connect body, breath, and voice in a new way.

I bring up this story to illustrate the fact that healing the fifth chakra involves a variety of levels simultaneously, ranging from physical to mental. It includes eliminating sound pollution, giving attention to our bodies, opening the voice through toning, chanting, or singing, learning clear communication skills, and quieting ourselves enough to listen to the subtler vibrations and messages within. Each of these basic principles is explored more fully below.

THE VIBRATING BODY

Since our bodies are the resonating chambers of the sounds we make, it is essential to work through bodily tensions. Release of tensions and held emotions restores the natural reflexive and vibratory nature of the body. Without this work, it is unlikely that the throat chakra would be free of constraints or that we would be living deeply in our truth. The reclamation of the body is the restoration of our unique vibration.

> There is no greater and more living resonator of sound than the human body. Sound has an effect on each atom of the body, for each atom resounds.
>
> HAZRAT INAYAT KHAN

Stanley Keleman, in *Your Body Speaks Its Mind*, describes a simple process for getting in touch with our basic pulsating vibration:

> If you hold your breath and pay attention to your chest and abdomen, you will feel the coming and going of excitement. If you clench your fist or tighten your thigh muscles and sustain the contraction, you will feel a fine vibration throughout your entire organism. If the vibration deepens, you'll begin to experience it as a pulsating. Sustain the contraction until the pulsating deepens, then let it go, and you become aware of a streaming: an internal flowing which is difficult to see but which you can feel.[5]

It is this streaming which is the signature of our aliveness and individuality. Whenever a powerful urge to move forward is contained, we can feel the streaming of energy pulsating through our bodies. We may also feel it after physical exertion or emotional expression, such as after a good run, a good cry, or a powerful sexual experience. This brings us to a vital experience of *self in connection*, where we are open to our own vibratory resonance.

Many people are afraid of containing this much charge. For some (especially those typically overcharged) having energy means having to immediately do something with it. If we express ourselves before our truth is fully ripened, then our actions are out of sync with our potential fullness. This is commonly experienced as *poor timing*.

Years ago, I habitually pushed myself in my work rather than waiting for my organic fullness to motivate me. I would end up running into a kind of creative bankruptcy, emptiness of ideas, and lack of energy. When I rushed myself ahead of my own natural rhythm, I felt unprepared, stressed, anxious, and even a bit breathless. We push our timing out of sync because of financial pressure, emotional insecurity, fear, hunger for power, and the excessive rule of the mind as it orders our bodies with its barrage of "shoulds." As the lower chakras become strong, the security from chakra one allows proper timing to occur, the emotional stability of chakra two lets our feelings become ripe and full, the sense of our own power from chakra three does not need to prove itself, and chakra four balances mind and body. At this point we can dance to the rhythm of our own personal vibration as it resonates with the environment and the people around us.

EXERCISE

Allow yourself to move freely around the room with your eyes closed. Try to move from the natural inclinations of your body, rather than from the decisions from your head. After your body begins to loosen up, accompany each movement with an abstract sound that emanates from the movement. Let yourself be open to an experience of "movement making sound," and look for a place where the movement and sound are a coordinated vibration that runs through your whole being. Let yourself enjoy the experience and see where it takes you.

CLEANING OUT THE FIELD

In addition to tuning into our own vibration, we need to pay careful attention to the outer vibrations that we experience daily. What is the level of sound and media pollution to which you are exposed? What kind of rhythms does your body experience in terms of eating, sleeping, sexuality, activity, and rest? What kind of vibrations do you find incompatible with the resonance of

Sound awareness is especially important, for although we easily close our mouth and eyes to what we don't want to take in, we can't really close our ears. Nature did not give us earlids. Our ears remain open and working even when we sleep.

STEVEN HALPERN

your own consciousness? How can you reduce or eliminate toxic noise and toxic people from your environment?

Soundproofing walls and windows, wearing earplugs around loud machinery, shortening unwanted phone calls, and allowing personal rhythms to settle into soothing and regular patterns all help protect our vibrational field. This acts as preventive medicine. Eliminating distracting patterns enables us to better hear ourselves and others on a deeper and subtler level.

In this day and age, however, it is difficult to eliminate sound pollution and still live in an urban environment. Since we can't always screen out harmful noise, it becomes essential to take time each day to be perfectly quiet. We need a period of time when we don't answer the phone, cannot be interrupted, and can meditate in silence with earplugs or listen to soothing music under headphones. Periodic weekends in the country, where background noise resonates in a completely different rhythm, can help our vibrational field to retune itself, much like resetting a thermostat. Without this, we eventually tune out unwanted sound and simultaneously tune out large portions of our consciousness as well.

DEEP LISTENING

Listening is an essential part of communication. In taking the time to be quiet, we are able to truly listen to ourselves. The chatter of the mind eventually dies down and the song of the heart pours forth. In this opening into silence, the upper and lower chakras can enter into resonance with each other, connecting mind and body.

In silence, inner listening forms the bonding of heart and mind.

EXERCISE

Sit in a quiet place by yourself and let your mind become quiet. See how many layers of sounds you can detect around you. Listen to the sound of your own breathing, the rhythm of your heartbeat, and the blood pulsing in your ears. Hear the birds, the distant traffic, the sound of the wind. Then let all these sounds blend into one general sound, where the rhythm of your breath and the subtle movements of your body become part of the sound around you.

As your body merges with this sound, allow it to subtly move with this rhythm. See where the movement takes you, being careful to stay with the overall sound you hear.

TONING

Toning encourages the basic vibration within you to come out through your throat as sound. Toning does not force the voice into specific words, melodies, or sounds, but works with both body and breath to create pure expression, devoid of intellectual meaning or aesthetic appeal.

When we move physically, or are moved emotionally, it's natural to make sound. We squeal with pleasure when we're excited or groan when we're hurt. When we exert ourselves, we seem to have more strength if we grunt. Unfortunately, we get embarrassed by these sounds and learn to stifle them, closing down the throat chakra.

EXERCISE

Toning is best done after a brief period of warming up the body. Stand erect and stretch upward, reaching for the sky. Stretch to the right and left, forward and back, loosening the torso. Let your body shake and bounce, letting out any sounds that want to emerge. Shake your legs out, swing your arms. Let your body become loose and vibrant.

> Pain frequently is the result of tension, and groaning is nature's way of relieving it.
>
> LAUREL ELIZABETH KEYES

When you feel sufficiently warmed up, stand with both feet planted firmly on the ground, and bring your arms back to your sides or lift them above your head. Close your eyes and listen to the sounds within you.

Take a deep breath and open your mouth, letting the breath out in as full a sound as possible. It may come out as a groan, a squeal, a guffaw, or any manner of strange sounds. Or there may be a variety of sounds that change from one moment to the next. Just let them emerge without judgment, opening to the spontaneity of expression as much as possible.

After a while, you will find that the tone settles into a note that feels particularly right for you—a note that you can sustain. You may need to experiment with many notes to find this special tone. Allow yourself to sing this note as fully as you can, reaching for resonance, relaxing your diaphragm, throat, and chest. See if you can feel where the sound originates in your body. Is it coming from your throat? Your chest? Your belly? Your head? Try to let it come from your whole body at once, moving any body part that seems disconnected until it is integrated into the sound as well.

Eventually, the release of the tone will settle naturally to a place of quiet. Notice how your body feels, what you can hear. Notice how present you feel. Write or draw in your journal, and feel the flow of creativity that often is released by this exercise.

CHANTING AND USING MANTRAS

Chanting is a more sophisticated form of toning. Chanting lulls the vibrations of our body and consciousness into resonance by the rhythmic repetition of a simple phrase or sound. This rhythm refines our awareness. The sounds used in chanting may have specific meanings that we wish to instill into our consciousness—as with repeating affirmations about things we would like to change, or may have no meaning and therefore bypass the conscious mind entirely. Both, however, are rhythmic experiences where the conscious mind does not have to think very much. This allows us to surrender to a deeper resonance or enter a trance state. Here our individuated consciousness expands to merge with the greater consciousness and rhythm of life.

> The mantra is not merely a technique of awakening; it is actually and in itself a state of being indicative of the presence of divinity.
>
> AJIT MOOKERJEE

Mantras are chants uttered silently in the mind. They replace the ceaseless rhythm of our busy thoughts, and therefore cleanse, simplify, and order the mind. *Mantra* literally means "instrument of the mind." Transcendental Meditation (TM) is a meditation technique where one mentally repeats a certain sound that is individually given by a teacher or guru. Research has shown that silently chanting one's mantra creates a meditative state by synchronizing brain waves between various lobes of the brain.[6]

In a world where we are constantly bombarded by dissonance, intoning a mantra can be another way to recalibrate our basic vibrational essence. Through mantra meditation, we eventually enter a quiet and rhythmic state, emptied of the disjointed mental garbage we pick up throughout the day and filled with a well-tuned attentiveness that brings greater alertness and sensitivity. Some yogis believe that chanting mantras releases a "liquid nectar" in the pineal gland that contributes to the alteration of consciousness. This may be due to the rhythmic play of the tongue against the roof of the mouth, which is believed to release the "nectar."[7]

Each chakra has a specific mantra sound. The list below gives both the seed sounds from the ancient tantric texts—believed to access the elemental qualities of the chakras—and the vowel sounds, which resonate in the body itself. For the Westerner, the vowel sounds produce a stronger experience, but I encourage you to experiment with both and find what works best for you.

- **CHAKRA ONE:** Seed sound Lam (*lahm*), vowel sound Ohh (as in *road*)

- **CHAKRA TWO:** Seed sound Vam (*vahm*), vowel sound Oooo (as in *rule*)

- **CHAKRA THREE:** Seed sound Ram (*rahm*), vowel sound Ahh (as in *father*)

- **CHAKRA FOUR:** Seed sound Yam (*yahm*), vowel sound Ayy (as in *play*)

- **CHAKRA FIVE:** Seed sound Ham (*hahm*), vowel sound Eeee (as in *sleep*)

- **CHAKRA SIX:** Seed sound Om (*ohm*), resonant sound Mmm

- **CHAKRA SEVEN:** No seed sound given, resonant sound Nngg (as in *sing*)

Leah Garfield, author of *Sound Medicine*, suggests chanting the seed sounds in a specific rhythm nine times each, with a full minute of silence between each chakra.[8]

To chant the vowel sounds, begin with some simple stretching exercises, and then sit or stand comfortably so that the breath is deep and full. As you chant the vowels, remember to open up to both the resonance of the voice and the vibration of the body where the chakra resides. Let the sound come out as fully as possible, for a minimum of one whole minute when by yourself. With a group, stagger the breaths and continue the sound even longer.

CREATE YOUR OWN MANTRA

After chanting the vowel sounds and experiencing the way they resonate within each of your chakras, you may wish to try creating a silent mantra to use in meditation. The following technique is designed to create a mantra that resonates with the chakras you would most like to improve.

Pick the sounds that go with one, two, or at most three of the chakras you feel need the most attention. Put the sounds together in a way that is pleasing to you. For example, if you want to work on the first and fourth chakras, you would pick the sounds *Ohh* and *Ayy*. Then your mantra might sound something like *Ayoh, Ayoh, Ayoh*.

Then sit in silent meditation mentally intoning the sound you have created. Feel it resonate within the chakras you have picked. Imagine them expanding or clearing. (This exercise works best when it is used consistently over a period of time.)

COMMUNICATION

So far we have listed techniques to tone the chakra in general, which allows the sound to come through our bodies more easily. Now we turn to the more specific aspect of the throat chakra: communication itself. If you find you are having trouble getting your point across to someone, it may be that you have not understood his point. Often, a person cannot truly listen until they feel they have been heard. We have previously applied the art of listening to the sounds around and within us. Now we apply that deep listening to communication with others.

THE NEED TO BE HEARD

One of the most profound human needs is the need to be heard. When this simple need is met by attentive, empathetic listening, we feel complete and ready to move onward. It is amazing how much healing can take place when our story, feelings, or opinions are simply heard, even if there is no change in the circumstances. The need to be heard validates our truth, our individuality, and our very existence. If we cannot be heard,

> If you wish to be understood, seek first to understand.
>
> STEVEN R. COVEY

we cease to exist in anything but our own minds. We feel crazy, doubtful of our own inner voice, and of our reality. When we cannot trust our experience, we split off from the body and, hence, split off from reality.

The need to be heard is often more important than finding solutions. This is a frequent dynamic with couples. If one partner cannot do anything about the problem his spouse is having, he does not want to hear about it. What is often more important than fixing the problem is acknowledging the other person's feelings. This simple practice can go a long way toward healing situations and facilitating good communication.

Karen and George were clearly immersed in this dynamic. George was frequently away on business; Karen kept the house while he was gone, minded the children, and tried to pursue her own career as a seminar coordinator in her copious free time. Needless to say, it was more difficult for Karen to do her work when George was away, but since George earned the primary money for the family, they saw no way to avoid his frequent absence. Karen needed to complain about her situation to George, but because he saw no way to change it, he refused to hear about it. Instead she needed him to simply acknowledge the difficulty it made for her, even if he could not change it. Then she would stop harping on it all the time, and stop making him feel worthless for the work he was doing.

In turn, George wanted Karen to understand that he was not exactly having fun on his business trips. He didn't like being away from home and felt pressured and underappreciated in his job. Since she didn't want him to go away in the first place, she in turn did not want to hear about his experience. So they closed themselves off from each other even during the brief periods they had together, as neither was able to express or feel heard about their primary concerns. As a result, their connection was seriously strained. Although they could not change their immediate circumstances, getting them to simply listen and acknowledge each other's realities helped tremendously to improve their basic connection and cooperation with each other.

ACTIVE LISTENING

Active listening enables another person to have the experience of being heard. In active listening, we quiet ourselves and turn our entire focus of energy toward the other person. As she speaks, we may nod or say "mmhm" to let her know that we are still with her, but we do not interrupt or make any comments. When the speaker is finished, we ask if she is complete. We may then want to ask questions or clarify something, but we still refrain from making comments, suggestions, arguments, or judgments.

When we feel that we understand what the speaker has said, we then respond by explaining what we have just heard, but in our own words. We might respond with a statement like, "What I hear you saying is that you're tired of always being the one to initiate talks about our relationship, and that it feels like I don't really care if I never share the things I feel with you." In this response, you are simply repeating what you have heard regardless of whether or not you agree with it, or have a counterpoint to offer. In repeating what you have heard, it is also important not to parrot the exact words, but to phrase your response in a way that communicates your own understanding of what has been said.

Your co-communicator then has a chance to let you know whether or not you heard her correctly. She might say, "That's close, but not quite right. It's not that I think you don't care at all, but that I don't *know* whether you care—that I don't know where I stand. When you don't let me know how you feel, I imagine the worst." If there is a correction, it is important to try again to see if you now understand correctly.

"So when I don't communicate with you about how I feel, you don't know for sure where you stand with me, and that makes you likely to imagine that I might not care."

"Yes, that's what I'm trying to say."

Only when the first speaker is satisfied that she has been truly heard is it time for the second speaker to share his own truth.

"If you're satisfied that I heard you correctly, then I would like to share with you how it is for me. Is that OK?"

"Yes, go ahead."

"The way it works with me is that I am least likely to communicate when I care the most. It's as if caring makes it too scary to let you know how much things matter to me. I know it sounds ridiculous, but where I am right now, when my heart chakra feels exposed and vulnerable, I retreat into silence until I know it's safe to come out."

"So, I hear that it's hard for you to communicate when your feelings are really engaged and your heart is open. You feel safer in silence."

After both people are satisfied that they have been fully heard (and this may go back and forth several times before it is complete), they can begin to create a solution that will address both concerns.

"When you're not sure where you stand with me, I would love it if you would just say to me, 'I'm not sure where I stand right now.' That would clarify what's going on."

"And when you retreat into silence because you're scared, I want to encourage you to tell me that you need to be quiet, instead of just retreating, which makes me feel shut out. If you say you need space, I can understand and not interpret it as a rejection."

It is equally important to listen to yourself while you are speaking. If we are experiencing difficulties in communication, it can be helpful to record our conversations with others, or our solo practice conversations, to hear nuances and subtleties. How would it feel to receive the words you are speaking? What can you hear between the words as you listen to your own voice? How can your communication become more direct and effective?

WRITING

Writing is a form of communication that transcends time. With pen in hand (or computer keyboard) we can sit in silence until the right words come, write them down, change them around, or say exactly what we please and throw it out before it unnecessarily hurts anyone's feelings. For those who have trouble communicating on the spot, it helps to take time to write out your feelings on your own time.

David found himself tongue-tied whenever his wife got angry. She was a Challenger-Defender who was quick with words and a master at argument. He was an Endurer/Masochist, a silent type who, without arguments to defend himself, would quietly nod in her presence, shrug his shoulders, and pretend to agree with her. Hours later he would review the conversation in his mind and think of all the juicy comebacks he could have said, and feel lost and helpless. His only comeback was to be passive-aggressive and emotionally removed, which of course only perpetuated the dysfunctional dynamic.

I encouraged David to sit down and write about his unexpressed and unresolved issues with her, using several forms of communication. The first form was for the purpose of finding his own voice. He was to begin by writing what he wished to tell her without censoring it. He could use any words he wanted, let out his anger without holding back, and go on without interruption for as long as he needed. It did not have to be a coherent argument—it was just for venting his feelings. This form was not given to her, but was used just to prime the pump and loosen the throat chakra from its habitual constriction.

Then, I asked him to read his writing aloud to me so I could be an active listener and let him feel what it was like to be heard. In being heard, he could experience how to use the power of his voice to find resonance and completion. He could learn to better trust his own voice.

He was then able to take what he had written and find ways to communicate the salient points without the heat of emotion, so that the words might better meet their target. With this clarity, we began role-playing a dialog between him and his ex-wife, so that he could practice sticking to his truth in the face of opposition, while I gave the kind of answer he usually received from her. He was then ready to try the dialog in real life. Much to his surprise, he found her far more able to listen to him now that he was clear on what he wanted to say, and said it firmly and directly, without the urgent press of feelings that previously tied him in knots.

Writing can also be helpful when communicating with people who are truly unable to hear what we need to say. They may no longer be living, may be geographically unavailable, or may not wish to be in contact with us for reasons of their own. These reasons need not keep us in an unresolved state, and working through all but the last steps of the above process can help us complete our own process and feel more resolved in the situation. If the person is still alive, it may be useful to send a revised letter even if we know they will not respond.

Unfinished conversations tend to continue in our mind, distracting us from being fully present. This exercise clears the throat chakra of unfinished conversation, letting us clear the disk so that it has room to store new information. We can then listen with an open mind.

MUSIC

If chanting, toning, and mantra meditation have the capacity to affect our innermost being, then music must have a profound effect on our entire mind–body system. Music can move us to tears, fill us with joy, inspire our body to shake and dance, or calm and excite us. Music in the background of movies and television plays our emotions like an instrument. Music sells products in advertising, and entertains, teases, inspires, and unites. Songs are the spiritual record of humanity, recording its trials and triumphs, and a binding thread of communities, religions, and political movements. One way to destroy a culture is to destroy its music.

> Music is a cry of the soul. It is a revelation, a thing to be reverenced. Performances of great musical works are for us what the rites and festivals of religion were to the ancients——an initiation into the mysteries of the human soul.
>
> FREDERICK DELIUS

Music deliciously combines upper and lower chakra experiences. It bathes the body in rhythm and resonance, while entertaining the mind with its complexity of meter, melody, instrumentation, and message. Music unites the soul of the body with the mind and spirit.

Shamanic medicine works in part on the principle of resonance through music and drumming. Music can put us into a trance, where the body lets go and enters into a different state of consciousness. In trance, we are able to transcend the ego and find a broader, spiritual state more conducive to healing.

Technically speaking, music travels across auditory nerves to the thalamus in the brain, which affects our emotions. The thalamus then stimulates the cortex, which sends responsive impulses back to the thalamus and hypothalamus. This circuit, known as the *thalamic reflex*, produces foot tapping and body swaying as the music intensifies. Surrounding the thalamus is the limbic system. This is the part of the brain that is most connected to emotions and to the endocrine system, which affects the chakras and influences our involuntary processes of breathing, heart rate, circulation, and glandular secretions.

Hal A. Lingerman, in *The Healing Energies of Music*, suggests using various kinds of music to invoke or heal specific emotional states.[9] He lists specific pieces to express or calm anger, to heal depression or boredom, or to balance hyperactivity, as well as music for the basic elements and for harmonizing the home and other environments. While his information is too extensive to include here, I suggest experimenting with some of his suggestions.

CONCLUSION

In the philosophies of India, sound is considered the primordial ingredient of creation. Sound, crafted from the cosmic drum of Shiva in the celestial realms, was given to Brahma and Saraswati, the pair of deities that rule over creation and beginnings. The divine order of the universe, the essence of spirit, and the element of sound are intricately connected. Without sound, the universe will collapse again into nothingness, stolen by Mother Kali in her final act of destruction. With sound, we are given the power to create from within ourselves using the same primordial energies that create the world around us and indeed, our very selves. With sound, we are given the tools to avert destruction.

> All the tragedy in the world, in the individual and in the multitude, comes from lack of harmony. And harmony is best given by producing harmony in one's own life.
>
> HAZRAT INAYAT KHAN

The fifth chakra facilitates a profound passage between the abstract information of conception, image, and idea, and the manifested realm of the material world. It takes us through the heart, where we communicate and connect with each other; through our power where we command and contain; through our emotions; and down into the coordination of the cells within our bodies. On the spiritual plane, sound brings us up through the lower chakras (using body, movement, will, and breath) into resonance and harmony, information and understanding. It is the prime transmitter of consciousness itself. Although sound may be the primordial ingredient of existence, it is consciousness—created from its vibrational impact—that creates and maintains the very web of life.

CHAKRA SIX

Seeing Our Way Through

SIXTH CHAKRA AT A GLANCE

ELEMENT
Light

NAME
Ajna (to perceive and
command)

PURPOSE
Pattern recognition

ISSUES
Image
Intuition
Imagination
Visualization
Insight
Dreams
Vision

COLOR
Indigo

LOCATION
Forehead, brow, carotid
plexus, third eye

IDENTITY
Archetypal

ORIENTATION
Self-reflection

DEMON
Illusion

DEVELOPMENTAL STAGE
Adolescence

DEVELOPMENTAL TASK
Establishment of personal
identity
Ability to perceive patterns

BASIC RIGHTS
To see

BALANCED CHARACTERISTICS
Intuitive
Perceptive
Imaginative
Good memory
Good dream recall
Able to think symbolically
Able to visualize

TRAUMAS AND ABUSES
What you see doesn't go with
what you're told
Invalidation of intuition and
psychic occurences
Ugly or frightening
environment (war zone,
violence)

DEFICIENCY
- Insensitivity
- Poor vision
- Poor memory
- Difficulty seeing future
- Lack of imagination
- Difficulty visualizing
- Poor dream recall
- Denial (can't see what is going on)
- Monopolarized (one true right and only way)

EXCESS
- Hallucinations
- Delusions
- Obsessions
- Difficulty concentrating
- Nightmares

PHYSICAL MALFUNCTIONS
- Headaches
- Vision problems

HEALING PRACTICES
- Create visual art
- Visual stimulation
- Meditation
- Psychotherapy
  - Coloring and drawing, art therapy
  - Working with memory
  - Connecting image with feeling
  - Dreamwork
  - Hypnosis
  - Guided visualizations
  - Past life regression therapy

AFFIRMATIONS
- I see all things in clarity.
- I am open to the wisdom within.
- I can manifest my vision.

SHADES OF INDIGO

Monica's image of herself was a shocking contrast to the person who sat in front of me. A stunningly attractive woman, she was graceful, articulate, and dynamic. I found her immediately likable, so I was surprised to find that she felt lonely and isolated, unable to find a partner or close friends.

Contrary to my impression, her self-image was abhorrent. She avoided social gatherings because she was, in her own words, "so obscenely fat" that she was embarrassed to appear in public. This of course kept her home alone on weekends, ironically "eating her heart out" to fill her loneliness. Monica carried a mere twenty pounds above the popular ideal of women's bodies, yet to her, the extra curves weighed far more than that. Try as she might to fit the image that popular culture had programmed into her consciousness, she could not. The mere *effort* of doing so pulled her out of her natural self, overriding the basic messages of the body. Every Saturday night, her body staged a food rebellion, sabotaging her attempts to force it into submission. Despite her efforts to diet and become slim, her body followed the image she held of the fat girl which was fast becoming a self-fulfilling prophecy. She was convinced that no one would have the slightest interest in an overweight woman, and her isolation became false proof that her theory was correct. The vicious cycle of giving up her natural self to fit an outer image she could not achieve plunged her into shame, reinforcing the negative image that perpetuated the whole cycle. She was a victim of the *image syndrome*.

Stuart also complained about loneliness. Unlike Monica, his self-image was not particularly negative, but his image of an acceptable girlfriend fit only the narrowest of possibilities. He was unable to see beauty in women of various shapes, sizes, or ages, and would have confirmed Monica's belief system entirely, had they ever met. As a result, the women who were attracted to Stuart were rejected from the start as unsuitable. In fact, to hear him talk, it was as if they did not even exist as he constantly cried, "Nobody loves me!" When I pointed out to him that many women were interested in him, Stuart replied that "they didn't count." The idealized women of Stuart's imagination were more real to him than anyone he might meet.

William was able to create a reality that matched the image he carried. He had a prestigious, well-paying job, an attractive wife and home, kept his body in good shape, and lived up to the image he had adopted for himself in every way he could. Still William was unhappy. As he grew older, there were emotional stirrings within that kept sabotaging his perfect image. His marriage showed signs of strain, he was starting to drink too much, and he lived daily with an angst that he could neither name nor overcome. William was living his image instead of his true self, living by outer direction instead of inner feelings. Having successfully followed his illusion to fruition, he was now experiencing a rude awakening at the midpoint of his life. As he looked beneath the surface, he discovered he was totally mystified about who he really was. He needed to learn a whole new way of seeing in order to recognize the person that dwelt within.

Each of these stories is about what can happen when consciousness gets wrapped around an image. While the issues described contain other chakra dynamics as well, each of these people needed to confront the discrepancy between image and reality and learn to see at a deeper level.

When our illusory images are reinforced by the culture at large, this becomes very difficult to do. We are bombarded daily by images that tell us how to look, how to feel, how to behave, what to buy, where to go, and even what to see. We drive down the freeway without noticing the bill-boards of slim ladies and muscled men holding cigarette packs, even though our mind is unconsciously programmed with these pictures. As I write this, my son is glued to the TV. He is being programmed with the values inherent in the shows he watches, which compete with our attempts to influence his conscious mind in other ways.

Our thinking process is believed to be 90 percent visual. The images around us parade through our fantasies and dreams, our conscious mind and our unconscious behavior, affecting all that we see and do. They distort the nature of what we see, creating illusions that we then take for reality. What light can we shine through the sixth chakra to illuminate this problem?

I like to think of the sixth chakra as a metaphoric stained glass window through which the light of consciousness shines on its way to manifestation. When the sun shines through colored glass, it projects the image of the stained glass on whatever solid surface it hits. The light of consciousness shines through the pictures we hold in our minds, shaping what we create. These images are also filters through which we see things, sometimes distorting our perceptions.

Stuart projected his inability to love upon the women he met. Monica created a self-image out of her basic shame. William was outgrowing his false self and his image was shattering like glass. The awakening of consciousness requires clearing the third eye of illusion so we can see what is within and around us without distortion.

The Sanskrit name for this chakra, *ajna*, means both "to perceive" and "to command." We see images with our physical eyes, but the third eye center holds those images in memory, which can distort our perceptions. From these perceptions, we command our reality.

UNFOLDING THE PETALS

BASIC ISSUES OF THE SIXTH CHAKRA

Pattern Recognition

Archetypes

Symbols

Images

Dreams

Intuition

Transcendence

Vision

Clairvoyance

Illusion

OPENING THE THIRD EYE

As we enter the brow chakra, we look back at the steps behind us with new vision. Adding indigo to our ever-expanding bridge we now have enough colors to see that we are, indeed, building a rainbow. Once we see what the pattern is becoming, we can intuit the steps necessary to complete it. Our sight gives us guidance. We can see where we have been, where we are now, and predict where we are going. This consciousness lets us know what to do, which explains why the sense of sight is classically related to the third chakra, even though the sixth chakra is about *seeing*.[1] Without vision our actions are mere impulses, but with vision they become creative acts of will in the service of transformation.

> Psychic development cannot be accomplished by intention and will alone; it needs the attraction of the symbol.
>
> C. G. JUNG

The element of this chakra is *light*, a higher and faster vibration than that of sound in the chakra below. Through light, we are blessed with the ability to see, to take in from a distance the shape and form of things around us. This miraculous act of seeing is the basic function of this chakra, but this implies far more than seeing with our physical eyes. Physical perception tells us *that something exists*, but only the inner sight can tell us *what it is*.

While our physical eyes are the organs of outer perception, the sixth chakra relates to the mystical *third eye*—the organ of inner perception. The third eye witnesses the internal screen where memory and fantasy, images and archetypes, intuition and imagination intertwine on endless display. By watching the contents on this screen, we create meaning and bring it to consciousness. The purpose of the sixth chakra is to see the way, and bring the light of consciousness to all that exists within and around us.

PATTERN RECOGNITION

We see the way by learning to recognize patterns. Patterns reveal the identity of a thing—what it is, what it is for, how to relate to it. Too often, we look at something only until we recognize the pattern and then we stop. We see someone coming toward us from across the street. We look at the hair, the body, the walk, trying to distinguish the pattern until we see who it is. We say, "Oh, that's Kevin," at which point we often stop taking in new information. Opening the third eye allows us to continue to look; we see beyond and perceive ever deeper patterns and meaning.

> The eyes are the gateways to the soul.
>
> WILLIAM SHAKESPEARE

Pattern recognition is like playing a game of connect the dots. At first we see only a jumble of dots and numbers on the page. But as we make connections between the dots, an image forms. Even before all the dots are connected, we can guess the image because we recognize it.

At a critical point in the assembling of information, the incomplete pattern reveals the whole. While each of our chakras brings us information, it is the task of chakra six to assemble that information into meaningful patterns. This self-reflection leads to self-knowledge and wholeness.

Pattern recognition requires the ability to see simultaneously into past, present, and future. When your friend launches into an all-too-familiar tirade about how he hates his job, you can predict what he is likely to say next because you've heard it all before. As a result, you may stop listening to him, and might not even notice if he says something new. We take information from the past and project it onto the future.

Recognition can shut off the possibility of new information, or it can spare us an experience we would rather avoid. Our interpretation of the pattern will decide which we choose. If I find myself in a relationship that reveals a dynamic I have been in before, I do not need to continue the whole relationship to find out what's likely to happen. I can choose to remove myself from the distant or deceitful lover as soon as the pattern becomes clear. Once we recognize a pattern, we can intuit what it will become and guide our actions accordingly. This is the beginning of wisdom.

In the recognition of patterns, we find our way to *insight*. Insight is the ability to see *within*, the "aha" of recognizing a pattern, seeing where it relates to the larger picture, seeing what it means. It is within the self that the information from our experiences has been gathering and is stored in our memory. It is only by seeing within that we can cross-reference that information and recognize meaningful patterns.

Each time we recognize a pattern, we move toward wholeness. This wholeness has an identity, which gives it both meaning and purpose. Opening the third eye allows us to see the big picture, transcend our ego-centricity, and find the deeper meaning inherent in all things. As inner sight develops, illusions are shattered, dreams are integrated, clarity begins, and consciousness extends yet another step beyond what was available through the lower five chakras alone. We now access the broad vision that enables us to see our way toward completion.

ILLUSION

In perceiving patterns we often run into *illusion*—the demon of the sixth chakra. Illusion wrests our consciousness from open-minded perception, fixing it upon a frozen image. An illusion is a static image, displaced in the stream of time, and is for that reason unreal. The illusion I hold of how something *should* be is usually an image of what it currently is *not*. My attachment to it pulls me out of present time, where I might see realistically. My fixation on my body ten pounds thinner fails to appreciate my body the way it is now. My illusion of how a relationship should be makes me criticize all the places my relationship falls short of that image, and I fail to see the meaning these issues might have for me. The three people described at the beginning of this chapter were all suffering from illusion, fixated in an image that kept them from living clearly and authentically.

Illusions are held in place by an investment of psychic energy. When we fixate on an image, everything becomes food for its embellishment. If we think someone dislikes us, we take the slightest disharmony as proof. A hypochondriac takes the slightest ache as proof of illness. When we invest in an illusion, it ties up our energy and perpetuates the attachment. The more we are attached, of course, the more energy we need to invest, and it is here that we run into the danger of obsession. Since illusion does not feed back the energy we invest, it does not bring satisfaction or completion and, like an addiction, continues to lure us into its false promises.

Anya escaped the unpleasant dramas of her family by reading romance novels as she grew up. Without consciously realizing it, she had adopted the illusion of the love affair that leads to the "happily ever after" model of marriage. As an adult, she invested all of her time and energy into her husband and family, never considering that the marriage might not last. As she was so invested in this image, she could not afford to look at the serious shortcomings of her marriage. She was in denial about her husband's abuse of herself and her children, and this denial pushed her to invest ever more energy in trying to please him, hiding the abuse from her friends, and maintaining the outer image of a happy family. As this investment took away from her social life and her financial viability, it became even more important to uphold the marriage, and her denial deepened. She obsessed about her husband constantly, always thinking about his needs at the expense her own.

Maria was abandoned by her father and was left with an angry mother. To make it worse, her father returned and left again several times before he finally disappeared forever. Maria can remember the time she spent, as a child, gazing out the window, watching for his car and wondering if he was ever coming back. Eventually, she recognized the pattern and realized that, even if he appeared once in a while, he was gone for good. Now an adult, Maria obsesses about her boyfriend abandoning her. No matter how much he assures her of his intentions, she interprets the slightest withdrawal as a sign that it's over, super-imposing a past pattern on the present situation. Sometimes she feels compelled to drive by where he works just to see his car, as if the presence of the car gives her reassurance. Both the car and the abandonment are illusions through which she tries to find some homeostasis.

When illusion is fed by a sixth chakra excess, it becomes obsession or delusion. Obsessions fix an unusual amount of energy on a particular issue; delusion assembles elaborate illusions around a central theme. Removed from the grounded connection of the first chakra, the upper chakras spin wildly, like an engine with the clutch disengaged—lots of activity with no forward movement. The more we invest in an illusion, the harder it is to let go of it. The investment seals the energy into the illusion, giving it archetypal proportions. Sealed in, we are trapped into repetitive cycles that keep us from true understanding.

ARCHETYPES

As bits of information assemble and begin to reveal the identity of the whole, we enter the world of archetypes. If we see a cat when connecting the dots, we recognize it because we have seen cats before. It may be a black cat or a tiger, a skinny kitten or a tailless manx, but all fall into the same archetypal category of *cat*.

The archetype is a composite of images and experiences that are constellated by a common theme. Archetypes are like morphogenetic fields that shape our understanding. Like the strange attractors of chaos theory, they cannot be seen directly, but are apparent in the events of our lives. Someone who is chronically driven to self-sacrificing benevolence may be overly influenced by the positive

> Psychologically... the archetype as an image of instinct is a spiritual goal toward which the whole nature of man strives.
>
> C. G. JUNG

aspects of the Great Mother archetype. Someone who lives in fear of being devoured by women may be suffering from the negative side of this archetype, the Terrible Mother. Stuart was so seduced by his inner anima archetype that his fantasy woman possessed his heart and no real woman could compete.

> The archetype, a precipitate of all human experience, lies in the unconscious, whence it powerfully influences our life. To release its projections, to raise its contents into consciousness, becomes a task and a duty.
>
> JOLANDE JACOBI

Archetypes can be symbolically represented by what is called the *archetypal image*. When an archetypal image is not fully integrated into the ego, then we are subject to illusion. For example, the Hero archetype represents the quest to achieve something extraordinary. William's drive toward success was a partial reflection of the Hero's quest, but his ego was so fused with an image of conformity that it negated the possibility of anything extraordinary. As a result, his success had a feeling of emptiness and left his soul thirsting for deeper meaning. Sorting out this difference allowed William to access the deeper archetypal energy of the Hero in a conscious way and orient his life toward more soul-fulfilling achievement.

Each of the chakras can be correlated to an archetype, as shown in figure 6.1. In addition, each chakra has the archetypal energy of its associated element (*earth, water, fire, air, sound, light,* and *thought*). The chakra system itself is a still-larger archetypal pattern, similar to Jung's archetype of wholeness, the Self. Jung saw the totality of the Self as the central archetype of order in the psyche, the formative principle of individuation.

Individuation itself is also an archetypal process, and though it differs from person to person, there are common elements that comprise the archetypal pattern. The process of individuation mirrors the unfolding of the chakras, where we reclaim the shadow, establish our autonomy, integrate our anima and animus, express our individuality, recognize our archetypal influences, and integrate all these elements into a greater wholeness. To recognize an archetypal energy is to recognize its pattern and meaning, and then guide ourselves accordingly. To recognize the pattern of individuation (or chakra unfolding) as it occurs in our lives allows us to see where we are,

7		Sage/Master
6		Seer
5		Artist
4		Healer
3		Hero
2		Lover
1		Earth Mother/Provider

FIGURE 6.1. ARCHETYPES OF THE CHAKRAS

where we are heading, and what we need to do to get there. Thus insight directs action.

In the sixth chakra we move into our *archetypal identity*. This identity is gained through the recognition of images and symbols that appear in our lives through dreams, imagination, art, relationships, or situations. Recognizing the archetypal significance of these symbols brings us into a larger spiritual framework. We enter a broader context of understanding, and a deeper recognition of who we are and what our purpose is. This is the essential work of developing our archetypal identity.

Alexandra was having difficulty dealing with the loss of vitality and libido that sometimes accompanies menopause. She continually felt like she was "dying" and gradually withdrew from her outer life. When I compared her process to the archetypal experience of journeying to the Underworld—the mythical land of death and rebirth, as represented by the Greek myth of Persephone, or the Sumerian myth of Inanna—it made it easier for her to cope. She could give her experience a meaning beyond her immediate suffering. She could accept it as an inward journey that had a beginning, an end, and a sacred purpose, as part of the quest for deeper wholeness and Self-reclamation.

The unconscious, as the totality of all archetypes, is the deposit of all human experience right back to its remotest beginnings. Not, indeed, a dead deposit, a sort of abandoned rubbish heap, but a living system of reactions and aptitudes that determine the individual's life in invisible ways. Archetypes are simply the forms which the instincts assume.

C. G. JUNG

Since the archetypes are embedded in a larger field, they carry a numinous energy. When we encounter them, we may feel a strong psychic charge, imbuing everything around us with great significance. They also carry a meaning and a purpose that dictates smaller details within. If we see in ourselves the archetype of a Teacher, Healer, Mother, Father, or Artist, we are gaining, with that recognition, an inherent set of instructions and energy. Although some of those instructions may direct us to more information, it is the archetype itself that really directs us. A pregnant woman, knowing she is going to be a mother, reads books on raising children, or takes birthing classes. She also has within her certain instinctual responses toward mothering that appear on their own when she gives birth. A healer trains himself in his disciplines, finds others in his trade, and seeks out those in need. But the healer also has a certain innate sense of health and disease and an attraction to the art that may be recognized throughout his life. A visual artist sees the world in terms of color and shadow, shape and composition, using her creative identity to make archetypal statements with her art. The instructions embedded within an archetypal energy not only give us meaning, but also direction.

The archetypal identity we acquire at this level becomes, for better or worse, a mode of perception. The healer and the artist look for different details in the same situation. We might ask then, is the archetype not just another illusion or distortion of our ability to truly see? It can be, but in recognizing the archetype, it becomes possible to recognize the filter as well and correct our perceptions accordingly. Knowing that I overidentify with the positive aspects of the Mother archetype, I can see the denial of my own shadow; I can recognize the program that says I have to be there all the time for each and every demand. I have a name for it, a way of perceiving it, a means for understanding. I can trace its meaning through my past to my own mother, to her mother, and on back through time. In the recognition of my archetypal influences, I am freer to create new behavior; without recognition, I am not even aware that I am making choices—my current behavior seems the only option.

Knowing our archetypal influences helps clarify our modes of perception. It clarifies our purpose in life and attracts the things we need in order to fulfill that purpose. It also keeps us from being unconsciously ruled by the archetype, and makes its energy available to us for our growth. The archetype then becomes an ally rather than an invisible dictator.

Unconscious subroutines in our behavior and belief systems are fueled by archetypal energies. Jung called these subroutines *complexes*. They are the things we habitually do or think even though we may know better, such as compulsively going off our diet time and again, being hurtfully critical of our children, sabotaging our relationships when they are going well, or avoiding success when it is just around the corner. Complexes are always formed around an archetypal matrix, and becoming aware of this matrix helps us break the cycle.

William found that even after he realized he had been following an image, he could not let go of his perfectionism. Intellectually, he could see that it was not necessary to maintain the image, but emotionally he was terrified to let go of it. As a Rigid/Achiever, he carried a deep need to impress his father. Even though his father was no longer living, the archetypal Father energy within his psyche still drove his feelings and behavior. As he individuated from his actual father, and claimed his own expression of the Father archetype, he could loosen his father's rigid influence on his behavior.

The archetypal level is simultaneously immanent and transcendent. It is immanent when we experience it as something inside that we bring forth from within ourselves. Even if we do not recognize an archetype, it can still be a constellating force in our behavior. A wife who unconsciously resonates with the archetype of the Lover may repeatedly have affairs on the side. The archetypal Artist is often miserable in a structured job. A childless woman possessed by the Mother archetype will continually take care of others even to her own detriment. Bringing our archetype to consciousness helps us embrace its energy in a conscious way.

An archetype is transcendent in that it resonates with a larger meta-structure, similar to the way our bodies are embedded in the physical world. We are not the only healer in the world as the tradition of healers goes back to the beginning of human life. We are not the first to become a father. Our image of Father, from our own father to all the fathers we have known through friends, movies, and literature, brings us information about how to be a father. The archetype of the Mother exists all around us, from the ancient goddesses to women comparing detergent on television commercials. An archetype has many forms of manifestation, but behind each is a common concept.

The archetype is transcendent because it is bigger than we are. It is immanent because it is an element of who we are—yet only one element, as we may embody several archetypes at once. We may be both Artist and Father, Trickster and Lover, Mother and Child. Archetypes may fight within us as the perpetual child fights the responsibilities of parenthood or as the Lover who desires connection fights with the Hermit who wants to be alone. In these apparent contradictions, it is important to find a way to honor each of the archetypal energies that cry for recognition. Rejecting them only sends them to the shadow realm where we energize the archetype's negative side. Then the Good Mother becomes the Bad Mother, angry and resentful of her children if she does not get the freedom she needs. The Lover becomes distant and moody if he does not get the time alone that he needs.

Archetypal energies are found at the core of all mythology and religion. Imbued with a powerful energy that resonates deep in our psyches, embracing the archetype is a spiritual experience, and opens us up to the spiritual states associated with the upper chakras. Christ, Buddha, and Pan, Aphrodite, Isis, and Mother Mary—all are archetypal principles that resonate not only with the forces of nature around us, but also with deep elements of our own psyche. In this resonance, the archetype holds great power. Over time, archetypes get invested with collective psychic energy, and strongly influence the culture.

Our best access to archetypal understanding and to the development of our archetypal identity is through the awareness and integration of symbols.

IMAGE AS SYMBOL

We enter the symbolic realm as we move above the heart chakra. Our language is made of sound symbols and our letters represent those sounds. In the visual realm, symbols speak to us as representations of powerful archetypal energies. We see them in our fantasies and dreams, we wear them in our jewelry, scribble them on our notes, and use them in our logos. Symbols are an immediate, whole-brain way of communicating about deep archetypal energies.

> Archetype is concentrated psychic energy and symbol provides the mode of manifestation by which the archetype becomes discernible. We can never encounter an archetype, only its symbol.
>
> EDWARD WHITMONT

Symbols are the means through which the mind perceives archetypal energy. Likewise, archetypes, which are by definition nonphysical templates for psychic energy, become integrated into consciousness through symbols.

Symbols emerge when we recognize a pattern. Spirit does not always speak to us in verbal language but has a more archetypal language spoken through symbols. If we are to develop an *archetypal identity*, then we must learn the language of symbols.

Symbols emerge from the unconscious through dreams and fantasies, creation of art, and chance encounters. As I began work on this chapter, I started a period of purification where I cleared interruptions and stepped up some of my spiritual practices. Two days later I found a complete, five-foot snake skin at the edge of my garden which confirmed that I was, indeed, shedding my old skin in the service of transformation. The fact that it appeared in my garden—a place where I cultivate the growing of things— brought me another symbol to contemplate. What do I want to cultivate in my life? What have I cultivated in the past that I want to leave behind?

When snakes first begin to shed their skin, there is a period when it slides over their eyes and they are unable to see very well. Once the skin has been shed, a new clarity returns. This reflected the period I had just gone through, where I was unsure of my voice and anxiously seeking my clarity. Finally, the snake is a symbol of the Kundalini energy that runs through the chakras, and as I enter the final chapters of this book, my internal Kundalini is entering a new level. The skin now sits on my personal altar, which displays many symbols of things I want to honor and bring into my life.

This is a small example of how to work with symbols that appear in life. The most potent source of these symbols is our dreams.

DREAMS

Dreams link the conscious and unconscious mind. Thus they link the lower and upper chakras, which are crucial both to our awakening as conscious individuals and to the connection of that consciousness with the dynamic ground of Earth and Nature.

Dreams speak to us in the symbolic mode of the upper chakras, but what they symbolize is the connection between our "lower" processes (instincts, feelings, and impulses) and the larger archetypal world of spirit. Dreams unlock the mystery that unites soul and spirit, individual and universal, into a dynamic and synthesized whole. They are a sixth chakra contribution to the goal of realization, which will comprise our final step on the Rainbow Bridge.

> The whole creation is essentially subjective, and the dream is the theater where the dreamer is at once scene, actor, prompter, stage, manager, author, audiences, and critic.
>
> C. G. JUNG

Dreams present alternatives to ordinary reality. In order to have vision, imagination, clairvoyance, and insight, we need to be able to think in new and creative ways. Dreams open the way for us to see things in a new light, revealing hidden feelings and understandings, desires and needs, rejected selves, unused talents, and missing pieces of our wholeness. They are often profoundly irrational images that uproot the conscious mind and open it to something larger.

Dreams often bring us answers to problems that our conscious mind could not solve and so become powerful spiritual teachers. Many scientific and technological discoveries are made through dreams, where answers to problems appear in symbolic form. Mendeleyev conceived of the periodic table of the elements in an afternoon dream he had after falling asleep to the precise arrangement of chamber music. Neils Bohr dreamed of race horses traveling on a track and was inspired to build his model of the atom with orderly orbits of subatomic particles. The invention of the sewing machine was crystallized by a dream where cannibals poked its inventor with spears that had holes in the *points*, bringing the essential key that had eluded inventors for fifty years.[2] Dreams are representations of our inner world as it struggles with the demands of the outer one.

Dreams are the psyche's way of maintaining homeostasis—of compensating for the lack of balance as we adjust our lives to external realities. They communicate essential information to the conscious mind about our health, relationships, work, growth, and almost any other area in which we might inquire. Jeremy Taylor tells the story of a woman, Barbara, who dreamed she opened a purse that was full of rotting meat. Her dream group worried that the purse represented her uterus and that she might have cancer. With no prior physical symptoms, the dream image resonated enough to make her go in for a checkup. The first one revealed nothing, but egged on by the dream she sought another opinion. She did, indeed, have cancer, and was able to remedy the situation just in time. Had she waited any longer, she was told it would have been too late.[3]

Dreams are a primary experience of transcendent consciousness. In dreams, there is no linear time or limitation to logical space. We can fly upside down, or can be on a mountain one minute and in the office the next. Dreams take us beyond the limits of the body, where physical ability is no longer a

The dream is a little hidden door in the innermost and most secret recess of the soul, opening into that cosmic night which was psyche long before there was any ego consciousness, and which will remain psyche no matter how far our ego consciousness may extend. All consciousness separates; but in dreams we put on the likeness of that more universal, truer, more eternal man dwelling in the darkness of primordial night. There he is still the whole, and the whole is in him, indistinguishable from nature and bare of all egohood.

C. G. JUNG

consideration. Dreams may also bring us into the body, by giving us symbolic information about its needs or by allowing us to practice movements and feelings that are denied our body in waking life. Thus dreams are an essential link between somatic and transcendent experience.

Dreams have fascinated philosophers and psychologists for millennia. As a healing force for the evolution of consciousness, they will be explored again when I talk about healing through the sixth chakra. In order to understand dreams, we must be able to embrace symbols as representations of archetypal energy and use our intuition to find their meaning.

INTUITION

Intuition is the unconscious recognition of pattern. It is one of the four functions of Jungian typology (the others being *sensation* and *feeling*, related to the first two chakras, and *thinking*, which relates to chakra seven). Intuition, like energy in the lower chakras, is basically passive. Those who try to force intuition know full well it does not behave according to will, but rather by a process of openness and receptivity.

Intuition is a leap toward wholeness from fragmentation.

The development of intuition enhances our psychic abilities and is a central function of chakra six. If we are shut off from our unconscious process and live almost entirely in our conscious mind, then our intuition will be undeveloped and become what Jung calls an *inferior function*. Without intuition, we cannot grasp the whole or the essence of something. We cannot surrender to the resonance of a more immediate truth and understanding than that which is available to us through the rational, conscious mind. Since intuition is passive, it requires surrender, just as opening to the elements of earth and water requires a surrender to gravity and flow. We need intuition to embrace the mystery that opens us to the larger, cosmic world.

We live in a culture that favors logic over intuition. As children, we are not taught to value our intuition and our hunches are often discounted if we cannot logically defend our reasoning. As a result we often discount our own hunches because we do not believe we could actually know things through nonlogical means. This internal invalidation suppresses our psychic abilities.

The rational mind (from *ratio*, "to count") thinks in pieces. One piece follows another, leading us logically from one thought to the next. While the rational mind may synthesize a whole from its individual pieces, it is poorly suited for grasping larger wholes on an immediate, experiential level. To grasp concepts of cosmic and transcendent consciousness—the realms associated with the upper chakras—we must have a more direct means of perception. This is the purpose of intuition.

Sri Aurobindo has described intuition as the flash of a match in the darkness.[4] For one brief moment, the whole room comes to light. We can see its size and shape and the furniture and objects within it as an immediate whole experience. The flash of intuition is a momentary illumination of the psyche that reveals its underlying wholeness. As we grow in awareness (especially through meditation practices), we learn to sustain these illuminated moments for longer and longer periods.

CLAIRVOYANCE

Sixth chakra development opens us to the possibilities of *clairvoyance*, which means "clear seeing." Clairvoyance opens inner sight to nonphysical planes, allowing us to see auras and chakras, past and future events. It begins with the development of intuition, and is a matter of learning to focus internal attention on something long enough to illuminate its patterns. As we gain awareness of our own conscious process, we gain the ability to focus that awareness where we choose. Once we find our own light, we can shine that light on whatever we wish to see.

Spiritual growth often requires us to break free of established patterns. This can be frightening—so frightening, in fact, that many people never attempt it at all, preferring instead to cling to the familiar realms of the lower chakras. How do we maintain our ground in the face of the unknown territory of transformation? We rely on intuition. Intuition then becomes the ground of the transpersonal psyche. It makes the unknown knowable.

Clairvoyance, like intuition, is developed through a conscious surrender to the unconscious mind. We

> The body itself is a screen
> to shield and partially reveal
> the light that's blazing
> inside your presence.
>
> RUMI

must let go of preconceived notions and allow the integrating power of the Self to move us toward wholeness. Developing clairvoyance requires trust, practice, opening to the inner feelings, voices, and images that come unbidden into our consciousness.

TRANSCENDENT FUNCTION

It is important at this point to take another look at our chakra structure and see where we are. As we pass the neck and enter the head, we transcend the physical world of time and space and enter the nonphysical, symbolic realm of the mind. Chakras six and seven together correspond to the areas that Jung called the supra conscious, or that others have called transcendent, transpersonal, or cosmic consciousness.

For in transcending the opposites by uniting them in himself, the symbol maintains psychic life in a constant flux and carries it onward toward its destined goal. Tension and release—as an expression of the living movement of the psychic process—are enabled to alternate in a constant rhythm.

JOLANDE JACOBI

The lower two chakras were the realm of instincts and the unconscious mind, which flowed with gravity according to their own nature. At chakra three we awakened to an egoic consciousness—a sense of separate self with a will to resist or direct the instinctual flow. Chakras three, four, and five are largely run by that egoic consciousness as it interacts with the outer world and integrates experience on the inner planes (see figure 0.8).

The realm of transpersonal consciousness is a realm that is beyond both ego and instincts yet reflects and combines both. In this reflection we can see that chakras six and seven are the *mental mirrors* of the lower and middle realms, respectively. Chakra six symbolically reflects the *unconscious* while chakra seven is the realm of *conscious* understanding. Chakra seven is the central processing unit (CPU) that finds meaning in the images chakra six brings forth from the lower realms, and incorporates them into an ever-growing body of understanding.

The ancient tantric texts that depict the chakras show their major *nadis* (channels of energy) as figure eight patterns that wrap around the chakras. The two nadis, *Ida* and *Pingala*—said to be the polar opposites, solar and

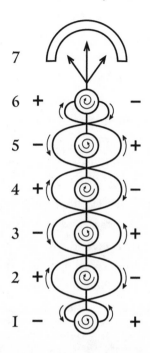

The Ida and Pingala
ascend and descend
in a spiral pattern,
contributing to the
chakras' spin. The
Sushumna travels
up the center.

lunar, masculine and feminine—begin at the first chakra and meet again at the sixth, polarizing each of the chakras in between and contributing to their spin (see figure 6.2). The fact that they meet in chakra six tells us that both dualities are present and united before the energy moves to the transcendent, nondualistic nature of the crown chakra. Therefore, chakra six is the ground in which dualities meet and become transformed. Among these are the dualities of conscious and unconscious.

Since the upper two chakras are associated with the realm of transcendent consciousness, they transcend the limitations of time and space (so important to the body) and their scope moves beyond the purely personal to a more universal, cosmic realm where awareness fuses diverse elements of experience into a unified whole.

Transcendent function is a term used by Jung to describe the psyche's ability to reconcile and synthesize opposites through the use of symbols. When this occurs we have a transformation of attitude. We move from a smaller place of either-or—in which there is internal conflict, contradiction, and repression—to a larger perspective that widens our vision. In technical terms, the purpose of the transcendent function is "to resolve the thesis of pure nature and its antithesis of the opposing ego into the synthesis of conscious nature."[5] In other words, we resolve the struggle between the conscious ego and the repressed instincts by a synthesis that includes both. Once resolution has occurred, we can use the energy of our instincts consciously and harmoniously, and stop being used by them. The transcendent function, therefore, is less a function of rising above our conflicts, than of coming to a perception in which those conflicts resolve into complementary aspects of our wholeness.

The transcendent function combines the unconscious aspects of the lower chakras with a vision of wholeness that can be embraced by the conscious mind, and hence the entire Self. It brings us to an entirely new vista—an emergence into a larger sphere of understanding. It is the final step in the individuation process (if, indeed, individuation is ever finalized). It is our gateway to the final step across the bridge—the gateway to self-reflection and self-knowledge.

Just as mantras were the focusing device of the fifth chakra, symbols are that of the sixth—most specifically the symbol of the *mandala*. Yogis sometimes practice *yantra yoga*, the yoga of meditating upon a symbol or mandala as a way of focusing the mind into clarity. Jung interpreted the appearance of mandalas in dreams as resolutions of opposites and symbols of wholeness.

As consciousness integrates more and more of its elements into a pattern of wholeness, the balance of opposites within takes its place around the Self as center, rather than the ego. The instincts are the center of the unconscious, and the ego is the center of the conscious mind, but the Self is the archetypal mystery that is at the center of the whole being. It is not a point, not a thing, not a place—but the cohesive force of wholeness, drawing together its various essential parts, much as the sun holds the planets in their orbits.

Jung says, "With the birth of the symbol, the regression of the libido into the unconscious ceases. Regression changes into progression, blockage gives way to flowing, and the pull of the primordial abyss is broken."[6] In the creation of the mediating symbol, our major polarities finally crystallize into understanding and lead us into conscious realization.

VISION

The final outcome of working through the sixth chakra—with its archetypes and images, dreams and fantasies, symbols and illusions—is the emergence of a personal vision. As we see more and more of ourselves, we see more deeply into people and situations around us. As we expand our internal picture into a larger, more comprehensive worldview, we inevitably begin to create a vision. This vision can address world problems and how they might be changed for the better, or it may only address something within our own lives. It may be as large as a vision to create a new society, or as focused as one about relating to our spouse differently. It is not the size or scope of the vision that is important, but the ability to see a new way of being.

Vision uses imagination to create something that has never been seen before. Its image, held in our mind, becomes the blueprint for our construction of reality. It becomes the new picture, the new stained glass window, through which the light of our consciousness will shine. The inner vision is the strange attractor that shapes the chaotic fluctuations of our lives.

> We participate in the forming of the future by virtue of our capacity to conceive of and respond to new possibilities, and to bring them out of imagination and try them in actuality.
>
> ROLLO MAY

What's the difference between vision, a positive aspect of chakra six, and illusion, its demon? Both are pictures held in the mind, and both shape our behavior. But vision leads us forward and illusion holds us back. A vision is a possibility, a goal to inspire us, constantly changing and evolving. We know a vision isn't real, and yet we believe in its potential. An illusion tends to be held as a certainty and forced into place—something we believe is real and unchangeable. An illusion binds the energy; a vision consciously directs it.

It takes vision to rebuild our Rainbow Bridge, to lead a life rich with meaning and purpose. It takes vision, both personal and collective, to change the many dysfunctional aspects of our world that keep us enmeshed, trapped, and disengaged. Vision is an essential part of the healing process.

No matter how abstract or specific our vision is, it can only begin with changes we make in our own lives. To create change, we need to be able to imagine it. We need an image, symbol, or sign that can steer the psychic energy of consciousness and activity toward a new manifestation. We need a shaper of reality—a goal for the future that draws forth its needs from the present. With this image in consciousness, the unformed chaos of our lives takes shape.

With the healing of the sixth chakra, we are able to create vision. We are able to form, consciously, the path to the future and liberate ourselves from the grips of the past. Our vision makes the difference.

GROWING THE LOTUS

DEVELOPMENTAL FORMATION OF
THE SIXTH CHAKRA AT A GLANCE

AGE
Adolescence

TASKS
Independence
Originality

NEEDS AND ISSUES
Self-reflection
Freedom and responsibility
Identity vs. role confusion

A child's imagination is almost constantly engaged. Uncluttered from fixed knowledge about the way things are, their imagination is free to explore new possibilities. In their innocence, children often see clearly to the heart of things, free from the illusions of how things "should be," freer to perceive them as they are. The innumerable "what ifs" that delight childhood curiosity openly explore possibilities as they try to decipher the patterns that influence their lives. This is spirit moving toward its natural goal of liberation and understanding. It is essential to support this imaginative creativity if the child is to remain open to the expansion of his or her own spirit.

Pattern recognition is a skill that develops throughout life. From the recognition of mother's face to the trancelike dance of

> Man's need to understand the world and his experience in it symbolically as well as realistically may be noted early in the lives of many children. ... It is the root of all creativity ... fed ... by the power of the initially imperceptible archetypes, working from out of the depths of the psyche and creating the realm of the spiritual.
>
> JOLANDE JACOBI

family roles, the assimilation of patterns moves from the simple to the complex. Each pattern perceived tells us something about ourselves, and something about the world around us. Each piece becomes part of the inner matrix of understanding that is constantly forming as we learn and grow. This is an innate process of human consciousness that is always engaged at some level.

So what marks the specific development of the sixth chakra?—the ability to think symbolically and abstractly. For Piaget, this is the period of *formal operations* (age twelve and up), where a child becomes more concerned with form than content, and where he begins to think like a scientist, to reason and philosophize about his life. At this stage a child can reason about something he has not actually experienced. He can live in the symbolic realm.

This awakening occurs when we realize that all that we perceive is not necessarily about us—and there are greater patterns beyond the high school social club, the family, or even the community. Strangely enough, this also creates a need to further define oneself as we adjust our ego to this larger vista and to the adolescent's rapidly changing physical body. It seems that the further the child can reach beyond himself, the more uncertain he becomes about his own identity.

Erikson marks adolescence as the stage where *identity vs. role confusion* becomes the dominant concern. At this time, there is an increased search for a meaningful personal identity, because, as we all know, the one Mom, Dad, or society have crafted is usually unacceptable. A meaningful personal identity at this stage needs to have epic proportions—it needs to resonate with the Self in a powerful way, and take that Self someplace larger. It needs to give direction to the powerful surge of energy that occurs when physical growth tapers off and sexual energy ripens. The energy previously used by the organism for physical growth that does not express itself sexually now moves into mental development.

In the search for a meaningful identity, we often see adolescents engage in a kind of archetypal hero worship. Boys worship baseball stars or archetypal figures from movies, such as Batman, Jean Luc Picard, or Rambo. They dye their hair orange and comb it into spikes, shave their heads, or pierce various parts of their anatomy, depending on the trend at the time. Young girls model themselves after fashion models, fantasize about marrying movie stars, or imitate hard-line feminists. They try on different roles as if they were auditioning for a play, and indeed they are, for the next stage of life is beckoning and it seems we can only be a part of it if we identify which role to play.

It is unfortunate that in this culture the search for personal meaning in terms of archetypes has become so crass. Our children, robbed of the rich archetypal heritage of mythology, are left to find their models from MTV. Rambo has replaced the mythic Hero and Barbie dolls, the spirit of Aphrodite. The entry of the adolescent into the larger community takes place at the mall, while school curricula remain unimaginatively fixated on a rational mode of thinking that does not allow for new identities.

Still, the archetypes parade through. Luke Skywalker meets his archetypal teacher, Yoda, and transforms the dark side of his father. Frodo, in *Lord of the Rings*, inspires pursuit of the Hero's Quest. These archetypal dramas have a marked impact on the creation of identity in the adolescent even if their symbolism is not consciously understood. As Erikson has said, "In searching for the social values which guide identity, one therefore confronts the problems of *ideology* and *aristocracy*. . . . In order not to become cynically or apathetically lost, young people must somehow be able to convince themselves that those who succeed in their anticipated adult world thereby shoulder the obligation of being the best."[7]

As imagination constitutes a major petal in the sixth chakra, the adolescent often scoffs at the older generation's *lack of imagination*. When mental apparatus opens with an explosion of imagination, Mom and Dad indeed seem pretty square. Never mind that they may have already tried all the things the adolescent finds so new and exciting—the old ways seem much too constricting for the youth as their sixth chakra awakens. They must experiment with their widening realm of possibility.

It may seem contradictory that the persona is initially formed at the fourth chakra stage and yet personal identity becomes so important again in chakra six. But there is a big difference between them. In the fourth chakra, we form our social personality relatively unconsciously. We imitate what we see around us, we adapt and conform. We do what works—what gets us love and approval. We are not aware of the range of choices that are possible.

During the peak of adolescence there is a reevaluation of the adopted persona. Suddenly there is a wider range to choose from, and we have creativity from chakra five to help us. This time the choice is relatively conscious. It is less likely to be about pleasing parents and more about one's identity with peers and cultural icons. It is more future oriented—changing who we have been to who we want to become. The new identity must have some kind of meaning. The search for this meaning leads us to the seventh chakra.

ADULT DEVELOPMENT

In the adult, the awakening of symbolic communication and the embracing of one's archetypal identity usually occur after a midlife crisis (if not in adolescence). Previously adopted roles no longer satisfy and their dissolution plunges us into unknown depths where clarity and certainty are nonexistent. Attachment to a previous identity may have denied other important aspects of ourselves that now taunt us in our dreams and fantasies and force us to open to a larger possibility of being.

Sixth chakra development is usually referred to as spiritual awakening. We suddenly see with new eyes, experience profound insight, change our perspective and attitude, or receive a vision. It can happen at any time in life, but like the light of most dawns, it is often preceded by darkness. It is darkness that makes us reach into the depths of our soul beyond where we have been before, in order to create a new reality. It is always darkest before the dawn.

TRAUMAS AND ABUSES

It is only by the distinct power of the intellect that we speak of visualization as something separate from the rest of experience. In truth, our visual process is directly linked with what we feel, think, and express. Seeing something out of the corner of our eye will make us jump or catch our breath. Alluring images can stimulate sexual arousal. Violent images might make us feel nauseous or frightened.

If visual memory is so linked with our somatic experience, then it follows that abuses to any of the chakras—to the body, the emotions, one's autonomy, one's heart, or the freedom of expression—will affect the opening of the sixth chakra as well. This is the library where we store the images that link with experience. If it is full of negative experiences, then we may unconsciously censor parts of the library.

If the feelings associated with an image or memory are unpleasant, there are only two ways to avoid those feelings: We can either *repress* the memory or we can *dissociate* from it. In repression, we close down our perceptive abilities and put blinders on the range of what we see. In dissociation, we inhibit our ability to make sense of the images we see—we strip them of their meaning and value, while our unconscious reactions continue disconnected from any conscious understanding.

Sandra's father repeatedly beat her mother, and Sandra herself was often verbally threatened. Witnessing the violence was enough to convince her to behave flawlessly in order to stay out of trouble. Yet as she witnessed the blows, her own body experienced fear and helplessness. She could not trust her father in his rage, nor could she trust her mother to defend her if the need arose, as her mother obviously failed to defend herself. Sandra was dependent on them for support and this produced an unbearable contradiction. Since this kind of fear energizes the body for action, yet there was no permissible action she could take, Sandra could only maintain psychic equilibrium by pretending not to see it. She

Being simultaneously present with body-feelings, visual pictures are found welded with somatic states. Retaining and reproducing a visual picture, therefore, means retaining and reproducing a body-state.

AKHTER AHSEN

repressed the memory. She instead remembered her father as loving and kind. As an adult, when her husband became violent with her teenage daughter, she failed to take action. When the abuse was later reported by a neighbor, Sandra remained mystified and defensive, emphatically arguing in her husband's defense about what a good man he was and how he loved his daughter. While there may have been elements of his love that were indeed there, she could not see the reality before her. She could not separate the love from the abuse, and instead saw and defended her own illusion.

The memory of her father was quite active, buried in Sandra's psyche. She was plagued by dreams of being chased by dark figures and her body was contracted and small, her voice timid. Her brow was furrowed around the sixth chakra, and she had worn thick glasses since early grammar school. In most respects, she was the ideal mother, doing everything she could for her daughter. But she had closed down a portion of her psyche, which kept her from seeing clearly and from recognizing an important pattern pertinent to her daughter's well-being.

Tom, on the other hand, reported horrendous memories from his childhood as if he were rattling off a laundry list, with obvious *dissociation*. Tom was highly creative, artistic, and elegant, but had a streak of coldness in his relationships that made one shudder. He failed to understand why his successive partners were always angry with him—he was unaware of the effect his words and actions had on a person, and instead faulted his partners' emotional weakness. His pattern in relationship persisted unacknowledged and unchanged. He could not "see" what he could not feel.

With repressed memories, we close down our sixth chakra, making it deficient. With dissociation, we lose our ground and the sixth chakra becomes excessive—bombarded with images that clutter up the psyche but never reach understanding.

An environment with daily scenes of suffering makes us close down our sixth chakra, and can even diminish the ability to see with our physical eyes. If someone has worn glasses since childhood, it can be worthwhile to explore what was going on in the family when the vision problems first developed. What was it they did not want to see? What was the contradiction? What is the illusion they carried away with them, and what might be the underlying truth?

There are also times when a child is told she did not see what she thought she saw. "Daddy's not drunk on the couch, he's just tired." "Mommy isn't upset with you, she's just having a bad day." "We're a very happy family and we all love each other very much." These are the kind of illusions that get stated verbally or are acted out by the family in their daily drama. Since contradiction is so difficult for the young child to live with, it is easier for her to deny her own perception.

In the recovery process, John Bradshaw talks about "moving from the illusion of certainty to the certainty of illusion."[8] Falsely remembering our past as safe and secure might be an illusion of certainty. When we really look back at the events accurately, we often see that this was most certainly an illusion. At this point, there is an awakening of clarity that allows us to see many things about our life from a new perspective.

Children are naturally sensitive. In the absence of direct knowledge, they rely on their intuition to assess a situation. A child may sense family secrets, but with no data to back it up she starts to distrust her intuition. As a result, it does not develop as much as other functions.

Shame

Shame produces intense self-scrutiny. Shame-based people feel compelled to look and perform as perfectly as possible at all times. As a result, the vision is turned inward in a paralyzing cycle of self-monitoring and is less available for looking outward. When the eyes do look outward, they often look for clues as to how we're doing, what's wanted of us, whether we're safe. When this self-scrutiny program is lodged in the sixth chakra, it takes up most of the chakra's "disk" space, blocking new information.

In addition, severely shame-based people cannot look you in the eye. When the self is considered basically flawed, we shield our eyes to prevent anyone from seeing in, as if they might see our own negative, internalized images. If we cannot meet another's eyes, we can neither see nor be seen accurately. We close the blinds on this essential window to the soul and become psychologically blind as well.

EXCESS AND DEFICIENCY

DEFICIENCY

If the sixth chakra becomes deficient, then its associated faculties remain undeveloped. There is poor intuitive ability, often with a compensating focus on the rational thought process. The person may seem psychically insensitive or "head-blind." This is the dinner guest who doesn't notice that his hosts are looking at their watches and clearing their throats, hinting that it's time to leave. This is the man who wants a date but cannot ask, and fails to see that the woman next to him is actually flirting. When head-blind, we fail to notice the subtle nuances of mood, often including our own. We might not notice until far too late that we had an intuition that something might not work out. With a deficient sixth chakra, we miss the subtleties of our own process (see figure 6.3).

> What is to give light must first endure burning.
>
> VICTOR FRANKL

If memory is poor in general, then the sixth chakra may have been closed down for protection. In this case, there may be some repressed memory, and the effort to keep it buried uses up a good portion of the chakra's storage capacity.

People with sixth chakra deficiency have difficulty visualizing or imagining things differently. They cannot imagine what the living room would look like painted blue, cannot imagine life other than the way it is, and cannot imagine themselves behaving differently. This person may say, "That's just the way I am," and leave it at that. Difficulty with visualization is also frustrating when trying to follow guided meditations or creative visualizations. Such people will often avoid techniques that employ such practices. If we cannot imagine change, it is less likely to occur.

When contents of the unconscious are repressed, it may be difficult to remember one's dreams. We may think we have no dreams (when, in actuality, everyone dreams each night) or we may be unable to retain our dreams in waking consciousness. Unfortunately, this cuts off an important key to accessing the deeper self. This may be due to a sixth chakra deficiency, or it may simply be that the person is using the sixth chakra so much in their waking life that it is less active at night.

If there is difficulty visualizing, imagining, or dreaming, there is more likely to be a strong belief that we see "the one true, right, and only way." *Monopolarization* refers to the state of mind that cannot see the other side. Unable to imagine differences, we must deny or invalidate them. This produces a spiritually closed mind that prefers to remain in the familiar rather than expand into the unknown. If the lower chakras have not provided the security needed to let go, we prefer to stay within the range of the familiar.

Of course, much of what we refuse to see comes under the heading of *denial*. Denial insists that something does not exist—that we do not have a drinking problem, that we are not overly attached to our relationship, that we are happy when we are not, or that the world has no environmental problems. Denial is both personal and collective. In denial we are held by the demon of illusion—held in a fantasy world that keeps us from having to take action in our lives.

EXCESS

When the image or memory of an event is disconnected from the rest of experience, the energy that is split off is invested in an image. When numerous dissociated images do not get grounded in experience, an excessive condition develops in the sixth chakra. These elements may haunt the person in dreams, appear as obsessive fantasies, or become full-blown delusions or hallucinations. This can run the gamut from mild neurotic annoyance to full-blown psychosis (see figure 6.3).

Such people appear to be laboring under the burden of too much psychic input. They will come up and tell you, often with wild darting eyes, what everyone is thinking about them or that certain events will happen. They may have many visions, but their visions are farsighted, blind to the realities close at hand. This is the person who is going to make a fortune with their new project when they can't even pay this month's rent, or the one who is already fantasizing about their wedding with a person they've only dated a few times. I call it "vision blindness," as if the image they see blinds them to everything else.

Excess energy in the sixth chakra happens when energy is withdrawn from the lower chakras. Without the grounding that brings limitation and

Figure 6.3. Sixth Chakra Excess and Deficiency

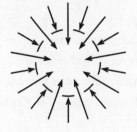

Excess

Poor discernment leaves a person overly bombarded with psychic input, diminishing clear seeing.

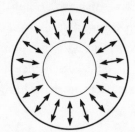

Deficiency

An excessive boundary keeps one from seeing out. Self-reflection is very narrow and egotistical.

simplicity, a person can get lost in the boundlessness of the upper chakras and have no way to sort it out. They may overidentify with archetypal energies and have too little personal ego to balance it. One may think they are Jesus, Cleopatra, or the next president, but have little awareness of their effect on their closest friends. The archetypal fantasies are used to buffer the weak ego and bring feelings of importance and power. They may discover some element of their past lives, and then attribute every current problem to unresolved issues from this memory. "I don't get along with Sarah because she was my mother in a past life and tried to kill me because she had too many children." (These fantasies may, however, reveal elements of the current issue.)

As I do psychic readings in my own work, I am constantly amazed and shocked by the power some people give to a psychic reader. I am usually tipped off to a sixth chakra excess when the person sits down and tells me with wide-eyed seriousness every detail of a former reading as if it were gospel. The sixth chakra is wide open, without discernment or discrimination. It is important to remain open to psychic, nonrational input, but equally important to rationally sort through it. Lack of discernment reveals poor sixth chakra boundaries, which allow it to become overloaded.

This is not to deny the possible value of intuition, past life memories, precognition, telepathy, or any other psychic arts. With sixth chakra excess, however, the ability to discern truth from fantasy becomes impaired. The universality of the sixth chakra opens to the vastness on the astral plane where anything goes without the testing ground of the lower chakras. This is a dangerous state.

The absence of energy in the lower chakras makes it easy to come and go from the body and so this person may indeed be receiving psychic input. This does not mean that all their input is accurate however, or that the perceived patterns are getting integrated into consciousness. Such people can often become "channelers," people who have the ability to leave their body and let other entities come through them. Opinions on the value of channeling vary from person to person. Whether the information channeled is from a separate, discorporate entity, one's unconscious or higher self, or subject to the whim of the imagination, there is no doubt that in some cases, accurate information can come through. There is also no doubt that inaccurate information can come through. As with any psychic activity, there must be a testing ground that sorts through what is said with discrimination. The excessive sixth chakra wants to bypass this process.

When one is bombarded by psychic input, it is difficult to concentrate. Intrusive elements distract us when we are trying to think clearly, and they may be accompanied by anxiety, which makes it difficult to sit still and let the mind settle. There is a classic metaphor that describes meditation as analogous to letting a muddy glass of water sit still long enough to let the mud settle and the water become clear. In this analogy, the excessive sixth chakra person is one who cannot afford to let the mud settle. If it did, it might reveal whatever they are trying to repress. Unable to settle, they are unable to ground and so the psychic energy remains in the upper chakras, looping through the infinite realm of imagination.

Having an excessive sixth chakra does not necessarily mean that one is highly developed psychically. Psychic development requires the ability to ground information, discern, decipher, and use it wisely in daily life. Instead, excess is a kind of runaway psychic energy, a car without brakes, a mind that is open but kaleidoscopic.

ELEMENTS OF BOTH

Recurrent nightmares can result from either excess or deficiency. As intrusive elements of consciousness, they can be seen as dissociated fragments rising up from the unconscious that cannot be integrated into waking life. If the chakra is very closed down, it may be that the dreams are attempting to bring the unconscious material to light. Therefore, one must compare the presence of nightmares to other elements of the sixth chakra checklist before determining the state of the chakra.

As usual, it is possible to have characteristics that are both excessive and deficient. One may have incredible dream recall, and yet be head-blind or have difficulty visualizing in waking life. One may be highly psychic or intuitive and still engage in denial. One may be imaginative, but insensitive to others.

BALANCED CHARACTERISTICS

Balanced characteristics include intuitive perceptive abilities that enhance one's functioning and the ability to be imaginative and creative. A balanced sixth chakra is able to calm the mind and see clearly, without having personal issues or lower identities in the way. It can think symbolically, imagine different outcomes, and find a guiding vision that gives meaning to life.

RESTORING THE LOTUS

HEALING THE SIXTH CHAKRA

For most people in our culture, sixth chakra work is less a matter of healing than it is of development. As children and young adults, we are not taught to use our intuition, to think mythically or symbolically, or even to believe in the possibilities of psychic awareness. Development of the sixth chakra requires overcoming this bias and disbelief, and then applying focus, practice, and discipline to developing our awareness. Learning to see is a matter of learning how to look and of having the patience to look long enough to find what you are seeking.

> When we do not properly understand but merely reject the mythic consciousness, we deprive ourselves of the possibility of psychic and social integration. The mythic consciousness is as necessary as the mental consciousness.... We can ignore these structures at our own peril.
>
> GEORG FEUERSTEIN

As our visual thought process is so intimately linked with the rest of our personal experience, each step in our healing process—whether of body, emotions, mind, or personal relationships—brings clarity to the larger picture we are trying to see.

As part of a culture largely disconnected from our ground in the form of earth and body, most of us lack the stable base necessary to effectively open the upper chakras. They remain only partially awakened and our task at this level (assuming we have done our grounding work) is to stimulate their awakening so they can better serve the integration of the Self.

As this awakening proceeds, we resolve the contradictions between perception and the rest of experience. When these elements fall into alignment, the flow of the psyche through the chakra system as a whole becomes ever more fluid and dynamic, awake and aware, integrated and whole.

DREAMWORK

The most potent place to begin development of the sixth chakra is through dreamwork. Dreams teach us to think symbolically, to see and integrate what is hidden, and to access the archetypal realm that dwells both within and without. Dreamwork is a broad topic that deserves volumes of its own. What follows below are some brief guidelines to get you started.

The first step in working with dreams is to learn to remember them. If we cannot pull our dreams into waking consciousness in the morning, then we are not successfully getting across this essential link in the bridge—the link between conscious and unconscious. Here are a few suggestions:

1. Make an affirmation as you fall asleep each night that you will remember your dreams.

2. Before you go to sleep, review your day in reverse, starting with the most recent event and moving back through the day to its beginning.

3. When you wake, do not move your position before mentally reviewing the dream in your semiconscious state. Only when you have reviewed the dream entirely do you let your body move. If you have already rolled over, return to the position you were sleeping in and the dream may come back.

4. Keep writing implements by your bed and create the habit of writing down whatever you can remember, even fragments. Once the psyche knows that attention is being paid to dreams, recall usually improves dramatically.

5. Some say supplements such as vitamin B or melatonin increase dream activity and recall. Use of marijuana and alcohol tends to suppress it.

FURTHER SUGGESTIONS

When you write down your dreams, write them in the present tense, such as, "I am going down the stairs to the basement. I see a hooded figure coming toward me. I feel scared and want to run but I can't move." Use as much detail as you can—describe colors, tastes, sounds, and especially feelings. Draw pictures of symbols and images when possible.

Regard the dream as a composite of your own psyche. Each person, animal, or thing in the dream is an aspect of yourself, including inanimate elements such as cars, houses, rocks, bodies of water, tools, or any other strange object that shows up. Cars are often the vehicle we use to move through life, and houses the structure of our psyche, but guard against standard interpretations of symbols such as those found in dream books. What the dream means to you personally is far more significant.

People you recognize from waking life can also symbolize parts of you. Friends, children, partners, parents, or hated enemies (especially!) can represent aspects of self such as the inner ally, the inner child, the anima or animus, the internalized parent, or the shadow. Shadow elements—dark or scary figures or people we strongly dislike—are best befriended rather than banished or conquered, as they have something to teach us. Ask them why they are there and what they want from you.

Your point of view in the dream is known as the *dream ego*. Examine the state of the dream ego—is it scared, excited, perplexed, angry? What is the dream ego trying to accomplish in the dream? How is it going about doing this? What is blocking this accomplishment?

Set up a dialog between various parts in the dream. Yes, you can have a dialog between the dream ego and the toaster, the tree, or the demon that is chasing you. Allow the dream ego to take the part of other elements of the dream, such as the tree you climb upon, the wall that blocks your progress, or the gun that is pointing at you.

Finally, it is helpful to share your dreams with others. If you sleep with someone, make a morning ritual of sharing your dreams. Find a dream group who can help you enact your dreams more fully and see aspects you may have missed. Make art from your dreams, draw pictures, write poetry or stories. Be creative in bringing your dream elements into waking life. You will develop a valuable language with which to communicate both to your deepest self and to the world of spirit.

STUDY MYTHOLOGY

If we are to expand into archetypal understanding and develop our own archetypal identity, we need to have a body of knowledge from which to understand our symbols. Myths are the record of archetypal elements in the human psyche—they reveal the dance of these archetypes on the transpersonal plane of collective consciousness. The stories of the gods and goddesses, mythic heroes, harpies, dragons, snakes, and other totem animals all describe the way archetypal figures have arranged themselves in the field of human consciousness. Knowledge of these stories stimulates our imagination, brings context and connectedness to our healing process, and opens us to a spiritual realm. It is essential for finding deeper meaning in the rest of life. It is also essential for bridging the internal and the external during the seventh chakra step into universal consciousness.

VISUAL ART

Many people claim that they have difficulty visualizing, which leaves them at a disadvantage for creative visualization, guided meditation, clairvoyant reading, or trance work. If you are one of these people, do not despair, there is hope. Even if you consider yourself the world's worst artist, you can stimulate your visual thinking process by creating art. The purpose here is not to create something to hang on your wall or give to friends, but to use visual art as a way to tap the unconscious, stimulate visual thinking, and have fun all at the same time. Here are some suggestions for the nonartist.

DRAWING YOUR CHAKRAS

Get a large piece of newsprint and some crayons, chalk, markers, or pens. Go into a meditative state and sense the energy in each chakra, one at a time. Focusing on the first chakra, feel whether it is open or closed, tense or alive, solid or fluid. Then take the colors that you feel best represent the energy inside, and draw whatever shapes express the feeling you have there. You might draw big black blocks, yellow swirls, pink circles, or whatever abstract forms seem to best state how you feel in that area of your body and life. Then do the same for the second chakra, placing it above the first on the paper. Repeat for each chakra, and when you are finished, take a look at it. What are the energetic lines that stand out? Are you more open at the top than the bottom? Are you constricted and dense, or so light that you're hardly there? Are the chakras connected to each other, or is there a break between some of them? If you were to meet this person, what might your reaction be? What areas need to be worked on, as revealed by your drawing?

COLLAGES

If you have trouble getting in touch with your feelings, want to work through a particular issue, or are terrified by placing actual color on paper, then you can also make collages. Pick a theme you want to work on, such as relationships, work, body image, communication, personal power, or dreams, and get a stack of old magazines, a large piece of paper or cardboard, some glue, and a pair of scissors. Cut out the pictures (and captions, too) that resonate with what you are feeling or wanting. Arrange them on the page, glue them down, and create a piece of art on which you can meditate. You can continue to add to this whenever you want as it reflects your change and growth.

MANDALAS

Jung described the mandala as a symbol that reflects wholeness. Mandalas are geometric designs that emanate from a center. They can be made with a compass and ruler and colored in any way you prefer. You may choose to do one mandala for each chakra, the first in a red scheme, the second in oranges, the third in yellows and golds, etc. The mandala—in process or as a finished form—can then be used when meditating on the associated chakra.

VISUALIZATION

When we visualize, imagine, or remember, we use a process very much like the one used to see psychically; the difference is the subject in question. If I close my eyes and remember what I saw on my walk yesterday, or close my eyes to imagine a walk I would like to take tomorrow, the process within is similar—I visualize elements that are not physically present. Memory is based on what we have seen, but so is our projection of future events—the only difference is the arrangement of their elements.

This means that if we want to develop our psychic abilities, it helps to learn to visualize. We can begin with a simple visualization exercise: Imagine a glass and fill it with water. Imagine it full, half-full, empty, or filled with red, blue, muddy, or clear water. Imagine an antique etched glass with designs on the outside, and then imagine the glass breaking. You can embellish this kind of exercise any way you want—the trick is to focus your attention on forming images at will.

We can also remember a dim image and allow it to fill out with details. What did you have for breakfast yesterday morning? What color were the dishes? What clothes were you wearing? Who else was in the room? What was the weather like outside? How many lights were on? We can use this technique to embellish our dream recall. "I am walking alone in the woods." What kind of woods? What season is it, what time of day? What kind of trees are there? What colors are you wearing in the dream? Each of these questions is asked not to find a answer, but to paint the canvas of the imagination.

We can also let a particular image like a rose or a house become a symbol for something we would like to look at. Imagine your best friend as a house. What color would the house be? What kind of condition would it be in? How many rooms are there? How would they be decorated? Who would live there? What would the yard look like? Would friends visit the house often? Would they feel welcome?

If we use a rose as a symbol, look at how open the rose is. What color is it and how many petals are open? How strong is the stem, how deep the roots? Is it in a sunny garden with other roses, or is it thorny and alone? Is the soil fertile and soft, or hard and rocky? How does this kind of information represent your friend? Or yourself?

Creative visualization is a technique for imagining the things we would like to manifest in our life and giving them the focus and attention needed to bring them about. Once we learn to visualize simple things, we can then visualize, in technicolor detail, the things we want and need. This creates the stained glass window through which we shine our consciousness in the act of creation.

The best way to visualize creatively is to lie down and relax deeply. Use a few yoga stretches or your standard meditation technique to relax, or perhaps

> Creative visualization is magic in the truest and highest meaning of the word. It involves understanding and aligning yourself with the natural principles that govern the workings of our universe, and learning to use those principles in the most conscious and creative way.
>
> SHAKTI GAWAIN

a few minutes of simply watching your breath. Then allow the thing, event, or situation you are seeking to play upon your imagination. Imagine it as if it were already here, as if you are actively engaged with your fantasy. Allow yourself to feel, on a physical/emotional level, your body's response. Soak your cells in that feeling; allow it to resonate with each chakra. Allow yourself to enjoy the process—do not make it an effort.

When you feel that your mind and body have thoroughly soaked up the visualization, it is time to let it go. If we do not let it go, it is like writing a letter that we never mail. Sometimes I put a glowing sphere around my image and imagine that it is a balloon floating off into the sky. As I let go of it, I tell myself that it is now on its way to manifestation and turn my attention to something else. (Otherwise, I am not letting it go.) I affirm my trust that my vision will manifest in the form and time that is most appropriate for all concerned.

GUIDED VISUALIZATIONS AND TRANCE JOURNEYS

There are many wonderful tapes on the market now that take us on illuminated journeys through archetypal realms, seeking visions, spirit guides, healing, and exploration. Friends can guide us on exploratory journeys using a variety of techniques, from reading aloud a journey written in a book to composing a journey complete with music, drumming, singing, or chanting.

It is also interesting to have a friend create an astral journey out of an archetypal myth. First, find a myth that speaks to you with a poetic telling that is rich with imagery. Then put yourself in a comfortable, relaxed state where you will not be disturbed, and have a friend read you the myth *as if you were the main character*. If it is the myth of Persephone's journey to the Underworld, for example, imagine that you are one of the main characters in the myth, such as Persephone being abducted, Demeter losing her daughter, or Hades stealing his bride. Allow your friend to read it as a guided visualization in the second person: "Now you are on the hillside, picking flowers. Suddenly you feel a draft of cold air coming up from the ground." Your friend should allow periods of silence so you can deeply explore the feelings aroused by the myth. Be sure to take the myth to its completion, for the resolution of the story contains the healing and teaching we seek.

Another option is the trance journey, where we create our own guided journey that unfolds in the moment. To facilitate an altered state, it is helpful to play drumming, chanting, or instrumental music in the background. Pick a theme for entering the journey (a visit to the akashic records, a journey to the Underworld, seeking a spirit guide, etc.) and allow the images to form as if walking through a dream. As images or figures appear in your imagination, interact with them. Give them gifts, ask them questions, dance with them, or embrace them. Allow yourself to learn what they can teach you. When you return, be sure to write down what you have learned in your journal while it is still fresh in your mind. You may find that the insights keep coming even though you are no longer in trance.

DEVELOPING INTUITION

Whether we are aware of it or not, our intuition is available all the time. The problem is whether we *listen* to it or not. In order to listen to it, we must validate that it has the potential to give us useful information. We must believe that it is there and is viable. We need not rely on it exclusively, as we can and should double-check the information our intuition gives us, but we can honor the hunches that lead us in the right direction.

> By learning to contact, listen to, and act on our intuition, we can directly connect to the higher power of the universe and allow it to become our guiding force.
>
> SHAKTI GAWAIN

As intuition is a passive, largely unconscious experience, it cannot be forced. Instead we must tune in deeply to our feelings, listen to our guts and to the nonrational parts of our thinking process. We must enter a state of openness and trust. If we do not trust ourselves or our surroundings, we will have difficulty trusting our intuition.

Who in your past has invalidated your intuition? What beliefs do you hold about its power? How much do you trust your intuitive process and what are the grounds upon which you base your trust or distrust?

Clarissa Pinkola Estes tells a story in *Women Who Run with the Wolves* about a young girl who, upon her mother's death, received a couple of small dolls to put in her pocket. As her mother lay dying, she was told that these dolls would answer her questions by jumping up and down in her pocket. This is a metaphor for that turbulent gut feeling we get when something is not right. How often we override that sensation and push ourselves forward, only to regret it later!

As a tool for our intuition, we can create imaginary symbols to speak to us, such as the dolls mentioned above. Others use an inner guide, wise woman or sage, angel, or animal totem as a symbol of their intuition. With a clear visualization, you can ask your guide any questions you might have. The answers come from within yourself, but often the guide can be the symbolic vehicle to translate that information into a form you can receive.

CLAIRVOYANCE

Clairvoyance is French for "clear seeing." It involves looking into the clear spaces around an object, rather than at the solid shapes of the material world. Clairvoyance is what remains when we clear illusions out of our own mind and look directly at the energies swirling about us. It enables us to see auras, chakras, and the subtle energy dynamics that flow within, around, and between people. Clairvoyance can be developed by anyone—it does not require a special gene or talent, though some people take to it more easily than others.

Clairvoyant abilities are developed through a combination of all these exercises. Being able to visualize helps us see answers to questions that arise, and following our intuition helps us make sense of what we see so we can apply it appropriately.

In my workshops on the sixth chakra, we begin with a combination of meditation and visualization. People then pick a partner and attempt to read each other's chakras. To do so, they sit in chairs opposite each other, close their eyes, and allow images to form in response to questions. Such questions might include: "What chakra is this person having the most trouble with? What kind of energies or fears are blocking that chakra? Where do they come from?" As images form, they are reported back to the person being read. "I see in the heart chakra a door that's loose on its hinges. I see a kind of darkness near the back on the left." The impressions may not always be visual, as some people are more kinesthetic or aural. "When I look at your third chakra, I feel in my own body an excitement of energy moving upward." "When I try to sense your first chakra, I hear the message that you do not ever feel safe in the world." Information can come to us in a variety of ways.

I am always amazed at how a few simple warm-up visualization exercises, such as coloring the chakras, and others listed above, allow people an immediate experience of clairvoyance. When they feed their impressions back to their partner, they are amazed at their accuracy. This does not make them experienced readers overnight, but it does allow some validation of their psychic abilities so they can begin to use them more often. Like a muscle, our vision gets stronger when we use our third eye.

VISION QUEST

To have a vision is to carry within us a source of inspiration and power. Like a guiding light, it illuminates our path and helps us sort out the many decisions we must make. Vision gives meaning and purpose to our life, shaping and transforming the world around us. Vision creates the strange attractors that shape chaotic energies into definable patterns. For some, vision comes easily, rising unbidden from the depths of consciousness to clarify our purpose or understanding. For most people, however, vision needs to be sought, invited, cultivated, and celebrated.

Native American religions and other forms of nature spirituality have a tradition known as the *Vision Quest*. A Vision Quest is a ritual of purification and listening, an open but focused search for spiritual teaching and guidance. It involves a willingness to humble oneself, embrace personal ordeal, and undo the connection to civilization that so blinds our sight long enough to see clearly into the patterns of the natural world. As a solo rite, it is a deep embracing of Self for the purpose of expanding into creative, archetypal, and universal identities.

What follows is a brief outline of a Vision Quest experience, not a full set of instructions. There are many variations and many groups who facilitate such quests, allowing you, the quester, to be free of mundane details and enter fully into the process. These groups also provide worthwhile guidance, ceremony, and support.

The Vision Quest usually includes three basic phases. In the first phase we sever ourselves from the world as we know it. We leave our city, home, and friends, and go far enough out into the wilderness so that there is no evidence of humans. A special place is chosen for the quest, one that has beauty and power, isolation and challenge. As we leave the known world, we psychologically sever ourselves from our mundane concerns, letting go of the daily worries that usually occupy our mind.

One enters the wilderness alone on a Vision Quest, with only a minimum of equipment. During the heart of the quest, which should be a minimum of three days but can be longer, the quester abstains from food. Fasting on the quest is a way of purification and of weakening normal ego defenses so we become open to more subtle planes.

During the heart of the quest, one enters a sacred dimension, outside the limitations of time and space, opening fully to spirit. The first day may be spent in walking meditation, searching for the right spot in which to focus one's attention. The second day may be spent sitting in a sacred circle created on the chosen spot, chanting, meditating, praying, and listening. One creates their own private ceremony to connect with the spirit of the place and ask for what they are seeking.

During this phase any number of things might happen. One may encounter their own psychological demons. One may meet animal spirits, have an experience with the wind, or have powerful dreams. There may be an experience of personal ego death, with a period of emptiness and loss that is eventually followed by a psychological rebirth filled with vision and understanding.

When the solo time is done and the spirit of the place has been thanked, it is time to return. Whether with a group or with a friend camping nearby, the quester then returns ceremonially to share the vision and wisdom that was gained. The group or friend can then help facilitate the transition back to civilization, where the vision can, over time, be implemented.

The important thing about a Vision Quest is to undo our usual way of looking at things. Our attitudes are reinforced by the culture, which impacts us daily with images, conversations, and experiences. During a Vision Quest, we consciously choose to enter the darkness in order to find and receive the light of new consciousness.

LIGHT

Exposure to the full spectrum of sunlight is essential to our health. Unfortunately, as civilization progresses, we spend more and more time indoors under artificial lights (especially fluorescents), exposed to frequencies of light that are not conducive to health. As the disappearing ozone layer allows greater risk of harm from the sun's ultraviolet rays, we cover our bodies with clothing, sunscreen, sunglasses, and hats that further block our exposure to full-spectrum light. While this may be necessary to some degree, we are losing valuable exposure to frequencies of light that promote well-being.

> Since the pineal is primarily regulated by environmental light changes, we are artificially manipulating and desensitizing its function much of the time by the widespread use of artificial lighting in our indoor and outdoor environments.
>
> JACOB LIBERMAN

Jacob Liberman, in his book *Light: Medicine of the Future*, states that we not only suffer from malnutrition but also from "malillumination." Insufficient exposure to full-spectrum sunlight can cause symptoms such as depression, chronic fatigue, higher levels of stress hormones such as ACTH and cortisol, as well as higher cholesterol levels. Studies of children have shown that improper lighting greatly contributes to hyperactivity, learning disorders, visual difficulties, nutritional problems, and even tooth decay.[9]

Psychologists have identified a depressive condition related to the changes of the seasons called *seasonal affective disorder (SAD)*, where people become lethargic and depressed during the winter months when there is less light. The effect of significantly increased exposure to full-spectrum lighting is so dramatic for people with this condition that it has become the treatment of choice. Could it be that the Prozac nation is suffering from light deprivation due to the predominance of indoor lifestyles?

Light enters the body through the eyes, which send signals directly to the hypothalamus, which, in turn, regulates the body's autonomic nervous system and endocrine system (both of which influence the chakras). The pineal gland, associated with chakra six, is a light-sensitive organ responsible for the production of *melatonin,* which regulates sleep cycles and helps coordinate the body's biological functions with the external environment. Over one hundred bodily functions have been correlated with diurnal cycles. When we alter this rhythm with artificial lighting, jet lag, or irregular hours, we throw off the body's central coordination. As Jacob Liberman describes it,

> All the body's systems relate to each other in a constant state of flux, with the hypothalamus at the center. The hypothalamus interfaces between mind and body, coordinating the readiness of both, affecting our consciousness, and thereby controlling our constant state of pre- paredness. This critical maintenance of body harmony is effected by synchronizing the body's vital functions with the environmental con- ditions, or, as some people say, "becoming one with the universe."[10]

MEDITATION

Meditation improves our focus and concentration. For most people, rising to the upper chakras requires a regular process of meditation. To open inner sight requires an ability to calm and control the mind and keep it one- pointed. Like a flashlight in the darkness, our focus illuminates what we need to see.

Meditation is mentioned here because it is an important element in psy- chic development. However, as it is primarily an activity of seventh chakra work, a more detailed discussion of meditation methods and techniques can be found in the chapter chakra seven, on page 422.

CONCLUSION

Ascending to the sixth chakra opens us to transcendent realms beyond ordinary awareness. This expansion can radically shift our perspective of daily situations and bring profound insight and vision. It can also elevate our understanding to broader levels, allowing us to embrace a much larger system of being than we have ever encountered. In expansion of consciousness, chakra six takes us to a beautiful world of colors and symbols, dreams and fantasy, archetypes and images. The possibilities expand through imagination, which stimulates creativity. Our new vista gives us increased understanding, as we not only perceive the patterns around us, but also perceive our own place and purpose in them.

> But the Self, as an inclusive term that embraces our whole living organism, not only contains the deposit and totality of all past life but is also a point of departure, the fertile soil from which all future life will spring.
>
> JOLANDE JACOBI

Chakra six prepares us for the final passage on the Rainbow Bridge. With its focus on archetypes, it lays the groundwork for understanding the intricate dance of divinity and consciousness that we shall encounter in the next chakra.

CHAKRA SEVEN

Opening to the Mystery of Heaven

SEVENTH CHAKRA AT A GLANCE

ELEMENT
Thought

NAME
Sahasrara (thousandfold)

PURPOSE
Understanding

ISSUES
Transcendence
Immanence
Belief systems
Higher Power
Divinity
Union
Vision

COLOR
Violet

LOCATION
Cerebral cortex

IDENTITY
Universal

ORIENTATION
Self-knowledge

DEMON
Attachment

DEVELOPMENTAL STAGE
Early adulthood and after

DEVELOPMENTAL TASK
Assimilation of knowledge
Development of wisdom

BASIC RIGHTS
To know and to learn

BALANCED CHARACTERISTICS
Ability to perceive, analyze,
   and assimilate information
Intelligent, thoughtful, aware
Open-minded, able to question
Spiritually connected
Wisdom and mastery, broad
   understanding

TRAUMAS AND ABUSES
Withheld information
Education that thwarts curiosity
Forced religiosity
Invalidation of one's beliefs
Blind obedience (no right to
   question or think for oneself)
Misinformation, lies
Spiritual abuse

DEFICIENCY
- Spiritual cynicism
- Learning difficulties
- Rigid belief systems
- Apathy
- Excess in lower chakras—
  materialism, greed,
  domination of others

EXCESS
- Overintellectualization
- Spiritual addiction
- Confusion
- Dissociation from body

PHYSICAL MALFUNCTIONS
- Coma
- Migraines
- Brain tumors
- Amnesia
- Cognitive delusions

HEALING PRACTICES
- Reestablish physical, emotional
  connection (excess)
- Reestablish spirit connection
  (deficiency)
- Learning and study
- Spiritual discipline
- Meditation
- Psychotherapy
  - Examine belief systems
  - Develop inner witness
  - Work with higher power

AFFIRMATIONS
- Divinity resides within.
- I am open to new ideas.
- Information I need comes
  to me.
- The world is my teacher
- I am guided by higher power.
- I am guided by inner wisdom.

SHADES OF VIOLET

THE SEPARATION OF SPIRIT AND MATTER

Western civilization is founded on the belief system that spirit and matter are separate and distinct. The earth is treated as an inanimate object to be used wastefully, at our own lack of discretion. Science examines the world rationally and methodically, pointedly avoiding the more nebulous issue of spirit. Corporations are built to enhance their economic prowess, often with little regard for the spiritual well-being of their workers or the environment.

People who give spirituality a high priority are often considered fringe members of society. For many seekers and respected masters, spiritual practice is seen as antithetical to mundane existence. Monks leave their homes and families and renounce all worldly pursuits in order to obtain enlightenment. Nuns cloister themselves to be closer to God. New Age ascension philosophy advises transcending the body and becoming nothing but light. Eastern philosophies tell us to let go of worldly attachments.

> We are no longer concerned with the dualistic opposition between God and man, but with the immanent tension in the God image itself. ... This inner non-equilibrium, the glorious imperfection of life, is the effective principle of evolution. God is not the creator but the mind of the universe.
>
> C. G. JUNG

The separation of spirituality from the rest of life leaves us spiritually homeless. In reflection of the archetypal divorce between Earth Mother and Sky Father, we are taught to seek enlightenment by denying the basic nature of our biological existence. This chasm between Heaven and Earth creates a corresponding abyss between spirit and soul that many fall into as they engage in ascetic practices, sign their will over to gurus, and disengage from the world. Denying our basic nature in order to achieve unity is a contradiction steeped in dualistic thinking, which will never lead to unity or wholeness.

The seventh chakra is about merging with divine consciousness and realizing our true nature. The petty concerns that occupy the bulk of our waking life often distract us from remembering who we truly are beneath the jobs and the cars, the kids and the clothes. It is important to know that we are children of the divine seeking our way back home—that there is a deeper meaning to life that underlies all of existence.

What is valid about this myth of separation is that we do need to disconnect from the *illusions* and *attachments* we place between ourselves and the divine, from the substitutions we use to fill the emptiness of our soul.[1] I believe the ultimate source of these soul wounds stems from stripping our ordinary existence of its spiritual meaning, leaving the average person without purpose or direction.

The crown chakra is the thousand-petaled lotus. Most people think of the petals as reaching up into the heavens; actually, the lotus petals turn downward like a sunflower, dripping nectar into the crown and down through the chakras. In this way, the two ends of the spectrum are profoundly connected. How can a lotus bloom without roots in the earth? How can it reach heaven if its roots are not deep and wide?

The Rainbow Bridge, like any bridge, is about connection. The two ends of the spectrum connect the individual self with universal creation. The middle section of the bridge takes that combination out into the world, through appropriate action, right relationship, and creative contributions. Our purpose in the seventh chakra is to contact the divine, but also to manifest divinity in our bodies and actions and so transform the world. In the seventh chakra, we see divinity in all matter and in all its infinite arrangements. Crossing the Rainbow Bridge is about stretching to connect the limited with the infinite, while still retaining both qualities. It is through that stretch that we grow.

To arrive at the fully blooming lotus crown chakra, our stem needs to be connected all the way to Earth, our roots deep in the ground. Through this connection, our lotus is nourished and continues to bloom, its petals ever unfolding. Our purpose is indeed to liberate the spirit, but if we are to avoid getting lost in the infinite we must retain a home to which the spirit can return. This is the challenge of a psychologically balanced seventh chakra.

UNFOLDING THE
THOUSAND-PETALED LOTUS

BASIC ISSUES OF THE SEVENTH CHAKRA

Consciousness

Awareness

The Witness

Belief Systems

Operating Systems

Universal Identity

Attachment

Higher Power

Transcendence

Immanence

Divinity

Information

Intelligence

Meaning

Unity

It is the tremendous experience of becoming conscious, which nature has laid
upon mankind, and which unites the most diverse cultures in a common task.

C. G. JUNG

CONSCIOUSNESS

Consciousness, the final frontier. That vast and indispensable key to the ultimate mystery, endless and unfathomable. The very thing that allows us to look into the mirror of the soul and perceive our own existence. Consciousness is both our final destination and the means of travel.

What is it that is reading these words right now, sorting them out, making sense of them? What is it that drew you to read this book, choose your partner, walk the path you travel each day? What is it that sees, hears, remembers, feels, thinks, and moves your body through its daily activities? To answer this is to find the final piece of the Rainbow Bridge.

We think of consciousness as our thoughts, but thoughts are what consciousness creates, not what it is. We think of consciousness as our perceptions, but there is a faculty that not only perceives, but also remembers, discriminates, and integrates our perceptions. Who or what does this?

> The act of individual consciousness reflecting upon its own immensity is the mystery of the crown chakra. To realize that consciousness flows through every quantum of life around us, and to behold the same presence within our own consciousness, this is enlightenment.

We feel the pull of consciousness on our emotions, but who or what feels those emotions, and how do we experience feeling? This is the mystery that we embrace in the crown chakra—a mystery that can only be experienced, not explained.

To become aware of our own consciousness is to witness a miracle. That your mind can decipher these strange shapes on the page, put them together into words, and then into concepts, and action—this is a monumental skill. That we can contain within us the words to hundreds of songs, identify countless voices over a telephone—even these mundane skills are miraculous. That we can run our own programs and rewrite them at the same time, that we can learn vast quantities about any subject we study, and transform that knowledge into creative expression, these are phenomenal accomplishments. Though we have computers that can calculate beyond our human abilities, we have yet to create a machine remotely as sophisticated as the human brain.

Mystic sages describe consciousness as a unified field in which all of existence is embedded. Sentient beings have the capacity to tap into that universal field of intelligence, where vast stores of information reside, much as a personal computer can access the Internet. How much consciousness we can tap into depends on our apparatus. A hand calculator can't utilize as much information as a personal computer, and therefore can't access the Internet or store research notes. A monkey can't tap into the same magnitude of consciousness as a human, and is unable to do mathematics or write poetry.

Opening the crown chakra is about expanding our awareness so that it can embrace a larger portion of the universal field of consciousness. This occurs through meditation, spiritual practice, mystical experiences, altered states of consciousness, study and education, and the elusively simple but profound act of paying attention.

DIVING IN THE RIVER OF CONSCIOUSNESS

Erich Jantsch, the late systems theorist, has outlined three distinct system levels of human consciousness: the *rational*, the *mythical*, and the *evolutionary*.[2] If we imagine life in all its complexity as if it were water flowing in a riverbed, we can illustrate each of these levels as distinct operating systems that organize information and experience.

> In a world which is creating itself, the idea of divinity does not remain outside, but is embedded in the totality of self-organization dynamics at all levels and in all dimensions.
>
> ERICH JANTSCH

We begin by sitting on the river bank and watching the water flow by. This represents the *rational system*, where knowledge comes through science and other logical, empirical means. The essential activities of the rational mode are observation and enactment. Our method of inquiry is characterized by an *I-it* relationship—subject to object. We do things to *it* and observe *its* reaction. We observe and measure the water's rise and fall, the stream bank and its erosion, the leaves and sticks that go by. We learn as much as we can from *outside* the stream, but as we lean closer and closer to the water in an attempt to understand its deeper mysteries, *we eventually fall in*. Immersed in the river, our perspective shifts dramatically. This plunges us into the *mythical system*.

Many people choose to remain on the stream bank, forever gathering data. They think they will gain enlightenment simply by accumulating information. They watch and learn but never become a part of something larger.

When we fall into the river, we shift from *observation* to *experience*. Immersed in the flowing water, we are no longer on the outside looking in, but are part of the mythical aspect of the stream, a force greater than ourselves. It cannot be explained in terms of gallons of water or rate of flow, but it comes through the realm of experience. If we embrace this mythic level and choose to swim in the river for a while, we no longer view our relationship with the river as *I* and *it*, but as *I* and *thou*. Here, subject embraces subject. The river has a life force of its own—it is going somewhere and taking us along with it. We can foolishly try to swim upstream, or we can allow its force to take us on a journey.

Archetypal consciousness emerges when we enter the river. At the archetypal level we identify with the river, identify it as the force that is taking us along our path, identify with its fast and slow places, its dangerous rapids and sensuous pools. We identify and embrace.

Our collection of data gathered at the rational level now assembles itself into an intuitive whole, a complete gestalt that involves mind and body simultaneously. It helps to know if a waterfall or rapid lies ahead. This knowledge is our foundation, the necessary lower chakra orientation of consciousness. Still, it tells us little about how to swim, a skill we can only learn by getting wet. Once swimming, we cannot explain how many gallons of water to push with our hands or even how often to stroke. We can only learn by feel and by doing, as it is with the stream of life as well.

At the mythic level, we battle forces that have lives of their own. In order to survive, we must become one with a force, but we have to leave the stream bank in order to have this experience. This is the aspect of spirituality that involves *letting go*. The stream bank is our familiar world, our rational mind, our safety, and security. It is our body of knowledge. As we enter into mythic

Without evolutionary inquiry, we lack a sense of direction; without mythological inquiry, we lack a sense of systemic existence. Without both, we separate ourselves from the world we live in.

ERICH JANTSCH

consciousness, the rational system does not disappear but is transcended by a deeper experience.

Becoming "one with the river" does not mean that we lose ourselves. If we simply gave up and surrendered to the water we could drown or be dashed on the rocks! This is the challenge that most of us meet on our spiritual path. How do we become one with a force greater than ourselves without losing ourselves? Our third chakra *will* has to engage and drive the feet to kick. We have to learn our relationship to the river and interpret our many feelings that tell us just how to move among the rocks. Once we jump fully into the stream of energy flowing through our bodies and our lives, we are forced to deal with larger challenges. We are forced to evolve.

By this merging—not just jumping in but learning to swim until it is a glorious free-flowing dance—we enter the third level of consciousness: the *evolutionary system*. At this point *I* and *thou* become *we*. This is the expansion into universal mind, the union with the divine, and the all-inclusive state of being where system boundaries have dissolved and reformed to a greater and deeper whole. Again, we do not lose the *I*, we reframe it. The *I* now includes the all. Here is our final transcendence into cosmic consciousness.

Many spiritual disciplines, especially those oriented toward ascendance, advise us to give up the self, to surrender all to a master, guru, or a particular concept of God.[3] While it is important to give up attachments to the lower egos, what is really called for is to become one *with* the divine. There is no *we* without an *I*. To become one with the divine is not to abandon the Self (as archetype of wholeness) but to realize that divine consciousness is who that Self really is.

To become one with the divine is to dissolve or transcend the boundaries that keep us separate. These boundaries exist in our mind alone. What we do need to give up is our attachment to the stream bank, our refusal to take the plunge and get wet, to take the chance on the unknown. We need to give up our clinging to the rational mode when it is unable to give us the deeper meaning of what it is like to be in the stream.

THE WITNESS

Sometimes the consciousness within is referred to as the witness. The witness sits behind our normal activity, watching without judgment the changing emotions, the flurry of thoughts, the impulses, and attachments. The witness is something above and beyond the body and its experience,

> What we seek is the very essence of that which is seeking.

beyond memories and dreams, even though it silently observes all these events. The witness may be the soul essence that has lived beyond this lifetime. It may be a divine intelligence that is larger than the Self. To become aware of the witness is to become aware of the essence that dwells within. The witness is the core of the Self, an indestructible spark of divinity.

To embrace the witness is to embrace the underlying reality of our being. The witness can be both objective and subjective. It can detach from the places where we suffer, and it can teach us how to swim in the stream when we are flailing about. The witness is the eternal guide, an invaluable friend, the deep inner awareness of the Self. Exercises for embracing the witness are included at the end of this chapter. For now, as you read through the rest of these words and as you put down the book and go about your life, be aware of the witness inside you. Just be aware.

BELIEF SYSTEMS

If we continue the analogy of chakras as programs on disks, plugged into the overall system as needed, then the crown chakra can be seen as the *operating system*. In a computer, the operating system enables us to read a program and make use of it. It interprets the instructions of that program. In other words, it makes meaning out of them. The prime activity of the seventh chakra is to derive meaning.[4]

Meaning tells us how to orient. It tells us how to interpret something, how to react, how to organize our experience. It gives purpose to our lives by creating a larger context in which to view our own existence. Most people, when something happens to them, want to discover its meaning. If you have an unusual pain in your body, you go to a doctor to find out what it means. If

> It is not only for unanswered questions that we seek knowledge, but also for the examination of unquestioned answers.

you get laid off your job, you want to know whether this means your work was poor, the economy is deteriorating, or whether the universe is telling you to change careers. In the human psyche, meaning gets assimilated into a set of beliefs. These beliefs then become the operating system that runs all the other chakra programs.

Our beliefs are made of interpretations of our experience. After beliefs are formed, the reverse is true—interpretation is based on belief, forming a continual feedback system. When Susan was a child, she was constantly disappointed. Her parents would repeatedly promise her something—a gift, a special outing—and then break their promise. She formed the belief that no one could be trusted. Now, she takes the slightest hesitation in someone's voice as proof that they are going to betray her. Her belief influences her interpretation of present situations. Since this is her operating system, she operates from a place of mistrust.

> The universe is exactly the way we think it is and that's why.
>
> JOHN WOODS

Our beliefs are based on concepts we have formed. Thus *conception* is the beginning point of all that we manifest. We have to conceive of something before we can do it.

When the egg and sperm come together in biological conception, there is very little material substance but a great deal of information. The DNA in the egg and sperm contain the "in-form-ation" (means of forming inside) that organizes the tissue into a particular form.[5] Likewise, our beliefs and concepts are *ordering principles* for information. They allow us to organize our data and give us guidance on how to behave.

The nature of our belief system determines our interpretation of any event that we experience. This interpretation is the governing principle in the way we order our life.

The "little engine that could" *believed* it could make it. The optimist who believes that this is the best of all possible worlds has a different interpretation than the pessimist who is afraid he is right. Our beliefs shape our reality and our reality shapes our beliefs.

Joan, for example, has had a number of negative experiences with men, including two incidences of rape. She holds a belief that men are selfish, dangerous, and less spiritually evolved. Nicole, on the other hand, holds a belief that she is nothing without a man, that she is incomplete alone, and she is always looking for Mr. Right. They are talking to each other at a party, when an attractive man walks up to them and begins flirting. What do you think might happen? Joan sees this as an interruption of her conversation, feels insulted, and becomes rude. Nicole is delighted and cuts off her conversation with Joan to speak to the man, an action that Joan interprets as *his* fault. Picking up these attitudes, the man naturally turns his attention toward Nicole and ignores Joan. One event is interpreted in two different ways, and these interpretations in turn then influence the man's behavior, which supports their beliefs.

The journey downward from the crown chakra begins with the conception of an idea. This conception is the supreme *bindu*, the dimensionless point of consciousness from which everything originates. From conceptualization we generate images in our sixth chakra. We have discussed how the light of consciousness shines through those images like stained glass, giving them potential for manifestation. The images that we carry then generate our story—our verbal litany of beliefs that we describe to others. Our story generates certain kinds of relationships, which stimulate various activities, feelings, and finally bodily experiences as manifestation descends from the conceptions of consciousness down through the chakras.

If we want to see what consciousness looks like, we need only look around us. All that we see began with conception—the buildings designed by architects, the people walking down the street, the trees and flowers that grew naturally from seeds. To see the nature of our own consciousness is to see its reflection in our own creations—the faces of our family, the way we care for our homes, the expression of our bodies, the things we create. As consciousness within changes, these outer manifestations change as well. In therapy, it is easier to generate shifts in consciousness than applying those insights to changing one's life. Nonetheless, the outer changes are impossible without the inner awakening.

The reprogramming work in the crown chakra requires an examination of our belief systems, for they are the primary structures that generate our reality. Often invisible, our belief systems are so much a part of us that we fail to recognize their existence. The awakened crown chakra questions any and all of our belief systems, constantly reprogramming and upgrading the operating system that runs our lives.

UNIVERSAL IDENTITY

Each of the identities explored in the lower chakras can be seen as metaphoric layers of clothing. Let us review these identities once again now that we are at the end of our journey.

The first chakra brought us our *physical identity*, where we identify with the body and its needs and abilities, as well as the physical world around us. The physical identity is oriented toward *self-preservation*.

> There is an unfolding of the one to a condition where it can be known——unity becomes recognizable.
>
> C. G. JUNG

At the second chakra we picked up our *emotional identity*, feeling the sensations of the physical body and transforming them on an unconscious level into value-oriented meaning. What feels good, we value, what feels bad, we devalue and move away from. The emotional identity sparks desire and motivation, which serve as fuel for the will in the chakra above. Our drive here is toward *self-gratification*.

As the will develops, our autonomous, separate self awakens. This is the birth of the *ego identity*, the executive element of the Self. The ego begins to split off from the unconscious drives as it orients to the outer world. It is primarily concerned with *self-definition*.

At the fourth chakra, we moved into our *social identity*, where the ego identity expands to include relationships with others. Here, the lower chakra drives, if satisfied, are ready to take a backseat as we move toward service to others. The reflexive quality of this identity is *self-acceptance* which is essential to acceptance of others.

The fifth chakra brought us our *creative identity*. Our awareness of the world beyond ourselves has grown and we seek to make a contribution to its culture, its arts, to the creative process in general. What is inside has had time to develop into *self-expression*.

Chakra six "dumped us in the river," where we entered the mythic realm of the *archetypal identity*. Here we begin to identify with the transpersonal, mythic forces that guide our world and lives. As we see ourselves reflected in these mythic forces, we enter a transpersonal *self-reflection*. The archetypal experience brings us a way to conceptualize and experience divine energies.

In the crown chakra, we come to the final and largest identity, that which identifies with all of creation, the *universal identity*. As our conscious-

> Universal Nature deposits certain habits of movement, personality, character, faculties, dispositions, tendencies in us, and that is what we usually call ourselves. . . . What is left of ourselves in the midst of all this? Not much, to tell the truth, or everything, according to the level switched on by our consciousness.
>
> SRI AUROBINDO

ness expands, our understanding embraces an ever larger scope. As we discover the immensity of the system we are embedded in, we identify with our universal connection. Our information can now encompass knowledge of distant galaxies thousands of light years across, as well as the dance of subatomic particles existing within each cell of our body. We embrace the story of evolution that covers billions of years, and realize we are part of the entire web of life—animals, plants, mountains, and seas. This vast identification can occur only through consciousness itself, through information. I can embrace my evolutionary history because I have learned about it. I can imagine spiral galaxies because I have seen pictures of them. I can connect with the larger world when I transcend my ego and realize the larger meaning of existence. This is the common theme in mystical experiences: the disidentification with the smaller ego states, and the recognition of a unitary identity with the entire creation.

Each of these identities moves from something innately individual—as unique and singular as our bodies—toward the universal. At the outer extreme of the crown chakra, individuality is completely transcended and absorbed within the larger field of the divine, expressed by the Buddhist maxim *Thou Art That*. The purpose of the crown chakra, of meditation, and indeed, of most spiritual disciplines is to break the limited bond with the lower identities and realize this universal identity.

Each of these identities is, in fact, a belief system and a means of interpretation. Take a relationship. A feeling-identified person will carry on a long-distance relationship even though it is not practical, so long as the feelings are strong enough. A sensate type, to whom practicality is more important, may end the relationship regardless of the level of feelings. If you live in your social identity, then you interpret the relationship in terms of your social role. If it fails, then you think you have failed in your role, or the other person has failed in his or her role. If you live in your creative identity, then you question whether the relationship supports your creative work. In archetypal identity, you may see the relationship as an archetypal dance between Mother and Child, between a Dark God and a Maiden Goddess, or between a Hero and his conquest.

In the universal identity, the operating system transcends all these interpretations and simply witnesses the incredible dance of the cosmos in its myriad manifestations. In this identification, we let go of attachment and control and instead open to miraculous witnessing. It is here that we truly "let go and let God."

To realize one's universal identity is to recognize our many identities as suits of clothing. This does not mean that we discard these clothes—I happen to enjoy my clothing very much, and there are few places I feel comfortable naked. Likewise, I need my ego and persona when I give a lecture. I need to identify with my body when it's tired. Yet I also need to know that these identities are options that only represent parts of a larger wholeness. They are clothing I can put on and take off when appropriate, because they are not the sole statement of who I am.

Realizing one's universal identity requires a foundation of the lower identities to be in place. We are less likely to search for cosmic consciousness while in the midst of an emotional or physical identity crisis. We are far more stable when lower-order needs are satisfied.

ATTACHMENT—DEMON OF THE CROWN CHAKRA

The demon of the crown chakra is attachment. While attachment is necessary for making and maintaining commitments essential to the lower chakras, it inhibits our ability to expand in the crown chakra. Attachment denies the constantly fluid state of the universal system. It keeps us anchored in time, unable to move forward, trapped in a small place, unable to embrace a larger place. In Eastern religions, attachment is seen as the basis of suffering.

Attachment is a slippery demon. It is not something we can live entirely without, as we need to keep some healthy attachments to our children and loved ones, our goals and agreements. I once heard a story of a yogi who meets a master and asks for teaching. The master asked him to prove his sincerity by renouncing his wife and family, which the yogi did immediately as proof of his nonattachment. Is it truly a spiritual act to abandon people who needed him so that he could pursue his own desires for enlightenment? In my view, I think not. It was just a transfer of attachment. True non-attachment would have been to say, "I have responsibilities right now. I will come when the time is right."

> Through pain and not getting what I want and expect, I learn the most about my attachments and about myself, and thus I can grow.
>
> CHARLES WHITFIELD

For some, letting go of attachment is synonymous with letting go of responsibility. It can become a means of escape. When the going gets rough, we simply let go of our connection rather than work through sticky issues. In so doing, we experience freedom but sacrifice growth.

In the truer sense of the word, letting go of attachment is about how we direct our psychic energy. To let go of attachment is to release our *fixation* upon something external, to relinquish our need to control, our desire for a certain outcome. Attachment is our way of not trusting the wisdom of the universe while it actually tries to teach us something. We stay attached because we are defending against our suffering, rather than seeing that suffering as a teaching. Attachment says we are certain we know what is best. It does not allow the humility that opens us to something larger.

Like all demons of the chakras, attachment itself is a teacher. As I began this chapter, I lost the love of someone to whom I was very deeply attached. (Was I being tested?) My attachment left me distracted in my work, suffering in my soul. I prayed to be free of it, did rituals around letting go of it, but it failed to budge. I remained attached—fighting it all the while. Finally a friend advised me not to fight it so much and just let it take its course—to grieve. Fighting was only increasing the attachment. Instead we have to address the underlying factors that empower the attachment. What purpose does it serve? What is the pain that wants to be soothed? Who is it that is suffering? The loss forces us to redirect our energies. What does it push us toward? What is the lesson it teaches us? Addressing our underlying needs will ease our attachments to what we cannot have.

Attachment fixates our energy outside the Self. Rather than focus on the object of attachment—the lost lover, the lost opportunity, the elusive reward—we should redirect the psychic energy to the Self. We can look once again for the inner witness. Who is it that is attached? What underlying belief supports this attachment? What purpose does this belief serve? What are its benefits? What are its costs? Which is greater?

Suffering may force a new perspective and perception about what is reality. It can weaken the ego through repeated frustration just enough to allow a giving up or surrendering, which opens the person to the possibility of transcending his or her previous belief systems and levels of consciousness.

CHARLES WHITFIELD

We can also become attached to belief systems. In the 1600s, the Catholic church was so attached to the idea that the sun revolved around the earth that Galileo was silenced and punished for saying otherwise. The father of someone I knew was so attached to the belief that his gay son was a sinner that he refused to see him as he lay on his deathbed with AIDS, denying them both a powerful moment of completion. Certainty can be one of the greatest tickets to ignorance. When we are sure that we know something, we run the risk of closing down the crown chakra. New information requires us to expand our belief system, and the refusal to do so closes our system.

Another word for attachment is *addiction*. We become attached because it serves our purpose to do so—not because we are right, or because something or someone is necessarily right for us, but because we are unconsciously using that attachment to avoid some aspect of our growth.

Avoidance is another form of attachment, only in reverse. With avoidance, we are attached to *not* having something, most often attached to our unwillingness to deal with sticky or messy situations in which we feel inadequate. Almost anything said about attachment can equally apply to avoidance, and what is being avoided is equally pertinent to our growth. It is interesting to note that in relationships, one person's avoidance often becomes another's attachment. These situations can often be remedied by having both sides move toward the center.

With both attachment and avoidance, there needs to be a willingness to release, a willingness to either face something or let go. This often needs to happen at the third chakra ego level, which is most involved with holding on and letting go.

> With the silent mind comes a widening of the consciousness and it can turn at will towards any point in the universal reality to know there what it needs to know.
>
> SATPREM

HIGHER POWER

The modern twelve-step movement, designed to assist people in their recovery from addictions and other disorders, puts great emphasis on connecting to a higher power. Many people see this element of the twelve steps as the most essential piece to recovery, while others find it a turnoff because of their previous experience with religion.

Opening up to a higher power, and to the mystical and transcendental side of spirituality in general, requires the ability to surrender. Only by surrendering our attachments, our unworkable belief systems, our addictive habits, and our need to control, can we truly experience the magnitude of our universal identity. Only then do we open to the abundant possibilities that exist.

Our earliest experience with higher power came from our parents. As children, they were like gods—all-powerful, all-knowing. When we were helpless babies, they clothed and fed us. They were our first teachers, our protectors, our providers. If it was safe to trust our parents and to surrender to their love and guidance, then the crown chakra is comfortable opening to a higher power. If childhood was not safe, then surrender becomes a very difficult thing to allow. Original trust issues must be reexamined in a new light and reapplied.

Surrendering to a higher power does not require us to relinquish lower states, but does involve a release of that which separates us from the rest of creation. To surrender is to release our defenses, to let go of attachment, to trust the universe. As we let go of the small places we hold so tightly, we are lifted and carried into grace.

TRANSCENDENCE AND IMMANENCE

The crown chakra is a two-way gate to the beyond. It opens outward, beyond ourselves to the infinite, and it opens inward and downward to the world of visions, creation, and eventual manifestation. Eastern philosophies stress transcendence as the goal and essence of the crown chakra, indeed of the chakra system itself. Transcendence is a cleansing bath in the waters of spirit, a blissful relief from that which binds us to limitation. The purpose of moving up through the chakras is one of constant transcendence, where each new plane encompasses the chakra below in a larger framework. The experience of transcendence is one of liberation.

Transcendence is the path of liberation. Immanence is the path of manifestation. To embrace them both is to see the divine within and without as an inseparable unity.

Eventually we have to come back down as expansion of consciousness is of greatest value when applied. Light shining in our eyes can be blinding, but light focused on something that needs illumination is a blessing. Immanence is the light of divine consciousness shining out from within. It manifests the presence of the divine within, the divinity of the Self in its wholeness. From the perspective of immanence, deity exists in everything living and nonliving. To speak with you is to speak with the God/dess nature within you. To grow a garden or raise a child is to see deity manifested in its multiple forms. To speak your truth is to let the deity emanate from within you.

A friend once said to me, "Why bother with creation? Why not just go straight to the source?" Being a great lover of creation as well as the force behind it, I pondered this a while. Should one ignore the beauty of the rivers, lakes, and oceans because they are not the clouds? Should we look only at the sun instead of the delicate play of light in the flowers? Should we ignore the child and go straight to the mother? If I write a book, do I want people to ignore it and instead call me on the telephone? Absolutely not! Creation is the expression of the divine, and it is often more profound, refined, and detailed than the source itself, which is enormously vast and abstract.

One of the differences between soul and spirit is that the soul is an expression of immanence within the individual, whereas the spirit seeks transcendence and universality. The soul is like a gatherer of spirit, forming the abstract into a composite being. In fact, the spirit may or may not be individual at all as it can take on many forms. Like consciousness, spirit seems to be a field that we tap into and carry within ourselves. The soul is enhanced by the presence of spirit, as if spirit is the essence from which it forms. Spirit is anchored and expressed through soul, which gives it embodiment, meaning, and purpose. Soul tends toward manifestation and spirit toward liberation.

To achieve transcendence is to enter the realm capable of embracing the whole. To bring that divine state of awakened consciousness down into our bodies and act upon it is to experience immanence. As the vehicle that brings the gods back down to earth, immanence is the restoration of the sacred.

EMBRACING THE GODS

How would you behave if you knew you were a god or a goddess? How would you treat yourself, how would you treat others? What kind of consciousness would you hold about your smallest actions if you knew their effects influenced the entire rest of creation? If your lapses of consciousness could mean countless deaths? If your awakenings could bring joy to the multitudes? What kind of mindfulness would that inspire?

> We make our destinies by our choice of gods.
>
> VIRGIL

I often ask my clients these questions as they pose pertinent inquiries into the nature of deity. It is my sincere belief that each one of us, and every living thing as well, is an element of the divine. Unfortunately, our divinity is often forgotten, contracted by fear, buried in shame and doubt, or confined by the boundaries of the personal ego.

As Stewart Brand says in *The Millenium Whole Earth Catalog*, "We are as Gods and might as well become good at it."[6] The concept of being an actual god or goddess opens us to a greater divine force and to a position of greater responsibility. That sense of responsibility requires enormous commitment to consciousness. It requires us to pay attention at all times.

How much do we pay attention to the smallest details when we are in the presence of our beloved? How much do we pay attention to what we put in our bodies when sick? What do we say when defending something that really matters? These moments receive our undivided attention because they are special. To embrace the deity within and realize it is always present is to realize that all moments deserve that kind of attention.

The mythological significance of the Rainbow Bridge is that it connects us to the gods. To walk across the bridge, embracing each step as we go, is to reclaim our connection to the divine source. The ultimate realization is not merely to connect *but to become*. In this way our expansive transcendence becomes immanence. This is the essence of grace.

God is as close to us as we can risk being close to our real self.

The gods of ancient mythology embody archetypal energies that are pure in form and potent in power. They express the universal one in its infinite emanations. The merging of consciousness with the omnipresent one is a state of enlightenment that few attain, and even fewer keep. For most of us, it is far beyond our reach even to glimpse, let alone to stay there. But to consciously embrace divinity in its infinite manifestations on a daily basis is an act of worship that elevates our consciousness into the realm of the sacred. As it says in the *Brihadaranyaka Upanishad*:

Whoever worships another divinity than his self, thinking, "He is one, I am another," knows not. . . . One should worship with the thought that he is one's self, for therein all these become one. This self is the footprint of that All—just as verily, by following a footprint one may find cattle that have been lost. . . . He who reverences the self alone as dear—what he holds dear, verily, will not perish.[7]

GROWING THE LOTUS

AGE
Early adulthood and throughout life

TASKS
Intellectual independence
Spiritual connection
Development of worldview
Education
Ego Transcendence
Maturation
Wholeness

NEEDS AND ISSUES
Spiritual freedom
Intellectual stimulation
Spiritual practice

Seventh chakra development builds our cognitive structure, our set of belief systems, our understanding of the world, and our ability to question and think for ourselves. There is no concrete developmental stage for this, as it happens in different ways from the moment of birth until the day we die.

The main activity of this cognitive structure is learning. Through learning we expand our horizons, master our relationship to objects and persons, and grow toward understanding and wisdom. Learning constantly adjusts what we know, constantly upgrades our cognitive matrix.

There is, however, a change in the orientation of what we learn that occurs at various stages depending on the individual. In the seventh chakra

> Our consciousness does not create itself——it wells up from unknown depths. In childhood it awakens gradually, and all through life it wakes each morning out of the depths of sleep from an unconscious condition.
>
> C. G. JUNG

stage we consciously crave a deeper understanding and connection to the underlying fabric of existence. This is the spiritual awakening that begins with such basic questions as, "Why are we here?" "What does it all mean?" "What is the source?" From early childhood on, children may ask these questions as passing curiosity. "What does it mean that Grandpa died?" asks the grandson. "What is spirit?" my son used to ask.

There is a deeper thirsting that also stirs at the onset of adolescence and comes to the fore when the child is liberated from the family and begins her own life. At this point the family, which has been the guiding matrix (for better or worse), retreats into the background of internalized values as the young adult seeks her own operating system. The absence of the family system creates both the need and the possibility for something new.

If the crown chakra is healthy, it will naturally seek knowledge throughout life. If the parents were somewhat relaxed in imposing their own belief system, it is more likely that a person will remain flexible and allow their beliefs to grow and change. If parents are fixated in a single belief system, the emerging adult may also fixate at various places, only upgrading their beliefs when suffering and frustration force them to do so.[8]

The difference between sixth and seventh chakra awakening is found in the amount of ego involved in the questing. Early and middle adolescence may be a time of searching for an archetypal meaning or identity, but this identity is ultimately a personal one. "Who am I in the greater scheme of things?" In the seventh chakra, there is a shift beyond ego as the search for meaning goes above and beyond the Self. Not so much "Who am I?" but "What does it all mean?"

> We either get success or lessons. If we learn our lessons successfully, we get both.

Since most of this expansion and questioning occurs after children leave home, the best we can do for them is to provide a healthy foundation for the crown chakra. We can do this by stimulating the intellect and organizing opportunities for learning and information, such as classes, books, and exposure to new experiences. It is essential that we give them both permission and encouragement to question, as well as discussions that answer their questions or help them find their own answers. We can model the value of learning, thinking, reading, and questioning. We can also model the practice of spirituality without forcing it. What the child chooses for herself will then be infinitely more real and of lasting value—we need only make available as broad a range of choices as possible.

TRAUMAS AND ABUSES

Abuses to the crown chakra are subtle but profound. They occur at any age and in many ways and fixate the crown chakra in either an open or closed position. This limits the possibilities for focus and concentration (too open) or for expansion (too closed).

WITHHOLDING INFORMATION, INVALIDATING BELIEFS

Children sense, on an intuitive level, everything that is going on around them. They usually lack the ability to understand what they sense and constantly seek information to fill in the blanks. Many parents choose to withhold information from a child, believing it is for their own good. Benny asks where babies come from and he is told, "the stork brings them." Children ask why Daddy is passed out on the couch and may be shamed for their questions. Sometimes children ask questions their parents literally cannot answer and are either told untruths or shamed again. "What do you want to know that for? What, are you stupid or something?" Rare is the parent who says, "I don't know. But here is a way you might find out." Children may long to study something their parents think is a waste of time or inappropriate for their gender. They may be denied access to information that helps them develop.

> A psychoneurosis must be understood, ultimately, as the suffering of a soul which has not discovered its meaning.... We cannot tolerate lack of meaning.
>
> C. G. JUNG

After seeing an *I Love Lucy* rerun on television, a friend's son asked his dad if the world was in black and white when his dad was a kid. His parents could have laughed and ridiculed their son for such a silly conclusion, shaming his very thought process. They might have said, "What a stupid question! What's the matter with you?" or further humiliated him by talking to another adult, "Honey, can you believe what Johnny just asked me? He thinks the world's just like the television!" If this happened often enough, the boy would learn to doubt his own thinking and keep his beliefs to himself. Instead my friend validated how his son might come to that conclusion, and carefully explained the difference between black-and-white and color photography.

Children are constantly hungry for knowledge, and withholding it deprives the child of proper mental nourishment. When information is withheld, the child either makes it up himself or stops asking. In either case, the searching stops and the crown chakra ceases to draw in new information and shuts down.

Poor education damages the curious mind. Most of our school systems fail to change as fast as the culture and poorly stimulate and support a child's natural hunger for knowledge. Schools too often make learning a tedious, boring task rather than a joyous exploration.

> What we have not conquered in the past returns again and again, each time with slightly different faces but fundamentally always the same, until we have confronted the ancient knowledge and untied it.
>
> SATPREM

SPIRITUAL ABUSE

When I recently gave a lecture at a New Age convention, I was accosted at the door by a viciously angry woman with a Bible. She came within inches of my face telling me how I would go to hell if I so much as entered the hall because it was full of devil worshippers. She tightly clutched the hand of a freckle-faced, red-haired boy of about seven, whose eyes were as big with fear as his body was lifeless and pale. I watched them both for a while as she accosted each attendant who tried to enter, and when I tried to simply meet the boy's eyes and smile, she roughly pushed him behind her. His face is forever stamped in my mind.

Children are often forced into unrealistic purity due to their parents' shame. Austere practices, angry tirades in the name of God, excessive authoritarianism, punitive practices in the name of religion, insistence upon perfection, and teaching a child that they are full of sin, all close down the crown chakra, produce shame and fear, and ensure that this person will have a harder time opening to any kind of spirituality in the future.

Some children are forced to adopt spiritual belief systems that do not come from their own unfolding. Take the example of Brian, who from a young age was forced to dress up in a three-piece suit and accompany his mother daily as she went door-to-door proselytizing for her church. Brian experienced constant shame as doors were slammed in his face and as children he knew taunted and teased him. He was not allowed to celebrate his birthday, Christmas, or any other holidays that were important to his classmates. He was not old enough for structured spirituality to have any interest or meaning for him, and what he did experience was negative and unpleasant. When he struggled with a heroin addiction as an adult, he found the whole idea of turning to a higher power repulsive and thus denied himself a possible key to his recovery.

Structured religion is often age-inappropriate. Young children do not experience spirit by sitting on hard pews, listening to words they do not understand, or being frightened into submission. Children brought up in a healthy and loving environment, however, are naturally connected to spirit. More often than not, it is adults who have forgotten that connection who project their alienation onto their children.

If spiritual practice does not include love and respectful regard for the individuality of another, then I consider it an abusive practice. Children are defenseless against that abuse. Instead they live in fear, guilt, and shame—demons of the lower chakras that bind them at these levels. Only by working through these issues can they open to their own personally fulfilling spirituality. On the other hand, it is also a deprivation not to expose the child to any religious choices. He needs to be offered a sufficient variety of spiritual options, or his road to his own spirituality will be made longer.

EXCESS AND DEFICIENCY

DEFICIENCY

If the crown chakra is closed down, the liberating current cannot finish its journey and we fail to achieve freedom. The transformative energies that rise through the body cannot come fully to consciousness, and do not get realized (see figure 7.1). Patterns in our lives will repeat again and again as they continually try to come to consciousness. Without the awareness of the crown chakra, we are more likely to be ruled by our unconscious.

> To make of the intellect a competent servant instead of an incompetent master must be a major goal of continuum philosophy.
>
> JEAN LIEDLOFF

THE KNOW-IT-ALL

My client Jane asked her mother to read a book on her religion, which differed from the one in which she was raised. Her mother refused to read the book, saying she already knew all she needed to know about God and was not interested. My client was not trying to change her mother's religion but only wanted her to understand her own views. How can one claim to know all there is about the infinite?

The opposite of infinite knowledge and possibility is fixation on a single point of view as the one true right and only way. As the mind closes to new information, skepticism may become part of the identity. Jane's mother had firm beliefs but refused new knowledge. John Bradshaw describes this in terms of mystified religion: "Cultic authoritarian religion creates a kind of cognitive closure. The language is so pat, so clear and rigid, that it closes off areas that the mind would naturally be stimulated to investigate."[9]

THE NEED TO BE RIGHT

I had an extremely bright friend who was "always right." He took it upon himself to tell everybody around him what they were doing wrong and how they could fix it. He was very perceptive about certain things, made an excellent critic, and usually, he *was* right. Still he was unhappy because few

FIGURE 7.1. SEVENTH CHAKRA EXCESS AND DEFICIENCY

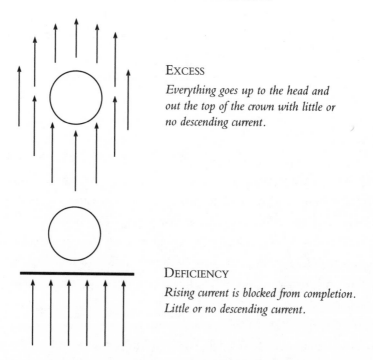

EXCESS
Everything goes up to the head and out the top of the crown with little or no descending current.

DEFICIENCY
Rising current is blocked from completion. Little or no descending current.

people wanted to be around him. Finally, someone pointed out that it seemed he would rather be right than happy, rather be right than have friends. This produced a value shift in his operating system that allowed him to operate in a new way.

Being right supports the delusion that we know everything. It also supports the ego, for in being right we get to make others wrong and come out smelling like a rose. This only creates separation and does not reflect the unity and expansion of the crown chakra. If you catch yourself doing this, stop and ask yourself, "What gives me the final authority on what's right? Right according to whom?" To accommodate multiple operating systems is to embrace the fact that there are many ways of being right.

FAILURE TO LEARN

Learning is a process of incorporating change as a result of experience. Without the liberating current, it may be difficult to change. If the crown chakra is closed down, it may be difficult to understand or retain new information. If the condition is chronic, there may be learning difficulties. At other times we are simply too distracted, attached, or skeptical to be able to learn something new. New information may be resisted because it erodes our belief systems—if we are overly identified with these beliefs, new information poses a threat.

BELIEF IN LIMITATIONS

It is amazing how vehemently people will defend their belief in limitations. "There's no way I'll ever get out of debt." "No matter what I do, I always end up alone." "No one can go to school while raising kids. I'm stuck in this job forever." Even when you describe situations where people have broken these limitations, the person will find a reason why it will not work for them. Belief becomes a self-fulling prophecy. This is another version of thinking that we know it all, but how can we know all the possibilities in an infinite universe?

SPIRITUAL SKEPTICISM

Some people are attached to the belief that nothing exists outside of the tangible, material world, a belief held by the bulk of our scientific establishment for hundreds of years. When extreme, spiritual skepticism reveals a deficient seventh chakra. If we cannot open to spirit, we cannot trust a higher power or open to the unknown. When there is spiritual skepticism, there is a preponderance of doubt, which is one of the five enemies to mindfulness in Vipassana meditation. (The other four are desire, restlessness, hatred, and sloth.) However, a certain amount of skepticism is a healthy thing—in fact, too little discrimination indicates an excessive crown chakra.

EXCESS

As the crown chakra is so often considered the be-all and end-all of the chakra system, it may seem odd to think of it as excessive. Once again, we must remember that excessive does not mean full and open, but overly invested with energy that is used as a defense (see figure 7.1). Excess in the crown chakra is quite common, as we pull ourselves up into our heads to avoid feelings and to distance ourselves from worldly demands. The person who is out of touch with her body and emotions or who feels powerless or lonely may be, of necessity, sending the unresolved energy up to the crown. Certainly this is the case with the Schizoid/Creative types, who find their reality in the world of the mind.

OVERINTELLECTUALISM

Over dinner, Frank rambled on about his latest insights, thinking he was charming us all by showing off his brilliant intellect. Although quite bright, he failed to notice that eventually no one was listening. While his wife had an excess to drink, Frank had an excess in the crown chakra.

"I think therefore I am" characterizes this pattern. The wheels of the mind are always turning, and such people can be highly intelligent and very knowledgeable. Building on their strengths, they overdevelop the intellect at the cost of their other parts, such as the body, emotions, or the heart. The world of the intellect is safe, fascinating, and ego inflating, but does not necessarily include an intelligence that operates wisely in real-life situations (just as Frank did not notice how bored his guests were).

> The intellect does indeed do harm to the soul when it dares to possess itself of the heritage of the spirit.
>
> C. G. JUNG

Excessive intellectualism is a chronic condition in our Western culture. Showing off what we know is made a virtue calculated by the number of obscure references, degrees, and learning institutions cited. Knowledge is power, but can be elusive and distracting if it is not grounded in wisdom and understanding.

SPIRITUAL ADDICTION

In some cases, spirituality becomes an addiction for the person with an excessive crown chakra. Used as an escape from some of the more demanding tasks of the lower chakras, one can run after a guru, thump their Bible on street corners, go to one meditation retreat after another, or rely on psychedelic drugs to get that spiritual high.

Spiritual purity is another form this addiction can take. Vows of poverty, chastity, and obedience are vows to keep the first three chakras deficient.

Fasting, ascetic practices, self-annihilation, and endless sacrifice can produce a high as well as an ego-inflating righteousness.

If these practices are sensibly applied to improving one's life, then the crown chakra is appropriately doing its job of evolving the soul in its journey. But if a person's life remains disordered and they escape into spiritual addictions, then their growth is arrested just as it would be with any addiction.

FEELING OVERWHELMED

When I first compiled all the information for this book, I felt overwhelmed. Even when I had finished the first draft, I got headaches thinking about how I was going to fit all that information into a single manuscript. It was hard to think clearly about how to pull it all together. Too much information, without proper organization, can be overwhelming.

When excess energy flows to the crown (as it does naturally with the Schizoid/Creative structure, or during stress or crisis), confusion, frustration, or dissociation can result. This happens to all of us from time to time, but when the stress is chronic, these states become part of the operating system. Then the crown chakra goes into a state of rapid free spin, similar to the obsessive state of chakra six. We have an excess of energy in the head but cannot think straight. We have too much information, yet do not know what to do. Many people get headaches when this happens, as the upward pressure builds up at the crown, unreleased. When the body is frozen, it is less able to handle a charge, and the excess goes to the head, where it creates confusion. At this point, it is time to do some grounding, meditation, or vigorous exercise to calm or discharge the excess energy.

PSYCHOSIS

Psychotic disturbances arise from a vast range of causes, and there is no simple statement that can be made toward their cure. They are mentioned here simply to place them in perspective as generally revealing an excess in the upper chakras. When feeling overwhelmed becomes a severe and chronic state, then the organization of the operating system may break down entirely. A person may approach or develop psychosis.

The lower chakras are primarily the realm of *neurotic disturbances*. I define neurotic behavior as those patterns we continually repeat even though they fail to work. Neurotic patterns are fueled by drives that have not yet come to consciousness, and are thus restricted to repetition. *Psychotic disturbances*, by contrast, are characterized by a break from reality and from the grounded aspects of the lower chakras. They most often manifest as a *lack* of predictable patterns and a failure to contain one's energy appropriately. Therefore, psychosis is an excess of the upper chakras, where the fifth, sixth, and seventh chakras manifest as voices, hallucinations, or delusional belief systems. Psychosis is an *excess* of the liberating current with too little grounding, which results in a lack of focus and containment. Neurosis is a *deficiency* of the liberating current with too little consciousness, which results in compulsive repetition.

RESTORING THE LOTUS

HEALING THE SEVENTH CHAKRA

Restoration of the seventh chakra is about awakening to the reality of our spiritual nature. As we eliminate the demons of fear, guilt, shame, grief, lies, illusions, and attachments, we are liberated from the habitual patterns of our thoughts and are free to experience consciousness as an infinite source. This realization brings dissolution of our separateness and insight into deeper levels of truth. Like the sixth chakra, it is less a matter of healing than it is of developing a capacity that has previously been asleep. If there is healing involved, it is to remove ourselves from the constant demands of the outside world, rid ourselves of false beliefs, and experience a personal and direct connection with divine source—in whatever form it may speak to us. We open this chakra by developing the capacity for stillness and concentration, for which there is no better tool than meditation.

Integrate around the convulsions of the mental and vital ego? As well moor a boat to the tail of an eel.

SRI AUROBINDO

MEDITATION

Meditation is a technique for energizing, calming, and clarifying the mind. Its purpose is to train the mind to enter subtler states of consciousness and transcend the petty concerns that usually occupy the mind, allowing us to access a deeper, grander state of awareness. Of all the methods for healing and developing the crown chakra, meditation is perhaps the most potent tool available. If universal consciousness is the system in which we are all embedded, and the mind an organizer of its components, then a technique that brings calm, order, and clarity to that mind also brings order and clarity to everything else as well. Those who practice meditation on a regular basis usually report an increased level of functioning in many aspects of their life, not just their thinking processes. Increased physical health and well-being, greater productivity in their work, better concentration, increased creativity, and more personal satisfaction are some of the effects that have been reported.[10]

There are countless techniques that one can use to obtain a meditative state. The following shows the broad range of techniques possible (but is not an exhaustive list). For those who say they cannot meditate, perhaps a different technique will help.

- Nonspecified, free-flowing movement, either as a quiet flow (Authentic Movement) or a rapid discharge (Rajneesh's Chaotic Meditation)

- Regulating and watching one's breath

- Gazing at an image, such as a flame, mandala, or symbol

- Uttering a mantra, phrase, or affirmation

- Observing the witness

- Following one's thoughts

- Walking silently and mindfully

- Concentrating on a concept or problem (such as the Zen koan "What is the sound of one hand clapping?")

- Intent listening to sounds or to music

- Visualizing moving energy up and/or down your body (running energy)

- Guided visualizations or trance journeys

- Simply relaxing and letting oneself be receptive to whatever comes through.

You will notice that some methods involve a *concentrative meditation*, where one focuses attention on a particular device, such as sound, image, or activity, for the purpose of making the mind one-pointed and shutting out all distractions. Other methods are *receptive meditations*, where one opens to the flow of thoughts, feelings, or impulses and follows wherever it might lead. There are three general stages in concentrative meditation, as described by Patanjali's *Yoga Sutras*: *dharana* (concentration), *dhyana* (meditation or merging), and *samadhi* (ecstasy).[11] In concrete terms, this involves focusing awareness on an object, allowing it to merge with the object, and experiencing the state of mind that arises when total absorption occurs and there is no longer a sense of subject and object, but only a sense of being. (Receptive meditation is described more fully in the section on mindfulness.)

The techniques that work best are subject to your basic character and needs at the time. If you are trying to calm your thoughts in a crisis, it may help to count your breaths, as even, regular breaths will calm the body. If it is so difficult to sit still that you do not meditate at all, you might try a moving or walking meditation. If your mind has a lot of chatter, you might try a mantra meditation, which sets up a rhythmic entrainment in your mind that brings harmony to your thoughts and actions. If you are trying to cleanse yourself of the stress you bring home from work, it is helpful to run energy through the body, as if taking a shower in sensation and light.

Meditation can have profound results. As our thoughts often keep us engaged in repetitive patterns and limited beliefs, meditation can yield a mental silence that allows us to access a deeper wisdom, a deeper state of consciousness. As we quiet the mind, we have the option to disengage our habitual responses—anger or judgment, fear or desire—and free ourselves from these patterns. As we disengage, we become lighter, emptier, and more able to access the transcendental states of universal consciousness.

Meditation can bring previously buried unconscious material from the lower chakras into consciousness. Thus meditation also serves the ascending, liberating currents as it refines our vibrations chakra by chakra, yielding deeper understanding and self-knowledge. Once we allow the constant chatter of the mind to subside, the deeper whisperings underneath emerge, just as dreams do when our conscious mind is asleep.

Emerging material from the unconscious can produce various results, however. We may be bombarded with feelings, sensations, or information we are not equipped to handle, or we might be freed of material that was unconsciously holding us back. If our work in the lower chakras has formed a foundation for higher consciousness, we will have the tools and context necessary for handling difficult material. If not, we can go to someone trained to help. In my opinion, it is not advisable to simply ignore it (as some spiritual teachers might advise), but to use the information to work through the knots of our psychic being. They may have somatic (physical), emotional, or symbolic aspects. I also want to stress that I am referring here to the larger pieces of material. It is not necessary to seek help for everything that comes through—just those things that repeat or have a strong psychic charge.

> What we have not conquered in the past returns again and again, each time with slightly different faces but fundamentally always the same, until we have confronted the ancient knowledge and untied it.
>
> SATPREM

Meditation can also serve the descending current of manifestation. This is the aspect that Sri Aurobindo called the *transforming force*. It is that which begins where other yogas end, illumining at first the summit of our being, then descending from level to level, gently, peacefully, irresistibly. It is this which will universalize our entire being, right down to the lowest layer.

Descending meditation reaches into the superconscious layer above the head and pulls down the force of awareness chakra by chakra, nourishing each center from the infinite source above. As we are bringing higher consciousness to lower centers, we are bringing a numinousness into our body, which results in immanence and grace in our being. It is this descent of consciousness that we will examine in the final chapter.

MINDFULNESS

Mindfulness is the essential key to living a conscious life. It is the fundamental quality to cultivate in the crown chakra, for it becomes the lens that guides the journey as well as the healing salve for the scrapes and bruises that we get along the way. Most of those scrapes occurred because of a lack of mindfulness.

Mindfulness means paying attention. It involves noticing the subtle flavors and textures of each moment and appreciating their many interwoven levels of meaning without getting attached to any particular one. Mindfulness takes our entire awareness into the present moment, enabling full experience. In that fullness, mindfulness brings us satisfaction in life as we are immersed in the incredible richness of each moment. Mindfulness does not forget the past or the future but brings them together in the present. We keep them consciously in sight as ways to enhance the meaning of the present. If I am watching a client have a breakthrough, my knowledge of where they have been and the freedom they will soon experience enhances the power of that moment. I do not need to rush to the past or future, but simply be with them in their present experience, knowing that it will take them where they need to go. Mindfulness underlies the concept "Waiting Is" (from Robert Heinlein's *Stranger in a Strange Land*). In waiting, we are not putting our attention on the future, but experiencing the perfection of the unfolding present.

Mindfulness has many enemies, including dissociation, presumptions, numbness, impatience, fear, and all the demons of the chakras. Each of these

> Mindfulness . . . has to do with examining who we are, with questioning our view of the world and our place in it, and with cultivating some appreciation for the fullness of each moment we are alive. Most of all, it has to do with being in touch.
>
> JOHN KABAT-ZINN

> When we commit ourselves to paying attention in an open way, without falling prey to our own likes and dislikes, opinions and prejudices, projections and expectations, new possibilities open up and we have a chance to free ourselves from the straightjacket of unconsciousness.
>
> JOHN KABAT-ZINN

enemies disconnects us from our experience of the present, occupying valuable disk space in our operating system. Each is a defense against the power of conscious living, which requires both sensitivity and responsibility. When we operate by habit, we allow our mind to disconnect and are no longer engaged in the present. When we operate on presumption, we are not allowing the present moment to unfold uniquely. When numb, we shut off valuable information and rob ourselves of the fullness of experience. If we are impatient, we are rushing to the future, not realizing how rich the present is. If we are afraid, we cannot fully engage and instead contract our attention.

Mindfulness brings us an immensity of information. Its enemies constrict information, leaving us with half-truths, misunderstandings, partial pictures, ignorance, and false impressions. Full information is equal to intelligence. To live intelligently is to avoid suffering and live with grace and ease.

Mindfulness does not have to *do anything*—it is instead a state of observation. It does not judge, value, negate, or applaud. It simply witnesses.

EXERCISE TO DISCOVER THE WITNESS

This can be done in meditation (followed by journal writing) or in conversation with another. The purpose is to disconnect from our normal vantage point long enough to recognize the reality of the essential self underneath.

MEDITATION METHOD: Choose a scene, story, or situation that has an emotional charge for you, one that has brought you difficulty. Let the scene run through your mind as if you were watching a video and had a remote control unit in your hand, from which you may pause, rewind, or fast-forward at any time. Watch the drama from the eyes of the witness.

Simply begin at the beginning, observing your baseline state of being, and let the drama play while you observe your reactions. When you get to a part that affects you strongly, push the imaginary pause button. Stop and observe your reaction. What is going on in your body? What are your feelings? What are your sensations? What meaning do you derive from your feelings? What are your impulses?

In a journal, write down your answers as if you were describing a third person. "She is feeling very nervous. Her palms are sweaty, and she feels afraid that someone is going to criticize her. She wants to run away." Then you can return to the movie and play out the next scene, repeating the same steps. Stop whenever there is a charge and record your experience. Notice that it is the witness who does the observation and writing.

After you have run through the scene, it is time to meet the witness. In the first person, write the viewpoint of the witness. What observations does the witness want to share about this person? What does it notice? What truths are apparent here? The witness might say, "I'm surprised she's so nervous. I see that she's afraid, but I want to tell her there's no real danger. She's done this job successfully many times before."

It is important to remember that the witness is not the judge. If the critic wants to appear in the guise of the witness, merely turn the witness on the critic. For example, if you find yourself writing, "She looks pretty stupid up there being so scared," then you know your critic has taken over the witness stand. Let the witness then observe and write about the critic. "I see that there is a need to pass judgment. I see that there is someone who does not understand her fear." We can witness our witnesses in multiple layers until we get to an *objective core Self*. This core Self has much wisdom. We know it when we find it.

WITH ANOTHER: Pick a scene, story, or situation that troubles you. Sit opposite a friend or therapist and tell them about it in the first person, sharing your feelings and thoughts. The listener merely acknowledges but does not interrupt. When you are finished, go sit next to the friend and retell the story in the third person, from the perspective of an objective witness. "She then had to go down and confront her boss, and this made her really angry. She did not like being angry because anger has always gotten her into trouble in the past."

As a final step, the friend can ask the witness for any further observations or insights about the person, and what the witness may have experienced while watching.

HIGHER SELF

When we cannot see our way out of the forest, we may need to climb to the top of the mountain to get a clearer view. Having regained our bearings, we can then chart a course that takes us where we want to go. By the same token, communing with the Higher Self can give us valuable insight when we cannot see our way through a difficult situation. Often, it just requires a change in perspective.

There are many opinions about just what the Higher Self might be. Some say it is communing with divine intelligence, God or Goddess, disembodied masters who act as guides, or an unconscious aspect of our own mind. Others say that it is just another aspect of the Self—the one that emerges naturally when the needs and wishes of the lower chakra identities have fallen away (see *Transcending the Lower Egos*, page 431). How we define it is of little importance, for it remains an unprovable mystery. What is important is that it is an archetype that allows us to *receive information*. That information can then be used for healing and guidance to bring us closer to wholeness.

EXERCISE FOR GUIDANCE FROM THE HIGHER SELF: TALKING TO GOD OR GODDESS

WITH A FRIEND OR COUNSELOR: Create a mental image of your concept of deity. It may be a round, stout Earth Mother, an old man with a white beard, a bright star, a fountain of light, or an astral cloud. It does not matter as long as it is an image *you can relate to*, one that carries wisdom and compassion for you. Describe your image of deity to your friend.

Next, think of an issue in which you seek guidance. Phrase your concern in terms of a question that can be posed to this higher being. "What is it that I need to understand in this difficult situation I'm in?" "How do I find out where my path needs to go right now?" It is helpful to ask "mature" questions, rather than petty ones like, "Does he love me?" After all, we are talking to a deity and we do not want to waste its time. Then tell your friend your question.

After you have described your deity and named your question, change places with your friend. Imagine now that you are this God/dess you have envisioned. Really feel it; immerse yourself in the experience. When you feel fully connected to this image, allow your friend to ask you, as God/dess, the question you raised earlier. Then allow yourself to answer as the deity might. Speak to your friend as if she were you. Have her remember and record what you say.

ALONE: If you would like to do this exercise alone, you can play both parts yourself. Image your concept of God/dess, and write your question on a piece of paper. Allow yourself to take on the God/dess form and read the question. Answer as you would above, either remembering the answer or allowing a tape recorder to record it. Then do some journal writing on whatever has come through.

NONATTACHMENT

It is fine and good to say that we should practice nonattachment as a way to lessen suffering and become mindful. But how do we do this when we are really attached to something? How do we unhook and return to our wholeness? If we force ourselves to avoid thinking about something, we are only increasing our attachment by the very effort of avoidance.

JOURNAL EXERCISE TO LOOSEN ATTACHMENT

Close your eyes and drop down into your body. Think of your object of attachment and the pain you have over losing it. Allow yourself to sink into that discomfort, into the sadness, into whatever feelings it brings up. Contact your witness as you observe yourself in these feelings. What does your witness notice?

Next, write down exactly what it is you are attached to, and the many levels of attachment that may go with it. For instance, if you are attached to a person, write down not only the person's name, but the qualities that are important to you. Write down the parts of the relationship to which you are attached, the things you find especially hard to let go of. Then, write down the parts of yourself that benefit from these qualities that you think you may be losing. If it is a job opportunity you are attached to, write down the things you expected that job to bring. Are you attached to success, money, prestige, or benefits? What part of you especially needs these things?

You can also get attached to sets of feelings. Perhaps you are attached to the feeling of victimization and anger that a situation brings up for you, and now you are attached to the resentment. Maybe you are attached to being right, to winning, or to doing something a certain way.

Once you have become clear about just what it is you are attached to, allow your witness to listen to the stories you are telling yourself about this loss. Perhaps you think it is your only opportunity to get something, or perhaps you think you will never be whole without it, never be able to love again, create again, have freedom again. Listen to these stories and let your witness assess their accuracy. Sort out the feelings from the truth. Write down the truth next to these statements when you can.

Next make a list of what this attachment is costing you. How much of your energy gets invested here, and where does that energy come from? If you had that energy back, what would be a more appropriate thing to do with it? If your job was taking you away from your family, see if you can imagine taking that energy back and putting it into your family. If your habit was costing you your health, imagine transferring that energy to healthier practices. If your relationship was interfering with your job, imagine putting that energy back into your work.

Finally, write down reasons why a higher wisdom may have separated you from this attachment. Find a form of God/dess to talk to (see exercise, page 428) and ask them to illuminate the meaning of this loss. It may bring forth an old childhood wound that needs healing; or it may teach you compassion; it may guide you in another direction. How can you apply this lesson?

When the journal work is done, it is time to go into meditation and withdraw the energy from your attachment and transfer it to more appropriate places. With your eyes closed, return for a moment to the feeling you had or would have had if life had gone as you planned it (i.e., without the loss of this attachment). Soak your cells in that feeling. Notice what you like about it—the high excitement, the sense of completion, or importance.

Next, in your mind's eye, move this object, person, or event back from yourself, making a clear separation. Thank it for the lessons it brought you. As it moves away, imagine that you are unhooking chords of energy, like taking the hook out of a fish you are throwing back in the water. Reel in these chords, pulling the energy back into your immediate field. Next, call in images of the things you need to give energy to. See your family, your work, your health, or whatever is most appropriate receiving new amounts of energy from you. Pull these things into your field and let the chords of energy connect with them instead. If there is still a feeling of emptiness, think of ways you might fill it—activities, practices, or other people with whom you can spend time. Allow the good feeling you began with to return as you imagine these other elements in your life. Soak your cells in this feeling, and from this place of strength, say good-bye to whatever needs to be released. You will now be in a larger, fuller place. Thou Art That! (With small adjustment, this meditation and journal exercise can be used equally for avoidance instead of attachment, as they are two sides of the same coin.)

> He who knows others is wise, but he who knows himself is enlightened.
>
> LAO TZU

TRANSCENDING THE LOWER EGOS

Opening the crown chakra is like taking off our clothing and experiencing the joy of being naked. The following meditation helps us drop the sheaths of identity associated with the lower chakras and embrace our universal identity.

Sit quietly in a comfortable meditation posture. Take a few deep breaths and allow yourself to let go of external distractions. With each inhalation, bring your attention inside yourself. With each exhalation, let go of the external world—anything that worries you, anything that is not part of this exercise, or is not part of the present moment. When you feel comfortably centered, you may begin.

STEP ONE: *Let go of anything that is not your body.* The body lives in present time and is a boundary between inner and outer worlds. As you let go of all that is *not* your body, allow your awareness to come fully *into* your body. Feel its length, its solidity, its width. Feel its edges and boundaries, insides and outsides. Feel it as the home you live in, as the cloak of the spirit and soul that makes them feel warm and safe.

Now feel the part that is sensing your body. Feel the presence of the resident dweller inside your body. Allow yourself to embrace that resident, embrace its energy, its existence. Think about how your body has changed shape over the years and how the resident has always remained. Notice how they are not the same. Ask the resident to come with you on a journey. Thank the body for holding you and allow yourself to go deeper.

STEP TWO: Now allow yourself to feel the emotions inside your body. What are you feeling right now? Feel the swirl of longings and fears, of joy and pain, and witness for a moment the extent of all the emotions that you experience in the course of a day, week, year, or lifetime. Feel the person inside who experiences these emotions. Imagine that these emotions are like a ride in an amusement park, full of ups and downs. Feel the indwelling spirit as the one who goes on the ride, but separate from the ride itself. Feel the choice that can be made about going on the ride. Allow yourself to say no to the ride, to disconnect and go someplace new, to go on a different ride. Embrace the inner Self and let the emotional body settle into the physical body. Prepare to move on.

STEP THREE: Now allow yourself to view, like watching a movie, the activities that you go through in your life. See yourself doing tasks at work, making supper, going for a walk. See yourself in your actions and reactions. Allow yourself to see the person that *responds*. See how many of those reactions are automatic, how many are based in emotions, how many are just physical habits. See how much the ego is hooked into these actions. Who is it that is doing these things? Allow yourself to see the person who acts and reacts as separate from the actions themselves. See the actions as choices. Allow yourself to choose nonaction. Embrace the indwelling spirit and let the actions fall away. Prepare to move on.

STEP FOUR: See yourself interacting with others. Take a moment to see yourself as they see you, as if you are watching from their eyes. What kind of person do you see? What is the role that he or she tends to play? Are there many different roles? Now see yourself from inside like a puppet master working the strings of a puppet, conducting the persona. See how the person behind the role is not quite the same as the role itself. Who is it that is playing that role? Embrace the puppet master and let the persona fall away. Prepare to move on.

STEP FIVE: Now see before you the things that you have created in your lifetime. See the school projects, the interior decor of your home, the artistic endeavors, the business projects, the events you generated, and even the situations that you have created. See the *I* that did the work of those creations, whether they were good or bad. See the *I* as a generator that can create many more things, but as something separate from the creations themselves. Acknowledge all you have done and allow yourself to leave those creations behind. Prepare to move on.

STEP SIX: Now see yourself as floating on a sea of archetypal energies, riding on the waves as each one peaks and falls, carrying you with it. See the archetypal forces that have run through your life—the cultural energies of male and female, the presence or absence of the shadow, the dance of archetypes in your family, your relationships. Feel how the culture has influenced the shape of this archetypal flow. Feel how you, in turn, are trying to shape it. See the thrust of your life as part of an archetypal urge to complete—maybe as the Hero, the Teacher, the Rebel, or the Lover. See how you have embraced this archetypal motif and how you have carried it, how it has carried you. See how these archetypal motifs are culturally influenced—that the culture is the sea with its waves rising and falling with different periods of history. Realize that there is still another presence within that has gone on this great ride—one that is separate from the archetypal energy, one that may have ridden many different waves over millennia of lifetimes, one that can choose which ride to go on. Allow yourself to let go of these energies and rise out of the sea. Prepare to move on.

STEP SEVEN: Feel the presence that has gone with you on this journey. Feel the lightness that comes when the body, the emotions, the actions, the persona, the projects, and the archetypal forces drop away. Allow yourself to expand beyond the earth, beyond the solar system, beyond the galaxy, and feel the connection with all of creation. Feel yourself as divine intelligence, pure awareness, as God or Goddess. See how small the other identities look from this perspective. Embrace the Self that still remains. This is your ultimate reality. *Thou Art That.*

EXAMINING OUR BELIEF SYSTEMS

As we expand our consciousness, our belief systems grow and expand. The greatest enemy to that expansion is the limiting beliefs we carry, such as "I can't do it. It'll never happen. It is impossible, illogical, I don't deserve it. You can't. I never, etc., etc., etc." What we in fact discover is that anything is possible. Impossibility negates the infinite potential of spirit.

To examine our belief systems, we need to follow our thoughts from conception back to their source. When I examine my beliefs, I might ask, "When did I first get that idea?" And then, "Where did those thoughts come from at the time? And those thoughts, before that?" Eventually we work our way through the outer influences of parents, peers, literature, or loved ones, to where we ask ourselves: "Is this really a belief that I have constructed of my own experience?" We can further ask which aspects of our experience led to this belief, and if our experience contradicts it, what is a more appropriate belief? Moreover, what beliefs did we bring to that experience at the time that may have influenced our interpretation? The process may indeed be labyrinthine, but it eventually leads to a deeper core experience. Released from the cloak of beliefs and interpretations, we are more directly connected with inner truth.

> Psyche and world form an inseparable unity rather than an irreconcilable duality.
>
> C. G. JUNG

EDUCATION AND INFORMATION

One of the purposes of consciousness is to bring us *information* to conduct our lives. The seventh chakra feeds on information, just as the first chakra feeds on food and touch or the fourth chakra on love. If the chakra is deficient, then it needs to be fed. If we find ourselves confused and ignorant, unable to think for ourselves, or not knowing which way to turn, then maybe we need more information.

Information can come in a variety of ways. It can come from teachers we meet along the path, from our Higher Self, from books, institutions, experience, and exploration. But the main thrust of the life force—indeed of evolution itself (simplistically stated)—is to become smarter, to obtain more and more information, and incorporate that information into ever more sophisticated systems of understanding.

Therefore, it behooves us to feed ourselves with information as a way of enhancing the crown chakra. Consider taking a new course of study or reading some new books. Tackle a subject that interests you and learn all you can about it. Working through this book or any good course of therapy is a way to learn about yourself and decipher the mysteries within. Knowledge of the world around us and the world within us are both paths to the mastery of *self-knowledge*, the goal of the seventh chakra.

RELIGION AND SPIRITUALITY

The word *religion* comes from the Latin, *religare*, which means "to re-connect." Ideally, its purpose is to facilitate a reconnection with spirit, with soul, and the vital and eternal aspects of life. Religion is the psychic structure many have chosen as the vehicle for connection, as an over-arching operating system that holds a set of instructions for dealing with the world. Religion can be the activity of the crown chakra in the same way that going to work every day can be the structure of chakra one.

> The elevation of psychic wholeness occurs only when energy previously invested in an external deity is withdrawn and returned to its source in the psyche.
>
> C. G. JUNG

While an adequate discourse on the topic of religion is too much for this chapter, I mention it here because it is one of the many petals of the seventh lotus, a powerful psychic structure that either liberates or imprisons our crown chakra. As a belief system, religion can obscure our experience or it can open us to wider vistas.

The drive toward religion comes from each of the chakras. For some it may come from a need for security (chakra one), or emotional fulfillment (chakra two), or a sense of power, community, or creative expression (chakras three, four, and five). For others it brings illumination or a chance to contact the ultimate source, however we experience that to be (chakras six and seven).

While respecting the seventh chakra right to choose one's own form of religion, I do feel compelled to mention that, within the context of any religion, one can adapt the outer structure of the religion as a defense. Religion negates spirituality when it becomes a structure for denying our feelings, avoiding the challenges of life, controlling others, or for ego-inflating righteousness. These are the traps of religion, the demons of attachment that parade as moral fortitude and obscure true spirituality.

On the positive side, religion does give us a structure, and, even more important, a practice, whereby we can let go and open ourselves to deeper states of experience, awareness, and understanding. It also gives us community and the support that comes from friends on a similar path. That support can be invaluable in times of crisis and difficulty or when the path seems most obscure. Practices such as meditation, singing in a choir, rituals, *puja* (offering), yoga, or community service ground religious values in real life experience. They are *the walk that goes with the talk*, the bones that allow the body to have a meaningful and solid form. Religion without a practice is but a set of ideas and concepts. Religion *with* a practice (or even a practice without a religion) is an active experience that can further the evolution of the soul and the world in which it lives.

CONCLUSION

Restoration of the Sacred

Along our journey from birth to wherever we are right now, we encounter obstacles and difficulty. The traumas and abuses we suffer as children, the lack of consciousness with which we operate, the blind spots of our culture—all these serve to shut us down and twist our path off its basic course. Yet, the archetype of the Self contains the program to become whole, much like a seed contains the program to become a flower. Each time we work through a piece of our past, we return to the original pattern and pick up our evolutionary process from where it was interrupted. We reclaim a piece of our body's reality, and so reclaim a piece of the temple. We break down the barriers that keep us from experiencing love, barriers that obscure the truth of our divine nature. We break through the illusions that keep us from seeing clearly, from deep understanding.

> Enlightenment or awakening is not the creation of a new state of affairs but the recognition of what already is.
>
> ALAN WATTS

Each piece we reclaim unfolds a petal of a chakra. Some pieces unfold several petals, or maybe several chakras, and bring deep restoration. Each piece allows us to live a fuller and richer life—bringing us deeper meaning about ourselves and the world in which we are embedded.

It is not so much a matter of trying to get somewhere as it is removing the blocks to seeing that we are already there. The goal is not to climb to the crown chakra as quickly as we can, thinking our journey comes to an end in some conceptual enlightenment, but to be as conscious as possible about the entire journey—to bring as much depth and wisdom as we can to each and every level. Even if we do manage to uncover the obstacles that keep us from the cosmic realization of our divine and universal Self, even if we do manage to find some kind of enlightenment for moments, days, or years, what then? Is there not a world around us lost in despair and crying for wisdom? Is there not a life yearning to be fully lived?

THE RETURN TRIP

Having climbed to the top in our journey thus far, we now begin the *descent* of consciousness. This, you will remember, is our manifesting current. As we all know, the landmarks on a return trip look a bit different from the first time around. As we unfold the chakras developmentally, from the base to the crown, our energy evolves into ever more efficient and complex levels. At each level we encounter a kind of realization: The infant gradually realizes that he is a separate being; the lover realizes that his partner has a reality different from his own; the visionary has a sudden flash of intuition and realizes some new perspective.

> The psychic realization or discovery of the soul is not then the end for the seeker, it is only the very small beginning of another voyage which is made in consciousness instead of in ignorance.
>
> SRI AUROBINDO

As we grow *up*, we simultaneously meet energy coming down from the top. We have said how pure awareness meets the body and allows us to operate it, that visual awareness stimulates movement and desire, and that language allows us to control our actions and conceptualize a self beyond immediate needs and impulses. How is this different in the journey downward?

In the journey up, we have access to the raw properties of the upper chakras, such as visual perception or language, but we are not yet *organized* on those levels. Our center does not operate from that state. The infant sees, but does not have a storehouse of images from which to make sense of what he sees. The toddler babbles, but does not yet think about what he is saying. The child loves, but does not yet understand the intricacies of relationships. You might say the access to the upper chakras is unconscious—it filters down, but we do not live there. We get a paycheck from the boss, but we do not own the company.

The journey upward allows us to access higher levels of organization and complexity, each one a new realization, a shift in perspective, a transformation. In the journey downward, however, we bring that higher awareness *into* our lower chakra activities. Instead of forming our decisions by feelings, we can base them on principles. Instead of repeating impulsive patterns, we can devise a strategy. Instead of merely *discovering* who we are, we can *create* who we are. Our principles, strategies, and creations include the lower levels, embellishing rather than denying them.

The energy coming up from the ground is dynamic and expansive. It is the energy stored in matter, full of potential for transformation into heat, light, activity. The energy coming down from the top is systematic and calm. It organizes, orders, governs. Yet without energy coming up from the bottom, there is nothing to organize, nothing to govern. Without energy coming down from the top, the ground energy turns into chaos and dissipates into nothingness.

Figure 8.1 shows how the chakras might appear once full realization has occurred.

The crown chakra is not merely a state of understanding, but a state of being. Consciousness is not a thing, but an experience. When we have fully arrived at this level, without denying or skipping over the levels below, we have arrived at a fully conscious state of being. What we can then bring down to the sixth chakra is not just an ability to see, but illumination. Illumination is like using an overhead light instead of a flashlight, where we see the whole instead of a part. With the understanding gained in the seventh chakra, we not only see the whole but also know what to make of it. As my friend and colleague Jack Ingersoll has said, "Vision transforms illusion into enchantment."[1] From illumination we create true vision.

Illumination brings inspiration to our creativity. Instead of unfolding our creative process by trial and error, we create from a place of vision. Our words have wisdom, clarity, and purpose. We know what we want to communicate. We understand what is being said, on an archetypal and a literal level.

When we bring our awakened consciousness down to the heart chakra, we bring the understanding necessary for compassion. Understanding allows us to see beyond our own needs in a relationship. We are able to bring the objective witness to our struggling process within, or to the trials of another. The wisdom to create lasting relationships is gained from experience and working through our own material. The calm that comes when the upper chakra awareness descends brings stability to our loving. Centered and balanced in ourselves, we demand less from our partner.

Figure 8.1. The Complete Journey

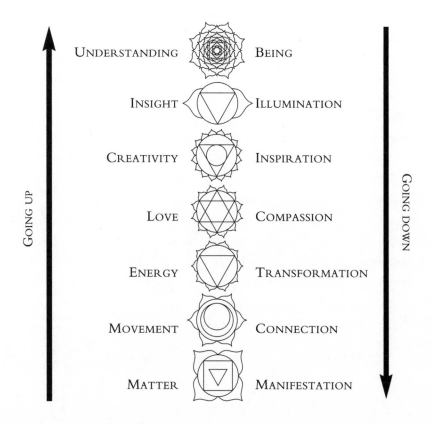

When we bring consciousness to our power, we have not only activity, but directed transformation. Instead of blindly acting through trial and error, we now use our intelligence to create a strategy. We make a plan to guide our actions. With vision, inspiration, communication, and love, we can energize that plan and direct it with clear intent.

We can now bring new awareness to our emotions and sexuality, deepen the texture of our experience, and broaden our understanding. We meet emotions with compassion. We express our sexuality with love and communication. The impulse to reach out can now make solid connections with emotional rapport, sensate awareness, new levels of empathy.

Finally, at the base chakra, these qualities become a part of our ability to manifest—where our conception, vision, inspiration, compassion, transformation, and connection enter into physical reality. We bring an expansive awareness deep into the body with love, connection, feeling, and aliveness. For it is indeed consciousness that makes the body fully alive, and the body that gives consciousness a place to live.

You may be thinking that this is all too ideal. How many people achieve total consciousness? Do we have to wait for enlightenment to have any of these qualities? I certainly hope not, or it would be very discouraging.

Enlightenment comes in pieces. It happens a little bit every day. Each time we have even a small insight, we have an expansion of consciousness that can then be applied wherever it is needed. Each time a feeling comes to consciousness, an image communicates meaning, a relationship gives us a lesson, or a success or failure gives us feedback about our actions, we gain a piece of wisdom that we can bring down through our chakras. Though we have talked about the chakras individually, remember that we are a complete, indivisible system. What affects one part affects the whole. As we change ourselves, so do we change the world.

PUTTING IT ALL TOGETHER

As you have been reading this book, you may have found yourself saying, "Boy, I really need to work on this one." "That sounds like my wife or husband; he's an excessive this or that." "I'd like to use some of this with my clients." If so, you have probably already been doing some of the work by just getting an idea of where the issues are. You may have a sense of where you are blocked or strong, what is excessive or deficient. You now need to look at each chakra in relationship to the others. It is time to embrace the whole.

MAKE AN ASSESSMENT

The following describes a method for assessing which chakras are excessive or deficient, and listing the issues of concern.

To begin, take a piece of paper and divide it into four columns labeled *Issues*, *Strengths*, *Excess*, and *Deficiency*. Next, go through the lists at the beginning of each chapter, and write down the words that apply to you. You may even come up with issues that are not listed, which is fine if you feel like it belongs in that chakra. Feel free to emphasize or qualify where appropriate. This is your statement—it is not a standardized personality test.[2] To double-check your results, have a friend who knows you well do an assessment of you, then compare.

This not only gives you an analysis of your overall pattern, but also provides a graphic list of the issues you need to work on, including the strengths you can rely on while doing this work.

Figure 8.2, on the following page, is a verbatim example from a volunteer.

FIGURE 8.2. ASSESSMENT EXAMPLE

CHAKRA	ISSUES	STRENGTHS	EXCESS	DEFICIENCY
SEVEN	None	Good belief system		Overly intellectual
	Love immanence and transcendence	Possibly delusional		
	Love the beyond, through the stargate			
	Presence of Divinity			
SIX	Not remembering dreams	My best chakra!		Nearsighted
	Imaginative	Intuitive		Memory?
	Can think symbolically	Perceptive		
	Fair memory			
	Good at visualization			
FIVE	Finding my own voice	Good listener	Talk too much	Fear of speaking?
	Neck hurts	Good singer	Interrupting	
		Can write well	Too loud	
FOUR	ALL!	Devotion	Codependency	Isolation
	Relationships	Love and trust	Poor boundaries	Narcissism
	Intimacy	The heart	Clinging	
	Self-love	Empathetic	Jealousy	
	Caring		Overly sacrificing	
THREE	Self-esteem	Responsible	Need to be right	Passive
	Power/ego	Reliable		
TWO	Need	Good social skills	Emotional	Fear of sex
	Movement	Emotions as allies		Dependency?
	Clumsy			
ONE	Trust	Good health	Hoarding (pack rat)	Manifesting
	Family	Practical		Focus and discipline?
	Boundaries	Grounded		Disorganized

Looking at this assessment, many things are readily apparent. There are far more characteristics listed for chakras four through seven, so the overall energy is stronger in the upper chakras. Chakras six and seven are clearly the strongest, so those strengths can be used to work on the lower chakras. The lower chakras are weaker, with the avoidant and compensating responses of deficiency and excess clearly apparent.

This person does not *inhabit* her lower chakras very much. Since the lower chakras are less developed and the upper chakras are strong, it is no surprise that the main issues center around the heart, where the upper and lower chakras seek balance. She may find that the issues of the heart resolve more by strengthening the lower chakras than by working on the heart directly, as it is already excessive. In other words, by getting into her body, she may feel more comfortable with movement, be less afraid of sexuality, and become more assertive, all of which will help balance the tendency to cling, be emotionally dependent, or have poor boundaries.

After you have completed this part of the assessment, you may wish to do some journal writing on the feelings, situations, or developmental material relating to those chakras, as well as engage in some of the suggested healing activities. My intention here is to present you with information you can use in whatever way feels most comfortable, but because the person is so different, I cannot prescribe a comprehensive treatment plan. A few general principles, however, can provide some language with which to talk about the overall structure.

TOP DOWN, BOTTOM UP, INSIDE OUT, AND OUTSIDE IN

Assessing your patterns shows where in your system the energy is strongest and weakest. Like Robin Hood who stole from the rich to give to the poor, we need to use the excessive energy to build up the deficient energy. If we are excessive in the sixth chakra, we can use that excess to visualize a healthy body or a better relationship. If we are strong communicators, we can use that skill to increase our sense of power or improve our relationships. If we are highly disciplined, we can use that discipline to do physical exercises or meditative practices.

In addition to the five basic character structures, there are also four basic patterns of unbalanced energy distribution through the chakras. They are named for the direction in which one's energy *needs to move* in order to achieve balance (excess toward deficiency). It must be emphasized that the following descriptions are stereotypical, and that your own pattern may be more subtle.

Where the attention goes, the rest of the energy is sure to follow.

TOP-DOWN SYSTEMS

If you live in your head, dealing with your body and the physical world only when you have to, then you have a top-down chakra system. Your assessment would reveal excessive upper chakras and deficient lower ones. Top-down people are usually *thinking-intuitive* types. They think first and act later (if at all), and often have difficulty being spontaneous and playful. After much pondering, they *decide* how to feel about something. They are often highly complex and intelligent people.

The natural tendency of top-down people is to move energy upward, but their *growth and balance* comes from moving it downward and connecting with the body. For example, the Schizoid/Creative individual who habitually moves energy upward would be considered a top-down energy system, because they are energetically top-heavy and will benefit most by developing the lower chakras.

This type usually suffers from early childhood difficulties that threw them out of their bodies and into their heads. They tend to pick jobs that are intellectual or analytical—teaching, computer programming, writing, counseling, and nonperforming arts, such as painting. They are oriented toward *self-reflection* and *self-expression*.

BOTTOM-UP SYSTEMS

Bottom-up systems, by contrast, are energetically bottom-heavy. Their tendency is to stay in the repetitive, familiar patterns of the lower chakras, while their growth comes from moving energy upward in the current of liberation. They are the *feeling/sensate* types who are more likely to be ruled by emotions and instincts than by cognitive process. They are less likely to discuss their decisions with others, and tend not to question their lives very much, preferring instead to keep things steady and not "rock the boat." They tend to have simple expectations from life, and are satisfied with sticking to regular routines.

Stereotypes of this pattern may be seen in the sports jock who lives for physical activity and belittles his wife's meditation class, or the laborer who just wants to work by day, watch TV at night, and wait for retirement to buy his boat. It may be the outdoorsman who loves nature, but has little interest in things of the intellect. In women, it may be the empty-headed ingenue whose primary concern is physical appearance, or the classic housewife who is content to stay home and keep house, with little interest beyond the mundane.

Bottom-up types generally enjoy physical activity such as exercise, sexuality, making things with their hands, cooking, or giving massage. (This does not mean that everyone who enjoys these things fits this pattern.) They keep their nose to the grindstone, tend to conform, and are predictable and reliable. Bottom-up structures are concerned mostly with *self-preservation* and *self-gratification*. Ruled by the unconscious, they often do not know why they do what they do, and may function by impulse, following the path of least resistance. It may not even occur to them to question their impulses, or ponder the meaning of life. Their energy tends to remain in the lower chakras unless stimulated by outside influences such as a relationship, a crisis, illness, or injury.

This structure is most likely to result from a strict parent who curtails the natural expansiveness of the child. "Sit still. Do what you're told. Be quiet. Don't even think about doing that." Their parents may have punished, ridiculed, or restricted creative behavior and experimentation. Some families model this kind of structure, teaching that life's rewards are found only in hard work, obedient behavior, and minimizing expectations.

INSIDE-OUT SYSTEMS

Inside-out systems are energetically centered in the middle ego centers, and their growth comes from extending this energy downward into the deeper self and upward toward the spirit and intellect. They have overall balance between the upper and lower chakras, but they are poorly connected to either end. They tend to take their bodies for granted and avoid introspection.

If the middle chakras are blocked, the energy is held in the middle of the body and kept from the periphery. This is evident in the Endurer structure, who has trouble finding his ground or bringing his feelings to consciousness, and who keeps his energy bound at the will. If the middle chakras are open, then these types tend to be ego- and action-oriented extroverts who like to engage life—socialites, performers, middle managers, or bureaucrats. They are not particularly interested in either their bodies or spiritual matters. They are more interested in the outside world of politics, business, relationships, or the performing arts. They are the doers who find their identity in activity yet may be unaware of their inner life. The Achiever and the Challenger-Defender may fall into this category.

Many such people take their bodies for granted unless something goes wrong, and they may have no interest in spirituality until some crisis forces them to search and question. This is the most common pattern in mainstream American culture.

OUTSIDE-IN SYSTEMS

These systems may be acutely aware of both their head and their body, with neither connected to the other. There is a great chasm of emptiness in the middle, especially at the heart. They may be highly sensitive physically, with allergies, irritations, or chronic pains, or even obsessed with their body in some way, such as with dieting or hypochondria. Their upper chakras tend to be highly developed and they are intelligent, creative, and intuitive. Disconnected from the integrative middle, this type tends toward introversion. There may be traumas that are repressed from memory, or serious wounds to the heart. Their growth comes from establishing deep relationships, from opening up and reaching out.

The Oral structure may fall into this category as they are collapsed in the heart, although Orals can also fall into any of the above categories, depending on their defense system. In extremes, this configuration can signify serious dissociations. I have seen it in multiple personality disorders, obsessive-compulsive disorders, and borderline personality disorders.

BALANCED SYSTEMS

It is possible to be relatively balanced through the chakras without being an enlightened master. People who have worked on their own healing or were lucky in their upbringing may be relatively balanced. What would this look like?

A person who is balanced in their chakra distribution would be well grounded and in touch with their body and exhibit relatively good health and vitality. They would be aware of their feelings without being ruled by them, sexually content without being driven. With a balanced third chakra, they would have confidence and purpose without dominating others. The heart would be compassionate and loving, yet centered and peaceful. Such a person could communicate feelings or ideas with equal truth and clarity, and be able to listen to others. The upper chakras would bring imagination, wisdom, and a personal connection with spirit.

This is an ideal for which we can hope to strive. By using our strengths to counteract our weaknesses and holding ourselves in loving compassion and understanding, we all have the means to achieve it. It only takes time, patience, and dedication.

USING THE ASSESSMENT

This assessment should give you a good idea of where the energy in the system is most present, and where it needs to move in order to achieve balance. Many people have reported to me that they achieved profound results just by visualizing or kinesthetically moving their energy in a new direction. This is especially true for ungrounded types who have never considered sending their energy downward.

WHEN IN DOUBT, WORK FROM THE GROUND UP

When I work with someone new, I usually start with grounding exercises and work my way up. This is generally a safe approach that helps to get the client in her body, and teaches some basic ways to create anchoring and safety. With grounding exercises, I can establish boundaries, get a sense of where the energy is blocked, and focus the person's life energy into the here and now, so we can work with it. It is also helpful to do drawings of the body or do the body dialog from my book *The Sevenfold Journey* (see page 71).

If the person is so frightened of having anything to do with her body that she cannot concentrate on the exercises, then starting with grounding is contraindicated. In this case I use conversation to establish trust and gather historical material. I ask the person to *imagine* roots anchoring her to the earth, or assign physical tasks to do at home such as working in a garden, getting a massage, or doing simple stretching exercises.

Once the ground begins to connect, the direction the work needs to take usually reveals itself. Emotions may arise; thoughts may bring associations with relevant material from the past; bodily sensations may become apparent. Dreams during the week may also give direction. If in doubt, I wait to see what emerges. I do not force a "healing agenda" on my clients, but follow their own pattern of unfolding, assisting and encouraging where needed.

At this point, the work depends entirely on the person's structure and the practioner's style. Hopefully, you will find suitable methods and techniques in this book. The main thing to remember is that body, soul, mind, and spirit, together with the seven chakras, are all one indivisible whole. Even when working with a part, all the other parts are present and participating. The whole must be kept in mind at all times as the guiding archetype of the Self.

KUNDALINI AWAKENING

Benjamin thought his wife, Marlena, was going mad. He complained that she was keeping him awake by thrashing and kicking all the covers off the bed. "She keeps twitching," he said, "as if someone were giving her periodic little shocks. She says she can't help it." She complained that her left foot and leg were tingling and aching, and she felt intense heat all through her body. Periodically, her whole torso would shake violently, sometimes only for a few seconds, and at others for nearly an hour. "And she's all over the place emotionally," he went on. "Sometimes she's scared and clings to me like a little girl. At other times she's blissed out. She tells me she's seeing colors and light when she closes her eyes, and sometimes she makes these strange sounds. I can't figure out what's going on, and I'm really concerned."[3]

> As one opens the door with a key, so the yogi should open the gate to liberation with Kundalini. She gives liberation to the yogi and bondage to the fool.
>
> HATHA YOGA PRADIPIKA

Classical psychologists would be tempted to say that, indeed, Marlena was having a psychotic break. Psychosomatic twitches and pains, voices, hallucinations, extreme mood swings, and dissociation all seem to indicate a serious disturbance. Yet, when viewed from a different light, these symptoms can reveal a radically different diagnosis—Marlena *could* be experiencing a Kundalini awakening.

In Hindu mythology, Kundalini is a serpent goddess who lies asleep at the base of the spine, coiled three and a half times around the first chakra. Her full name is Kundalini-Shakti, and she represents the unfolding of the divine Shakti energy, the energizing potential of life itself, a living Goddess who enlivens all things. Under certain circumstances, the Kundalini energy awakens and begins to rise through the body, piercing and opening the chakras as she moves in her undulating, snakelike fashion. As she releases stored and blocked energies, her movement can be quite intense, sometimes painful, and often leads to mental states that seem out of this world. Circumstances that stimulate Kundalini awakening are many and varied, but are usually triggered by such things as extended periods of meditation, yoga, fasting, stress, trauma, psychedelic drugs, or near-death experiences.

Even mundane experiences can trigger this unpredictable goddess. About seventeen years ago, I had my first Kundalini experiences after falling off a horse and bruising my tailbone. I had been practicing yoga and meditation for a few years, so I was somewhat prepared. My experience was less intense than most, but included several months of sleeping only four hours a night, a strong desire to meditate for long periods of time, an uncharacteristic lack of interest in sex, and a period of heightened sensitivity and creativity. I was taking clairvoyant training at the time, and had an incredible upsurge in my psychic abilities. I have had milder and shorter Kundalini experiences after watching a frightening thriller movie that stimulated my survival chakra, or by going without food for longer than normal. I also experienced Kundalini energy when I was pregnant with my son, mostly during the first trimester.

Kundalini is a condensed, primal force, similar to the potential energy found in matter. When released, it creates a vertical connection between the chakras by opening the subtle channels known as *nadis*, most specifically, the central channel that moves up the spine, called *sushumna*.[4] If we put water through a small hose at very high pressure, the end of the hose will undulate like a snake. Similarly, the intense energy of Kundalini undulates in the body as it rises through the chakras.

Kundalini can also be seen as the result, rather than the cause, of the chakras connecting with each other. Theoretically, as the chakras enlarge, the spinning of one can enhance the spinning of the one above or below it. Any energy spinning along the edge of a chakra could get swept upward (or downward) in a serpentine motion by the chakras, as their spinning changes direction from clockwise to counterclockwise[5] (see figure 6.2).

Kundalini is basically a healing force, though its effects can sometimes be quite unpleasant. Such effects may last for minutes, days, months, or even years, as documented in the well-known case of Gopi Krishna, who spent years dealing with Kundalini.[6]

If you find yourself dealing with uncomfortable Kundalini symptoms, the following suggestions and resources may be of help.

1. *Attend to the body.* Purify the body as much as possible by abstaining from substances such as recreational drugs, tobacco, alcohol, and

caffeine. This may include prescription drugs as well. Watch your diet and avoid food additives, high sugars, or greasy foods. Eat well, with a strong focus on protein, which is generally grounding. Get massage and vigorous exercise, if possible.

2. *Reduce stress.* You may be in for a major spiritual transformation. If so, you need to make some room for it. It may take time to make the necessary changes in your life. You may even be incapacitated for periods of time. You may need to devote more time to your spirituality or health. If possible, schedule a spiritual retreat for yourself—a period away from your usual life where you can allow the Kundalini energies to run their course and where you have the leisure to contemplate their meaning.

3. *Find support.* Find others who have knowledge of this experience, and friends with whom you feel spiritually aligned. (See sources on page 474.)

4. *Educate yourself.* Read about Kundalini. Find out about the spiritual system of yoga. Learn about the chakras.

5. *Treat underlying psychological issues.* As Kundalini brings up unresolved issues (which it surely will) this is an excellent time to deal with them. It will make the ride a lot smoother. Find a therapist you can work with or a support group.

6. *Examine your spiritual practices.* You may need to stop meditating for a while if it increases unpleasant Kundalini symptoms. Let the process you have already awakened catch up with your body and psyche. If you have not been practicing meditation, yoga, or some spiritual practice, it may be time to begin. The proof is in the pudding—see what increases or decreases the unpleasant effects.

7. *Practice grounding.* Kundalini is most difficult when the energy is moving upward without enough energy moving downward to balance. Refer to grounding exercises in this book or in my book *The Sevenfold Journey*, and practice them daily. Investigate the possibility of first chakra issues that need to be resolved in order to give a firmer base.

8. *Practice yoga*. Hatha yoga helps to strengthen the body, purify the *nadis* (subtle channels), and awaken the chakras. The spontaneous movements *(kriyas)* triggered by Kundalini awakening often resemble or result in classic *asanas* (yoga poses), so you can help clear the way for Kundalini's smooth passage by taking on a regular yoga practice. Yoga is so popular now that there are classes in most areas, and you can sample various kinds of yoga until you find a style and a teacher that suit you.

If Kundalini symptoms are uncomfortable, I do not recommend Kundalini yoga classes, as they are designed to heighten, not diminish, this energy. However, a qualified Kundalini yoga instructor may have good advice for you if you are experiencing unpleasant symptoms.

SHIVA—COUNTERPART TO KUNDALINI-SHAKTI

Kundalini-Shakti is the upward current that breaks out of restricted matter and moves toward the infinite. Shiva, her counterpart, is the source of the downward current. He is the Hindu god of destruction, partner to the great Mother Kali. Shiva destroys ignorance, attachment, and illusion. In this act, he brings realization of the eternal consciousness within that can never be destroyed.

Shiva, like many archetypes and gods, has a dark and a light force. In his active principle, he is called *Rudra*, the howler or weeping one—a fierce destroyer, searing ignorance in a single glance with lightning that emanates from his third eye. Yet Rudra was also the lord of song, healing, sacrifices, and prosperity, simultaneously seen as the remover of pain. In his later aspects, Rudra was given the name Shiva, meaning *Lord of Sleep*, representing the "non-dual, undifferentiated state of peace."[7] In this form, he is the ultimate transcendent deity of all knowledge, the merging of the individual with the divine, representing limitless bliss.

When activated by Shakti, Shiva moves into manifestation as *the dance* (Shiva Nataraja) and is often shown dancing on a corpse, which represents forgetfulness. Without Shakti, it is said that Shiva is but a corpse.

The Shiva principle is the axis of manifestation developing from the point-limit (bindu), the center of the universe.

ALAIN DANIELOU

When enlivened by Shakti, "The dance of Shiva suggests the primordial rhythm of the divine Heart whose pulsation initiates each and every motion on the universe."[8] Together Shiva and Shakti are the primordial emanations of life itself, the cosmic parents inherent in all creation.

In their coupling, Shiva is the pure consciousness that meets and tempers the raw, vital energy of Shakti. Shiva is the static masculine principle that moves toward form and order, whereas Shakti is the dynamic feminine, moving toward freedom and chaos.[9] Often worshipped as the Shiva lingam (male symbol of creation), Shiva represents the piercing nature of consciousness that impregnates the seeker with potent awareness.

Shiva can be a tempering force for the violent ravages of Kundalini-Shakti. To bring consciousness down from the top is to bring calm and order to her chaotic energies. When we deal with Kundalini, we are dealing with difficult, unrefined, and unconscious energies. As Kundalini rises, she "cooks" the grosser levels into the refinement of the higher chakras. Shiva, however, *is* that refinement. He brings order and peace to her restless wildness. Perhaps Kundalini is most unruly when she is longing for her partner.

To invoke the energy of Shiva is to call upon the transcendent bliss of the crown chakra and bring it down through the body. This invokes the manifesting current, which brings form, simplicity, and grounding. The union of these two forces synthesizes the cosmic principles of male and female, upper and lower, form and chaos, transcendence and immanence, into a single dynamic essence.

TANTRA—MEETING AT THE HEART

The philosophy of Tantra, which most people mistakenly think is only about sex, is actually about weaving. The word *Tantra* literally means "loom" and the verb *tan* means "to stretch." Tantra is the spiritual practice of weaving together opposite energies, specifically the upward and downward currents of Shakti and Shiva. Sexuality, as a subset of Tantra, is a sacred act that embodies this union on the physical plane. The ultimate balance of these two forces,

> Thus the yogin, who, through the stirring of the energy, dwells steadfastly at the junction of the twofold movement of emanation and resorption, is returned to the primordial oneness, the vibration of the universal heart.
>
> LILIAN SILBURN

however, occurs when we bring them through all the chakras and balance them in the heart.

Tantra seeks to obtain enlightenment not by renunciation, but by embracing the full experience of living. Tantra delights in the senses, desires, and feelings, and is focused on the expansion of consciousness that comes from a dynamic, sensate connection to life. Tantra does not advise us to cease action but to transform our acts into creative evolution. Tantra is the harmonious weaving of primordial opposites: mortal and divine, male and female, Shiva and Shakti, spirit and matter, Heaven and Earth.

We have stated that the heart chakra is the central integrating chamber of the chakra system. Through the bonding power of love, all things eventually find their way to connection and wholeness. The crown brings us *realization*—the understanding that allows us to embrace the whole. The body is the temple where all things come to rest and fruition. Without integration, the temple is empty and the spirit is homeless. The heart, as integrator, is thus the ultimate center of the Self.

> The union of two triangles symbolizes the union of Shiva-Shakti manifesting in the objective universe. When the two triangles are separated and form an hourglass pattern . . . they represent dissolution: time and space cease to exist.
>
> AJIT MOOKERJEE

What does it mean to bring ourselves into the center at the heart? It means that we feel our bodies and their needs and emotions, and bring these feelings to a place of wisdom and understanding. It means that we consider our actions for their effects on others, yet maintain an awareness of the individual Self. It means that we embody our wisdom by not blindly accepting beliefs without testing them with the body's truth. It means that we approach all life—in the Self and with others—with compassion and love. It means we dwell in a place of peace and balance, alive yet calm, changing yet stable.

I believe that at this point in history, we are desperately being called upon to rise to the level of the heart from our collective immersion in the third chakra. Presently, world issues center around power and aggression. We live in the shadow of potential nuclear holocaust. Western civilization has exalted the cult of the individual. We have worshipped the Hero's quest. We have achieved technological prowess.

It is now time to court the next stage of the Hero's quest: the *return*. This is where the fruits of individuality and power are brought home to benefit the community—a distinct movement from third chakra to fourth. We must realize that as individuals, our possibilities are limited, but as conscious members of a larger community, we have unlimited potential. In the quest for enlightenment, the final responsibility is to return to the world and become part of the *evolutionary system*.

Only love can lift us out of the violence, aggression, and coldhearted individualism that typifies our time. Only love can reweave the original fabric of wholeness that has been severed, in ourselves, and among each other. This is the vital piece of the Rainbow Bridge that needs to be emphasized at this time. As the bridge is created by each one of us, only we, as conscious, integrated individuals, can open our hearts to make the connection between Heaven and Earth a living reality.

TEMPLE FOR THE GODS

In Norse mythology, the giants built the palace Valhalla as an abode for the gods. The Rainbow Bridge was the means of getting to Valhalla. However, the giants had requested a payment for their work—Frejya, the goddess of love. We cannot have another build our temple for us, nor can we afford to pay for it by sacrificing love. If we are to invite divine energies to manifest within us, then we must build our own temple.

> Spirituality is the awakening of divinity in consciousness.
>
> HARISH JOHARI

In the seventh chakra discussion, I described consciousness as a universal field accessed through the individual psyche. I also noted how the amount of consciousness we can access depends upon our intelligence and state of mind. The divine, however, is more than just consciousness. In its full spectrum, the divine is also beauty, sound, love, energy, feeling, and form—elements reflected in each chakra. To tap into the *full* spectrum of divinity, we need to build a temple within ourselves that is capable of receiving and transmitting each one of these frequencies. Only then can we fully access the many levels in which divinity manifests.

Each chakra represents an essential chamber in the temple of the Self. Each one houses an aspect of the sacred and is necessary for wholeness. The more we clean and properly decorate the temple, the more we court the presence of the divine.

We build a temple to the gods by creating, clearing, and restoring each of the chambers of the chakras. Only when we have built a foundation and reclaimed our life force from the ground up are we truly able to handle the manifestations of divine consciousness. How fully we can bring forth divinity depends on how thoroughly we develop the seven chambers inside. Once we open to the gods, our job is then to bring them forward through our own sacred living and enhance the journey for others. Only by going on the journey ourselves can we guide others. Thus, the journey across the Rainbow Bridge becomes a sacred quest for the evolution of humanity.

ENDNOTES

INTRODUCTION

1. Tantrik Purnananda-Swami, *Sat-Chakra Nirupana* [Description of and Investigation into the Six Bodily Centers], translated by Arthur Avalon (see below).

2. Arthur Avalon, *The Serpent Power* (New York: Dover Publications, 1974).

3. Ancient tantric diagrams had varied color associations for the chakras. For more information on the "etheric body" colors and the chakras, see Valerie Hunt's paper "A Study of Structural Integration from Neuromuscular, Energy Field, and Emotional Approaches," available through the Rolf Institute, Boulder, Colorado, or see my book *Wheels of Life* (St. Paul, MN: Llewellyn, 1987), 327.

4. Stanley Keleman, *Patterns of Distress: Emotional Insults and Human Form* (Berkeley, CA: Center Press, 1989), 9.

5. See Alexander Lowen, *Language of the Body* (New York: Collier Books, 1958), or Wilhelm Reich, *Character Analysis* (New York: Farrar, Strauss, and Giroux, 1949).

6. The first three orientations—self-preservation, self-gratification, and self-definition—were first correlated to "lower forces" by Jacqueline Small, in her book *Transformations* (Marina del Rey, CA: DeVorss & Co., 1982).

7. Margaret Mahler, *The Psychological Birth of the Human Infant: Symbiosis and Individuation* (New York: Basic Books, 1975), 54.

8. Ken Wilber, *The Atman Project* (Wheaton, IL: A Quest Book, 1980), 7–29.

9. J. Marvin Spiegelman and Arwind U. Vasavada, *Hinduism and Jungian Psychology* (Phoenix, AZ: Falcon Press, 1987), 48.

CHAKRA ONE

1. Erik Erikson, as quoted by Barbara and Philip Newman, *Development Through Life: A Psychosocial Approach* (Chicago: Dorsey Press, 1975), 182.

2. Ashley Montagu, *Touching: The Human Significance of the Skin* (New York: Harper & Row, 1971), 77–78, lists several such studies. Most had a 100 percent death rate.

3. Susan Kano, *Making Peace with Food* (New York: Harper & Row, 1989), 40.

4. This term was coined by Pamela L. A. Chubbuck, Ph. D., in her private teaching.

CHAKRA TWO

1. People involved with sadomasochistic sexuality (S&M) will obviously take issue with this statement. For some people, pain enacted under certain conditions is pleasure. This shadow side of sexuality is a complicated issue involving more than just the pleasure/pain dynamic; it also involves psychological issues of power and submission. Intense sensation is sometimes required to combat numbness, and pain is intense sensation. There are people for whom pain invites expansion in cases where numbness and contraction have previously ruled.

2. Hal Stone works especially with voice dialog, and his books, written with Sidra Stone, include *Embracing Our Selves* and *Embracing Each Other* (see Bibliography).

3. According to Erikson, we are still in the trust vs. mistrust dilemma at this age. If I were to distinguish the second chakra along these lines, I would add a stage called separation vs. attachment, the healthy resolution of which would be autonomy, which brings us to the next stage, which challenges us to keep that autonomy in the onslaught of shame and doubt.

4. Margaret Mahler, *The Psychological Birth of the Human Infant: Symbiosis and Individualism* (New York: Basic Books, 1975), 53–54.

5. Ashley Montagu, *Touching: The Human Significance of the Skin* (New York: Harper & Row, 1978), 209.

6. Daniel Goleman, *Emotional Intelligence* (New York: Bantam Books, 1995), 225.

7. Jean Liedoff, *The Continuum Concept* (Reading, MA: Addison-Wesley, 1975), 32.

8. Marion Woodman, *Addiction to Perfection* (Toronto: Inner City Books, 1982), 36.

9. Alice Miller, *The Drama of the Gifted Child: The Search for the True Self* (New York, Basic Books, 1981).

10. Alexander Lowen, *The Betrayal of the Body* (New York: Collier Books, 1967), 2.

11. Peter Levine, *Waking the Tiger: Healing Trauma: The Innate Capacity to Transform Overwhelming Experiences* (Berkeley, CA: North Atlantic Books, 1997).

CHAKRA THREE

1. Laurence Boldt, *Zen and the Art of Making a Living* (New York: Penguin Arkana, 1993), xlvi.

2. Ibid., 152.

3. Ibid., 134.

4. John Pierrakos, *Core Energetics: Developing the Capacity to Love and Heal* (Mendocino, CA: Life Rhythm Publication, 1987), 286.

5. Rollo May, *Love and Will* (New York: Delta, 1969), 27.

6. Ibid., 218.

7. Ibid., 193.

8. Just as will is built upon pleasure (moving from the ground upward), so is pleasure only present in coordination with will (the descending current moving downward). Sexual coercion is a prime example of this, where a normally pleasurable activity is robbed of pleasure because the will is not in accordance with the act.

9. Alexander Lowen, *Language of the Body* (New York: Collier Books, 1988), 200.

10. Robert Bly, *Iron John* (Reading, MA: Addison-Wesley, 1990), 110–111.

11. Starhawk, *Truth or Dare* (San Francisco: Harper & Row, 1987), 71.

12. Ibid., 81.

13. Alice Miller, *Drama of the Gifted Child* (New York: Basic Books, 1981), 39.

14. Alice Miller, *For Your Own Good* (New York: Basic Books, 1983), 59.

CHAKRA FOUR

1. *San Francisco Chronicle*, May 11, 1994, A8. Other statistics in the same article show that each day in America 9 children are murdered, 13 die from guns, 30 are wounded by guns, and 1,200,000 latchkey children come home to a house in which there is a gun.

2. Details of archeological research supporting the existence of extended worship of the Goddess archetype is too lengthy to include in this discussion. For more information, refer to Riane Eisler's *The Chalice and the Blade* (San Francisco: HarperCollins, 1991), or Elinor Gadon's *The Once and Future Goddess* (New York: Harper & Row, 1989). These are but a few of the many books on the subject.

3. C. G. Jung, "Transformation Symbolism in the Mass," from *Structure and Dynamics of the Psyche*, as quoted by Aldo Caratenuto in *Eros and Pathos* (Toronto: Inner City Books, 1985), 25.

4. Thomas Moore, *Soul Mates: Honoring the Mysteries of Love and Relationship* (New York: HarperCollins, 1994), 23.

5. Ibid., 19.

6. Jean Piaget, as quoted in *Psychological Development: A Life-Span Approach* (New York: Harper & Row, 1979), 173.

7. While the masculine/feminine characteristics listed here may seem hopelessly sexist, they do reflect collective concepts that must be integrated before we can escape such sexism and incorporate both qualities into our psyche, regardless of gender.

8. Harville Hendrix, *Getting the Love You Want* (New York: Harper & Row, 1988), 38.

9. Alice Miller, *For Your Own Good* (New York: Basic Books, 1981), 115.

10. Steven R. Covey, *The Seven Habit of Highly Effective People* (New York: Simon and Schuster, 1989), 79–80.

CHAKRA FIVE

1. These statistics and more are from Steven Halpern, *Sound Health* (San Francisco: Harper & Row, 1985), 11–12.

2. Mikol Davis and Earle Lane, *Rainbows of Life: The Promise of Kirlian Photography* (New York: Harper Colophon, 1978), 47.

3. Ibid., 58–61. When the couple changed to pleasant thoughts, their auras flowed into one another, even though they were not physically touching. During unpleasant thoughts, they remained distinct.

4. Erik Erikson, *Childhood and Society* (New York: W.W. Norton, 1964), 259.

5. Stanley Keleman, *Your Body Speaks Its Mind* (Berkeley, CA: Center Press, 1975), 36.

6. Harold Bloomfield, et al., *Transcendental Meditation: Discovering Inner Awareness and Overcoming Stress* (New York: Delacorte Press, 1975).

7. Randall McClellan, *The Healing Forces of Music* (New York: Amity House, 1988), 61.

8. Leah Garfield, *Sound Medicine* (Berkeley, CA: Celestial Arts, 1987), 73–77.

9. Hal A. Lingerman, *The Healing Energy of Music* (Wheaton, IL: Quest Books, 1983).

CHAKRA SIX

1. In the Tantric texts, chakras one through five are correlated respectively with smell, taste, sight, touch, and hearing. There are no physical senses correlated to the upper chakras.

2. These tales are described in greater detail by Jeremy Taylor, *Where People Fly and Water Runs Uphill* (New York: Warner Books, 1992).

3. Ibid., 13.

4. Satprem, *Sri Aurobindo, or the Adventure of Consciousness* (New York: Harper & Row, 1968).

5. Gerhard Adler, as quoted by Jolande Jacobi, *The Way of Individuation* (London: Hodder & Stoughton, 1967), 18.

6. C. G. Jung, *Psychological Types*, from *The Collected Works of C. G. Jung, Volume 6* (Princeton, NJ: Princeton University Press, 1971), 325.

7. Erik Erikson, *Childhood and Society* (New York: W.W. Norton, 1964), 263.

8. John Bradshaw, *Bradshaw on: The Family*, PBS Broadcasting.

9. Jacob Liberman, *Light: Medicine of the Future* (Santa Fe, NM: Bear & Co., 1991), 59–60.

10. Ibid., 36.

CHAKRA SEVEN

1. Once again the reader is reminded that I speak of soul as that which organizes itself toward the body, feeling, and form. Spirit is more abstract and universal and wants to expand. When soul is disconnected from spirit, it becomes lifeless and dull. When spirit is disconnected from soul, it lacks depth and texture, and becomes diffuse and ineffective.

2. Erich Jantsch, *Design for Evolution* (New York: George Brazillier, 1975).

3. As God is by nature unlimited, a "particular concept of God" is by nature limiting, and therefore a contradiction that renders the definition false.

4. Meaning derives from the Old English *maenan*—to recite, tell, or state an intention, hence to intend. Meaning tells us what something's intention or purpose is.

5. Alexander Maven has even suggested that the mystic union characteristic of the seventh chakra is directly analogous to a sperm penetrating an ovum. We take a long journey that only a few survive, and once we arrive we are absorbed completely and transformed into the beginning of something greater. We do not lose our identity (chromosomes) but merely redefine it to include an additional set. (In addition, this analogy gives a good argument for the feminine aspect of divinity, does it not?) From John White, ed., "Mystic Union: A Suggested Biological Interpretation" in *The Highest State of Consciousness* (New York: Doubleday/Anchor, 1972).

6. Stewart Brand, *The Millenium Whole Earth Catalog* (San Francisco: HarperCollins, 1994), i.

7. Brihadaranyaka Upanishad, 1 Adhyay, 4 Brahmana, verse 10ff; Max Müller, trans., *The Upanishads* (New York: Dover, 1962).

8. Studies have shown that children growing up in monogamous families with the same set of parents are more likely to become fixated in one way of thinking than children who grow up with coparents who remarry, nonmonogamous parents, or extended families. Magorah Maruyama and Erich Jantsch, eds., "Toward Cultural Symbiosis" in *Evolution and Consciousness* (Reading, MA: Addison-Wesley, 1976), 198.

9. John Bradshaw, *Creating Love* (New York: Bantam, 1992), 244.

10. Students International Meditation Society and Demetri P. Kanellakos, "Transcendental Meditation" in *The Highest State of Consciousness* (New York: Doubleday/Anchor, 1972).

11. H. Aranya, *Yoga Philosophy of Patanjali* (New York: State University of New York Press, 1983).

CONCLUSION

1. Personal correspondence.

2. If someone has created a more standardized personality test that reflects the chakras, I would be very interested in seeing it.

3. This particular story is a composite of typical Kundalini symptoms, taken from a number of documented cases from various sources.

4. The esoteric literature discusses many kinds of Kundalini risings, which travel through different *nadis*. The *sushumna* is the main, central channel, and characterizes the nature of the vertical rising.

5. There are many disagreements about the spinning of the chakras. Some say they all spin clockwise (see Barbara Ann Brennan's *Hands of Light* and Rosalyn L. Bruyere's *Wheels of Light*). I think this is energetically unrealistic as this contradicts the alternate motion of the *nadis*, Ida and Pingala (see page 359).

6. Gopi Krishna, *Kundalini: The Evolutionary Energy in Man* (Boston: Shambhala, 1971).

7. Alain Danielou, *Gods of India* (1995).

8. Lilian Silburn, *Kundalini: Energy of the Depths* (1988).

9. There are different opinions on this. Since the downward pointing triangle represents the feminine symbol of the yoni, and the upward triangle, the Shiva lingam, some (see Ajit Mookerji, *The Tantric Way*) say that Shakti is the downward current and Shiva is the upward. This goes against the classic interpretation of Kundalini-Shakti as a rising force and puts Shiva's home at the base of the spine, which is contrary to Shiva's basic attributes of pure consciousness. Yet, in classic pictures of the *muladhara* chakra, the Shiva lingam is shown upright, wrapped three and a half times around by the serpent Kundalini.

10. Ajit Mookerjee, *The Tantric Way* (Boston: New York Graphic Society, 1977), 9.

BIBLIOGRAPHY

CHAKRAS, ENERGY, AND YOGA

Aranya, H. *Yoga Philosophies of Patanjali*. New York: State University of New York Press, 1983.

Avalon, Arthur. *The Serpent Power*. New York: Dover Publications, 1974.

Brennan, Barbara Ann. *Hands of Light: A Guide to Healing through the Human Energy Field*. New York: Bantam, 1987.

———. *Light Emerging: The Journey of Personal Healing*. New York: Bantam Books, 1993.

Bruyere, Rosalyn L. *Wheels of Light: A Study of the Chakras*, vol. 1. Sierra Madre, CA: Bon Productions, 1989.

Couch, Jean. *Beginning Yoga: The Runner's Yoga Book*. Berkeley, CA: Rodmell Press, 1992.

Davis, Mikol, and Earle Lane. *Rainbows of Life: The Promise of Kirlian Photography*. New York: Harper Colophon, 1978.

Evola, Julius. *The Yoga of Power: Tantra, Shakti, and the Secret Way*. Rochester, VT: Inner Traditions, 1992.

Farhi, Donna. *Yoga Mind, Body & Spirit: A Return to Wholeness*. New York: Holt & Co., 2000.

Feuerstein, Georg. *The Shambhala Encyclopedia of Yoga*. Boston: Shambhala, 1997.

———. *Wholeness or Transcendence? Ancient Lessons for Emerging Global Civilization*. New York: Larson Publications, 1992.

Hunt, Valerie. "A Study of Structural Integration from Neuromuscular Energy Fields and Emotional Approaches." In *Wheels of Light*, vol. 1, by Rosalyn L. Bruyere. Sierra Madre, CA: Bon Productions, 1989.

Johari, Harish. *Chakras: Energy Centers of Transformation*. Rochester, VT: Destiny Books, 1987.

Judith, Anodea. *Chakra Balancing: A Guide to Healing and Awakening Your Energy Body*. (Boulder, CO: Sounds True, 2003).

———. *The Chakra System: A Complete Course in Self-Diagnosis and Healing*. Boulder, CO: Sounds True, 2000. Compact disc.

———. *The Illuminated Chakras: A Visionary Voyage into Your Inner World* (Sebastopol, CA: Sacred Centers, 2003). Twenty-eight-minute video.

———. *Wheels of Life: A User's Guide to the Chakra System*. St. Paul, MN: Llewellyn, 1987.

Judith, Anodea, and Selene Vega. *The Sevenfold Journey*. Berkeley, CA: The Crossing Press, 1993.

Kaptchuk, Ted J. *The Web That Has No Weaver: Understanding Chinese Medicine*. New York: Congdon & Weed, 1983.

Kraftsow, Gary. *Yoga for Wellness: Healing with the Timeless Teachings of Viniyoga*. Middlesex, England: Penguin Books, 1999.

Lasater, Judith. *Relax and Renew: Restful Yoga for Stressful Times*. Berkeley, CA: Rodmell Press, 1995.

McLaren, Karla. *Your Aura and Your Chakras: The Owner's Manual*. York Beach, ME: Weiser, 1998.

Mookerjee, Ajit. *The Tantric Way: Art, Science, Ritual*. Boston: New York Graphic Society, 1977.

Mumford, John. *A Chakra and Kundalini Workbook: Psycho-Spiritual Techniques for Health, Rejuvenation, Psychic Powers, and Spiritual Realization*. St. Paul, MN: Llewellyn Publications, 1994.

Saraswati, Swami Ambikananda. *Healing Yoga: A Guide to Integrating the Chakras with Your Yoga Practice*. New York: Marlowe & Co., 2001.

Shumsky, Susan G. *Exploring Chakras: Awaken Your Untapped Energy*. Franklin Lakes, NJ: Career Press, 2003.

White, John, ed. *Kundalini, Evolution and Enlightenment*. New York: Anchor/Doubleday, 1979.

Chakra One

Boldt, Lawrence. *Zen and the Art of Making a Living*. New York: Penguin Arkana, 1991.

Kano, Susan. *Making Peace with Food*. San Francisco, Harper & Row, 1989.

Liedloff, Jean. *The Continuum Concept*. Reading, MA: Addison-Wesley, 1975.

Roberts, Elizabeth, and Elia Amidon. *Earth Prayers from Around the World*. San Francisco: Harper San Francisco, 1991.

Chakra Two

Anand, Margo. *The Art of Sexual Ecstasy: The Path of Sacred Sexuality for Western Lovers*. Los Angeles: J.P. Tarcher/Putnam, 1989.

Bass, Ellen, and Laura Davis. *The Courage to Heal: A Guide for Women Survivors of Sexual Abuse*. New York: Harper & Row, 1988.

Borysenko, Joan. *Guilt Is the Teacher, Love Is the Lesson*. New York: Warner Books, 1990.

Davis, Laura. *Allies in Healing: When the Person You Love Was Sexually Abused as a Child*. New York: Harper Perennial, 1991.

———. *The Courage to Heal Workbook: For Women and Men Survivors of Child Sexual Abuse*. New York: Harper & Row, 1990.

Eisler, Riane. *Sacred Pleasure*. San Francisco: Harper, 1995.

Goleman, Daniel. *Emotional Intelligence*. New York: Bantam, 1995.

Jwala, with Robb Smith. *Sacred Sex: Ecstatic Techniques for Empowering Relationships*. San Rafael, CA: Mandala Books, 1994.

Kane, Evangeline. *Recovering from Incest: Imagination and the Healing Process*. Boston: Sigo Press, 1989.

Love, Patricia. *The Emotional Incest Syndrome: What to Do When a Parent's Love Rules Your Life*. New York: Bantam Books, 1990.

Montagu, Ashley. *Touching: The Human Significance of the Skin*. New York: Harper & Row, 1971.

Ransdale, David, and Ellen Ransdale. *Sexual Energy Ecstasy: A Practical Guide to Lovemaking Secrets of the East and West*. New York: Bantam, 1993.

Sanders, Timothy L. *Male Survivors: 12-Step Recovery Program for Survivors of Childhood Sexual Abuse*. Freedom, CA: The Crossing Press, 1991.

Chakra Three

Assagioli, Roberto. *The Act of Will*. New York: Penguin Arkana, 1974.

Bradshaw, John. *Healing the Shame the Binds You*. Deerfield Beach, FL: Health Communications Inc., 1988.

Covey, Steven R. *The Seven Habits of Highly Effective People*. New York: Simon and Schuster, 1989.

May, Rollo. *Love and Will*. New York: Delta, 1969.

Starhawk. *Truth or Dare: Encounters with Power, Authority, and Mystery*. San Francisco: Harper & Row, 1987.

Steiner, Claude. *The Other Side of Power: How to Become Powerful without Being Power Hungry*. New York: Grove Press, 1981.

Tavris, Carol. *Anger: The Misunderstood Emotion*. New York: Simon & Schuster, 1982.

Chakra Four

Adamson, Sophia. *Through the Gateway of the Heart*. San Francisco: Four Trees Publications, 1985.

Beattie, Melody. *Codependent No More: How to Stop Controlling Others and Start Caring for Yourself*. New York: Harper Hazelden, 1987.

Bradshaw, John. *Bradshaw on the Family: A Revolutionary Way of Self-Discovery*. Deerfield Beach, FL: Health Communications, Inc., 1988.

———. *Creating Love: The Next Great Stage of Growth*. New York: Bantam, 1992.

———. *Homecoming: Reclaiming and Championing Your Inner Child*. New York: Bantam, 1990.

Carotenuto, Aldo. *Eros and Pathos: Shades of Love and Suffering*. Toronto: Inner City Books, 1989.

Hendricks, Gay, and Kathlyn Hendricks. *Conscious Loving: The Journey to Co-Commitment*. New York: Bantam, 1990.

Hendrix, Harville. *Getting the Love You Want*. New York: Harper Perennial, 1988.

Mellody, Pia. *Facing Codependence*. San Francisco: Harper & Row, 1989.

Metrick, Sydney Barbara. *Crossing the Bridge: Creating Ceremonies for Grieving and Healing from Life's Losses*. Berkeley, CA: Celestial Arts, 1964.

Moore, Thomas. *Soul Mates: Honoring the Mysteries of Love and Relationship*. New York: Harper Perennial, 1994.

Sell, Emily Hilburn. *The Spirit of Loving*. Boston: Shambhala, 1995.

Stone, Hal, and Sidra Winkelman. *Embracing Each Other: Relationship as Teacher, Healer & Guide*. Novato, CA: Nataraj Publishing, 1989.

Chakra Five

Gardner, Kay. *Sounding the Inner Landscape: Music as Medicine*. Stonington, ME: Caduceus Publications, 1990.

Gardner-Gordon, Joy. *The Healing Voice: Traditional and Contemporary Toning, Chanting, and Singing*. Berkeley, CA: The Crossing Press, 1993.

Garfield, Laeh Maggie. *Sound Medicine: Healing with Music, Voice, and Song*. Berkeley, CA: Celestial Arts, 1987.

Gerber, Richard. *Vibrational Medicine*. Santa Fe, NM: Bear & Co., 1988.

Halpern, Steven. *Tuning the Human Instrument: An Owner's Manual*. Palo Alto, CA: Spectrum Research Institute, 1978.

Halpern, Steven, with Louis Savary. *Sound Health: The Music and Sounds That Make Us Whole*. San Francisco: Harper & Row, 1985.

Hamel, Peter Michael. *Through Music to the Self*. Boston: Shambhala, 1979.

Keyes, Laurel Elizabeth. *Toning: The Creative Power of the Voice*. Marina del Rey, CA: DeVorss & Co., 1973.

Leonard, George. *The Silent Pulse*. New York: E.P. Dutton, 1978.

Lingerman, Hal A. *The Healing Energies of Music*. Wheaton, IL: Quest Books, 1983.

Maidment, Robert. *Tuning In: A Guide to Effective Listening*. Gretna, LA: Pelican Publications, 1984.

McClellan, Randall. *The Healing Forces of Music: History, Theory, and Practice*. New York: Amity House, 1988.

Miller, Melvin E., and Susanne R. Cook-Greuter, eds. *Creativity, Spirituality, and Transcendence*. Stamford, CT: Ablex Publishing, 2000.

Stone, Hal. *Embracing Our Selves: The Voice Dialogue Manual*. Novato, CA: Nataraj, 1993.

Chakra Six

Ahsen, Akhter. *Basic Concepts in Eidetic Psychotherapy*. New York: Brandon House, 1973.

Feinstein, David, and Stanley Krippner. *Personal Mythology: The Psychology of Your Evolving Self*. Los Angeles: Jeremy Tarcher, 1988.

Foster, Stephen. and Meredith Little. *The Book of the Vision Quest*. Englewood Cliffs, NJ: Prentice Hall, 1988.

Gawain, Shakti. *Creative Visualization*. San Rafael, CA: New World Library, 1979.

————. *Living in the Light*. New York: Bantam, 1993.

LaBerge, Stephen. *Lucid Dreaming: The Power of Being Awake & Aware in Your Dreams*. New York: Ballantine, 1985.

Liberman, Jacob. *Light: Medicine of the Future*. Santa Fe, NM: Bear & Co., 1991.

Jung, Carl G. *Man and His Symbols*. New York: Doubleday, 1964.

Stevens, Anthony. *Archetypes*. New York: Quill, 1983.

Taylor, Jeremy. *Dreamwork: Techniques for Discovering the Creation Power in Dreams*. New York: Paulist Press, 1983.

————. *Where People Fly and Water Runs Uphill: Using Dreams to Tap the Wisdom of the Unconscious*. New York: Warner Books, 1992.

Wauters, Ambika. *Chakras and Their Archetypes: Uniting Energy Awareness and Spiritual Growth*. Berkeley, CA: The Crossing Press, 1997.

Williams, Strephon Kaplan. *Jungian-Senoi Dreamwork Manual*. Berkeley, CA: Journey Press, 1980.

Chakra Seven

Booth, Leo. *The God Game: It's Your Move*. Walpole, NH: Stillpoint, 1994.

Goldstein, Joseph. *The Experience of Insight: A Simple and Direct Guide to Buddhist Meditation*. Boston: Shambhala, 1983.

Kabat-Zinn, Jon. *Wherever You Go, There You Are*. New York: Hyperion, 1994.

Rama, Swami, Rudolph Ballantine, and Swami Ajaya. *Yoga and Psychotherapy: The Evolution of Consciousness*. Honesdale, PA: Himalaya International Institute of Yoga Science and Philosophy, 1976.

Satprem. *Sri Aurobindo, or the Adventure of Consciousness*. New York: Harper & Row, 1968.

White, John, ed. *Frontiers of Consciousness: The Meeting Ground Between Inner and Outer Reality*. Julian, CA: Julian Press, 1974.

————. *The Highest State of Consciousness*. New York: Anchor Books, 1972.

PSYCHOLOGY

General and Transpersonal Psychology

Assagioli, Roberto. *Psychosynthesis*. New York: Penguin Arkana, 1976.

Bynum, Edward Brude. *Transcending Psychoneurotic Disturbances: New Approaches in Psychospirituality and Personality Development*. Binghamtom, NY: Harrington Park Press, 1994.

Cortwright, Brant. *Psychotherapy and Spirit: Theory and Practice in Transpersonal Psychotherapy*. Albany, NY: State University of New York Press.

Eliade, Mircea. *Shamanism*. Princeton, NJ: Princeton University Press, 1964.

Levine, Stephen. *Healing into Life and Death*. New York: Anchor Books, 1987.

Mijares, Sharon G. *Modern Psychology and Ancient Wisdom: Psychological Healing Practices from the World's Religious Traditions*. New York: Haworth Integrative Healing Press, 2003.

Miller, Alice. *The Drama of the Gifted Child: The Search for the True Self*. Translated by Ruth Ward. New York: HarperCollins, 1981.

——. *For Your Own Good: Hidden Cruelty in Child-Rearing and the Roots of Violence*. Translated by Hildegarde Hannum and Hunter Hannum. New York: Farrar, Straus, and Giroux, 1983.

Ornstein, Robert E. *The Psychology of Consciousness*. San Francisco: Penguin Books, 1972.

Ratsch, Christian, ed. *Gateway to Inner Space: Sacred Plants, Mysticism, and Psychotherapy*. Dorset, England: Prism-Unity Press, 1989.

Small, Jacquelyn. *Transformers: The Therapists of the Future*. Marina Del Rey, CA: DeVorss & Co., 1982.

Thouless, Robert H. *An Introduction to the Psychology of Religion*. 3rd edition. London: Cambridge University Press, 1971.

Walsh, Roger N. and Frances Vaughan, Ph.D. *Beyond Ego: Transpersonal Dimensions in Psychology*. Los Angeles: J. P. Tarcher, 1980.

Washburn, Michael. *The Ego and the Dynamic Ground: A Transpersonal Theory of Human Development*. New York: State University of New York Press, 1988.

Wilber, Ken. *The Atman Project: A Transpersonal View of Human Development*. Wheaton, IL: Quest Books, 1980.

——. *No Boundary: Eastern and Western Approaches to Personal Growth*. Boston: Shambhala, 1985.

——. *Sex, Ecology, and Spirituality: The Spirit of Evolution*. Boston: Shambhala, 1995.

Somatic Psychology

Conger, John P. *The Body in Recovery: Somatic Psychotherapy and the Self.* Berkeley, CA: Frog, Ltd., 1994.

———. *Jung & Reich: The Body as Shadow.* Berkeley, CA: North Atlantic Books, 1988.

Hanna, Thomas. *Somatics: Reawakening the Mind's Control of Movement, Flexibility, and Health.* Reading, MA: Addison-Wesley Publishing Co., 1988.

Keleman, Stanley. *Emotional Anatomy.* Berkeley, CA: Center Press, 1985.

———. *The Human Ground: Sexuality, Self, and Survival.* Berkeley, CA: Center Press, 1975.

———. *Love: A Somatic View.* Berkeley, CA: Center Press, 1994.

———. *Patterns of Distress.* Berkeley, CA: Center Press, 1989.

———. *Your Body Speaks Its Mind.* Berkeley, CA: Center Press, 1975.

Levine, Peter, with Ann Frederick. *Waking the Tiger: Healing Trauma: The Innate Capacity to Transform Overwhelming Experiences* (Berkeley, CA: North Atlantic Books, 1997).

Lowen, Alexander. *The Betrayal of the Body.* New York: Collier Books, 1967.

———. *The Language of the Body.* New York: Collier Books, 1958.

Lowen, Alexander, and Leslie Lowen. *The Way to Vibrant Health.* New York: Harper Colophon Books, 1977.

McNeely, Deldon Anne. *Touching: Body Therapy and Depth Psychology.* Toronto: Inner City Books, 1987.

Pierrakos, John. *Core Energetics: Developing the Capacity to Love and Heal.* Mendocino, CA: Life Rhythm Publication, 1987.

Reich, Wilhelm. *Character Analysis.* Translated by Theodore P. Wolfe. New York: Farrar, Straus and Giroux, 1949.

———. *Children of the Future.* New York: Farrar, Straus and Giroux, 1983.

———. *The Function of the Orgasm: The Discovery of the Orgone.* New York: World Publishing Co., 1971.

Jungian Psychology

Carotenuto, Aldo. *The Vertical Labyrinth: Individuation in Jungian Psychology.* Toronto: Inner City Books, 1985.

Dourley, John P. *A Strategy for a Loss of Faith: Jung's Proposal.* Toronto: Inner City Books, 1992.

Hill, Gareth. *Masculine and Feminine: The Natural Flow of Opposites in the Psyche.* Boston: Shambhala, 1982.

Jacobi, Jolande. *Complex, Archetype, Symbol*. Princeton, NJ: Princeton University Press, Bollingen Series, LVII, 1959.

———. *The Psychology of C. G. Jung*. Translated by K. W. Bash. New Haven, CT: Yale University Press, 1951.

———. *The Way of Individuation*. Translated by R. C. F. Hull. London: Holder & Stoughton, 1967.

Jung, Carl Gustav. *Aion: Researches into the Phenomenology of the Self*. Princeton, NJ: Princeton University Press, 1959.

———. *The Archetypes and the Collective Unconscious (The Collected Works of C. G. Jung, Volume 9.1)*. Princeton, NJ: Princeton University Press, 1959.

———. *Dreams*. Princeton, NJ: Princeton University Press, 1974.

———. *Memories, Dreams, Reflections*. Edited by Aniela Jaffe. New York: Vintage Books, 1965.

———. *The Practice of Psychotherapy (The Collected Works of C. G. Jung, Volume 16)*. Princeton, NJ: Princeton University Press, 1966.

———. *Psychological Types (The Collected Works of C. G. Jung, Volume 6)*. Princeton, NJ: Princeton University Press, 1971.

———. *Psychology and Religion: West and East (The Collected Works of C. G. Jung, Volume 11)*. Princeton, NJ: Princeton University Press, 1958.

———. *Psychology and the East*. Princeton, NJ: Princeton University Press, 1978.

———. *The Structure and Dynamics of the Psyche (The Collected Works of C. G. Jung, Volume 8)*. Princeton, NJ: Princeton University Press, 1960.

———. *Two Essays on Analytical Psychology (The Collected Works of C. G. Jung, Volume 7)*. Princeton, NJ: Princeton University Press, 1966.

Jung, Emma. *Animus and Anima*. Woodstock, CT: Spring Publications, 1957.

McNeely, Deldon Anne. *Touching: Body Therapy and Depth Psychology*. Toronto: Inner City Books, 1987.

Moore, Thomas. *Care of the Soul: A Guide for Cultivating Depth and Sacredness in Everyday Life*. New York: HarperCollins, 1992.

Smith, Curtis D. *Jung's Quest for Wholeness: A Religious and Historical Perspective*. New York: State University of New York Press, 1990.

Spiegelman, J. Marvin, and Arwind Vasavada. *Hinduism and Jungian Psychology*. Scottsdale, AZ: Falcon Press, 1987.

Whitmont, Edward. *The Symbolic Quest: Basic Concepts in Analytical Psychology*. Princeton, NJ: Princeton University Press, 1969.

Woodman, Marion. *Addiction to Perfection: The Still Unravished Bride*. Toronto: Inner City Books, 1982.

Developmental Psychology

Erikson, Erik. *Childhood and Society*. New York: W.W. Norton, 1964.

Mahler, Margaret S., Fred Pine, and Anni Bergman. *The Psychological Birth of the Human Infant: Symbiosis and Individuation*. New York: Basic Books, 1975.

Mussen, Paul Henry, John Janeway Conger, Jerome Kagan, and James Geiwitz. *Psychological Development: A Life-Span Approach*. New York: Harper & Row, 1979.

Newman, Barbara M., and Philip R. Newman. *Development Through Life: A Psychosocial Approach*. Chicago: Dorsey Press, 1975.

Papalla, Diane E., and Sally Wendkos Olds. *A Child's World: Infancy through Adolescence*. New York: McGraw-Hill, 1986.

Piaget, Jean. *The Grasp of Consciousness: Action and Concept in the Young Child*. Translated by Susan Wedgewood. Cambridge, MA: Harvard University Press, 1976.

Piaget, Jean, and Barbel Inhelder. *The Psychology of the Child*. Translated by Helen Weaver. New York: Basic Books, 1969.

Evolutionary Psychology and Systems Theory

Jantsch, Erich. *Design for Evolution: Self-Organization and Planning in the Life of Human Systems*. New York: George Braziller, 1975.

————. *The Self-Organizing Universe: Scientific and Human Implications of the Emerging Paradigm of Evolution*. New York: Pergamon Press, 1980.

Jantsch, Erich, and Conrad H. Waddington. *Evolution and Consciousness: Human Systems in Transition*. Reading, MA: Addison-Wesley Publishing Company, 1976.

Neumann, Erich. *The Origins and History of Consciousness*. Princeton, NJ: Princeton University Press, 1954.

Teilhard de Chardin, Pierre. *The Phenomenon of Man*. New York: HarperCollins, 1959.

MISCELLANEOUS

Berman, Morris. *The Reenchantment of the World*. New York: Bantam Books, 1984.

Blair, Lawrence. *Rhythms of Vision*. New York: Schocken Books, 1976.

Bly, Robert. *Iron John*. Reading, MA: Addison-Wesley, 1990.

Gibran, Kahil. *The Prophet*. New York: Knopf, 1951.

Kosko, Bart. *Fuzzy Thinking: The New Science of Fuzzy Logic*. New York: Hyperion, 1993.

Addictions

Ash, Mel. *The Zen of Recovery*. New York: Tarcher/Putnam. 1993.

Bien, Beverly, and Thomas Bien. *Mindful Recovery: A Spiritual Path to Healing from Addiction*. New York: John Wiley & Sons, 2002.

Cunningham, Donna, and Andrew Ramer. *Further Dimensions of Healing Addictions*. San Rafael, CA: Cassandra Press, 1988.

Grof, Christina. *The Thirst for Wholeness: Attachment, Addiction, and the Spiritual Path*. San Francisco: Harper, 1993.

Kasl, Charlotte. *Women, Sex, and Addiction: A Search for Love and Power*. New York: Ticknor & Fields, 1989.

Whitfield, Charles, L. *Alcoholism and Spirituality: A Transpersonal Approach*. Rutherford, NJ: Thomas Perrin, Inc., 1985.

Kundalini

Greenwell, Bonnie. *Energies of Transformation*. Saratoga, CA: Shakti River Press, 1995.

Krishna, Gopi. *Kundalini: The Evolutionary Energy in Man*. Boston: Shambhala, 1971.

Kundalini Research Network, c/o Lawrence Edwards, Ph.D., 66 Main St., Bedford Hills, NY 10507, (914) 241-8510, www.kundalininet.org. (Website provides information, not referrals.)

Mookerjee, Ajit. *Kundalini: The Arousal of Inner Energy*. New York: Destiny Books, 1982.

Sannella, Lee. *The Kundalini Experience*. Lower Lake, CA: Integral Publishing, 1987.

Silburn, Lilian. *Kundalini: Energy of the Depths*. New York: State University of New York Press, 1988.

INDEX

Lowen, Alexander, on, *continued*
  Masochist character, 206
  Oral character, 140
  psychopath character, 317
  Schizoid/Creative character, 81
  theories of development, 38–39
Lower chakras, 6, 112, 185

M

Mahler, Margaret, 41, 125
Maidment, Robert, 330
Making Peace with Food, 80–81
Manasmus, 73
Mandalas, 360, 379
Manifestation, 14–15, 64–65. *See also*
  Current of manifestation
Manipura, 10, 38, 195
Mantras, 327–329
Masculine, 234–235, 237
Maslow, Abraham, 34, 38–39
Masochist/Endurer character, 22, 25,
  201–209, 332–333, 448
Mason, Marilyn, 198
Massage, 93–94
Mass communication, 289, 290
May, Rollo, on
  Eros, 161
  love, 178, 214, 241
  myth of baptism, 108
  powerlessness, 168
  vision, 361
  will, 178, 179, 188, 213
McClellan, Randall, 293, 322
Meaning, 30, 399–400
Meditation
  chakra six and, 387
  guided, 216, 378
  Higher Self, 428–429
  mantras for, 327–328
  mindfulness, 425–426
  nonattachment, 429–431
  observing the breath, 276
  techniques, 422–425
  transcendental, 327

transcending lower egos, 431–434
Vipassana, 418
The Witness, 399, 426–428
Memory, 15, 367–368, 370–371
Menopause, 349–350
The Millenium Whole Earth Catalog,
  409–410
Miller, Alice, on
  abuse, 252, 305, 307
  narcissistic personality, 133
  poisonous pedagogy, 189, 191, 201, 258
  self-esteem, 196
  truth, 310
Mind, 127, 233–234, 357
Mindfulness, 425–426
Mirroring, 126, 131
Monopolarization, 371
Montagu, Ashley, 124, 125, 128
Moodiness, 132
Mookerjee, Ajit, 291, 327, 456
Moore, Thomas, 12, 110, 231, 232, 239
Morals, 119
Mother
  child development and, 81, 84, 125–126
  "good" and "bad", 124
  infant development and, 68–69
Mother archetype, 350, 351, 352
Mother Goddess, 33
Movement
  chakra one excess and, 89
  emotional release and, 114, 158
  healing through, 151–152, 324
  letting go, 109
  reaching out and taking in, 237–239
  restoring flow of, 152–155
  restricted, 144, 145
Muladhara, 10, 38, 57, 61, 62
Music, 334–335
Myth
  archetypes and, 352–353, 377
  gods of, 410
  modern, 225–226
  rainbows in, 3–4
  study of, 377–378

Rape, 135–136. *See also* Sexual abuse
Rational consciousness, 396
Rational mind, 357
Realization. *See* Enlightenment
Rebirthing, 99
Reception and expression, 16, 17, 149
Regressive techniques, 99–101
Reich, Wilhelm, 21, 38–39, 121
Rejection, 258–260
Relationships
    balance in, 230, 237
    chakra one and, 81
    family, 250
    forming, 43
    freedom and attachment in, 239–240
    internalized, 256–258
Religion, 416, 435–436
Repression, 117, 130, 367–368
Resonance, 292–295
Respect, 193
Responsibility, 174, 175, 179
Reversibility, 303
Rhythm entrainment, 294
Rights, seven, 26–28
Rigid/Achiever character, 22, 25,
        260–262, 264–265, 268
Rilke, Rainer Maria, 228
Roots, reclaiming, 61–62
Routines, 249–250
Rumi, 357

S

Sacred marriage (Hieros gamos), 14, 236
Safety, 170, 216–217
Sahasrara, 11, 39
Satprem, 407, 414, 424
Schizoid/Creative character, 21–22, 24,
        81–85, 86–87, 446
Screaming, 311
Seasonal affective disorder (SAD), 386
Second chakra. *See* Chakra two
Secrets, 308–310
Self
    archetype of, 438

    ego and, 177
    heart as center of, 456
    Higher, 428–429
    identity and, 30
self
    beholding, 232–233
    environment as, 68–70
    false, 209, 216
    love beyond, 281–282
Self-acceptance, 32, 43, 273–275, 299, 402
Self-definition, 31, 42, 186, 402
Self-esteem, 180–181
Self-expression. *See also* Creativity
    chakra five and, 296, 402
    creative identity and, 304
    development of, 44
    identification with, 32
    thinking-intuitive people and, 446
Self-gratification, 31, 402, 447
Self-image, 340–342
Self-knowledge, 33, 44
Self-love, 231–232, 255
Self-negating beliefs, 191
Self-preservation, 402, 447
Self-reflection, 33, 44, 232–233, 403, 446
Sensation, 110
Sensory deprivation, 197–198
Sensory-Motor period, 70
Sensory reception, 128–129, 197–198
Separation, 41, 123, 170, 226, 393
The Serpent Power, 5
The Sevenfold Journey, 95, 453
The Seven Habits of Highly Effective People,
        182, 280
Seven identities, 29–34, 44, 364, 402–404.
        See also specific identities
Seven rights, 26–28
Seventh chakra. *See* Chakra seven
Sexuality
    abuse of, 133–135, 197, 254
    chakra imbalance and, 81, 145–146,
        147–148
    first sexual relationship, 47
    as forbidden subject, 309–310

ALSO BY ANODEA JUDITH

BOOKS

Chakra Balancing: A Guide to Healing and Awakening Your Energy Body

A complete home-study kit with beautifully illustrated chakra cards. 102-page workbook, 2 audio CDs, and 7 cards. Sounds True, 2003.

The Sevenfold Journey: Reclaiming Mind, Body, and Spirit Through the Chakras

A self-help workbook on the chakras, coauthored with Selene Vega, including over 120 photos. 294 pages. The Crossing Press, 1993.

Wheels of Life: A User's Guide to the Chakra System

A classic illustrated text, with over 150,000 copies in print. 480 pages. Llewellyn Publications, 1999.

OTHER PRODUCTS

A Beginner's Guide to the Chakras:
How to Heal Yourself Using Your Body's Energy Centers

A great starter for understanding the underlying energy dynamics of the chakra system. 73-minute audio CD. Sounds True, 2002.

The Chakra System: A Complete Course in Self-Diagnosis and Healing

Complete chakra instruction. 9-hour audio tape series (6 tapes) with booklet. Sounds True, 2000.

The Illuminated Chakras: A Visionary Voyage Into Your Inner World

Stunning visual meditation with 3-D animation and 5.1 surround sound. 28-minute DVD or VHS. Sacred Centers, 2003.

Wheels of Life Guided Meditations

Guided mediation. 75-minute audio CD. Llewellyn, 1987.

Chakra Prayer Flags

Limited edition flag sets. 7 flags per set.

Publications, products, articles, and information about workshops can be found at:

SACRED CENTERS
WWW.SACREDCENTERS.COM   (707) 823-8988